THE

BATTLE OF WATERLOO,

CONTAINING THE

SERIES OF ACCOUNTS

PUBLISHED BY AUTHORITY,

𝔅𝔯𝔦𝔱𝔦𝔰𝔥 𝔞𝔫𝔡 𝔉𝔬𝔯𝔢𝔦𝔤𝔫,

WITH

CIRCUMSTANTIAL DETAILS,

PREVIOUS, DURING, AND AFTER THE BATTLE,

FROM A VARIETY OF

AUTHENTIC AND ORIGINAL SOURCES, WITH RELATIVE

OFFICIAL DOCUMENTS,

FORMING AN HISTORICAL RECORD OF THE OPERATIONS

IN THE

Campaign of the Netherlands,

1815.

TO WHICH IS ADDED AN ALPHABETICAL LIST
OF THE OFFICERS KILLED AND WOUNDED, FROM 15th TO 26th JUNE, 1815,
AND THE TOTAL LOSS OF EACH REGIMENT,
WITH AN ENUMERATION OF THE WATERLOO HONOURS AND PRIVILEGES,
CONFERRED UPON THE MEN AND OFFICERS, AND LISTS OF REGIMENTS, &C.
ENTITLED THERETO.
ILLUSTRATED BY A PANORAMIC SKETCH OF THE FIELD OF BATTLE, AND A PLAN
OF THE POSITION AT WATERLOO, AND MOVEMENTS, WITH A
GENERAL PLAN OF THE CAMPAIGN.

BY A NEAR OBSERVER.

SEVENTH EDITION, CORRECTED AND IMPROVED.

LONDON:

PRINTED FOR JOHN BOOTH, DUKE STREET, PORTLAND PLACE;
T. EGERTON, MILITARY LIBRARY, WHITEHALL;
AND
MANNERS AND MILLER, EDINBURGH.

1815.

The most high, mighty, and most noble Prince Arthur, Duke, Marquis, and Earl of WELLINGTON. Marquis of Douro. Viscount Wellington of Talavera and of Wellington, and Baron Douro of Wellesley. One of his Majesty's Most Honourable Privy Council. Field Marshal of His Majesty's Forces. Colonel of the Royal Regiment of Horse Guards Blue. Knight of the Most Noble Order of the Garter. Knight Grand Cross of the Most Honourable Military Order of the Bath. Prince of Waterloo in the Netherlands. Duke of Ciudad Rodrigo, and a Grandee of Spain of the First Class. Duke of Vittoria. Marquis of Torres Vedras, and Count of Vimiera in Portugal. Knight of the Most Illustrious Order of the Golden Fleece. Of the Spanish Military Order of St. Fernando. Knight Grand Cross of the Imperial Military Order of Maria Theresa. Knight Grand Cross of the Imperial Military Order of St. George of Russia. Knight Grand Cross of the Order of the Black Eagle of Prussia. Knight Grand Cross of the Royal Portuguese Military Order of the Tower and Sword. Knight Grand Cross of the Royal Military Order of the Sword of Sweden. Knight Grand Cross of the Order of the Elephant of Denmark, of William of the Low Countries: Of the Annunciade of Sardinia: Of Maximilian Joseph of Bavaria. Of the Crown of Rue, the Family Order of the King of Saxony. The Order of Fidelity of the First Class of the Grand Duke of Baden, and of several others. And Commander of the Forces of his Britannic Majesty in France, and of the Army of his Majesty the King of the Low Countries, &c.

" Whoever gave more honourable prize
" To the sweet muse, than did the martial crew ;
" That their brave deeds she might immortalize
" In her shrill tromp, and sound their praises due?
" Who then ought more to favour her, than you,
" Most Noble Lord, the honour of this age,
" And precedent of all that arms ensue?
" Whose warlike prowess and manly courage,
" Tempered with reason and advisement sage,
" Hath filled sad Belgic with victorious spoil ;
" In France and *India* left a famous gage,
" And lately shook the Lusitanian soil."

" * * * * * * * * * * * * a noble peer,
" Great England's glory, and the world's wide wonder,
" Whose dreadful name late thro' all Spain did thunder,
" And Hercules' two pillars standing near,
" Did make to quake and fear :
" Fair branch of honour, flower of chivalry !
" That fillest England with thy triumph's fame,
" Joy have thou of thy noble victory,
" And endless happiness of thy own name
" That promiseth the same ;
" That through thy prowess and victorious arms
" Thy country may be freed from foreign harms,
" And *Britain's* great and glorious name may ring
" Through all the world, fill'd with thy wide alarms
" Which some brave Muse may sing
" To ages following."

EDMUND SPENSER, *Author of the Fairie Queen.*

First published in Great Britain in 2015 by Osprey Publishing,
Osprey Publishing, PO Box 883, Oxford, OX1 9PL, UK
Osprey Publishing, PO Box 3985, New York, NY 10185-3985, USA
E-mail: info@ospreypublishing.com

OSPREY PUBLISHING IS PART OF THE OSPREY GROUP

A CIP catalogue record for this book is available from the British
Library

ISBN: 978 1 4728 0589 8
E-pub ISBN: 978 1 4728 1304 6
PDF ISBN: 978 1 4728 1303 9

Originated by PDQ Digital Media Solutions
Printed in China through Worldprint

15 16 17 18 19   10 9 8 7 6 5 4 3

Osprey Publishing is supporting the Woodland Trust, the UK's
leading woodland conservation charity, by funding the dedication
of trees.

www.ospreypublishing.com

INTRODUCTION

The last shots of the battle of Waterloo were fired in the evening of Sunday 18 June 1815. Sometime between 9 and 10pm, the Duke of Wellington met his Prussian ally Field Marshal Gebhard Leberecht von Blücher near La Belle Alliance inn. Blücher embraced the duke and greeted him: 'Mein lieber Kamerad, quelle affaire!' Wellington later claimed that Blücher had spoken the only two French words he knew. With the British troops exhausted by their exertions during the day, they agreed that the late-arriving Prussian cavalry should clear the retreating French off the battlefield. This they successfully did until a halt was called around 11pm. Blücher hoped that the battle should suitably be named after La Belle Alliance. Others expected it to be called after the village of Mont St Jean, behind the British lines. Wellington preferred Waterloo – a village on the road north to Brussels – on the grounds that this name would prove easier for the British to pronounce.

The battle over, Wellington slept briefly before, in the early hours of Monday morning, he sat down to write his official dispatch to Earl Bathurst, Secretary of State for War. His dispatch, dated Monday 19 June, reached London late in the evening of Wednesday 21 June and was published in an extraordinary edition of the *London Gazette* on Thursday 22 June. By that time, news of the victory had already reached London, quashing the pessimistic rumours that had swirled around the city in the absence of anything definite. According to a note in this book, the Honourable Mr Butler and an Irish friend, travelling in the Netherlands for pleasure, heard news of the battle while in Brussels. They stayed to help the wounded straggling into the city, before leaving for Ostend on Monday. On the morning of Tuesday 20 June they sailed across the English Channel on board HMS *Leveret* to Deal, arriving in London at 4pm. They then quickly delivered their good news and dispatches to Lord Melville, First Lord of the Admiralty. Other accounts differ as to how the news first reached London.

The celebrations were immediate and intense. Britain had been at war with France with barely a break since 1793. Both Houses of Parliament met on Friday 23 June to give thanks, as did the Lord Mayor, Alderman and Commons of the City of London on 5 July. A Privy Council order of 29 June required churches, both established and dissenting, to read an official State Prayer, while William Wordsworth burst into lengthy verse, urging 'this favoured nation' to 'be conscious of thy moving spirit ... thy protecting care'.

The national newspapers devoted many columns to the battle and its aftermath, while printers quickly reproduced scenes of the battle and other images to sell to an eager public. Within a few weeks, two enterprising publishers put together a collection of 'accounts published by authority, British and foreign, and other relative documents, with circumstantial details, previous and after the battle, from a variety of authentic and original sources.' The book was evidently a success, for it went through seven ever-expanding editions in 1815, with three further editions appearing in 1816 and 1817. It is the seventh edition of this book you are holding in your hand.

The first part of the book opens with lengthy circumstantial detail of the battle incorporating information from various sources, notably an eyewitness account from a French officer. This is then followed by 'further particulars from different sources', including numerous letters that flesh out the detail in great depth. The sheer scope of these sources is a fine testament to the editors who so rapidly compiled this book. The second part mixes official and authenticated papers with personal letters and accounts drawn from both sides of the conflict. A panoramic sketch of the battlefield, a plan of the campaign in the Netherlands in June 1815 and a battle plan are interleaved into the text, the panoramic sketch referenced in the opening pages in great detail. In memory of the dead, lists of officers killed and wounded, with some biographical details of the fallen heroes, forms the final part. The last word goes to the Duke of Wellington, whose biography occupies the final page.

The earliest editions of this book were published for sale by the London businesses of John Booth of Duke Street, Portland Place, and Thomas Egerton of the Military Library in Whitehall (not to be confused with the Royal United Services Institute, a military research institute and library founded in Whitehall by the Duke of Wellington in 1831 and still in existence today). By the time of this seventh edition, Alexander Manners and Robert Miller from Edinburgh had been added to the title page, to be replaced in the next edition by John Fairbairn, also of Edinburgh.

Unlike the division that exists today between publishers who commission and promote a book, printers who typeset and manufacture it, and booksellers who sell it, these tasks were combined within single enterprises in the early 1800s. Our three publishers were all booksellers who also printed books on the premises. Looking through this edition, it is clear that different typesetters were involved, as the type size and style changes frequently. John Booth was a well-known London bookseller. Thomas Egerton's Military Library specialized in offering books to naval and military officers as well as publishing other titles, most notably the first three novels of Jane Austen. Alexander Manners and Robert Millers operated a bookshop at 208 High Street, Edinburgh, publishing a range of Scottish-related books, including Walter Scott's *Minstrelsy of the Scottish Border* and James Bruce's *Travels to Discover the Source of the Nile*.

This book would quite possibly have remained hidden in the catalogues of second-hand booksellers had not my mother, an inquisitive antique dealer in Guildford, Surrey, found a copy in a junk shop and given it to her history-loving son as a present. For years it sat on my bookshelves until the advent of the bicentennial of the battle provided the opportunity of seeing it back in print.

Simon Adams
London 2014

TABLE OF CONTENTS.

PART I.

TABLE OF CONTENTS.

PART II.
AUTHENTICATED, OR OFFICIAL PAPERS.

PART III.

CIRCUMSTANTIAL DETAIL

PREVIOUS, DURING, AND AFTER

THE BATTLE OF WATERLOO,

Containing also

FURTHER PARTICULARS, COLLECTED FROM THE
COMMUNICATION AND CORRESPONDENCE OF
SEVERAL OFFICERS OF RANK
AND DISTINCTION,

Who were occupied in different Parts of the Field of Action,

INCLUDING

A FRENCH OFFICER'S DESCRIPTION,

WHO WAS AN EYE WITNESS, &c.

ON the evening of Thursday the 15th of June,
a Courier arrived at Brussels, from Marshal Blucher to announce, that hostilities had commenced
The Duke of Wellington was sitting after dinner,
with a party of officers, over the desert and wine,
when he received the dispatches containing this unexpected news. Marshal Blucher had been attacked
that day by the French; but he seemed to consider
it as a mere affair of outposts, which was not likely to
proceed much further at present, though it might probably prove the prelude to a more important engagement.* It was the opinion of most military men in
Brussels, that it was the plan of the Enemy by a false
alarm to induce the Allies to concentrate their chief
military force in that quarter, in order that he might
more successfully make a serious attack upon some

* The first intelligence of the commencement of hostilities was known in London, at four o'clock on Tuesday afternoon, June 20, 1815. (*Vide Part* 2, p. 156.)

b

other point, and that it was against Brussels and the English army, that the blow would be aimed. The troops were ordered to hold themselves in readiness, to march at a moment's notice; but no immediate movement was expected, and for some hours all was quiet.

It was past midnight, and profound repose seemed to reign over Brussels, when suddenly the drums beat to arms, and the trumpet's loud call was heard from every part of the city. It is impossible to describe the effect of these sounds, heard in the silence of the night. We were not long left in doubt of the truth. A second courier had arrived from Blucher: the attack had become serious; the enemy were in considerable force; they had taken Charleroi, and had gained some advantage over the Prussians, and our troops were ordered to march immediately to support them: instantly every place resounded with martial preparations. There was not a house in which military were not quartered, and consequently, the whole town was one universal scene of bustle: the soldiers were seen assembling from all parts in the Place Royale, with their knapsacks upon their backs; some taking leave of their wives and children; others sitting down unconcernedly upon the sharp pavement, waiting for their comrades; others sleeping upon packs of straw, surrounded by all the din of war, while bât horses and baggage waggons were loading; artillery and commissariat trains harnessing, officers riding in all directions, carts clattering, chargers neighing, bugles sounding, drums beating, and colours flying.

A most laughable contrast to this martial scene was presented by a long procession of carts coming quietly in, as usual, from the country to market, filled with old Flemish women, who looked irresistibly comic, seated among their piles of cabbages, baskets of green peas, early potatoes, and strawberries, totally ignorant of the cause of all these warlike preparations, and gazing at the scene around them with many a look of gaping wonder, as they jogged merrily along, one after another, through the Place Royale, amidst the crowds of soldiers, and the confusion of baggage waggons.

Yet there was order amidst all this apparent confusion. Regiment after regiment formed with the utmost regularity, and marched out of Brussels. About four o'clock in the morning, the 42nd and 92nd Highland regiments marched through the Place Royale, and the Parc. One could not but admire their fine appearance; their firm, collected, steady, military demeanour, as they went rejoicing to battle, with their bagpipes playing before them, and the beams of the rising sun shining upon their glittering arms. Before that sun had set in night, how many of that gallant band were laid low! They fought like heroes, and like heroes they fell—an honour to their country. On many a highland hill, and through many a lowland valley, long will the deeds of these brave men be fondly remembered, and their fate deeply deplored. Never did a finer body of men take the field —never did men march to battle, that were destined to perform such services to their country, and to obtain such immortal renown! It was impossible to witness such a scene unmoved. Thousands were parting with their nearest and dearest relations, and to every British heart it was a moment of the deepest

interest.   Our countrymen were marching out to
battle—they might return victorious—and we proudly
indulged the hope of their triumph; but they were
going to meet an Enemy formidable by their numbers,
and their discipline; commanded by a leader, whose
military talents had made him the terror, and the
Tyrant of Europe, and whose remorseless crimes and
unbounded ambition had so long been its scourge.
Not only was the safety of our brave army at stake,
but the glory which Britain had so dearly purchased
and so nobly won — her prosperity — her greatness
—her name among other nations—the security and the
fate of Europe, depended upon the issue of that eventful contest, which was now on the eve of being decided.

Our troops, however, who had never known defeat,
were confident of success, under the command of
a General who had so lately led a victorious army
from the shores of the Tagus, over the Mountains
of the Pyrenees, and carried conquest and dismay
into the heart of France ; under whom they had
never fought but to conquer, and whom they now
followed to battle as to certain victory.   What could
not British soldiers do under such a general?   What
could not such a general do with such soldiers?   The
Duke of Wellington himself, with a candour and
modesty which does him the highest honour, made
an observation, which ought never to be forgotten.
" When other Generals commit any error, their army
is lost by it, and they are sure to be beaten ; when I
get into a scrape, my army get me out of it."

- Before eight in the morning the streets, which had
been filled with busy crowds, were empty and silent; the great Square of the Place Royale, which

had been filled with armed men, and with all the appurtenances and paraphernalia of war, was now quite deserted.

The Flemish drivers were sleeping in the tilted carts that were destined to convey the wounded—the heavy baggage waggons ranged in order, and ready to move when occasion might require, were standing under the guard of a few centinels; some officers were still to be seen riding out of town to join the army. The Duke Wellington had set off in great spirits, observing, that as Blucher had most likely settled the business himself by this time, he should perhaps be back to dinner. Sir Thomas Picton mounted upon his charger, in soldier-like style, with his reconnoitring-glass slung across his shoulder, gaily accosting his friends as he rode through the streets, left Brussels in the highest spirits never to return. It was on this very morning that Napoleon Buonaparte made the boast, that to-morrow night he would sleep at Lacken.*

After the army were gone, Brussels seemed indeed a perfect desert. Every countenance was marked with anxiety or melancholy—every heart was filled with anxious expectation. It was not, however, supposed that any action would take place that day. What was then the general consternation, when about three o'clock, a furious cannonading began!—It was certainly in the direction our army had taken—it came from Waterloo!—Had our troops then encountered

* A palace now belonging to the King of Holland, about three miles beyond Brussels, in an elevated situation, surrounded by beautiful grounds. It was fitted up with great magnificence by Louis Buonaparte, and Napoleon himself staid there in his progress through the Netherlands.

the French before they had joined the Prussians?—
Were they separately engaged?—Where?—When?—
How?—In vain, did every one ask questions which
none could answer—numbers of people in carriages
and on horseback set off towards Waterloo, and returned no wiser than they went, each bringing back
a different story—a thousand absurd reports, totally
devoid of foundation, were circulated—what you were
told one minute, was contradicted the next. According to some, Blucher had been completely beaten—
according to others, he had gained a complete victory;
—some would have it, that 30,000 French were left
dead on the field of battle—others, that about the
same number were advancing to surprize Brussels.
It was even said that the English army were retreating *in confusion*—but the bearers of this piece of intelligence were received with so much indignation, and
such perfect incredulity, that they were glad to hold
their peace. Some said the scene of action was
twenty miles off—others that it was only six. At
length intelligence came from the army, brought by an
officer who had left the field after five o'clock. The
British, in their march, had encountered the Enemy
on the plains of Fleurus,* about fifteen miles from
Brussels.—The Highland regiments received the furious onset of the whole French army, without yielding
one inch of ground. With resolute unshaken valour
they fought to the last, and fell upon the very spot
where they first drew their swords. The combat
was terrible—the enemy were in much more for-

* The French were not destined to be a second time victorious on the plains
of Fleurus. About the end of the 17th century, a great battle was fought there,
in which they completely defeated, instead of being defeated by, *the Allies.*

midable force than had been represented, and deriving confidence from their immense superiority of
numbers, they fought most furiously—Blucher was
separately engaged with another division of French
at some distance, and could give us no assistance.
Yet this brave handful of British had undauntedly
stood their ground, repulsed every attack, and were
still fighting with the fullest confidence of success.
In the words of this officer, " all was well."

Still the cannonading continued, and apparently
approached nearer.* The French were said to be 30
or 40,000 strong. Only 10,000 British troops had
marched out of Brussels—our army was unconcen-
trated—it was impossible that the cavalry could have
come up—the principal part of the artillery were at a
distance. Under such circumstances, it was impossible, even with the fullest confidence in British valour,
not to feel extreme anxiety for the army. Unable to
rest, we wandered about the Parc the whole evening,
or stood upon the ramparts listening to the heavy cannonade, which towards 10 o'clock became fainter, and
soon afterwards entirely died away.

No further intelligence had arrived—the cannonade
had continued five hours since the last accounts came
away. The anxiety to know the result of the battle
may be imagined.

Between twelve and one, we suddenly heard the
noise of the rapid rolling of heavy carriages, in long
succession, passing through the Place Royale, mingled with the loud cries and exclamations of the
people below. For some minutes we listened in

* Probably because in the stillness of evening, it was heard more distinctly.
There was no real change of position.

silence,—faster and faster, and louder and louder, the
long train of carriages continued to roll through the
town; the cries of the affrighted people increased.
In some alarm we hastily ran out to inquire the
cause of this tumult : the first person we encountered
was a scared Fille-de-Chambre, who exclaimed
in a most piteous tone — " ————————
———————— les François sont tout près—dans une
petite demi-heure ils seront ici ————————
———————————— Que ferons-nous, que ferons-
nous! ——————————————————— il faut
partir tout de suite." Questions were in vain—she
could only reiterate again and again,—" Les François
sont tout près—Les François sont tout près,"—and
then renew her exclamations and lamentations. As we
flew down stairs, the house seemed deserted, every
room door was open—the candles were left burning
on the tables—every body had run out into the
Place Royale—at the bottom of the stairs, a group
of affrighted Belgians were assembled — consternation pictured on their faces. They could only tell
us that intelligence had been brought, of a large
body of French having been seen advancing through
the woods to take Brussels, that they were within
half an hour's march of the city, (which was wholly
undefended), and that the English army was in
full retreat. " C'est trop vrai—c'est trop vrai," was
repeated on every side, " and the train of artillery that
was passing through (they said) was retreating!"—
We had soon, however, the satisfaction of finding
that this was not the case, that the artillery were
passing through to join the army, that they were not
retreating, but advancing ; and finding that the report

of the French being within half an hour's march of the city, rested only on the authority of some Belgians, our alarm gradually subsided—some people indeed took their departure—but as the French did not make their appearance, some went to bed, and others lay down in their clothes, by no means assured that their slumbers might not be broken by the entrance of the French.

In fact between five and six, we were roused by a loud knocking at the door, and the cries of " Les François sont ici—Les François sont ici." Starting up, the first sight we beheld, was a troop of Belgic cavalry—covered—not with glory, but 'with mud,* galloping through the town at full speed, as if the enemy were at their heels ; and immediately the heavy baggage waggons, which had been harnessed from the moment of the first alarm, set off full gallop down La Montague de la Cour, and through every street by which it was possible to effect their escape. In less than two minutes, the great Square of the Place Royale, which had been crowded with men and horses, carts and baggage waggons, was completely cleared of every thing, and entirely deserted. Again were the cries repeated, of " Les François sont ici!—Ils s'emparent de la porte de la ville!" The doors of all the bed-rooms were thrown open, the people flew out with their night-caps on, scarcely half dressed, and looking quite distracted, running about pale and trembling they knew not whither, with packages under their arms—some carrying huge heterogeneous collections of things down to the cellars, and others

* L'Oracle de Bruxelles said, that the Belgic troops had " covered themselves with glory."

loaded with their property flying up to the garrets.
The poor Fille-de-Chambre, nearly frightened out of
her wits, was standing wringing her hands, unable
to articulate any thing but " Les François—Les François!"—while the *Cuisiniere* exclaimed with more
dignity, " Nous sommes tous perdus."

In the Court-yard below, a scene of the most dreadful confusion ensued ; description can give but a
faint idea of the scuffle that took place to get at the
horses and carriages; the squabbling of masters and
servants, ostlers, chambermaids, coachmen, and gentlemen, all scolding at once, and swearing in French,
English, and Flemish; while every opprobrious
epithet and figure of speech which the three lan-
guages contained were exhausted upon each other,
and the confusion of tongues could scarcely have
been exceeded by that of the Tower of Babel.
Some made use of supplication, and others had re-
course to force; words were followed by blows.
One half of the Belgic drivers refused either to go
themselves, or let their *beasts* go, and with many
gesticulations called upon all the saints and angels
in heaven to witness, that they would not set out—no,
not to save the Prince of Orange himself; and neither
love nor money, nor threats, nor intreaties, could induce them to alter this determination. Those who
had horses, or means of procuring them, set off with
most astonishing expedition, and one English carriage after another took the road to Antwerp.

It was impossible for the people at Brussels, who
were wholly ignorant of the event of the battle, and
acquainted only with the disadvantageous circumstances under which it had been fought, not to fear

that the Enemy might at last have succeeded in breaking through the British, or at least the Prussian lines, or that Buonaparte, ever fertile in expedients, might have contrived to elude their vigilance, and to send a detachment under cover of night, by a circuitous route, to seize the unguarded city, the possession of which was to him of the highest importance. The news of the advance of the French—the alarming reports which had been brought in from all quarters during the night—the flight of the Belgic troops, and above all, the failure of any intelligence from our own army, tended to corroborate this last alarm, and it seemed but too certain that the Enemy were actually at hand. At length after a considerable interval of terror and suspense, an Aide-de-Camp of the Duke of Wellington arrived, who had left the army at four o'clock, and, to our unspeakable joy, this was found to be a false alarm. It had been spread by those dastardly Belgians whom we had seen scampering through the town, and who had, it is supposed, met with some straggling party of the enemy. It was also said, that a foraging party of French had come bravadoing to the gates of the city, summoning it to surrender. A considerable number of French, indeed, entered the town soon after; but they were French prisoners.* The Duke's Aide-de-Camp brought the welcome information, that the British army, though attacked by such a tremendous superiority

* The French themselves acknowledged their loss was nearly equal to ours; heavy as ours was, theirs was much more severe. Generals Dumoulin and Cambaceres, Aides-de-Camp to Buonaparte, arrived at Brussels as prisoners, 17th in the morning. Editor.

of numbers, and under every possible disadvantage, had completely repulsed the Enemy, and remained masters of the field of battle. The cavalry, or at least a considerable part of them, had come up at the close of the action, but too late to take any part in it: thus our infantry had sustained, during the whole of the day, the attack of the enemy's cavalry as well as infantry.

The Duke expected that the engagement would be renewed this morning; but the army was now collected, and joined both by the cavalry and artillery, and a more decisive engagement might be expected. The French had sustained a great loss in killed, wounded, and prisoners. The defeat which the Prussians had sustained could not, however, be concealed,* and the Belgians were filled with consternation and dismay. The corpse of the Duke of Brunswick had passed through Brussels during the night, and his fate seemed to make a great impression upon the minds of the people.† Waggons filled with the wounded began to arrive, and the melancholy spectacle of these poor sufferers increased the general despondency. The streets were filled with the most pitiable

---

* The war took a most ferocious character between the French and Prussians from the very beginning. Before the opening of the campaign, the 1st and 2nd corps of the French had hoisted the *black* flag. They openly avowed, that they would give no quarter to the Prussians, and in general they kept their word. The Prussian loss, in all the affairs together, is calculated at 33,120 men. E.

† In the spirit of the days of Chivalry, the Duke of Brunswick had taken a solemn oath that he would never sheath the sword, till he had avenged the insult offered to the tomb of his father. It is to be lamented, that he should have fallen without the satisfaction of knowing how full and glorious was the revenge for which he panted. The sincerity of the sorrow which even in a moment of such universal consternation, was every where testified for his loss, affords the highest eulogium on his virtues. Peace to his ashes! His death has been honoured by the best funeral oration—the lamentations of the people.

sights. We saw a Belgic soldier dying at the
door of his own home, and surrounded by his relatives, who were weeping over him; numerous were
the sorrowful groups standing round the dead bodies
of those who had died of their wounds in the way
home. Numbers of wounded, who were able to walk,
were wandering upon every road; their blood-stained·
clothes and pale haggard countenances, perhaps,
giving the idea of sufferings much greater than the
reality.

It is well known that on the forenoon of this day,
(Saturday), the Duke of Wellington fell back about
seven miles, upon Waterloo, in order to take up a
position more favourable for the cavalry, and from
which he could keep up the communication with
Marshal Blucher, who had retreated upon Wavre.

Never was there a more masterly or successful
manœuvre. By superior generalship, every plan of
the Enemy was baffled; although constantly on the
watch, he never had it in his power to attack our retreating army to the smallest advantage. The con-
fession escaped from Napoleon himself, that it was
on his part " *a day of false manœuvres.*" In the
mean time it is impossible to describe the panic that
the news of this retreat spread at Brussels. Nobody
could convince the Belgians that a retreat and a
flight were not one and the same thing; and, firmly
convinced that the English had been defeated, they
fully expected every moment to see them enter Brussels in the utmost confusion, with the French after
them: even the English themselves, who had the
most unbounded confidence in the British army and
its commanders, and who were certain that if they

retreated it would be with good order, steady discipline, and undaunted courage, began to fear that the
immense superiority of the Enemy had made the Duke
judge it prudent to fall back until joined by fresh
reinforcements.

There is a mistaken idea in this country, that the
French, that even Napoleon Buonaparte himself was
popular in Belgium. This was a moment when Hy-
pocrisy itself would have found it impossible to dissemble; and the dismay which reigned upon every
face, and the terror which filled every town and village, when it was believed that the French were victorious—the execrations with which their very names
were uttered—the curses, " not loud but deep," half
repressed by fear, betrayed how rooted and sincere
was their hatred of the tyranny from which they had
so recently escaped. There may be miscreants* *of
all ranks* in Belgium, as in other countries, whom the
hope of plunder and the temptations of ambition will
bring over to any party, where these can be obtained;
but by the great body of the nation, from the highest
to the lowest, the French government is abhorred,
and Napoleon himself is regarded with a detestation,
the strength of which we can form no idea of in this

* Among his papers taken after the Battle of Waterloo, was a list of eighty
inhabitants of Brussels, whose persons and property were to be respected by the
French army on its entrance into that city. Among these was a Flemish Nobleman, who had prepared a splendid supper for Buonaparte on the 18th. Of
the remainder, several of them had also prepared one for his principal
officers. Of this junto, the Nobleman who was to have been Buonaparte's
host, has fled. The others remained at Brussels on Saturday, apparently without
fear, although it is well known that the King of the Netherlands is in possession
of the list. It is also certain, that several Proclamations were found among
the papers of Buonaparte, addressed from Brussels, Lacken, &c. all prepared in
confident expectations of his success on the 18th, the capture of Brussels, and his
irruption into Flanders and Holland. Editor.

country. Their very infants are taught to lisp, these sentiments, and to regard him as a monster.

It would be endless to dwell upon every fresh panic. An open town like Brussels, within a few miles of contending armies, is subject to perpetual alarms, and scarcely an hour passed without some false reports occurring to spread general terror and confusion. Every hour only served to add to the dismay. So great was the alarm in Brussels on Saturday evening, that 100 Napoleons were offered in vain for a pair of horses to go to Antwerp, a distance of 30 miles; and numbers set off on foot, and embarked in boats upon the canal. In the afternoon, a violent thunder-storm came on, followed by torrents of rain, which during the whole of the night, when the army were laying unsheltered upon the field of Waterloo, never ceased a single moment. On Sunday the terror and confusion reached its highest point. News arrived of the French having gained a complete victory, and it was universally believed. A dreadful panic had seized the men left in charge of the baggage, in the rear of the army, and they ran away with a rapidity that could not have been surpassed even by the French themselves. The road between Waterloo and Brussels, which lays through the Forest of Soigné, is completely confined on either side by trees; it was soon choaked up; those behind attempted to get past those before—officers' servants were struggling to secure their masters' baggage—panic-struck people forcing their way over every obstacle, with the desperation of fear,—and a complete scuffle ensued, which might really be called a battle burlesqued, in which numbers of horses were killed, and some lives lost, not to mention the innumerable broken heads and black bruises sustained on the occasion.

The road was covered with broken and overturned waggons—heaps of abandoned baggage—dead horses, and terrified people. In some places, horses, waggons, and all, were driven over high banks by the road side, in order to clear a passage. The quantity of rain that had fallen, of itself made the roads nearly impassable, and it was impossible for the wounded to be brought from the field. Certainly these *Waterloo Men* who came flying into Brussels on Sunday, did not cut a very glorious figure!

At Antwerp, though more distant from the scene of action, the consternation was nearly as great. Long rows of carriages lined the streets, filled with fugitives, who could find no place of shelter; and people of rank and fortune were glad to eat and sleep in one and the same miserable hole, which at any other time they would have disdained to have entered. So great was the universal anxiety, that during the whole of Sunday, though the rain was almost incessant, the great Place de Maire was crowded with people, who stood from morning until night, under umbrellas, impatiently watching the arrival of news from the army, and assailing every body who entered the town with fruitless inquiries.

Our persons indeed, and our outward senses, might be in Antwerp or Brussels, but our whole hearts and souls were with the army. One common interest bound together all ranks and conditions of men. All other subjects—all other considerations were forgotten—all distinctions were levelled—all common forms thrown aside and neglected,—ladies accosted men they had never seen before with eager questions; no preface—no apology—no ceremony was thought of—strangers conversed together like friends—all ranks of people addressed each other without hesitation—every body seeking—every body giving information—and English reserve seemed no longer to exist.

It is impossible to imagine the strong overpowering anxiety of being so near such eventful scenes, without being able to learn what is really passing. To know that within a few miles such an awful contest is deciding—to hear even the distant voice of war—to think that in the roar of every cannon, your brave countrymen are falling, bleeding, and dying—to dread that your friends, even those dearest to you, may be the victims—to endure the long and protracted suspense—the constant agitation—the varying reports—the incessant alarms—the fluctuating hopes, and doubts, and fears—no—none but those who have felt what it is, can conceive or understand it.

This state of suspense had lasted three days. Continual vague and contradictory reports, and rumours of evil, were brought in, during the whole of Sunday, which only served to increase the general anxiety. At length, between nine and ten in the evening, some wounded British officers arrived on horseback from the field, bringing the dreadful news, that the battle was lost, and that Brussels was actually in the possession of the French! This was corroborated by fugitives from Brussels, who affirmed they had seen the French in the town; and one gentleman declared he had been pursued by them, half way to Malines. It was even asserted, that the French had

entered Malines: later accounts tended to confirm
these disastrous tidings, and Antwerp was filled with
consternation and dismay. Many people set off for
Holland, thinking Antwerp no longer safe. Through
the whole night, carriages filled with the wounded—
heavy waggons loaded with military stores—trains of
artillery and ammunition—Hanseatic troops to garrison it, in case of a siege, continued to pour into the
town. It was then, when fear almost amounted to
certainty, when suspense had ended in despair, after
a night of misery—that the great, the glorious news
burst upon us—that the Allies had gained a complete
victory—that the French—defeated—routed—dispersed—had fled from the field of battle—pursued by
our conquering troops. No words can describe the
feelings of that moment—no eloquence can paint the
transport which filled every breast and brought
tears into every eye. An express arrived at eight
in the morning, bringing a bulletin to Lady Fitzroy
Somerset, dated from Waterloo, the preceding night,
merely containing a brief account of the victory.
The tumults, the acclamations, the rejoicings which
ensued—the voluble joy of the Belgians, the more
silent heartfelt thankfulness of the British, the contending feelings of triumph, pity, sorrow, anxiety,
gratitude, and admiration, may be conceived, but
they cannot be described. A party of wounded
Highlanders, who had found their way on foot from
the field of battle, no sooner heard the news, than,
regardless of their sufferings, they began to shout
and huzza with the most vociferous demonstrations
of joy; and those who had the use of their arms,
threw their Highland bonnets into the air, calling

out in broad Scotch, " Boney's beat!—Boney's beat!
—huzza!—huzza!—Boney's beat!"

These Sketches of the Field on which the glorious battle of the 18th of June was fought, were
taken on the spot, from the summit of a perpendicular bank, immediately above the high road from
Brussels to Genappe, in the front of the centre of the
British position. The First Plate represents the
view as it appeared to the British Army, when
drawn up in order of battle, on the morning of
that memorable day, looking directly forward to the
hamlet of La Belle Alliance, fig. 1 and 2; and the
heights occupied by the French, fig. 3, 4, 5, and Plate
2nd, fig. 6. The Second Plate, taken from the same
spot, looking the contrary way, represents the ground
occupied by the British, with the farm-house of
La Sainte Haye, fig. 7, in front, and backed by the
Forest of Soignies, fig. 8 and 9, Plate 2. Each
plate forms a semi-circle, comprizing the whole
view which the eye can take in at once. The two
Plates join together at each end, as marked; (A
joining to A, and B joining to B,) forming a complete circle or panoramic view of the Field of Battle. Every house, every bush, every tree, every
undulation is distinctly copied from nature. There
is not a spot on which the eye can rest, that was
not immortalized by some heroic deed of British
valour, and scarcely a clod of earth that was not
covered with the wounded, and the dead bodies
of our countrymen, and their vanquished foes.

The ground on which the battle was fought, cannot
at most exceed two miles from North to South, including the whole from the rear of the British to the rear
of the French position. Vide plate and sketch, fig. 3,

4, 5, and 6, was the height occupied by the French, and plate 2; fig. 12, 13, 14, 15, the height occupied by the English. From East to West, from the extremity of the left to that of the right wing of the contending armies, is scarcely a mile and half in extent;* the smallness of the space on which they fought, and the consequent intermixture of the two armies, might have occasioned in some degree the sanguinary result of the battle. The French position was decidedly the best; the eminence they occupied was higher, and the ascent steeper than ours, and better adapted both for attack and defence. The battle took place at some distance from the village of Waterloo, which is situated behind the skirts of the Forest of Soigné, and is not seen from the field. It was occupied on Saturday, the night preceding the battle, by the Duke of Wellington, the principal officers of his Staff, the Prince of Orange, Lord Uxbridge, Sir Thomas Picton, Sir William De Lancey, and other general officers; their names, written in chalk, were yet visible on the doors of the cottages in which they slept. After the battle, those houses were filled with the most severely wounded of the British Officers, many of whom died, and are buried here.

The following is a tolerably accurate statement of the combined British, Hanoverian, and Belgic Army, under the command of Field Marshal the Duke of Wellington, K. G. and K. G. C. B.

  38,000 British.

   8,000 King's German Legion.

  14,000 Hanoverians.

  22,000 Belgian, Brunswick and Nassau Troops;

* The ground had not been measured; this computation is merely intended to give an idea of its extent; it does not profess to be correct.

forming a total of 82,000 men, of which 62,000 were Infantry, 15,000 Cavalry, and 5,000 Artillery, Engineers, &c. This calculation includes 15,000 men, who were employed in garrisons, and not present at either of the battles.

The French Army amounted to 130,000; and after the losses of the 15th and 16th, and the detachment of two corps under Marshal Grouchy, there must have remained at least 90,000 men, with which Napoleon took the field on the 18th of June; while, after allowing for our own losses on the 16th, detachments and casualties, the whole effective force of the united British and Belgic Armies, under the Duke of Wellington on that memorable day, did not amount to 55,000 men, who were divided into two Corps d'Armée, under the orders of General the Prince of Orange, K. G. C. B. and Lieut. Gen. Lord Hill, K. G. C. B. under whom the Infantry was commanded by

Lieut. Generals Sir Thomas Picton, K. G. C. B.

Sir Henry Clinton, K. G. C. B.

Baron Sir C. Alten, K. C. B.

Major Generals Sir H. de Hinuber, K. C. B.

Sir James Kempt, K. C. B.

Sir Colin Halkett, K. C. B.

Sir Denis Packe, K. C. B.

George Cooke.

Peregrine Maitland.

Frederick Adam.

Sir John Byng, K. C. B.

Sir John Lambert, K. C. B.

Colonels Baron Charles Ompteda,

Halkett, and

Mitchell.

The Cavalry was commanded by Lieut. General
the Earl of Uxbridge, K. G. C. B. and under him by
Major Generals Lord Edward Somerset, K. C. B.

     Hon. Sir Wm. Ponsonby, K. C. B.

     Count Sir W. Dornberg, K. C. B.

     Sir Colquhoun Grant, K. C. B.

     Sir R. Husse Vivian, K. C. B.

     Sir I. Ormsby Vandeleur, K. C. B. &
Colonel Baron Sir F. de Arentschildt, K.C.B.

The Artillery was commanded by Col. Sir George
Adam Wood, and the Engineers by Col. Smyth.

“ Never was the overthrow of a great army so
complete.   Of 40,000 cavalry, not 10,000 returned
capable of service, and of an immense artillery, only
12 pieces were saved.”

The road from Brussels to Genappe passes through
the little village of Mont St. Jean, (fig. 10, Plate 2,)
from which the French have named the battle, and
which was occupied by the British during the
whole of the day; and repeatedly and furiously,
though ineffectually, attacked by the Enemy. Count
D'Erlon headed a desperate attack against it, which
was repulsed by the British Army; and Napoleon
Buonaparte, in his own account of the battle, declares he was on the point of leading a general
charge of the whole French army against it in person,
at the very moment when the general charge of the
British Army and their Allies took place, which obliged
him to lead it in the opposite direction. All the inhabitants had fled from this village previous to the action,
and even Waterloo was deserted; but in a farm-house,
fig. 41, Plate 2, at the end of the village nearest
the field, one solitary woman remained, during the

whole of the day, shut up in a garret, from which she could see nothing, and without any means of gaining information of what was passing, while they were fighting man to man, and sword to sword, at the very doors; while shells were bursting in at the windows, and while the cannon-balls were breaking through the wooden gates into the farm-yard, and striking against the walls of the house. This woman was the farmer's wife: and when asked her motives for this extraordinary conduct, she replied with great simplicity, that she had a great many cows and calves, and poultry, and pigs—that all she had in the world was there; and that she thought, if she did not stay to take care of them, they would all be destroyed or carried off. The three rooms in the lower part of the house, nay even the stables and cow-houses, were filled with wounded British officers, among whom was Major-General Cooke, Lieut. Colonel Cameron, of the 85th, Major Llewellyn of the 28th regiment, and many others who had particularly distinguished themselves by their conduct in the field. The British position crossed the road to *Nivelles*, which branches off to the right, from Mont St. Jean (See Plan of Position); and sloping along, passes behind the wood and chateau of Hougoumont on the height, the most advanced post of the British army, fig. 11, Plate 2. In front, it occupied the farm of La Sainte Haye, fig. 7, Plate 2, extending to the left along the hedge, fig. 12, 13, 14, and 15, Plate 2, and a lane behind it, which was occupied by General Picton's division. Upon this height, a considerable part of our artillery was placed; but it was also dispersed in different parts of the field, and placed upon every little eminence,

with great judgment and effect.   The quarry, fig. 16,
17, 18, 19, 20, Plates 1 and 2, in front of the British
position, fig. 21, Plate 2, is a high perpendicular bank
cut down for the road to pass through : fig. 22, Plate
2, the top of the opposite bank, was also surrounded
with cannon.   The chaussée or paved road from Brussels to Genappe, fig. 23, 24, 25, 26, 27, Plates 1 and 2,
which passes nearly through the centre of the position
of both armies, proceeding directly forward from the
village of Mont St. Jean, leaves the farm-house of
La Sainte Haye, fig. 7, Plate 2, on the right, nearly
in the hollow, and again ascends to La Belle Alliance (fig. 1, Plate 1,) on the summit of the opposite
hill, which, with the heights on each side, were
occupied by the French.   This celebrated spot is
a small farm-house on the left side of the road,
pierced through in every direction with cannon-ball.
The offices behind it are now a heap of ruins, from
the fire of the British artillery.   Numbers of wounded
French officers crawled in here the night after the
battle, and on the morning of the 19th it was filled
with the dead and dying.   The little cottage, fig. 2,
Plate 1, on the opposite side of the road, is also
called La Belle Alliance, and forms a part of the
hamlet.   It was here, that Napoleon Buonaparte
stood in the proud confidence of success, after dis-
patching a courier to Paris, with intelligence, that
the battle was won—it was here, a few hours afterwards, when the battle was really won, that Lord
Wellington and Marshal Blucher accidentally met,
in the very moment when Napoleon, foremost in
the flight, and followed by his panic-struck army,
was driven along by their victorious troops.

After some skirmishing between the piquets, the French commenced the engagement about 10 o'clock, with a furious attack upon the post at the wood and garden of Chateau Hougoumont, fig. 11, Plate 2, which was occupied by General Byng's brigade of guards. It was a point of particular importance to the Enemy to gain this post, as, from its situation, it commanded a considerable part of our position; and accordingly it was furiously and incessantly assailed by large and reinforced bodies of the Enemy, and gallantly and successfully defended to the last by the British. Napoleon himself directed the charge of the French Imperial Guards against it;* but even though fighting under the immediate eye of their leader, they were broken, repulsed, and finally cut to pieces by the British Guards. Thirty pieces of our artillery played continually over this wood, to assist its defence, while the Enemy directed against it their hottest fire. *(Vide letters from officers in the Guards and General Alava's Spanish official account.)*

Every tree in the wood of Hougoumont is pierced with balls—in one alone, I counted the holes, where upwards of twenty had lodged: but the strokes which were fatal to human life, have scarcely injured them; though their trunks are filled with balls, and their branches broken and destroyed, their verdure is still the same. Wild flowers are still blooming, and wild rasberries ripening beneath their shade; while huge

* It is not true that Napoleon ever charged in person : he incessantly ordered his battalions to advance—to charge—to bear down upon the Enemy—he impetuously urged them forward—he inflamed their ardour by the recollection of past, as well as the prospect of present victory, and the promise of plunder and reward; but he never led them on to battle himself—he never once braved the shock of British arms.

black piles of human ashes, dreadfully offensive in smell, are all that now remain of the heroes who fought and fell upon this fatal spot. Beside some graves, at the outskirts of this wood, the little wild flower, "Forget me not," "Myosotis arvensis," was blooming, and the flaring red poppy had already sprung up around, and even upon them, as if in mockery of the dead. The Chateau itself, upon which the attack was first made by the French, now in ruins, is immediately behind the wood, by the side of the road to Nivelles. It was the beautiful country-seat of a Belgic gentleman, and was accidentally set on fire by shells, during the action, which completed the destruction occasioned by the cannonade. In the garden behind the house, the roses, orange-trees and geraniums were still flowering in beauty, and the fig-tree and the pear-tree bearing their fruits—a melancholy contrast to the ruined house, whose mouldering piles were still smoking, and to the scene of desolation around.

The poor countryman, who with his wife and infant family inhabited a miserable shed amongst the deserted ruins, pointed out with superstitious reverence, the little chapel belonging to the Chateau, which alone stood uninjured in the midst of these blackened walls and falling beams. There was something inexpressibly striking in the almost miraculous preservation of this simple sanctuary of piety, which the flames of war, and the hand of rapine, had alike spared; and it was affecting to see standing on the spot still reeking with human blood, and heaped with the dreadful and yet undecayed remains of mortality, the sacred altar of that blessed religion, which proclaimed, " Peace on Earth," and dispelled the horrors of death by the assurance of immortality.

A more mournful scene than this ruined chateau and wood presented, cannot possibly be imagined. Even when the heaps of dead were reduced to ashes,—the broken swords, shattered helmets, torn epaulets, and sabre, tashes bathed in blood, told too plainly the deadly strife that had taken place; and the mournful reflexion could not be repressed, that the glory which Britain gained upon this spot, was purchased by the blood of some of her noblest sons.

Here the standards of *the Invincibles*, inscribed with the names of Jena, Austerlitz, Wagram, and Friedland, were wrested from them. The Scotch Greys took one of the French Eagles; and Francis Stiles, a corporal in the 1st Royal Dragoons, took another.*

---

* *Extract of a Letter from Serjeant Ewart, of the Scots Greys, who took a French Eagle, dated Rouen, June* 18, 1815.—" The Enemy began forming their line of battle, about nine in the morning of the 18th: we did not commence till ten. I think it was about eleven when we were ready to receive them. They began upon our right with the most tremendous firing that ever was heard, and I can assure you, they got it as hot as they gave it; then it came down to the left, where they were received by our brave Highlanders. No men could ever behave better; our brigade of cavalry covered them. Owing to a column of foreign troops giving way, our brigade was forced to advance to the support of our brave fellows, and which we certainly did in style; we charged through two of their columns, each about 5,000; it was in the first charge I took the Eagle from the Enemy; he and I had a hard contest for it; he thrust for my groin— I parried it off, and cut him through the head; after which I was attacked by one of their lancers, who threw his lance at me, but missed the mark, by my throwing it off with my sword by my right side; then I cut him from the chin upwards, which went through his teeth; next I was attacked by a foot soldier, who, after firing at me, charged me with his bayonet—but he very soon lost the combat, for I parried it and cut him down through the head; so that finished the contest for the Eagle. After which I presumed to follow my comrades, Eagle and all, but was stopped by the General, saying to me, " You brave fellow, take that to the rear: you have done enough until you get quit of it;" which I was obliged to do, but with great reluctance. I retired to a height,

Here the brave, the lamented Sir W. Ponsonby fell, leading on his men to victory and glory.

The grief of his country and friends for his loss, will be aggravated by the knowledge that it is to be attributed as much to the fault of his horse, as to his too ardent courage, which carried him alone and unsupported into the midst of his enemies; the account

and stood there for upwards of an hour, which gave a general view of the field; but I cannot express the horrors I beheld: the bodies of my brave comrades were lying so thick upon the field, that it was scarcely possible to pass, and horses innumerable. I took the Eagle into Brussels amidst the acclamations of thousands of the spectators that saw it." Editor.

The Eagles taken, belonged to the 45th and 105th regiments, and were superbly gilt and ornamented with gold fringe. That of the 45th was inscribed with the names of Jena, Austerlitz, Wagram, Eylau, Friedland, &c. being the battles in which this regiment, called the *Invincibles*, had signalized itself. The other was a present from Louisa to the 105th regiment. One was much defaced with blood and dirt, as if it had been struggled for, and the Eagle was also broken off from the pole, as if from the cut of a sabre; but it was nevertheless preserved. It is worthy of observation, that the Eagles taken, were only given to their respective regiments at the *Champ de Mai*. On the 1st of June, they glittered over the heads of the vain Parisians, amid cries of *Vive l'Empereur*. Editor.

The Life Guards, the foremost in this important battle, by their physical power and courage, appalled the veteran enemy, although clad in mail, and in possession of that high mind (grande pensée), which devoted them to honour and the country. Often, in the conflict of " *La Belle Alliance*," did the Earl of Uxbridge turn his eye towards them, exclaiming, " Now for the honour of the Household Troops ;" and as often was his Lordship solaced by the brightest effects of glory under his eye. (*Vide Extract of a Letter from an Officer in the Horse Guards.*) Editor.

Captain Kelly, of the Life Guards, encountered and killed the Colonel of the 1st regiment of French Cuirassiers, in the battle of the 18th; after which he stripped the vanquished of his epaulets, and carried them as a trophy.

One man is known to have had three horses shot, and taken prisoner; but being rescued by Light Dragoons, returned and remounted to the charge.

Shaw in the Horse Guards, of pugilistic fame, was fighting seven or eight hours, dealing destruction to all around him; at one time he was attacked by six of the French Imperial Guard, four of whom he killed, but at last fell by the remaining two. A comrade who was by his side a great part of the day, and who is the relater of this anecdote, noticed one particular cut which drove through his opponent's helmet, and with it cut nearly the whole of his face at the stroke. Editor.

that has been given of the death of this gallant officer
is perfectly correct. He led his brigade against the
Polish Lancers, checked at once their destructive
charges against the British Infantry, and took 2000
prisoners; but having pushed on at some distance
from his troops, accompanied only by one Aide-de-
camp, he entered a newly-ploughed field, where the
ground was excessively soft. Here his horse stuck,
and was utterly incapable of extricating himself. At
this instant, a body of Lancers approached him at
full speed. Sir William saw that his fate was inevitable. He took out a picture, and his watch, and
was in the act of giving them to his Aide-de-camp to
deliver to his wife and family, when the Lancers came
up: they were both killed on the spot. His body was
found, lying beside his horse, pierced with seven lance
wounds; but he did not fall unrevenged. Before the
day was ended, the Polish Lancers were almost entirely cut to pieces by the Brigade which this officer
had led against them.

There is a considerable space of ground, and a
deep dell between the observatory and Hougoumont.
fig. 28, Plate 2. The peasant who had served
Napoleon as a guide the preceding day, was with
him during the principal part of the battle; and
from him we learnt that he often expressed surprize
that the Belgic troops did not come over to him.
Wherever the French encountered them, by his orders
they called to them to join and not to fight against
their Emperor. He had formed the idea of arming
the Belgic peasantry, and a considerable dépôt of
muskets was at Lisle for that purpose. Before the
engagement began, he addressed a short speech to

the soldiers, which was received with enthusiasm, promising them that Brussels and Ghent should be given up to plunder for three *hours*, according to some accounts—to others, for three *days*. He is reported to have said, " These English fight well, but they must give way soon;" and asked Soult if he " did not think so." Soult said, that he much doubted whether they would ever give way. " And why?" said Napoleon with his usual quickness. Soult replied: " he believed they would sooner be cut to pieces." Still Napoleon seemed to entertain the fullest confidence of victory, and at six o'clock jocularly observed that they should arrive at Brussels in good time for supper.

Soon after, the Prussians advanced from the wood at the bottom of the ravine, fig. 29, Plate 1, passing the little hamlet in the hollow, fig. 30, Plate 1, and advancing up the heights, fig. 31, 32, Plate 1, to the right flank and rear of the French position. At first he would not credit it—he angrily exclaimed, they were his own troops, they were French reinforcements advancing under Grouchy and Vandamme: but when the truth was forced upon him, when he perceived that they were really Prussians, his countenance changed, he turned pale, and faltered in his speech; and when he saw the impetuous charge of the Allies, and the confusion and discomfiture of his own troops, his alarm became extreme, and exclaiming, " Tout est perdu," he precipitately galloped from the field. It is, I believe, beyond a doubt that he was one of the first to set the example of flight. After relating these parculars, the guide, hearing some person speak of him

with contempt, cordially agreed with us that he certainly was a pitiful scoundrel, (" un vrai scélérat,")
for he had only given him a single napoleon for all
the trouble he had had with him.

At the commencement of the action the Duke of
Wellington on horseback, surrounded by his Staff,
stood on the high ground to the right of the high road
from Brussels to Genappe, fig. 33, Plate 2. To say
where he afterwards was, is impossible—it would be
more difficult to say where he was not; wherever his
presence was most requisite, he was to be found; he
seemed to be every where present. Exposed to the
hottest fire, in the most conspicuous position, he
stood reconnoitring with his glass, watching the
Enemy's manœuvres, and issuing orders with the most
intrepid coolness, while balls and shells showered
around him, and his Staff Officers fell wounded and
dying by his side. Sir William De Lancey received
the shot which occasioned his death while the Duke
was in close conversation with him, and many of his
escapes seemed almost miraculous.*

* At a critical part of the battle, he took his station on a ridge, and declared
he would not stir from it, nor did he stir till he quitted it in triumph. In the
whole of the contest, he performed all the duties a military man could per-
form. *He was General of Division, Commander of Corps, and Colonel of a Regiment!*
He at times headed several different regiments, and rallied them to the attack.
Towards the close of the day, Napoleon led an attack of the Imperial
Guards; they were met by the British Guards (who did not feel the panic,
which it was boasted these men had occasioned among the Prussians and
Russians), and overthrown in an instant, in the finest style. The position of
Waterloo was well known to his Grace: in the summer of last year, his Grace
went there in his way to Paris, and on that occasion took a military view of
it. He then declared, that if ever it should be his fortune to defend Brussels,
Waterloo would be the position he would occupy. His conduct on the 18th
had thrown all his former actions into the shade; he never moved, but in fire;
and when one of the hottest charges was made by the Enemy, he threw himself
into the hollow square that was charged. Editor.

He was once on the point of being taken prisoner by a party of cavalry; and at one time, perceiving the 52nd and 95th regiments waver and give ground under the attack of an overwhelming force, he rallied them, placed himself at their head, charged in person, drove back the Enemy, and restored the day: but the hand of Providence shielded him in that eventful hour, to be the Saviour of his Country,* and the Conqueror of that inveterate foe, who during a long succession of years had turned the whole force of his gigantic power to effect the ruin of England; and " while he heaven and earth defy'd," and sought once more

> " To wade through slaughter to a throne,
> " And shut the gates of mercy on mankind,"

he was destined to meet his final overthrow on that field, from which he escaped with life, but not with honour.

† " My heart (says the Noble Duke) is broken by the terrible loss I have sustained of my old friends and companions, and my poor soldiers; and I shall not be satisfied with this battle, however glorious, if it does not put an end to Buonaparte."—In a letter to his mother, Lady Mornington, the Duke pays a high compliment to Buonaparte—he says that he did his duty—that he fought the battle with infinite skill, perseverance, and bravery—" and this," adds the noble Duke, " I do not state from any personal motive of claiming merit to myself—for the victory is to be ascribed to the superior physical force and constancy of British soldiers. To his brother, the Hon. Wellesley Pole, he writes, " never had he fought so hard for victory, and never from the gallantry of the Enemy had he been so near beaten." Editor.

The Duke of Wellington, in a letter to the Earl of Aberdeen, writes, " I cannot express to you the regret and sorrow with which I contemplate the losses the country has sustained; none more severe than that of Gen. Sir A. Gordon. The glory resulting from such actions so dearly bought, is no consolation to me, and I cannot imagine that it is any to you ; but I trust the result has been so decisive, that little doubt will remain, that our exertions will be rewarded by the attainment of our first object; then it is that the glory of the actions in which our friends have fallen, may be some consolation to me." E.

Extract from Mr. Vansittart, the Chancellor of Exchequer's Speech.—The

The conduct of the Duke of Wellington on this memorable day, realised the fabled achievements of the hero whose prowess is celebrated in the strains of an old Italian poet:

" Il valoroso Duca d'Inghilterra
" Fece, quel dì cio che, in molti anni fero
" Già mole cavaliér' maestri in guerra."

MORGANTE MAGGIORE
PULCI.

While the battle raged with unceasing and unexampled fury in the right wing, it was scarcely less tremendous in other parts of the field. The farm of La Sainte Haye, fig. 7, Plate 2, whose walls and roof are pierced and battered through with cannon-shot, formed a prominent feature in the action. It was long and vainly attacked, until at length the ammunition of the troops who were defending it, was exhausted, without the possibility of procuring more, and they were consequently obliged to abandon it.

The Enemy's reserve were chiefly placed upon the heights on their right, fig. 34, Plate 1, as it was the great object of Napoleon, if possible, to turn the left British flank, and separate us from the Prussians, with whom

merit of our troops and our officers in this great battle, was briefly expressed in the modest simplicity of the Duke of Wellington's dispatch; but the whole might be seen to more advantage, by looking at the accounts of our Allies, and of the Enemy. It was, indeed a proud day when the Conqueror of Europe was destroyed by one battle. Editor.

The Editor begs to recommend to public notice, an octavo print of this Illustrious Commander, as the best likeness yet seen, and which bears this character from those who well know his Grace. The plate is the property of Mr. Martyn, the possessor of an ancient unique cameo ring on a fine sardonyx : the subject a Biga, with Victory in a Car, presenting a Laurel Crown to a Conqueror.

The Editor recommends this print with the tracing of this Gem, as a proper ornament to the present work. The price is 5s. 6d.; Proofs 10s. 6d.

d

we maintained a communication through Ohain on
our left. To effect this, the most desperate efforts
were made, column propelling column, and fresh
masses of troops continually pouring down, while their
artillery scattered destruction along our line. Major-
General Sir Thomas Picton's division, stationed along
the hedge, fig. 12, 13, 14, 15, Plate 2, and in the lane
behind it, sustained the chief brunt of this long and
tremendous attack, and unshaken maintained their
ground. Upon this spot thousands of our brave soldiers met a glorious death; their gallant leaders,
wounded and dying on the ground, still cheered on
their men to the charge. The 28th Regiment formed
into a square, repelled the furious attacks of the
French Cuirassiers,* whose armour inspired them with
confidence and courage; still they could not stand
the English charge with the bayonet, and again and
again they were repulsed by the 28th Regiment, with

* The Cuirassiers of the French Imperial Guard are all arrayed in armour,
the front cuirass is in the form of a pigeon's breast, so as effectually to turn off
a musket shot, unless fired very near, owing to its brightness; the back cuirass
is made to fit the back; they weigh from nine to eleven pounds each, according to the size of the man, and are stuffed inside with a pad: they fit on by a
kind of fish-scaled clasp, and are put off and on in an instant. They have helmets
the same as our Horse Guards, and, straight long swords and pistols, but no
carbines. All the accounts agree in the great advantage that the French cuirassiers derived from their armour. Their swords were three inches longer than
any used by the Allies, and in close action the cuts of our sabres did no execution, except they fortunately came across the neck of the enemy. The latter
also feeling themselves secure in their armour, advanced deliberately and steadily, until they came within about twenty yards of our ranks, as a musket-ball
could not penetrate the cuirasses at a greater distance. The cuirass, however,
was attended with one disadvantage; the wearer, in close action, cannot use
his arm with perfect facility in all directions; he chiefly thrusts, but cannot
cut with ease. They are all chosen men, must be above six feet high, have
served in three campaigns, twelve years in the service, and of a good character;
and if there is a good horse to be found, they have them. It is to be observed,
that a wound through a cuirass mostly proves mortal." Editor.

immense loss: their intrepid Colonel, Sir Philip Belson, had a horse shot under him.

It was in a more advanced part of the field (I believe, near the tree, fig. 35,) that the lamented Sir Tho. Picton fell, in the thickest of the fight, gloriously " leading up his division to a charge with bayonets, by which one of the most serious attacks made by the Enemy was defeated" (vide Duke of Wellington's dispatch): a musket-ball, which passed through his right temple, was cut out with a razor, on the lower and opposite side of his head, where it appeared just breaking through the skin : he never spoke a word after he received the wound.*

Fig. 36, 37, 38, Plate 2. A hedge completely trodden down, where the fighting was particularly severe, and the carnage was dreadful; in front of it, and between it and the hedge, behind fig. 12, 13, Plate 2, huge graves or rather pits are filled with hundreds of dead, where the victors and the

---

* After the 16th, this gallant officer's coat was observed to be most dreadfully cut. After his lamented fall, it was discovered that he had been wounded in the hip on the 16th by a musket-ball, a circumstance which he carefully concealed from every one but his servant ; the wound had assumed a serious aspect for want of surgical assistance, having been only bandaged by himself and servant as well as circumstances would admit." Editor.

" Towards the afternoon, when the 92d were reduced to scarce 200 men, a column of 2000 of the Enemy bore down upon them, when this chosen band charged this overwhelming force with their bayonets, penetrating into the centre of them; the Scotch Greys cheering the brave Highlanders, rushed forward to support them, driving the Enemy back with great loss." (Vide the letter of the 92d regiment.)

At the battle of Quatre Bras, in a similar manner the 71st repulsed the Imperial Guard, and when they were retreating, the piper suddenly struck up the Pibroch: at the well-known sounds, the Highlanders charged their astonished enemies, still followed into the thickest of the fight by the piper, who was hurried forward by the impulse of valour—and the French were almost to a man cut to pieces.

vanquished are promiscuously thrown; so lightly had the clay been laid over them, that from one a hand had forced its way above the ground, and in another, a human face was distinctly visible. Indescribable was the horror of these objects. Three weeks after the battle, the very gales of heaven were tainted with the effluvia arising from them : besides these tremendous graves, of which several hundreds might be counted, immense heaps of the dead were burnt in different places, and their ashes, mingled with the dust, are scattered over the field.

Fig. 39, 40, in the back ground, is a part of the ground where the British bivouacked on the night of the 17th, beneath a heavy and incessant torrent of rain. In the morning of the 18th, they were just preparing breakfast, and dressing their beef-steaks, when Lord Wellington's Aides-de-Camp riding up, called to them, " Stand to your arms; the French are advancing:" instantly breakfasts and beef-steaks were abandoned; wet, cold, and hungry, but bold and undaunted, our brave soldiers ranged themselves to face their foes, and during nearly twelve hours, without any other aid, maintained the unequal, and the glorious contest. Let it never be forgotten, that the united British and Belgic army on that day amounted to little more than half the Enemy.

It was the policy of the Duke of Wellington, when attacked by such a tremendous superiority of force, to act upon the defensive, until joined by the Prussians, whose progress had been impeded by the dreadful state of the roads. Just before they appeared, the Enemy, turning their artillery against the centre of our army near the farm of La Sainte Haye, made a desperate effort with the united cavalry and artillery to force that point. Our gallant troops, unmoved, received the shock, and after a long and dreadful contest, the French were compelled to retreat in confusion. At that moment, the Prussians were seen advancing up the heights, to charge the Enemy in flank. The fire of the Prussian artillery began to take effect. Blucher himself appeared in the field. The Duke, seizing the critical moment, ordered the whole body of infantry, supported by the cavalry and artillery* to charge. They rushed impetuously forward with the irresistible force of valour. The French gave way on every side; a total rout ensued. They fled in confusion back to their own country, leaving behind them the whole of their baggage, their artillery, their prisoners, and their wounded. It was then, at half past nine in the evening, that Marshal Blucher † and Lord Wellington accidentally met at La Belle

---

* The fire of the artillery had been terrible, and destructive all day, but at this moment, no idea can be conveyed of the shock and crush that was now felt from it. *Extract from a French officer's letter, who was in the battle.* Editor.

† This gallant Veteran, the moment he heard of the engagement, got up, mounted his horse, and led his troops to the field. He had been confined to his bed in consequence of the injury he sustained on the 16th, when his horse was killed by a shot, and fell upon him. As he lay upon the ground, unable to extricate himself, and covered by his cloak, which fortunately prevented the Enemy from recognizing him, the French Cuirassiers twice charged close past him, and he was on the point of being trampled to death by an advancing squadron, when he was rescued by a regiment of Prussian Hulans. With some assistance he instantly re-mounted another horse, and the first words this brave old officer spoke, were; " Now then, my fine fellows, let us charge them again!" " The horse which the Prince Regent presented to Marshal Blucher, on which he placed so high a value, was killed under him during the late battle." Marshal Blucher seemed to have been possessed of the spirit of prophecy, when he told the British officers after the review at Grammont, " that he should soon have the pleasure of meeting them in Paris." Certainly this prediction was verified, even sooner than his most sanguine expectations could have anticipated.

Alliance. It was in this miserable cottage, pierced through and through with cannon-balls, and deserted by all but the dead and dying, that their first interview took place, after four days of battle with the common enemy, and in the moment when victory had crowned their united arms. Both armies being on the same road, they decided that the British troops, who had fought for nearly twelve hours,* should relinquish the pursuit to the Prussians, who had come in at the close of the contest, in time to decide the victory and to share its glory. They parted: Blucher proceeded on his way, Lord Wellington returned to Waterloo. As he crossed again this fatal scene, on which the silence of death had now succeeded to the storm of battle, the moon breaking from dark clouds shed an uncertain light upon this wide field of carnage, covered with mangled thousands of that gallant army, whose heroic valour had won for him the brightest wreath of victory, and left to future times an imperishable monument of their country's fame. He saw himself surrounded by the bloody corpses of his veteran soldiers, who had followed him through distant lands—of his friends—his associates in arms—his companions through many an eventful year of danger and of glory: in that awful pause which follows the mortal conflict of man with man, emotions unknown or stifled in the heat of battle forced their way, the feelings of the man triumphed over those of the general, and in the very hour of victory, Lord Wellington burst into tears.

* At the close of the pursuit of the Enemy, the Duke of Wellington, finding the troops so exhausted as to be unable to proceed, recommended it to them to give the flying Enemy three British cheers before halting. Editor.

Thus ended a day as glorious in its achievements as important in its results, which at once averted the calamities that threatened the world, and altered the destinies of nations. Thus ended a contest, which has raised the glory of England to its highest pitch, and in which the last and most decisive proof was given, that in every age, and every country, under every disadvantage of numbers and situation, from the days of Cressy and Agincourt to the present times; on the burning sands of Egypt, and the sheltered shores of Italy; on the mountains of Portugal, the plains of Spain, amidst the rocks of the Pyrenees, the fields of Flanders, and the valleys of France; in foreign lands, and in their native soil; by land, and by sea; Englishmen have ever been victorious over their ancient and presumptuous foes.

The names of Alexandria, of Maida, of Vimiera, of Corunna, of Talavera, of Barrosa, of Albuera, of Salamanca, of Vittoria, of Orthes, of the Pyrenees, of Thoulouse, and finally, of Waterloo, will proclaim to future times, the deeds of British valour—deeds more like the tales of chivalry and romance, than the events of real life, and of civilized ages.

If it was a day of glory, it was likewise a day of sorrow for Britain; if we triumph in it as the proudest, we must also mourn it as the most bloody of all the battles that she has fought or won. Those who witnessed the most sanguinary contests of the Peninsular war, declared they had never seen so terrible a carnage; and the Prussians acknowledged that even the battle of Leipsic was not to be compared to it. The dead could not be numbered; and by those who visited this dreadful field of glory, and of death, the day after the battle, the spectacle of horror that it exhibited can never be forgotten.

The mangled and lifeless bodies were even then stripped of every covering—every thing of the smallest value was already carried off. The road between Waterloo and Brussels, which passes for nine miles through the thick shades of the Forest of Soigné, was choaked up with scattered baggage, broken waggons, and dead horses. The heavy rains and the great passage upon it, had rendered it almost impassable, so that it was with extreme difficulty that the carriages containing the wounded could be brought along. The way was lined with unfortunate men who had crept from the field, and many, unable to go farther, lay down and died:—holes dug by the road side, served as their graves, and the road, weeks after the battle, was strewed with the tattered remains of their clothes and accoutrements. In every village and hamlet,—on every road,—in every part of the country, for thirty miles round, wounded soldiers were found wandering; the wounded Belgic and Dutch stragglers exerting themselves to the utmost to reach their own homes. So great were the numbers of the wounded, that, notwithstanding the most active and unremitting exertions, the last were not removed from the field of battle into Brussels till the Thursday following.

It is impossible for words to do justice to the generous kindness, and unwearied care and attention, which the inhabitants of Brussels and Antwerp, and the whole of the Belgic people, exerted towards these poor sufferers. Nor should the humanity shown by the British soldiers themselves be unnoticed. The wounded of our army, who were able to move, employed themselves in tying up the wounds and administering to the wants of their suffering enemies*—a striking and noble contrast to the brutality with which the French had treated our prisoners.†

The desolation which reigned on the scene of action, cannot easily be described. The fields of high standing corn were trampled down, and so completely beaten into the earth, that they had the appearance of stubble. The ground was completely ploughed up in many places with the charge of the cavalry, and the horses' hoofs, deep stamped into the earth, left the traces where many a deadly struggle had been. The whole field was strewed with the melancholy vestiges of war and devastation—soldiers' caps pierced with many a ball, and trodden under foot—eagles that had ornamented them—badges of the legion of honour — cuirasses — fragments of broken arms, belts and scabbards innumerable—shreds of tattered cloth, shoes, cartridge boxes, gloves, highland

* *It is pleasing to add the testimony of a foreigner.* " The British regiments of infantry, which displayed such intrepid valour in the battle of the 18th, gave, after the action, the most affecting and sublime example ever offered to nations. They were seen forgetting their own wounds, and hardly escaped from the sword of the enemy, proceeding to afford all the succour in their power to those who had just endeavoured to cut them down, and who, in their turn, had fallen on the field of destruction. The conduct of the English army is mentioned with admiration, as uniting the heroism of valour, to the heroism of humanity." Editor.

† We forbear to dwell upon the horrid details of the merciless barbarity with which the French treated our prisoners: besides being stripped and plundered, exposed to the severest privations, and the grossest insults, many of our bravest officers, whose names respect for the feelings of their surviving friends forbids us to mention, were actually murdered in cold blood, after surrendering up their swords; such diabolical cruelty would be incredible, and for the sake of humanity, we would gladly doubt its truth, had we not incontrovertible proofs from many eye-witnesses of these brutal murders. *Vide letters from an officer of the Life Guards and of Light Dragoons.*

bonnets, feathers steeped in mud and gore—French novels, and German Testaments—scattered music belonging to the bands—packs of cards, and innumerable papers of every description, that had been thrown out of the pockets of the dead, by those who had pillaged them. French love-letters, and letters from mothers to their sons, and from children to their parents, were scattered about in every direction. Amongst the thousands that we examined, it was however remarkable, that we found only one English letter. It was from a soldier's wife to her husband.

Upon this field were performed deeds of valour as heroic as any which swell the page of history, which will for ever be buried in oblivion. Of those who performed them, many rest in the bed of honour, and those who survive, will never relate the story of their own achievements. Modesty is ever the concomitant of true courage; and thus actions, which could they have been witnessed, would have been the theme of an applauding world, are now unknown and unadmired. It is scarcely possible to notice the merits of any individual without injustice to others. It is difficult to say who were bravest, when all were brave; and who were greatest, amongst an army of heroes.

Never was there an attack more tremendous, nor a resistance more firm, unshaken and triumphant. The French army, infuriated by despair, animated by the promised plunder of Brussels, and filled with perjured traitors, who had betrayed their king and country, and who knew that their lives and fortunes depended on success, fought, from first to last, with the desperation of madness. But they could not wrest victory from the hands of the British. In every land and in every clime, wherever the French have appeared as oppressors, the British have sprung forward as deliverers—they have sought foreign lands, not as enemies but as friends—they have fought and conquered, not to destroy, but to save. It is but a few years since the late arrogant Ruler of France made the boast that he would invade this country—scatter its armies—dethrone its monarch—and march his victorious troops into its capital. His threats have recoiled upon himself; England has answered him not by words, but by deeds.—*His* country is invaded—his armies are scattered—he is himself dethroned, and the victorious troops of England are in his capital! It is to them we are indebted that he comes to our shores not as a conqueror, but as a suppliant, not as a tyrant, but as a captive. It is to them we owe our preservation—our very existence as a nation—our dearest liberties, and our proudest glories. Wounded thousands of that brave army are now enduring in lingering pain and confinement, the sufferings they have received in the service of their country. During years of hardships they have braved for her, in foreign lands, the dangers and the horrors of war. They have triumphed in many a well-fought field—they have sought every changing scene where honour was to be gained, or glory to be won. Oh! who, at this triumphant moment, does not feel it his proudest boast to be an Englishman!—Who can refuse a tribute of regret to the brave who have perished!—What heart does not swell with gratitude to that gallant army, whose heroic valour has raised their country to the highest pitch of glory, and to whom we are indebted, that while other nations sank beneath the yoke of despotism, and basely crouched at the feet of the Tyrant, England alone proudly defended her own rights—singly maintained the long and glorious contest—broke the spell which bound the kingdoms of Europe in ignominious slavery— and finally restored to the world, Peace, security, and independence!

> " England! be still, *even to thy latest* times,
> " The nurse of Heroes, and the scourge of crimes;
> " Still may thy patriot Sons, where'er they roam,
> " Diffuse abroad the rights they boast at home;
> " Still unseduc'd by glory's vain increase,
> " Make war thy pathway to the shrine of Peace;
> " Still guard the rights of Freemen against Slaves,
> " And rule, with Heaven's approval—proudly rule the waves!"
>
> T. MOORE.

London, Aug. 7, 1815.

FURTHER PARTICULARS,*

OF THE

BATTLE AND ITS CONSEQUENCES:

FROM

DIFFERENT SOURCES.

" It would be confessed that whatever the former fame of the Duke of Wellington might have been, yet, in all the various occurrences of his life, in all those great achievements which he had performed, and which had called for the thanks of the Nation, he had never before attained to a height of glory like the present.—And in all the great events which he had been engaged in, and those scenes that he had witnessed, it had never before fallen to the lot of this illustrious Commander to render so great a service to his country, so extensive a benefit to the world. —There was in the present victory an acknowledged pre-eminence over all those that had preceded it: but when we looked at its influence and combination, in which are bound up all the interests of the civilized world, it was almost impossible to conceive an idea adequate to its magnitude and importance.—The position of the Allied Army, previously to the late one, was a very peculiar one, and, without meaning to impute blame, or to suppose any neglect of security, he must say that the circumstance of the armies not being actually engaged in hostilities, necessarily led to a distribution of force for the more convenient obtainment of subsistence for so large an army. The whole line of troops destined to act upon France not being equally advanced, it was clearly not the interest of the Allies to become the assailants; the army, therefore, which was to act upon the offensive, making its point of union the point it chose for an attack, must have a great advantage over an army situated as the Allied Army was: and yet it was impossible to alter that position; for if Marshal Blucher and the Duke of Wellington had concentrated their forces, they must have left open a long line of country at the mercy of the Enemy, who might have made use of such a lapse for the most important ends: and therefore, not imputing any neglect of preparation to the Commander, it must be evident that the attacking army would have the advantage. With such a force on the frontiers of France, it was with Buonaparté a great object to attack it in some powerful point before the Combined Powers were all perfectly ready for operations; and accordingly he had acted with all the decision of character and energy of mind that he was known to possess, and as soon as he could leave Paris he joined his army, and directing it to the North commenced his operations. In considering the nature and

---

* The Editor has to acknowledge his obligations for the kindness and attention of his friends in procuring for him many of the interesting letters and anecdotes forming these particulars which precede the Official Documents, &c.

extent of the forces engaged, he must observe, that of the ten corps d'armée which France possessed, the five which were complete were united under Buonaparté, together with his guard, and other cavalry. These troops had certainly maintained their ancient character; and *one feature of the victory was, that it had been gained over the best troops of France, and that too, at a moment when they displayed all their ardour, and when their conduct even surpassed all that they had before performed; although this force did not amount to less than one hundred and thirty or forty thousand men, the flower of the French army!*—*That was a regular and disciplined army, even before the Bourbons quitted France, and for which, since the return of Buonaparté, every thing had been done to make it effective; it was the force which had been selected, and combined to act upon the northern frontier.* To particularize the conduct of any part of the Allied Army, would be invidious, where all had acquitted themselves with nearly equal bravery; but he might be allowed to say, that except the British part, (who themselves were only such as the country could spare at a time when a strong detachment of our veteran troops had been sent to America) nearly the whole was a green army: the Allies, particularly the Dutch, Belgians, Hanoverians, and troops of Nassau, were chiefly young soldiers; and deducting the absent corps, consisting of 25,000 under Prince Frederick, and the other corps distributed along the line to the northward, there was not in action a greater number than 64,000 men, to support the attack of the whole French army. He fully felt what we owed to the illustrious Prussians, who were ready to support the British army, and enabled them to make that movement, without which the Duke could not have obtained such an advantage over a superior force. The effort he made was crowned with success; and with his energy of mind, and example of person, it was certain that much would be effected.— But from that example *it was dreadful to reflect on the risks to which his valuable life was exposed; — in fact, such was the dauntless activity, that he was much more exposed than any private soldier, who could only bear the hazard of a single spot; but the Duke was every where, at least wherever danger was.*—Under the circumstances in which the Duke found himself at the end of the day, when the French had been repulsed, and Marshal Bulow advanced, he put himself in motion, and attacked the French; *their lines did not resist, as ours had done; he forced the second line, routed their whole army, and took more than half the artillery of their army and its ammunition.* — It was impossible to attempt to predict what would be the result of this victory; but this much was certain, that the Duke of Wellington had been enabled to follow the Enemy with an army that had been either fighting or marching the whole day before. The French had attacked with their usual temerity: by this he did not mean to censure them; Buonaparté was justified in his attempt; he had been driven back; but if he could have succeeded, the effect would have been fully equal to the sacrifice made to obtain the object." *Extract from Lord Castlereagh's Speech in the House of Commons, preparatory to his motion for a Vote of Thanks, June 23; which see, with the Officers included in the Waterloo Honours, at the end of this work.*

The whole of the mighty and important operations were carried on within a tract of country extending from Thuin to Ligny, about 20 miles, from Ligny to Waterloo about the same distance, and from Waterloo to Thuin, about 25 miles. There is no doubt, that Buonaparté would have been attacked as soon as the Russians had come up; but in point of fact, he commenced hostilities, without any menacing movement on the adverse side. He issued an Order of the Day on the 14th to his soldiers, appealing to their passions, by reminding them that that day was the anniversary of Marengo and of Friedland.* On the following morning, at day-light, he put the whole of his army in motion, and attacked the Prussian posts established on the Sambre; in the course of the day, he succeeded in driving them from that river, making himself master of the ground from Thuin to Fleurus. According to Buonaparté's account of the result, in the various contests on the 15th, the Prussians lost 2000 men, while the French only experienced a loss of 10 killed, and 80 wounded! Buonaparté also claims a victory on the 16th. He however admits, that he lost 3000 men on that day; but says he took many thousand prisoners, and 40 pieces of cannon! On Sunday the 18th, the grand struggle was made. The whole weight of the French force, with the exception of Vandamme's corps, was thrown upon the army of the Duke of Wellington, whose line was within fifteen miles of Brussels. The battle began about ten o'clock in the morning, with a furious attack on a post occupied by us in front of our right. This was supported by a very heavy cannonade upon our whole line, with repeated attacks of infantry and cavalry, until seven in the evening, when the Enemy made a desperate attempt to force our left, in which, after a severe contest, he was defeated, and retired in great disorder. This was the happy moment, seized by the genius and resolution of our unrivalled Hero, to advance his whole line of infantry, supported by cavalry and artillery, against the Enemy, who was unable to resist the English attack. The first line was driven back on the second, and the second was almost instantly broken. All was now total rout and confusion; artillery, baggage, every thing was abandoned; and the true British perseverance of General and soldiers was crowned with a success so much the more precious, as it had remained long in a state of the most awful suspense. The French fought with greater desperation than ever before witnessed; but it may be added, that after their rout, they became more completely broken than ever, threw away their arms by whole regiments, and were, in short, wholly dispersed and disorganised. The loss on the part of the British has been severe, but on that of Buonaparté it is almost beyond calculation. On all sides was seen a total disregard of personal danger. The leaders were mingled in the heat of the fray, like the meanest soldier. Marshal Blucher, it is said, was for some moments a prisoner. As to Buonaparté, he was more than once inclosed among the British troops, and disentangled, as it were, by miracle. He led on the Guard himself to the charge; and seemed to feel, that there could be no hope for his power, but in the absolute jeopardy of his life.

---

* Vide Documents in the French Official Accounts.

LETTER FROM AN OFFICER TO HIS FRIEND IN CUMBERLAND.

Camp of Clichy.

"All the sharers of my tent having gone to Paris, and my servant having manufactured a window-shutter into a table, and a pack-saddle into a seat, I will no longer delay answering your two affectionate letters, and endeavour to comply with your demand of an account of the battle such as it offered to my own eyes.

"On the 15th of June, every thing appeared so perfectly quiet, that the Duchess of Richmond gave a ball and supper, to which all the world was invited; and it was not till near ten o'clock at night that rumours of an action having taken place between the French and Prussians were circulated through the room in whispers: no credit was given to them, however, for some time; but when the General Officers whose corps were in advance began to move, and when orders were given for persons to repair to their regiments, matters then began to be considered in a different light. At eleven o'clock the drums beat to arms, and the 5th Division, which garrisoned Brussels, after having bivouacked in the Park until day-light, set forward towards the frontiers. On the road we met baggage and sick coming to the rear; but could only learn that the French and Prussians had been fighting the day before, and that another battle was expected when they left the advanced posts. At two o'clock we arrived at Genappe, from whence we heard firing very distinctly; half an hour afterwards we saw the French columns advancing, and we had scarcely taken our position when they attacked us. Our front consisted of the 3rd and 5th Divisions, with some Nassau people, and a brigade of cavalry, in all about 13,000 men; while the French forces, according to Ney's account, must have been immense, as his reserve alone consisted of 30,000, which, however, he says, Buonaparté disposed of without having advertised him. The business was begun by the first battalion of the 95th, which was sent to drive the Enemy out of some corn-fields, and a thick wood, of which they had possession: after sustaining some loss, we succeeded completely; and three companies of Brunswickers were left to keep it, while we acted on another part of the line: they, however, were driven out immediately; and the French also got possession of a village which turned our flanks. We were then obliged to return, and it took us the whole day to retake what had been lost. While we were employed here, the remainder of the army were in a much more disagreeable situation: for in consequence of our inferiority in cavalry, each regiment was obliged to form a square, in which manner the most desperate attacks of infantry and charges of cavalry were resisted and repelled; and when night put an end to the slaughter, the French not only gave up every attempt on our position, but retired from their own, on which we bivouacked. I will not attempt to describe the sort of night we passed—I will leave you to conceive it. The groans of the wounded and dying, to whom no relief could be afforded, must not be spoken of here, because on the 18th it was fifty thousand times worse. But a handful of men lying in the face of such superior numbers, and being obliged to sleep in squares for

· fear the Enemy's dragoons, knowing that we were weak in that
arm, might make a dash into the camp, was no very pleasant reverie
to soothe one to rest. Exclusive of this, I was annoyed by a wound
I had received in the thigh, and which was become excessively painful.
I had no great coat, and small rain continued falling until late the
next day, when it was succeeded by torrents. Boney, however, was
determined not to give us much respite, for he attacked our piquets
at two in the morning; some companies of the 95th were sent to
their support; and we continued skirmishing until eleven o'clock,
when the Duke commenced his retreat, which was covered by Lord
Uxbridge. The Blues and Life Guards behaved extremely well.

" The whole of the 17th, and indeed until late the next morning,
the weather continued dreadful; and we were starving with hunger,
no provision having been served out since the march from Brussels.
While five officers who composed our mess were looking at each
other with the most deplorable faces imaginable, one of the men
brought us a fowl he had plundered, and a handful of biscuits, which,
though but little, added to some tea we boiled in a camp-kettle, made
us rather more comfortable; and we huddled up together, covered
ourselves with straw, and were soon as soundly asleep as though
reposing on beds of down. I awoke long before day-light, and found
myself in a very bad state altogether, being completely wet through
in addition to all other ills. Fortunately I soon after this found my
way to a shed, of which Sir And. Barnard (our commandant) had
taken possession, where there was a fire, and in which with three or
four others I remained until the rain abated. About ten o'clock the
sun made his appearance, to view the mighty struggle which was to
determine the fate of Europe; and about an hour afterwards the
French made their dispositions for the attack, which commenced on
the right. The Duke's Dispatch will give you a more accurate idea
of the ground, and of the grand scale of operations, than I can do;
and I shall therefore confine myself to details of less importance
which he has passed over.

" After having tried the right, and found it strong, Buonaparté
manœuvred until he got 40 pieces of artillery to play on the left,
where the 5th division, a brigade of heavy dragoons, and two companies of artillery, were posted. Our lines were formed behind a
hedge, with two companies of the 95th extended in front, to annoy the
Enemy's approach. For some time we saw, that Buonaparté intended
to attack us; yet as nothing but cavalry were visible, no one could
imagine what were his plans. It was generally supposed, that he
would endeavour to turn our flank. But all on a sudden, his cavalry
turned to the right and left, and showed large masses of infantry, who
advanced up in the most gallant style, to the cries of " Vive l'Empereur!" while a most tremendous cannonade was opened to cover
their approach. They had arrived at the very hedge behind which
we were—the muskets were almost muzzle to muzzle, and a French
mounted officer had seized the colours of the 32d regiment, when
poor Picton ordered the charge of our brigade, commanded by Sir
James Kempt. When the French saw us rushing through the hedge,
and heard the tremendous huzza which we gave, they turned; but
instead of running, they walked off in close columns with the greatest

steadiness, and allowed themselves to be butchered without any material resistance. At this moment, part of Gen. Ponsonsby's brigade of heavy cavalry took them in flank, and, besides killed and wounded, nearly 2000 were made prisoners. Now Buonaparté again changed his plan of attack. He sent a great force both on the right and left; but his chief aim was the centre, through which lay the road to Brussels, and to gain this he appeared determined. What we had hitherto seen, was mere "boys play" in comparison with the "tug of war" which took place from this time, (3 o'clock) until the day was decided. All our army was formed in solid squares—the French cuirassiers advanced to the mouth of our cannon—rushed on our bayonets: sometimes walked their horses on all sides of a square to look for an opening, through which they might penetrate, or dashed madly on, thinking to carry every thing by desperation. But not a British soldier moved; all personal feeling was forgotten in the enthusiasm of such a moment. Each person seemed to think the day depended on his individual exertions, and both sides vied with each other in acts of gallantry. Buonaparté charged with his Imperial Guards. The Duke of Wellington led on a brigade consisting of the 52nd and 95th regiments. Lord Uxbridge was with every squadron of cavalry which was ordered forward. Poor Picton was killed at the head of our Division, while advancing. But in short, look through the list engaged on that day, and it would be difficult to point out one who had not distinguished himself as much as another. Until eight o'clock, the contest raged without intermission, and a feather seemed only wanting in either scale to turn the balance. At this hour, our situation on the left centre was desperate. The 5th Division, having borne the brunt of the battle, was reduced from 6000 to 1800. The 6th Division, at least the British part of it, consisting of four regiments, formed in our rear as a reserve, was almost destroyed, without having fired a shot, by the terrible play of artillery, and the fire of the light troops. The 27th had 400 men, and every officer but one subaltern, knocked down in square, without moving an inch, or discharging one musket; and at that time I mention, both divisions could not oppose a sufficient front to the Enemy, who was rapidly advancing with crowds of fresh troops. We had not a single company for support, and the men were so completely worn out, that it required the greatest exertion on the part of the officers to keep up their spirits. Not a soldier thought of giving ground; but victory seemed hopeless, and they gave themselves up to death with perfect indifference. A last effort was our only chance. The remains of the regiments, were formed as well as the circumstances allowed, and when the French came within about 40 paces, we set up a death-howl, and dashed at them. They fled immediately, not in a regular manner as before, but in the greatest confusion.

"Their animal spirits were exhausted, the panic spread, and in five minutes the army was in complete disorder: at this critical moment firing was heard on our left, the Prussians were now coming down on the right flank of the French, which increased their flight to such a degree, that no mob was ever a greater scene of confusion; the road was blocked up by artillery; the dragoons rode over the infantry;

arms, knapsacks, every thing was thrown away, and *" sauve qui peut "* seemed indeed to be the universal feeling. At eleven o'clock, when we halted, and gave the pursuit to Blucher's fresh troops, 150 pieces of cannon and numbers of prisoners had fallen into our hands. I will not attempt to describe the scene of slaughter which the fields presented, or what any person possessed of the least spark of humanity must have felt, while we viewed the dreadful situation of some thousands of wounded wretches who remained without assistance through a bitter cold night, succeeded by a day of most scorching heat; English and French were dying by the side of each other ; and I have no doubt, hundreds who were not discovered when the dead were buried, and who were unable to crawl to any habitation, must have perished by famine. For my own part, when we halted for the night, I sunk down almost insensible from fatigue; my spirits and strength were completely exhausted. I was so weak, and the wound in my thigh so painful, from want of attention, and in consequence of severe exercise, that after I got to Nivelles, and secured quarters, I did not awake regularly for 36 hours."

*Extract of a Letter from an Officer in the Guards.**

Bavay, June 21, 1815.

" I date my letter from the first town in France, we having this morning, for the second time, violated its boasted frontiers, and that too, in the very teeth of a triple line of fortresses, and on the anniversary of Vittoria, after a battle, which, notwithstanding the brilliant and most glorious tale of the 21st of June, 1813, must in every way rank above it, in the page of history.

" Assured of my safety, you will doubtless be anxious for an account of the three eventful days I have witnessed ; and therefore I lose no time in gratifying your curiosity, particularly as I am aware of your desire to be informed of every thing relating to your friends the Guards. We were suddenly moved from Enghien, where we had remained so many weeks in tranquillity, on the night of the 15th instant, or rather the morning of the 16th, at three o'clock. We continued on our march through Braine-le-Comte, (which had been the Prince of Orange's head-quarters,) and from thence on to Nivelles, where we halted, and the men began making fires and cooking. During the whole of this time, and as we approached the town, we heard distinctly a constant roar of cannon ; and we had scarcely rested ourselves, and commenced dressing the rations, which had been served out at Enghien, when an Aide-de-Camp from the Duke of Wellington arrived, and ordered us instantly under arms, and to advance with all speed to *Les Quatre Bras,* where the action was going on with the greatest fury, and where the French were making rapid strides towards the object they had in view, which was to gain a wood, called " Bois de

* Capt. Batty of the Grenadier Guards has also published an account of the affairs in the Netherlands, with a general plan of the whole campaign, of Quatre Bras and of Waterloo, which is strongly recommended to the notice of the reader.

e

Bossu;" a circumstance calculated to possess them of the road to
" Nivelles," and to enable them to turn the flank of the British
and Brunswickers, and to cut off the communication between
them and the other forces which were coming up. The order
was, of course, instantly obeyed; the meat which was cooking,
was thrown away; the kettles, &c. packed up, and we proceeded,
as fast as our tired legs would carry us, towards a scene of slaughter, which was a prelude well calculated to usher in the bloody
tragedy of the 18th.

  "We marched up towards the Enemy, at each step hearing more
clearly the fire of musquetry; and as we approached the field of
action, we met constantly waggons full of men, of all the various
nations under the Duke's command, wounded in the most
dreadful manner. The sides of the road had a heap of dying and
dead, very many of whom were British: such a scene did, indeed,
demand every better feeling of the mind to cope with its horrors;
and too much cannot be said in praise of the Division of Guards,
the very largest part of whom were young soldiers, and volunteers
from the Militia, who had never been exposed to the fire of an
enemy, or witnessed its effects. During the period of our advance from Nivelles, I suppose nothing could exceed the anxiety
of the moment, with those on the field. The French, who had a
large cavalry and artillery, (in both of which arms we were quite
destitute, excepting some Belgian and German guns,) had made
dreadful havock in our lines, and had succeeded in pushing an im-
mensely strong column of tirailleurs into the wood I have before
mentioned, of which they had possessed themselves, and had just
began to cross the road, having marched through the wood, and
placed affairs in a critical situation, when the Guards luckily came
in sight. The moment we caught a glimpse of them, we halted,
formed, and having loaded, and fixed bayonets, advanced; the
French immediately retiring; and the very last man who attempted
to re-enter the wood, was killed by our grenadiers. At this instant,
our men gave three glorious cheers, and, though we had marched
fifteen hours without any thing to eat and drink, save the water we
procured on the march, we rushed to attack the Enemy. This
was done by the 1st brigade, consisting of the 2d and 3d battalions
of the first regiment; and the 2d brigade, consisting of
the 2d battalion of the Coldstream and third regiment, were
formed as a reserve along the chaussée. As we entered the
wood, a few noble fellows, who sunk down overpowered with
fatigue, lent their voice to cheer their comrades. The trees were
so thick, that it was beyond any thing difficult to effect a passage.
As we approached, we saw the Enemy behind them, taking aim at
us: they contested every bush, and at a small rivulet running
through the wood, they attempted a stand but could not resist us,
and we at last succeeded in forcing them out of their possessions.
The moment we endeavoured to go out of this wood, (which had
naturally broken us,) the French cavalry charged us; but we at
last found the third battalion, who had rather *skirted* the wood,

and formed in front of it, where they afterwards were in hollow
square, and repulsed all the attempts of the French cavalry to
break them. Our loss was most tremendous, and nothing could
exceed the desperate work of the evening; the French infantry
and cavalry fought most desperately; and after a conflict of nearly
three hours, (the obstinacy of which could find no parallel, save in
the slaughter it occasioned,) we had the happiness to find ourselves complete masters of the road and wood, and that we had at
length defeated all the efforts of the French to outflank us, and turn
our right, than which nothing could be of greater moment to both
parties. General Picton's superb division had been engaged since
two o'clock P. M., and was still fighting with the greatest fury; no
terms can be found sufficient to explain their exertions. The fine
brigade of Highlanders suffered most dreadfully, and so did all the
regiments engaged. The gallant and noble conduct of the Brunswickers was the admiration of every one. I myself saw scarcely
any of the Dutch troops; but a regiment of Belgian light cavalry
held a long struggle with the famous Cuirassiers, in a way that can
never be forgotten; they, poor fellows, were nearly all cut to
pieces. These French Cuirassiers charged two German guns,
with the intent of taking them, to turn them down the road on our
flank. This charge was made along the chaussée running from
Charleroi to Brussels; the guns were placed near the farm-houses
of Les Quatre Bras, and were loaded, and kept till their close
arrival. Two companies, (I think of Highlanders,) posted behind
a house and dung-hill, who flanked the Enemy on their approach,
and the artillery, received them with such a discharge, and so near,
as to lay (with an effect like magic) the whole head of the column
low; causing it to fly, and be nearly all destroyed. We had fought
till dark; the French became less impetuous, and after a little
cannonade they retired from the field. Alas! when we met after
the action, how many were wanting among us; how many who
were in the full pride of youth and manhood, had gone to that
bourn, from whence they could return no more! I shall now
close my letter; and in my next, will endeavour to give you some
description of the 18th; for, to add to this account now, would be
but to harrow up your mind with scenes of misery, of which those
only who have been witnesses, can form an adequate idea."

Village of Gommignies, June 22, 1815.

" Having completed our day's march, I once more take up my
pen, and after giving you some of the leading features of the 17th,
shall do my best to relate to you, as far as lies in my power, the
most striking incidents of the glorious day of Waterloo. At day-
break, on the 17th, we were again under arms, having snatched a
hurried repose to our wearied limbs, on the ground near which we
fought. Uncertain as to the movements of the Enemy, or whether
they purposed renewing their attack, we were in a state of anxious
suspense: and the skirmishing at intervals in our front, made us
expect that something was about to be done; during all this time,

we were employed, by parties, in bringing in our wounded companions, whom the darkness had the night before prevented our finding, and in doing our best to be ready for any thing that might occur, and in assuaging, as well as we could, the sufferings of those around us. We succeeded in finding the bodies of our four officers, Captains Grose and Brown, Ensigns Lord Hay and Barrington, who were killed; and had the melancholy satisfaction of paying the last tribute of respect to their remains. They were buried near the wood, and one of our officers read the service over them. Never did I witness a scene more imposing; those breasts which had, a few hours back, boldly encountered the greatest perils, did no now disdain to be subdued by pity and affection; and if the ceremony wanted the real clerical solemnity due to its sacred character, it received an ample equivalent in this mark of genuine regard, and the sincerity with which we wished them a more immortal Halo, than that which honour will confer. The whole night was occupied in getting up the cavalry and artillery; and report said, that the Duke of Wellington had it in contemplation to become, in his turn, the assailant; be that as it may, we were ordered to fall back by the Charleroi road through Genappe, to our position of Waterloo. I will not invite you to accompany us on our march, which was only marked by fatigue, dust, heat, and thirst. After halting for a short time, to ascertain our actual position, we marched to it, and were greeted by one of the very hardest showers of rain I ever remember to have seen, which lasted nearly half an hour—it then ceased. The whole afternoon was taken up by the various divisions getting to their respective posts, and making active preparations for the expected attack on the morrow. Our position was a very compact one; the extreme left resting on Ter la Haye, the left centre on La Haye Sainte, and the right centre on Hougoumont; and the extreme right was thrown back to a certain degree, in consequence of a ravine, which would otherways have laid it open to the Enemy.

" We were posted near Hougoumont, into which the four light companies of the division of Guards, under Colonel M'Donald and Lord Saltoun, were thrown. The house had a large garden attached to it, laid out in the Dutch fashion, with parallel walks and high thick hedges, and was surrounded by an orchard. As the army fell back, the Enemy's cavalry attacked the rear, and there were constant skirmishes and charges of cavalry during the day. Towards seven o'clock in the evening the French cannonaded Hougoumont and our position for near an hour and a half, and were answered by the guns on the top of the hill in our front. We were moved back a little distance to get out of the exact range of the shot, and after continuing during the time I have above mentioned, eagerly awaiting a further developement of their attack, the firing ceased, and we continued till the morning in the situation we now held. The weather, which had hitherto been showery, became settled into a decided and heavy rain, which continued in actual torrents the complete night through, accompanied by a gale of wind and constant thunder and lightning. Such a night few have witnessed, it was one that imagination would paint as alone fit for the festival of the dæmons of death, and for the fates to complete the web of those brave souls whose thread of life was so nearly spun. After such a night of horrors and contending expectations, the dawn of any kind of day was welcome; it seemed, however, with difficulty to break through the heavy clouds which overhung the earth, and appeared so slowly, that it seemed as if nature reluctantly lent her light to assist at the scene of carnage and distress, which was to mark the history of this eventful day. Our artillery, which had the night before so admirably answered the fire of the French guns, was all placed on the heights in our front. It is here necessary for me to remark, that our position comprehended the two roads from Charleroi and Nivelles to Brussels, which united at the village of Mont St. Jean, and formed rather an acute angle, The Prince of Orange's corps composed the first line, with the whole artillery in its front, and Lord Hill's corps the right flank and second line.

" About a quarter past eleven o'clock, A. M. the battle commenced by the French making a most desperate and impetuous attack upon Hougoumont, against which, as well as La Haye Sainte, they directed their most furious efforts during the whole day. Hougoumont, however, appeared to be the principal object they had in view, since its possession would have uncovered our flank, and have afforded them a most fatal advantage over our line ; in a word, had it been lost, nothing short of its being re-taken at any rate could have repaired the misfortune. The French opened upon us a dreadful cross-fire, from three hundred pieces of artillery, which was answered with a most uncommon practice from our guns ; but to be just, we must own that the French batteries were served in a manner that was terrible. During this period, the Enemy pushed his troops into the orchard, &c. &c., and after its being contested for some hours, he succeeded in reducing our men to nothing but the house itself. Every tree, every walk, every hedge, every avenue had been fought for with an obstinacy almost unparalleled ; and the French were killed all round, and at the very door of the house, to which, as well as a hay-stack, they succeeded in setting fire; and though all in flames over their heads, our brave fellows never suffered them to penetrate beyond the threshold; the greatest part of the wounded on both sides were, alas, here burned to death!—In consequence of this success on the part of the French, the Coldstream and third regiment were ordered into the wood, from whence they drove the Enemy ; and every subsequent struggle they made to re-possess themselves of it, proved abortive. The places of these two battalions of guards were supplied by two of our gallant friends, the Black Brunswickers, who seemed, like salamanders, to revel in the smoke and flames. The 2d and 3d battalions of the first regiment were formed with the two battalions of Brunswickers into hollow squares, on the slope and summit of the hill, so as to support

each other; and in this situation we all lay down, till between
three and four o'clock P. M., in order to avoid the storm of death,
which was flying close over our heads, and at almost every moment carrying destruction among us : and it is, you will allow, a
circumstance highly creditable to those men, to have lain so many
hours under a fire, which for intensity and precision was never, I
believe, equalled; with nothing else to occupy their attention,
save watching their companions falling around them, and listening to their mournful cries. It was about the time I have just
named, that the Enemy, having gained the orchard, commenced
their desperate charges of cavalry, under cover of the smoke
which the burning houses, &c. had caused; the whole of which
the wind drifted towards us, and thus prevented our observing
their approach. At this period the battle assumed a character
beyond description interesting, and anxiously awful. Buonaparté was about to use against us an arm, which he had never yet
wielded but with success. Confidently relying upon the issue of
this attack, he charged our artillery and infantry, hoping to capture
the one, and break the other, and, by instantly establishing his
own infantry on the heights, to carry the Brussels road, and throw
our line into confusion. These cavalry, selected for their tried
gallantry and skill (not their height or mustachios), who were the
terror of Northern Europe, and had never yet been foiled, were
first brought up by the 3d battalion of the 1st regiment. Never
was British valour and discipline so pre-eminent as on this occasion; the steady appearance of this battalion caused the famous
Cuirassiers to pull up; and a few of them, with a courage worthy
a better cause, rode out of the ranks, and fired at our people and
mounted officers, with their pistols, hoping to make the face of
the square throw its fire upon them, and thus become an easy
prey: but our men, with a steadiness no language can do justice
to, defied their efforts, and did not pull a single trigger. The
French then made a sudden rush, but were received in such a
manner, and with a volley so well directed, as at once to turn
them; they then made an attempt on the 2d battalion, and the
Brunswickers, with similar success; and, astonished at their own
failure, the cool intrepidity of their opponents, and the British
cheers, they faced about. This same game was played in succession by the Imperial Horse Guards, and Polish Lancers, none of
whom could at all succeed in breaking our squares, or making the
least impression upon them whatever. During their attacks, our
cavalry rushed out from between the squares, and carried havock
through the Enemy's ranks, which were nearly all destroyed. I
cannot here resist relating an anecdote of Major Lloyd, of the
Artillery, who, with another officer, (whose name I could not
learn) was obliged to take refuge in our square at the time these
charges were made, being unable to continue longer at their posts.
There was a gun between our battalion and the Brunswickers,
which had been drawn back; this, Major Lloyd with his friend
discharged five or six times at the French cavalry, alternately

loading it and retiring to the square, as circumstances required. We could see the French knocked off their horses as fast as they came up, and one cannot refuse to call them men of singular gallantry; one of them, indeed, an officer of Imperial Guards, seeing a gun about to be discharged at his companions, rode at it and never suffered its fire to be repeated while he lived. He was at length killed by a Brunswick rifleman, and certainly saved a large part of his regiment by this act of self-devotion. Thus discomfited, Buonaparté renewed his cannonade, which was destructive to a degree, preparatory to an attack of his whole infantry. I constantly saw the noble Duke of Wellington riding backwards and forwards, like the Genius of the storm, who, borne upon its wings, directed its thunders where to burst. He was every where to be found, encouraging, directing, animating. He was in a blue coat, and a plain cocked hat, his telescope in his hand; there was nothing that escaped him, nothing that he did not take advantage of, and his lynx's eyes seemed to penetrate the smoke, and forestall the movements of the foe. How he escaped, that merciful Power alone can tell, who vouchsafed to the allied arms the issue of this pre-eminent contest; for such it is, whether considered as an action by itself, or with regard to the results which it has brought about. Upon the cavalry being repulsed, the Duke himself ordered our second battalion to form line with the third battalion, and, after advancing to the brow of the hill, to lie down and shelter ourselves from the fire. Here we remained, I imagine near an hour. It was now about seven o'clock. The French infantry had in vain been brought up against our line, and, as a last resource, Buonaparté resolved upon attacking our part of the position with his veteran Imperial Guard, promising them the plunder of Brussels. Their artillery covered them, and they advanced in solid column to where we lay. The Duke, who was riding behind us, watched their approach, and at length, when within a hundred yards of us, exclaimed, " Up, Guards, and at them again! " Never was there a prouder moment than this for our country or ourselves. The household troops of both nations were now, for the first time, brought in contact, and on the issue of their struggle the greatest of stakes was placed. The Enemy did not expect to meet us so soon; we suffered them to approach still nearer, and then delivered a fire into them, which made them halt; a second, like the first, carried hundreds of deaths into their mass; and, without suffering them to deploy, we gave them three British cheers, and a British charge of the bayonet. This was too much for their nerves, and they fled in disorder. The shape of their column was tracked by their dying and dead, and not less than three hundred of them had fallen in two minutes to rise no more. Seeing the fate of their companions, a regiment of tirailleurs of the Guard attempted to attack our flank; we instantly charged them, and our cheers rendered any thing further unnecessary, for they never awaited our approach. The French now formed solid squares in their rear, to resist our advance, which, however, our cavalry cut to pieces. The Duke now ordered the

whole line to move forward: nothing could be more beautiful.
The sun, which had hitherto been veiled, at this instant shed upon
us in departing rays, as if to smile upon the efforts we were making, and bless them with success.   As we proceeded in line down
the slope, the regiments on the high ground on our flanks were
formed into hollow squares, in which manner they accompanied
us, in order to protect us from cavalry—the blow was now struck,
the victory was complete, and the Enemy fled in every direction:
his *déroute* was the most perfect ever known; in the space of a
mile and a half along the road, we found more than thirty guns,
besides ammunition waggons, &c. &c.   Our noble and brave co-
adjutors, the Prussians, who had some time since been dealing
out havock in the rear of the Enemy, now falling in with our line of
march, we halted, and let them continue the pursuit.   Buonaparté
fled the field on the advance of the Prussians, and the annihilation of his Imperial Guard, with whose overthrow all his hopes
perished.   Thus ended the day of " Waterloo."   The skill and
courage of our Artillery could not be exceeded.   The brigade of
Guards, in Hougoumont, suffered nothing to rob them of their post :
every regiment eclipsed its former deeds by the glories of to-day;
and I cannot better close this than by informing you, that when we
halted for the night, which we did close to where Buonaparté had
been during a great portion of the battle, and were preparing our
bivouac by the road side, a regiment of Prussian lancers coming
by, halted and played " *God save the King*," than which noth:ng
could be more appropriate or grateful to our feelings; and I am
sure I need scarcely add, that we gave them three heartfelt cheers,
as the only return we could then offer."

Extract from a Letter by an Officer in the Guards.

" On the evening of the 15th, we heard that the French were
passing the frontiers, and we received orders to hold ourselves in
readiness to march; at two o'clock we received our orders to march,
and were off at three.   We passed through Braine le Comte, and
proceeded to a bivouac near Nivelles.   While we were setting ourselves down, an order came to move immediately to the left through
Nivelles—having passed it, we heard the firing very close, and soon
met many wounded Belgians coming in.   At five o'clock, General
Maitland galloped up, and ordered the grenadiers to drive the French
out of a wood, and in about half an hour we perfectly cleared it.
When we opened at the end of the wood, the Enemy threw in a most
tremendous fire of round and grape shot, from which we found it
necessary to retire.   We got out of the wood in another part, and
they immediately advanced columns to attack us, which deployed very
regularly, and drove us a short way back.   However, we advanced
again; and they gave way, and retired to their guns.   They then advanced upon us, and having driven us back a second time, their cavalry attempted to charge; but a square of *Black Brunswickers*
brought them up, while we were nimbly slipt into the wood on our
right, lined the ditches, and paid them handsomely.   Our loss was
very severe, and we found great difficulty in forming our line again.

At last we effected it with the third battalion of our regiment, and then we drove every thing before us. We kept possession of the wood all night. The Prussians and French had been engaged from two o'clock in the morning, in the position of Fleurus; and the former had been driven back. The French then tried to get possession of the road to Brussels. They had a severe contest with the Dutch, and one of our divisions, and had succeeded in driving the Dutch out of a wood, (Bossu I think it is called). We arrived at the very moment the French skirmishers were appearing. We dashed in and cut them up properly, though our loss was severe. Out of 84, I had only 43 left in my company.* At night the remains of the battalion bivouacked at the head of the road, and during the night we received a strong reinforcement. They call this the action of Quatre Bras (where two high roads cross). In the morning of the 17th, the Enemy made no further attempt against us; and as the Prussians had retired during the night, we did the same very leisurely, about 11 o'clock, taking up a position in front of a village called Waterloo, at a point where the high road or chaussée to Brussels crosses that from Nivelles to Namur. Here we remained quiet through the night, except that it rained more furiously than ever I experienced, even in Spain. We were quite wet through, and literally up to the ancles in mud. The cavalry were considerably engaged during the day of the 17th, but the Hussars could not make much impression against their heavy armed opponents. The Life Guards behaved most nobly, and carried every thing before them. The morning of the 18th dawned full of expectation of something decisive being done.

"But first I must give you some idea of our position. It ran from the Brussels chaussée to the right, about a mile and a half in length, and then turned very sharply to the right and crossed the chaussée from Nivelles to Namur, which two chaussées cross each other, so that we were nearly in a quarter-circle (like an open fan, the two outside sticks being the chaussées).

"At the turn and at the bottom of a slope was a farm and orchards, called Hougoumont. This was the key of our positions, and in front of our centre. On this point the most serious attack was made.

"At twelve o'clock the columns of the Enemy moved down from the heights which they had occupied during the night, and our artillery began to cannonade them most furiously, which their artillery returned; and it is said that 300 pieces were in use that day. The British infantry were drawn up in columns under the ridge of the position. We were at the turn or knuckle with two battalions of Brunswickers. The Third Regiment of Guards were in columns in front of the turn, and the Coldstream at the farm-house. The light infantry of the division were to defend the orchard and small wood next to it. The third division were in squares to the left of our squares, and under cover of the ridge.

"Unfortunately for us, during the cannonade the shot and shells which passed over the artillery, fell into our squares, and I assure you

---

* It appears by the Gazette, that the first regiment of Guards lost, in this affair, five officers killed and eight wounded: no official return has yet been made of the men; but report states that regiment to have lost 500 killed and wounded in this battle, exclusively of the action on the 18th.

I never was in a more awful situation.   Col. Cook (who commanded the battalion) was struck with a grape shot as he sat on the ground next to me.   The Enemy now made an attack with infantry and cavalry on the left, in hopes of carrying the chaussée to Brussels; but the artillery guns cut them to pieces every time they advanced. They then attempted to charge the guns with cavalry; but the squares of infantry kept up so smart a fire that they could never reach our guns, though the artillerymen were obliged to leave them to get out of our fire.   When the Enemy found the attempt fail on this point, he ordered an attack on the farm-house, which it was necessary for him to possess in order to turn the right of our position. There it was that the serious struggle commenced.   Two companies of light infantry, under Lord Saltoun, disputed the wood and orchard most gallantly, but were at last obliged to retire under cover of the house, when the Enemy were charged by the light infantry of the 2d brigade (the Coldstream and 3d), and driven back with great loss. At this period the Coldstream entered the house, which the Enemy set on fire by shells, but did not entirely consume it.   The Enemy were foiled in two repeated attempts, and were each time severely cut up by the artillery.   When they failed in their attacks upon our squares, the cavalry rushed out from between our squares and cut them up most desperately.   When he found these efforts vain, he began his attack upon the centre.   He first endeavoured to carry the guns with his cavalry, which came up most gallantly; but our squares sent them to the right about three times in great style. ` I never saw any thing so fine, the cavalry rushing out and picking up the deserted cannon.   After these failures he brought up his *Garde Impériale,* just opposite to our brigade, which had formed in line on their advancing.   We were all lying under shelter of a small bank, as they covered their advance with a most terrible fire of grape and musketry. Buonaparté led them himself to the rise of the hill, and told them " that was the way to Brussels:" we allowed them to approach very near*—when we opened so destructive a fire, that there were soon above 300 of them upon the ground, and they began to waver.   We instantly charged, but they ran as fast as possible.   The Duke of Wellington, observing this crisis, brought up the 42d and 95th, taking the Enemy in flank, and leading them himself quite close up.   The Enemy's column was entirely dispersed.   After this, we were again annoyed with grape and musketry, which obliged us to retire.   On fronting, we saw another heavy column of the *Chasseurs de la Garde Impériale.*   We immediately started at double quick time to meet them; but they had had such a proper reception just before, that they never let us come near them; and when they turned, the rout became general.   We ran on as fast as we could, and the cavalry started after them.   We got about two miles that evening, taking ourselves 30 pieces of cannon.   Nothing could be more complete and decisive.   Most fortunately the Prussians came on the field at this moment, and pursued the Enemy through the night."

* Those who witnessed this, speak of it as a most handsome affair. The Imperial Guard's charge was most furious; General Byng, from circumstances, could only receive them in line; the volley was destructive, literally knocking the mass back; nothing could exceed the effect, or be superior to this determined coolness. Gen. Byng, in the course of the day, had many narrow escapes; in one instance, a cannon-ball forced itself between his arm and side, rending a hole in his cloak, but did no other mischief than leaving a slight contusion in the hip.   Editor.

Extract of a Letter from an Officer in the Horse Guards.

" On the morning of the 16th, about 2 o'clock, the route came, and we; (the 2d Life Guards) marched from Murbecke at 7 ; and after a very long day's march, passed through Braine Le Comté and Nivelles, at which last place we heard a cannonade. As our army was then engaged with the French, we proceeded at a brisk trot, for several miles on the road from Nivelles, and halted for the night in a wheat field. Next morning, our men were drawn up in a line of battle fronting the wood where the French had retired ; but they would not venture to attack us. Lord Wellington by a *ruse de guerre*, however, drew them from the wood by a rapid retreat, for a few miles, towards Brussels ; which brought the French exactly on the spot where he wished to fight them, and where he might bring his cavalry into play. While retreating, we were overtaken by a violent thunder-storm and heavy rain, which rendered us very uncomfortable. During the whole, no man was lost, but the Blues lost three or four; the 1st Life Guards charged some of the French Lancers, and almost cut them to pieces. We were drawn up to give them a second charge, but they would not stand it. This evening, we bivouacked in a piece of boggy ground, where we were mid-leg up in mud and water. About 11 o'clock, the grand action commenced. We were very soon called into action, and charged the French Cuirassiers of the Imperial Guard, whom we almost cut to pieces. A second charge of the same kind, left but few of them ; but we suffered very much: we have with the regiment at present about 40 men. We know of 49 wounded, so that the rest must be either killed or prisoners. Lieut. Col. Fitzgerald was killed soon after the first charge. Capt. Irby was taken prisoner, as his horse fell with him in returning from the charge : he has since made his escape, and joined us; but they have stripped him of his sword, watch, and money, and had nearly taken his life. The heaviest fire was directed against the Household brigade the whole of the day; and it is astonishing how any of us escaped. At the conclusion of the battle, we were masters of the field ; and only one officer of the 2nd Life Guards, with two corporals and 40 privates, remained. There was no officer of the 1st Regiment, all, or most of them having been dismounted. The command of the two regiments for the night was given by Lord Somerset to the remaining officer of the 2d.* Col. Lygon had one horse shot under him, towards the conclusion of the battle, and the horses of several of our officers were wounded. Lord Welington was with the brigade the greater part of the day, during which time I saw him repeatedly. He seemed much pleased; and was heard to observe, to the general officer near him, that it was the hardest battle he had ever fought, and that he had seen many charges, but never any to equal the charges of the Heavy Brigades, particularly the Household. We made in all four charges; viz. two against cavalry, and two against the Imperial Guards."

Extract of a Letter from an Officer of the 6th or Inniskilling Dragoons.

Brussels, 21st June, 1815.

" Hostilities commenced on the 16th, by an attack on the Prussian advanced posts. Our army was put immediately in motion, and after two affairs, we retired to our position 14 or 15 miles from hence, and covering the great road to this place. Our right rested on a hill, our centre on another more advanced, forming part of the circumference of a circle; the left I did not see. The attack commenced on the right, but was soon transferred with great fury to the centre. The Enemy attacked in three solid columns of immense depth, supported by cavalry and artillery. Our infantry received them in line: behind the infantry, was Gen. Ponsonby's Brigade of Cavalry, consisting of the 1st Dragoons, the Greys, and Inniskillings:—when the infantry had given their fire, we charged through intervals, which the infantry made for us, in open column of half squadrons, and completely upset the Enemy's three massy columns, not leaving a man. Gen. Ponsonby and Col. Hamilton of the Greys being killed, the command of the brigade devolved upon me :—nothing could be finer than their conduct, or more successful. Our strength before the action was 1050; after it, about 100; " but many had been sent to escort prisoners." In killed, wounded, &c., we lost about two thirds. The Enemy reiterated his attacks on the centre with fresh troops, but without success. He then made a most desperate attack on the right, where my small brigade of 100 men was called to charge about 400 cavalry, supported by artillery and squares of infantry. I was told that every thing depended on our exertions— it was in leading my miserable remains, that I received my wound. The charge was not successful, indeed almost every man and horse was knocked down. Such butchery was never beheld—the day was long doubtful, but the fortunate arrival of the Prussians decided it."*

Extract from a Letter by an Officer in the Light Dragoons.

" That previous to the Horse Guards charge, on the 18th, his regiment was ordered to attack a body of Lancers and Cuirassiers, on whom they could make no impression : that numbers of their men having fallen, they were forced to retreat, when the French were ordered to charge in their turn, and from the superior weight of the horses and men, and their species of armour and weapons, he had the mortification to see them cut down numbers of his regiment: that being in the rear, he soon received himself so desperate a shock from one of the lancers as to plunge himself and horse into a deep ditch, with such violence that the horse never got out alive; while he, being thrown, fortunately escaped with life, though immersed in, and covered with mud and water : that

* This letter has previously appeared in a Scotch Newspaper, the officer's name is found to be Muter. Editor.

in his fall, the lancer attempted to run him through, luckily missed his aim, and only tore away part of the flesh of the arm : that finding himself in the midst of the Enemy, he had offered an officer to surrender, but who declined taking charge of him then, and ordered him to an adjacent field, where were several others under similar circumstances : that he had the mortification to witness from thence the overthrow of numbers of the men during their retreat, but at last to his great satisfaction saw the heavy brigade advance to the charge, who in their turn overthrew every thing in their way, literally rolling both men and horses of the French over to a considerable distance, by the tremendous force of their charge, and cutting down all before them. Seeing the face of affairs to be changed, he contemplated upon an escape; and having communicated his idea to a brother officer near him, they together made for another part of the field, and had hardly gained the summit of a steep bank, when looking back, they observed a small French detachment enter the field, and cut down in cold blood all the prisoners there, waiting for the orders of their captors, to the number of 30 or 40, while only himself and companion escaped."

42d Regiment.*

" The 42d regiment was ordered to advance along with a Belgian corps, to support the Prussians, who were under fire. In

Extract of a Letter from a Private of the 42d Regiment to his Father.

General Hospital, Antwerp, June 24, 1815.

" On the 15th, about twelve o'clock at night, we turned out, and at two in the morning marched from the city of Brussels, to meet the Enemy, who were advancing in great force on that city. About three o'clock in the afternoon of the 16th, we came up with them. Our whole force did not exceed 12,000 men, who were fatigued with a long march of upwards of twenty miles, encumbered with knapsacks and other luggage. The day was uncommonly warm and no water to be had on the road; however, we were brought up in order of battle. The French being strongly posted in a thick wood, to the number of 40,000 men, including cavalry and lancers, gave us very little time to look round us ere the fight commenced on both sides, in an awful and destructive manner, they having every advantage of us, both as to position and numbers, particularly in cavalry, and the British dragoons had not yet come up. The French cavalry charged the British line of infantry three different times, and did much execution, until we were obliged to form squares of battalions, in order to turn them, which was executed in a most gallant manner, and many hundreds of them never returned. Still they sent up fresh forces, and as often we beat them back. The battle lasted until it was quite dark, when the Enemy began to give way, our poor fellows who were left alive following them as long as they could see, when night put an end to the fatigues of a well-fought day. Thousands on both sides lay killed and wounded on the field of battle; and, as the greater part of the action lay in corn fields along a vast track of country, many hundred must have died for want of assistance through the night, who were not able of themselves to crawl away. I was wounded by a musket-ball, which passed through my right arm and breast, and lodged in my back, from whence it was extracted by a surgeon in the hospital of this place. Captain M. is most severely wounded, having several shots through his body, and the regiment, in general, are mostly cut off. We have heard, since we came here, that our fine brigade, which entered the field on that eventful day, consisting of the 3d battalion Royal Scots, 42d, 44th, and 92d regiments, are now formed into one battalion, not exceeding in the whole 400 men. Lord Wellington retired in the night to wait for reinforcements, and next day our cavalry and the rest of the army arrived. Thus I have given you as full an account of affairs, principally what I witnessed on the march, owing either to their own superior quickness, or to the want of ardour in the Belgians, the latter were left behind; and in a field of high standing corn, a column of French Lancers advanced upon them. Col. Macara ordered the regiment to form a square, in doing which two companies were left out, or were rather in the act of falling in, when they were pierced by the Lancers, and in one moment overwhelmed, and literally annihilated. The Lancers then attacked the square, and repeated the charge several times. One half of them were also mowed down, together with the brave Colonel; upon which Lieut.-Col. Dick took the command, though wounded by a musket-ball; he succeeded in rallying and forming them into a diminished square, and thus presented an undaunted resistance to the Enemy. The Lieutenant-Colonel was at length, from the loss of blood, carried from the field; but the gallant remnant of the men succeeded in putting the Lancers to flight."

79th Regiment.

" Of the 79th, not more than 96 non-commissioned officers and privates escaped unhurt on the 16th and 18th; the regiment on the 16th, before the battle, was 800 strong.

92d Regiment.

" The 92d, forming one of the regiments of the 1st Brigade along with the Scots (Royals), 42d and 44th, was suddenly ordered to Brussels, on the 15th, at night—after which they marched thirty miles, and came up with the Enemy about two or three o'clock on the 16th, and immediately marched into the field; but as the first division was only there with some Brunswickers, the 92d was ordered to take position in a ditch, to cover the guns and cavalry, as the junior regiment: in the mean time the other part of the division went a little to the left, to check the French infantry passing that way. The situation of this regiment was most unpleasant for upwards of an hour, but possessed of an ample view of seeing all that was going on, although exposed very much to the Enemy's guns, at this period, from the Duke and Staff being just in front of the regiment; and at this point, all the reinforcements passed to their stations. Very many of the Duke's Staff were then wounded. At this time the French cavalry began to attack a village; the Brunswick cavalry, then in front of the 92d, went to meet them: not being in sufficient strength, the Brunswickers retired upon the 92d in some confusion; we could not then give any help—the French cut down a great many of their rear men, and dismounted two guns. The Brunswickers passed round the right flank, intermingled with French; as soon

the 16th. Nothing can exceed the kindness and attention of the inhabitants of this city to our wounded men; the hospital is constantly filled with ladies and gentlemen, who, although speaking a different language, personally administer to our wants with the kindest attention, distributing clean shirts, bread, wine, coffee, tea, milk, and fruit of all sorts, with every requisite for our comfort and accommodation."

as they were cleared, the regiment fired. The grenadiers being wheeled back on the road which lined the ditch, we linèd, to enable them to fire as the French passed—the others to fire obliquely on the road—on those following the Brunswickers, the volley seperated the front charge from the rear by the gap which we made ; nothing was seen but horses and men tumbling over each other—the rear of the Enemy retreated, and the front dashed through the village, cutting down all stragglers. The Enemy's charge being repelled, we now prepared to charge, against a body of cavalry nearly in motion, supported by infantry—" Come on, my old 92d," was the word from the Adjutant-General Barnes— he then jumped from the ditch, and we charged beautifully ; Colonel Cameron led the regiment ; the Enemy's fire was severe : we then moved from behind a house, and passed the corner of a garden parallel to the road, when a volley was given by a column on the right, which was retreating to the wood—this fire killed our gallant Colonel Cameron, and did considerable execution.* This column kept the regiment five minutes before the garden could be cleared, to advance to the lines—the fire was now dreadful, and the regiment suffered much : the French at length retreated up to the side of the wood, still, however, keeping up a tremendous fire. The 92d had by this separated itself from the line, and not more than fifty left, when a regiment of Guards was sent to its relief—the men afterwards retired behind the houses, when the loss was found to be 28 officers, and 270 men. The Guards, however, were not allowed to keep possession of the position we had gained, five minutes.

" In the afternoon of the 18th, the regiment, which was then reduced to about 200 men, found it necessary to charge a column of the Enemy which came down on them, from 2 to 3000 men : they broke into the centre of the column with the bayonet; and the instant they pierced it, the Scotch Greys dashed in to their support, when they and the 92d cheered and huzza'd " Scotland for ever." By the effort which followed, the Enemy to a man were put to the sword or taken prisoners; after which the Greys charged through the Enemy's second line, and took the eagles.

" It was perhaps the most destructive battle ever fought. The loss fell almost entirely on our division, which, along with the Brunswick troops and some Prussians, was the only one up for the first two hours. The three Scotch regiments are nearly annihilated ! !—Ours had only six officers who escaped, and some are so dangerously wounded, as to give little hope of their recovery. We were amply revenged, however ; and gave the French a lesson, which they will not soon forget : but they are so strong

* Lieut. Col. Mitchel then took the command of the regiment, was soon wounded, and carried off the field, resigning the command to Capt. Holmes, the senior officer present. Capt. Holmes was soon after wounded, and carried off. Capt. Dugald Campbell then took the command, and he was soon wounded and carried off; the command thus devolved on the next senior officer present.

on this point, that, notwithstanding our giving them such a drubbing, his Grace found it necessary to occupy a better position, by retiring about a league and a half in the rear. He expected another attack, but it did not take place; and this gave time to Lord Hill and Blucher to operate upon the Enemy's flanks, which obliged him to retrograde. His Grace was strong enough to repel any attack that might be made upon him.

" You would be astonished how we could have borne the fatigue which we suffered. We marched from Brussels at one in the morning, and arrived at three o'clock in the afternoon at the place of action, having marched nine leagues. We were engaged in five minutes after, and continued so till night. I was wounded about half past eight, when I was obliged to walk six miles to the nearest village, where I lay in pain and sleepless till day-light. I was again obliged to walk to Brussels, seven leagues; not being able to bear the motion of a waggon. The exertion has done me no good. I am indeed surprised that I was able to stand it out. The poor fellows who had escaped, bivouacked in the field, without tents or baggage—last night the same—and it has rained incessantly. I am unable to give you the particulars of the action —it was altogether brilliant and decisive. The Highlanders, and Royals, in particular, behaved admirably. Our regiment was charged by a body of Cuirassiers of the Guard, and we gave them a noble peppering. We also charged a column of infantry, which we dispersed; on getting behind some hedges, they rallied, and gave us a terrible fire. It was here that our regiment suffered most. Cameron our gallant Colonel, (Vide Military Notices) and four other officers, fell almost at the same instant—this was about six o'clock. We drove them, however, from all the hedges, and advanced upon two guns, which began to open upon us with grape. These we also drove from two different positions. The French suffered prodigiously; but our cavalry and artillery not being up, we could do no more than repel their attacks.*

" The courier arrived in the Duke of Bassano's carriage. Our regiment was again engaged, and suffered severely. There is scarcely one officer left. Never was there a sight so touching, so extraordinary, as this town presents—the people in crowds going out to meet the wounded with refreshments, bandages, &c.—all the women employed in the kindest offices. I returned to the house of my former landlord, where I am treated as if I were his own brother. The French prisoners are treated by the populace in the most violent manner; the escort can with difficulty protect them from being attacked."

---

* The Scotch regiments, who had during the battle of the 18th, given such proofs of heroic intrepidity, offered a most sympathetic example in appearing to forget their wounds, to render services to their wounded Iron Foe, who, but the minute before had been attempting with all their might to destroy them. We know from respectable persons, that upwards of 500 of the French owe their lives to their generous enemies.

95th Regiment.

" The 95th received a charge of horse, and destroyed every one, making use of the horses to carry away their wounded."

Extract of a Letter—Artillery.

" The brigade attached to the second division of the army, behaved most nobly and effectively, and have obtained great reputation—they completely turned the Imperial Guards, led on by Buonaparté in person, when they were within forty yards.—Their gallant commander, Captain Napier, received several wounds about the head, body, and arms; his thigh broken in two places. I am happy to add, he is doing well.

" A foreign regiment of * * * * * * * * * *, extremely well horsed and appointed, and soldier-like, were ordered by the Commander-in-Chief of the cavalry, to place themselves under line, on the brow of a hill; and, from being raw soldiers, he would not put them to any difficult service, but gave the conditional orders, that if the charge he was about to make with an English brigade succeeded, they were then to ride in and cut away:—for the performance of this, the most earnest entreaty was made, and the strongest promise given, that every attention should be paid to the direction—the charge was made and completely succeeded, and the Enemy in the greatest confusion. The noble Earl then looked round for his gallant supporters—but they had turned their horses heads, and were trotting away towards Brussels; an Aide-de-Camp was immediately dispatched, and, notwithstanding that he even took the Colonel by the collar, to stop them was impossible; and it was then begged as a favour, and entreated of them, not to go further than Waterloo—it was all useless, to Brussels he would go, and to Brussels he went. This, although a great disappointment, was attended with such outré (and it may be said comic) effect, that every one who noticed it, notwithstanding their serious occupation, were convulsed with excessive laughter, and among them the noble Duke himself. The men, however, to do them credit, it is understood, have brought their Colonel to an account.

" The Irish howl set up by the Inniskilling Dragoons, and other Irish Regiments, is reported to have carried almost as much dismay into the ranks of the Enemy, as their swords The stubborn bravery and conduct of these regiments contributed much to the success of the day, it having been their lot to find themselves in the hottest part of the action, innumerable opportunities (particularly the Inniskilling) were afforded them of showing their devotion to their country's honour, and exalted sense of gallantry and duty." An officer of the Inniskilling says, " Our brigade charged, upset and completely destroyed three large columns of infantry; at least 9000. The old Inniskillings behaved most gallantly."

f

" His Royal Highness the Prince of Orange, hurried by ardour into the midst of the battle, was surrounded and taken by the French. The seventh battalion perceived the Prince's danger, hastened to his assistance, and succeeded in delivering him; his Royal Highness took off the insignia of his order, and threw it into the midst of the battalion, exclaiming : " Children, you have all deserved it ! "—It was fastened to their colours on the field of battle, amid cries of " Long live the Hereditary Prince ! " All the Belgians swore to defend, even to death, this mark of honour; and at this sublime moment, many of these brave men fell, while pronouncing this patriotic oath."

" Towards the close of the day, when he saw the lines were bending, he was at the head of his people, cheering and exciting them, amidst the hottest fire, when his Royal Highness received a musket-ball in his left arm, which lodged in his shoulder. (*Vide Dutch Account.*)

Extract of a Letter from an Officer, from the Bivouac near Landrecy.

" After our bivouac of the 18th after the battle, we marched to Nivelles, over the terrible field : so horrible a scene, scarcely any man ever witnessed ; the ground, for the space of a league, was covered with bodies, absolutely lying in ranks, and horses grouped in heaps, with their riders. Towards our right was a chateau, which during the battle took fire from the Enemy's shells; and in that state was heroically defended by Saltoun, and afterwards by the 2nd brigade of guards. The appearance brought to my mind St. Sebastian ; it was equally horrid, though on a smaller scale.—I did not mention to you, in my last, that towards the close of the action, we were engaged with the Imperial Guard. After seven hours dreadful cannonade, and during which we suffered very much from grape and shells, the French cavalry advanced in a gallop, in masses, up the slope of a gentle hill; they were arrested by a continual échelon of squares, whose cross fire cut them to pieces, our men standing like statues. After this succeeded a tiraillade (sharp-shooting) of about half an hour, when we all imagined the fight was over, and that it would die away with the night; but to our surprise, the head of an immense column of the Old Guard appeared trampling down the corn fields in our front: they advanced to within one hundred and fifty yards of our brigade, without attempting to deploy or fire a shot. Our wings threw themselves immediately forward, and kept up such a murderous fire, that the Enemy retired, losing half their numbers, who, without any exaggeration, literally lay in sections. Their loss in cannon is estimated at 160 pieces, and the Prussians take more every step they advance. I have now to tell you the lamentable loss of 32 officers of our regiment, which has left the command of the 2d battalion under Saltoun, and the third under Reeve, the two youngest captains. Maitland commands the division, and Fered the brigade, in consequence of General

Cooke's wounds. Colonel Cooke was struck by a cannon-shot on the shoulder, about a foot above my head; but I believe his case is not hopeless. Those who were at Vittoria, Albuera, and Leipsic, say, their fire was not to be mentioned, or the carnage to be compared to that of Waterloo.—The 73d regiment is commanded by Lieut. Robert Stewart, and the 1st light German battalion has only one captain left.—Milnes not being likely to recover, or Luttrell command for some time, I have this morning accepted the command of the regular light infantry company, instead of the supplementary one, which I commanded in the action. Greville is in company with me. We marched on the 19th to Nivelles, 20th to Binch, 21st to Bavay, and to-day to this place, 15 miles from Cambray, 5 miles from Quesnoy, and 10 from Landrecy. The Hussar brigade, and some light troops, with a corps of Prussians, observe Maubenge, and some Hanoverian cavalry are stationed round Quesnoy. The Prussians advance by Charleroi, Maubuge, and Landrecy, and Givet. I hope soon to date from Paris."

EXTRACTS FROM LETTERS RELATIVE TO THE CONDUCT OF THE 3rd BATTALION OF THE ROYALS.

Battle of the 16th.

"I have great pleasure in detailing the conduct of the gallant 3rd Battalion of the Royal Scots; and though I have been present with the regiment at the battles of Busaco, Salamanca, Vittoria, Fuentes d'Honor, both stormings of San Sebastian, the passage of the Bidassoa, &c. (in all of which they bore a most conspicuous part, and suffered most severely), I can assure you they never evinced more steadiness and determined bravery than at the late battle. About half-past one o'clock on the 16th, the battalion was taken from its place in the centre of the 5th division, by a movement to its own left, by order of Sir Thomas Picton, and instantly by command of that lamented officer brought into action by a charge upon a column of the Enemy: it succeeded beyond our most sanguine expectations in routing this column, who afterwards formed under the protection of their cavalry, and then commenced a most galling fire upon us, which we returned with the utmost steadiness and precision. The battalion was brought into action under the most trying circumstances imaginable, and continued so for a long time; but they never for one moment lost sight of that character which upon former trials they had so well earned and maintained. The ground through which they moved was planted with corn that took the tallest men up to the shoulders; and the Enemy by this, and the advantage of the rising ground, threw in volley after volley of grape and musketry, which did astonishing execution.

"After being engaged for some time in a line, the battalion was formed into a square to resist the Enemy's cavalry, who were then advancing in great force; and I have the pride of stating, that though charged six or seven times by an infinite superiority of numbers, the French cavalry never for an instant made the slightest impression upon the square of the Royal Scots.

" The high encomiums given to this battalion on the morning of the 17th, by the General Officers both of Brigade and Divisionn,for its conduct on the 16th, have made me very proud of being a Royal Scot. The Cuirassiers never were able to make the smallest impression upon our squares, nor did we lose one single man by the cavalry. We were at the very commencement of the action sent with Sir James Kempt's brigade, by order of Sir T. Picton, and remained apart from our own brigade the whole day. The 42d and 92d were chiefly engaged near a village, in which the Commander of the Forces remained with the head-quarters for a great part of the afternoon. Our battalion and the 28th formed one square, and it so happened that the Cuirassiers charged that part of the square in which the Royals were posted.

" On the afternoon of the 17th, the battalion, in concert with the rest of the army, retired through the village of Genappe, and took up the position of Waterloo, which was destined to add fresh glory to the British arms. About nine o'clock in the morning of the 18th, the battalion was attacked by the Enemy, and with very little interruption the entire day they formed a line of skirmishing in front of the brigade. I have often seen the battalion engaged ; but I must confess, on this trying day, they far excelled any thing I ever witnessed, and, indeed, so pleased was the late General Picton with their gallantry and good conduct, that he several times expressed it himself to them in the most flattering terms."

From an Officer to his Father (written on the field of battle), dated Les Quatre Bras, 19th June, 1815.

" England has to thank the talents of her comsummate General, and the bravery of the allied troops under his command, their steadiness, and great endurance of privation ; for yesterday's victory is equalled by none of modern days, except Leipsig.

" On the 14th, the French army transferred the seat of war from its own territory, to that of the Allies, by crossing the frontier in the direction of Fontaine St. Eveque, and moving in large masses on Charleroi and Fleurus. During the 16th, they succeeded in getting possession of these places, and in moving their whole army on the road from Charleroi to Brussels, with the intention of separating the English from the Prussian right, and carrying consternation to that city. The Guards moved from Enghien at three o'clock in the morning of the 16th, to Braine Le Comte, then to Nivelles, and from thence, (making all together 27 miles march) to Les Quatre Bras—a point where four cross roads meet, one leading from Charleroi to Brussels, immediately on our march. We found that we had come at the critical moment, when the Enemy were actually in possession of a large wood, commanding all four roads, and cutting off our communication with Marshal Blucher. The 3d division had been driven from the wood, and the Guards were ordered to re-take it. The Enemy's tirailleurs retired as we advanced, till at length we passed the wood, and found ourselves in the presence of an immense body of French cavalry ready to charge. From the difficulties of the ground, we could not manœuvre, and retired into the wood ; the cavalry charged in after us, did us no harm, and were all cut to pieces ; but their light troops advanced in such numbers, as to oblige us to evacuate the wood at ten o'clock, after four hours hard fighting, till night closed the business. We lost here in the first brigade, Lord Hay, Barrington, Brown, and Cross, killed; Askew, Adair, Miller, Streatfield, Townsend, Stuart, Croft, Fludyer, and Luthel, wounded. I received a contusion in my right instep from a musket shot, and a bayonet scratch over the eye; but neither of any consequence. At night, we bivouacked on the road; and in the morning of the 17th, retired on the Brussels road, to preserve our communication with the Prussians, who had been separately attacked, and had retired on the 16th, in the same direction. Lord Wellington took up a position with his whole army, near Braine la Leud, his right resting on the village of Waterloo, covering the approach from Charleroi; his left extending beyond, and covering the approach from Nivelles—the whole position 12 miles from Brussels, and covering it in those directions. The night of the 17th was a miserably wet piquet bivouac for me, the rain falling in torrents. At noon on the 18th the French made the most desperate attack with artillery, cavalry, and tirailleurs, ever witnessed. Our defence was equally terrible. The whole line was formed in squares and battalions; not one man fell back; the whole stood firm. The French cavalry repeatedly attacked échelon of squares after échelon, and were repulsed ten or eleven times with immense loss. Our squares stood in the face of shot, shells, and every thing else; which caused great destruction, without our being able to return a shot. At eight o'clock, the Enemy moved forward his old Guard, who were received by the first brigade of Guards, and a Dutch brigade, with Saltoun at their head, with such a fire, that they took to their heels—their whole army fled in the greatest disorder, and was followed in sweeping lines, as fast as the lines could move. Our cavalry cut them to pieces. The abandoned guns, carriages, knapsacks and muskets, choaked up the ground; and for five miles, in which we followed them last night, the field was covered with the bodies of Frenchmen only. The Prussians beat them in another attack of the same sort the same day, and took Napoleon's carriage and baggage. Napoleon commanded the army opposed to the Duke of Wellington, and both were in the field together. We are just going to move off in pursuit. I have not taken my clothes off, or changed, since I left Enghien; and don't know when I shall. I never was better in my life. On the 18th, we lost Doyly and Pardoe, killed—Gen. Cooke, Lieut. Colonel Cooke, Stables, Lutterell, Batty, and Ellis, wounded."

Extract of a Letter from Charleroi, dated June 20, in the morning.

The well-known sentiments of the Functionary who is the author of this letter, guarantees the authenticity of the details which he gives.

" The 14th in the evening, the Prussians were informed, that a movement was executing along the whole French line; and in fact, at seven *a. m.* on the 15th, the tirailleurs were upon Marchiennes-sur-Pont and Couillet. There were several affairs of out-posts, and the firing of musketry took place as far as the entrance of the wood of Gilly. The French remained masters of the town at eleven *a. m.*

" Buonaparté's army defiled during two days; he was himself at the head of the first column; he passed through here at three o'clock, as far as the wood of Gilly, where he took a position.

" About 6 or 7 *p. m.* he returned to lodge at Puissants, and set off again the next morning at 10, to direct the battle which took place from Ligny to Quatre-Bras.—I never in my life saw a finer French army, than that which he had this time.*

" It was wholly composed of veteran troops, and had a considerable *matériel.* Well, in twice twenty-four hours he has lost all. His soldiers began to arrive here on the 18th, at 7 *p. m.*, in the most terrible disorder. Three quarters of those who returned were wounded. The Generals and Officers were in the most cruel despair, and vented a thousand imprecations against this man, who cannot satiate himself with blood: they will not serve him any longer. Almost all the Colonels, Majors, and Generals, are either killed or wounded. In a word, of 40,000 cavalry who passed through here, not 10,000 capable of service have returned; they all threw away their arms, and every soldier said he was going home, and that nobody should ever bring him into the fire again.

" Officers have told me, that the retreat from Moscow was not near so terrible as this, because the Generals and Chiefs of Corps had abandoned every thing, and saved themselves as they could.

" Of the immense artillery which Buonaparté had, only twelve pieces of cannon have returned.

" From Quatre-Bras to Beaumont, you cannot take four steps without finding effects that have been abandoned. More than 100 caissons, loaded with ammunition, provisions, and money, were abandoned in the streets of Charleroi, which, in three hours, were all pillaged by the populace.

" I have just learned, that almost all the villages through which the French passed in their retreat, have been plundered. Marshal Blucher's corps is here, and the heads of his columns are advancing to Beaumont. The French prisoners taken by the Prussians, are sent to Tirlemont, Louvain, Liege, &c. Their number is immense; the artillery taken is sent to the rear of the army."

From a Correspondent at Brussels, June 22.

" After the action of the 16th, which was uncommonly obstinate and bloody, both armies retired a few miles. The French occupied a large wood near Genappe: the English took up a strong position, with a village called Waterloo in their centre, (which was head-quarters), about thirteen miles from Brussels, having the fine forest of Soigné, which extends from thence to the very gates of Brussels, in their rear. The Prussians, under General Bulow, were posted on the left of the Anglo-Belgic army, having the small town of Wavre for their head-quarters. All Saturday, the 17th, both sides were busy preparing for the terrible contest. A cannonade was kept up at intervals. The weather was sultry, with heavy showers and much thunder and lightning. The British artillery and cavalry (the want of which was severely felt on the 16th, had now come up, with the

---

* N. B. The writer has served several campaigns as a conscript.

27th, and some other fresh regiments. The ground being unequal, the little hills and swells were furnished with cannon. These preparations continued till about noon of Sunday the 18th, when the French debouched from their coverts, and were astonished, but not daunted, to find us so well prepared to receive them. They made their attack with more than their usual impetuosity, attempting to cut our line, and turn our left wing; in which if they had succeeded, they would have separated us from the Prussians. To effect this, they made the most astonishing and reiterated efforts, column propelling column, whilst their artillery and mortars scattered destruction along our whole line. They, in fact, did succeed in breaking up some of our squares of infantry, notwithstanding the most heroic acts of courage that ever were displayed in any battle. But the Enemy's columns were shaken; his men could no longer be made to stand; and his officers fought unsupported by their soldiers, like men in despair. At this critical moment, the grand and general charge was made. Our brave fellows poured down on the Enemy with irresistible force; and about nine o'clock, the French gave up the well-fought field, and retreated about six miles, leaving the ground thickly strewed with killed and wounded, arms, cannon, and baggage. How our great Hero of the battle escaped being killed or taken is wonderful, as he was never exposed so much before. He was seen with his spy-glass, viewing the manœuvres of the field, with the same *sang-froid* and self-possession that an astronomer might be supposed to view the satellites of Jupiter; whilst showers of balls and shells flew about him, with evident direction, and which killed and wounded several of his Staff. A select party of French cavalry cut their passage through our line of infantry, and were near succeeding in taking him prisoner. At one critical time, when our lines and squares were wavering, Lord Wellington himself, at the head of the 95th, charged and drove back the most advanced of the Enemy.

" The feats of particular regiments were also remarkable. The 28th, formed into a square, repulsed the repeated efforts of the Cuirassiers to break through them. The 73d did the same; it repulsed every thing until its flanks were opened by showers of grape.

" The three Highland Regiments, the 42d, 79th, and 92d, already thinned in the action of the 16th, and of which they bore the brunt, were now reduced to complete skeletons.—Such was also the state of the 44th after the action. Nor were the acts of the cavalry less meritorious, particularly the Heavy Brigade. The charge was led by the 6th, or Enniskillen Dragoons, with Lord Ponsonby at their head. They cut down every thing before them, and overturned the French chasseurs like nine-pins. It is said they actually made 3,000 prisoners. They were followed up with equal intrepidity by the Guards, the Scotch Greys, and the 1st Dragoon Guards: but to enumerate the particular deeds of each, would require the historic page to contain them. Suffice it to say, that all the British did their duty in the most exemplary manner, as they never fail to do: nor shall I tarnish so brilliant a battle by making any remarks on corps who might not have been so steady. As to the Enemy, it is but justice to say, his courage and conduct equalled, if not surpassed, the finest of his former exploits. It would be unworthy in us to wish to elevate our own character by traducing our enemies. For by how much his valour shall have been conspicuous, by so much the more glory will they have acquired who have beat him.   History will have a fine and just subject of praise in that of his Royal Highness the Hereditary Prince of Belgium.   Towards the close of the day, when our lines were bending, he was at the head of his people, cheering and exciting them, amidst the hottest fire ; in doing which, his Royal Highness received a musket-ball in his left arm, which ultimately lodged in the shoulder."

Extract of a Letter from a German Officer, July 16.

" I have visited the field of battle.* The sleep of the dead is sound.   On the spot where this day month thousands thronged and fought, where thousands sank and bled, and groaned and died, there is now not a living soul, and over all hovers the stillness of the grave.

" In Ligny 2000 dead were buried.   Here fought the Westphalian and Berg regiments.   Ligny is a village built of stone and thatched with straw, on a small stream which flows through flat meadows.   In the village are several farm-houses, inclosed with walls and gates. Every farm-house the Prussians had converted into a fortress.   The French endeavoured to penetrate through the village by means of superior numbers.   Four times were they driven out.   At last they set on fire the farm-houses in the upper end of the village with their howitzers ; but the Prussians still kept their ground at the lower end.   A whole company of Westphalian troops fell in the court-yard at the church ; on the terrace before the church lay 50 dead.

" In the evening the French surrounded the village.   The Prussians retired half a league: the position was lost; and it is incomprehensible why the French did not follow up the advantage they had obtained, and again attack the Prussians in the night.

" This was on the 16th.   The same day a French column marched by the high road of Charleroi to Brussels.

" At Quatre Bras, they found the Duke of Brunswick and the Prince of Orange.   Here the battle was as hot as at Ligny.   The Duke let himself be carried away by his ardour into the fire of small arms ; a musket-ball went through his bridle-hand, and entered the belly; the liver was penetrated : he fell, and breathed his last in ten minutes.   His sufferings were short.

" At the inn by the cross roads at Quatre Bras, the contest was the hottest.   Here are the most graves.   The wounded reeled into the inn yard, leaned against the walls, and then sank down.   There are still the traces of the blood on the walls, as it spouted forth from the wounds with departing life.

" Where the battle was, the fields are completely trodden down for a circuit of about a league.   On both sides of the high road, ways are made about 100 feet broad, and you can still follow the march of the battalions in all directions through the fine fields of maize.

" On the 18th, the battle was renewed four leagues nearer Brussels, on both sides of the high road.   The spot is a plain, sprinkled with

* Those who witnessed the field two days after the battle, state, that the spectacle was most horrible ; the contortion of the fallen, was inconceivable, and this horror was increased by the large masses of horses that fell.   Editor.

hillocks.   The diameter of the field of battle may be about a league
and a half. Buonaparté placed himself near the farm-house of Mont
St. Jean, on a rising ground, whence he could overlook the whole.
Beside him was one Lacoste, a Walloon, who now lives near the hamlet of Belle Alliance, and who was employed as a guide.   This man
told me as follows:—When the Prussians came out of the wood of
Fritschermont, Buonaparté observed them with his glass, and asked
one of his adjutants who they were.   The latter, upon looking through
his glass, replied, ' they are the Prussian colours.'   That moment
his face assumed a chalky whiteness, as if the ghost of the sainted
Queen of Prussia had appeared to him, whom he persecuted to death.
He said nothing, but merely once shook his head.

"When he saw that the battle was lost, he rode off with his general staff and the above guide.   He had told Lacoste, that he wished
to be conducted by a by-road to Charleroi.

" Genappe is an open market-town, a league and a half from the
field of battle, through which runs the Dyle, a small stream.   At the
lower end of Genappe, lies an iron forge, which it drives.   A quarter
of a mile lower lies the village of Ways, at which there is a bridge.
An officer had arrived at Genappe about five in the afternoon, with
orders to withdraw the baggage.   He had already considered the
battle as lost, because the reserves had been brought into the fire.
When the flight became almost universal, the military waggons were
driven 16 a-breast on the causeway.   In the narrow Genappe they
were wedged in together, and Lacoste relates that it took an hour and
a half to get through them.   It was half-past twelve at night before
they got out of the town, with 150 horses of the staff.   I asked him
why he did not take Buonaparté by the bridge of Ways, where nobody passed; he replied— ' I was not aware of this road.'

" Thus with all the maps of the war depôt, with all the engineer
geographers, who with their repeating circles can set off the geogra-
phical position of places even to a second, Buonaparté, with a
large Staff, here depended on the ignorance of a peasant, who did
not know that there was a bridge over the Dyle at Ways.   People
talk a great deal of military skill and military science, while often in
decisive moments the whole depends upon the knowledge of a very
common man.

" In the village of Planchenoit, the fourth of a league from Belle
Alliance, the Guards were posted. The principal house in the village
is nearly burnt down.   It is inhabited by a very intelligent farmer of
the name of Bernhard. He, like the others, had fled on the day of
battle; but witnessed, on an opposite height, the combat between
Bulow and the French reserve, and could give a very good description of it.   He carried me to the key of the position opposite Fritschermont.   He told me that the peasant who guided Bulow's army,
resolved not to come out of the wood at Fritschermont, but to descend into the valley lower down, and to penetrate by Planchenoit,
nearly in the rear of the French reserves. ' Then,' said he, ' we
shall take them all.'   The period was truly most critical when the
Prussians came to the attack.   Wellington was hard pressed, all his
reserves were already in action, he was already compelled to with-

draw some of his artillery, and a countryman from the vicinity of
Braine la Leud told me, that he saw some of the army (as he expressed
it) *en débandage*.   Buonaparté was probably only waiting for the moment when, with his Guards, he could decide the day.   We shudder
when we reflect, that at this important moment, all depended on the
local knowledge of a single peasant.   Had he guided wrong, had he led
them into the hollow way through which the cannon could not pass,
had Bulow's army come up an hour later, the scale had probably descended on the other side.   Had Buonaparté been victorious, and
advanced to the Rhine, the French nation would have been intoxicated with victory, and with what they call the national glory, and a
levy *en masse* would have been effected throughout all France.

   " How great soever the number of killed and wounded in a battle
may be, yet as compared with the amount of the armies engaged, it
máy generally be pronounced moderate.   However murderous our
artillery are, yet their operation is inconsiderable, as relative to the
great number of rounds.   At the battle of Leipsic, probably only
about one in the hundred of cannon and cartridge balls fired, took
effect.   The battle of Waterloo was more sanguinary from the smallness of the field of battle.   Probably every sixth man fell in it.

   " The disorder of a battle generally first originates with the runaways, who fly from an impression that all is lost, and who bawl this
out to others in order to excuse their own flight.   Although the
Prussian army, on the 16th, retreated only half a league from Ligny,
yet shoals of fugitives passed through Liege and Aix-la-Chapelle,
spreading universal alarm.   I fell in with some of them, 25 leagues
from the field of battle ; they asserted, that the French were within
a mile of Brussels, and their light troops already in the suburbs.
On the 18th, so early as five in the afternoon, French runaways
came to the inn at Quatre Bras, who had fled from the field even at
the time when circumstances seemed very favourable to them.

   " The idea of being cut off, operates very strongly upon men ;
should it get possession of the mass, then all order is lost, and the
army destroys itself.   Hence may be explained the great defeat of the
French on the 18th.   In Genappe, there was nothing but pell-mell
confusion, and they suffered themselves to be cut down like cattle.
In Genappe, eight hundred lay on the spot.   General Duhesme, who
commanded the rear guard, was cut down by a Brunswick hussar, at
the gate of an inn.—' The Duke fell yesterday, and thou shalt also
bite the dust :' so saying, the black hussar cut him down.   The fury
of the Brunswickers no longer knew any bounds.

   " Wellington's army consisted chiefly of young regiments.   What
supported them, was the confidence which they had in the talents of
their General.

   " The Belgians and Dutch, by the common victory in which they
participated, have been pretty well amalgamated and fraternised.
Besides, the nation feels itself honoured by its brave Prince."

Letter from Prince Bernhard of Saxe Weimar, to his Father.

Bivouac near Waterloo, in the Wood between Brussels and Genappe, June 19th, 1815.

" Dear Father,

" Thank God, I am still alive and have escaped unhurt from two bloody battles. The first was on the 16th of June, the second was yesterday. I beg when you read this, to take Ferrari's map in your hand. For four weeks I was in cantonments in Genappe, with the regiment of Orange Nassau, of which I am Colonel. On the 15th I was appointed Brigadier of the second brigade, of the division Perponcher; my predecessor had had the misfortune to break his leg. Besides my two battalions of Orange Nassau, I now had under my command three battalions of the Duchy of Nassau;—when my brigade was 4000 strong:—to-day I have not 1200 left!—On the 15th, the French fell upon the Prussian army, and pressed it very much. My brigade continued on the left wing of the Dutch army, the head-quarters of which were at Braine-le-Comte—my division lay in Nivelles. A battalion of Nassau were at Frasne, and also a battery of Dutch horse-artillery. When the Prussians retreated towards Fleurus, the post at Frasne was attacked and driven back. The infantry threw itself into a wood on the right, and the artillery retired fighting to Quatre Bras. At this important post, I had drawn my brigade together, and cannonaded the Enemy, whom I succeeded in keeping off. I maintained this post through the whole night. Towards morning, on the 16th, I was reinforced by a battalion of Dutch Yagers, and a battalion of Militia. Soon after arrived my General of division and the Prince of Orange. With the latter I went to the out-posts, and by this order undertook a reconnoissance, with a battalion and two cannon. Towards noon, the Enemy showed strong columns, and began to cannonade us. It is said he had three corps of his army engaged against us on this day. We had only five battalions to oppose to him, and the skirts of a wood to defend to the utmost.

" The Duke of Wellington himself was present at the beginning of the action; I kept my ground a long time against an enemy thrice my number, and had only two Belgic cannons to protect myself with. The Enemy took the point of a wood opposite me, and incommoded my left flank. I, without loss of time, took some volunteers, and two companies of Dutch militia, and recovered my wood at the point of the bayonet; I was at the head of the storming parties, and had the honour to be one of the first in the wood. In cutting away some branches, I wounded myself with my sabre very slightly in the right leg, but was not a moment out of battle:—it is in fact not worth while to mention this wound; I write to you about it only that you and my good mother may not be alarmed by exaggerated and foolish reports. While

I manfully defended my wood; the Enemy drove back our left wing as far as Quatre Bras. It was on this occasion that the brave Duke of Brunswick was killed by a ball, which entered his breast. Strong columns of infantry turned my right flank; I asked for orders how to act, but received none. When I saw myself surrounded on all sides, and my people had expended all their ammunition, I retreated in good order through the wood to the neighbourhood of Hautain le Val. The Hanoverian division Alten supported me, and recovered the wood, but lost it again; at last it was forced by the English with great loss, and maintained through the night. I bivouacked for the night in the wood. The Prussians retreated this day to Wavre, and on account of this retreat we were obliged to retire to the position near Mont St. Jean, between Genappe and Brussels; this was done on the 17th. We were obliged to bivouac for the night upon a very muddy soil, in the most dreadful rain. Yesterday about 10 o'clock began the decisive battle, which was completely gained towards evening by Wellington over Napoleon in person. (A hundred and) sixty cannon are the fruit of this bloody victory. I commanded on the left wing, and was charged to maintain a village and a position. With a great loss of men I succeeded. The victory was still doubtful, when, about 4 o'clock, the Prussians under Generals Bulow and Ziethen arrived upon our left flank, and decided the battle. Unhappily the Prussians who were to support me in my village, mistook my Nassauers, whose uniform is still very French, though their hearts are true German, for Frenchmen, and made dreadful fire upon them. They were driven from their post, and I rallied them a quarter of a league from the field of battle. My General of division, whose first brigade was wholly destroyed, is now with me. I must conclude, because I have just received orders to proceed to Nivelles in pursuit of the Enemy. Farewell, dear father; salute my mother, my sister-in-law, my brother, and all my friends; and be assured that I will do every thing to be worthy of you.

The Colonel and Brigadier,
Bernhard of Saxe Weimar.

Extract of a Letter from an Officer in the Army of the late Duke of BRUNSWICK.

Brunswick, June 29, 1815.

" —— On the 15th, in the evening, about ten o'clock, a letter was brought from the Duke of Wellington's office, which contained an order, that all the troops might be concentrated at the Allée Verte, near Brussels, on the following morning at day-break. Orders were accordingly given, and sent off as fast as possible: but, the dislocations being rather at a great distance, the troops could not arrive before 5 o'clock ; when the Duke, on the instant, marched through Brussels, and so on to the road to Waterloo. Directly afterwards, the Duke of Wellington followed, and, after showing a letter to the Duke, changed his horse; they then set off together, and were as fast as possible followed by their suites. About 10 o'clock, we arrived at Quatre Bras, where we found part of the Nassau troops engaged, and heard that the French advanced very fast, and were exceedingly strong.   We then went on a hill to observe their approach ; but hardly had they perceived the number of officers, but the rascals fired at us with grenades : so we were obliged to leave the spot, and I narrowly escaped being killed.   About 12 o'clock we returned; and the Duke strongly expressed his wish of having an opportunity of meeting the French in equal force with his troops.   To his great satisfaction, the Royal Scotch, the Hanoverians, and his own corps, arrived betwixt one and two o'clock.   Tired and hungry as they were, they sang as they passed the Duke, abusing and swearing against Buonaparté, wishing that they might soon meet him, and have an opportunity of setting the soldiers of the *Grande Nation* to rights. Hardly had we marched half an hour, when we saw the French expecting us on a hill.   The Duke of Wellington then ordered to collect the troops as quick as possible, and to prepare for battle. At 2 o'clock all was ready, and the attack began.   The battle was very bloody, but we compelled the Enemy to retreat.   About half past four the French advanced again, and appeared double the number of the Allied Army ; but no fear was shown.   The cannonade began most horribly, which in some respects put the train and baggage in confusion : however, the troops stood, and fought like lions ; so the French were again obliged to retreat, and were driven back to their position.   Here they had a great advantage, being covered by a little wood, where they had placed all their artillery and riflemen.   The Duke of Wellington most likely knew this, and ordered a fresh attack, to get the French out of the wood. The troops advanced, the Brunswick division on the left wing. When *they* came near the wood, the French commenced a horrible fire with artillery and case-shot, which occasioned a great loss to our corps.   In this attack, which was about 7 o'clock in the evening, the Duke was unfortunately killed on the spot by a case-shot. At this moment I was not far from his highness, and ordered our small carriage, thinking that he was only wounded—when, alas ! to my inexpressible sorrow, I found he was dead.   My feelings I cannot describe, but you will be able to form to yourself an idea."

Letters written from Fleurus.

June 17, 1815.

" The French armies have again immortalized themselves on the plains of Fleurus.

" We entered Belgium on the 15th.   The Enemy was overthrown in a first affair upon every point where he attempted to resist us.

" Before Charleroi, several of his squares were broken and taken by some squadrons only: one thousand seven hundred prisoners only could be saved out of five or six thousand men, who composed those squares. Yesterday (the 16th) we encountered the whole of the Enemy's army, in its position near Fleurus; its right, composed of English, under the command of Wellington, was in front of Meller, its centre at St. Amand, and its left at Sombref, a formidable position, covered by the little river Ligny.

" The Enemy occupied also the little village of Ligny, in front of this river. Our army debouched in the plain, its left under Marshal Ney, by Gosselies, the centre where the Emperor was, by Fleurus, and the right under General Girard, upon Sombref. The actions began at two o'clock upon the left and centre. Both sides fought with inconceivable fury. The villages of St. Amand and Ligny were taken and re-taken four times. Our soldiers have all covered themselves with glory. At eight o'clock the Emperor, with his whole guard, had Ligny attacked and carried. Our brave fellows advanced at the first discharge upon the principal position of the Enemy. His army was forced in the centre, and obliged to retreat in the greatest disorder; Blucher, with the Prussians, upon Namur, and Wellington upon Brussels.

" Several pieces of cannon were taken by the Guard, who bore down all before them. All marched with cries a thousand times repeated of ' *Vive l'Empereur!*' These were also the last words of the brave men who fell. Never was such enthusiasm; a British division of five or six thousand Scottish was cut to pieces; we have not seen any of them prisoners. The Noble Lord must be confounded. There were upon the field of battle eight enemies to one Frenchman. Their loss is said to be fifty thousand men. The cannonade was like that at the battle of Moskwa.

" This morning the (17th) the cavalry of General Pajol is gone in pursuit of the Prussians upon the road to Namur. It is already two leagues and a half in advance; whole bands of prisoners are taken. They do not know what is become of their commanders. The rout is complete on this side, and I hope we shall not so soon hear again of the Prussians, if they should ever be able to rally at all.

" As for the English, we shall see now what will become of them. The Emperor is here."

Some private letters from the army give the following particulars :—

" The English are retiring upon Brussels by the forest of Soignies; the Prussians are falling back upon the Meuse in great disorder.

" The 17th at 11 P. M. the Emperor had his head-quarters at Planchenoit, a village only five leagues from Brussels. The rain fell in torrents. His Majesty was fatigued, but he was very well.

" Count Lobau, who was marching with the 6th corps upon Namur, was, with his van-guard, only half a league from the town. Five battalions are gone from Lille to escort the prisoners taken on the 15th and 16th."

Telegraphic Bulletins, from Paris, dated the 17th, at 2 o'Clock, and transmitted to Lille and Boulogne the 18th, at 4 in the Morning.

" On the 15th the French army forced the Sambre and entered Charleroi, made 1500 prisoners, took 6 pieces of cannon, and destroyed four Prussian regiments.   We have lost very few men.
" On the 16th, his Majesty the Emperor gained a complete victory over the English and Prussians united, commanded by Lord Wellington and Prince Blucher."

Restitution of Works of Art * carried off by the French.*

Aix-la-Chapelle, July 25th.

" By an official letter from the Counsellor of State, M. Ribbentrop, Intendant-General of the army of the Lower Rhine, dated Paris, July 15, I have received information, that his Excellency Field-Marshal Prince Blucher of Wahlstadt, immediately after the taking of Paris, ordered that all the works of art and literature which are there, and which had been previously carried off by the French from the States of his Prussian Majesty, should be seized and restored to the places from which they were taken.   For the execution of this order, a Special Committee has been appointed at Paris, under the direction of an Intendant-General, and at the same time a line of conveyances from Paris to the Rhine.   The first convoy left Paris on the 16th; among the articles which it brings, is the invaluable picture of St. Peter, which Rubens presented to Cologne, his native city, and which the audacious hands of our enemies ravished from the sacred and classic soil.   Orders have also been given, that the beautiful columns of granite and porphyry, carried off by the same sacrilegious hands from the sanctuary of our Cathedral at Aix-la-Chapelle, and placed afterwards to support the arched roof of the Hall of Antiquities at Paris, shall be pulled down, and brought back to Aix-la-Chapelle.   I had particularly requested our illustrious Field-Marshal, immediately upon the taking of Paris, to cause these two articles to be restored ; he has immediately complied with this desire, and has thus acquired a particular right to the gratitude of the cities of Cologne and Aix-la-Chapel e. You see, Prussians of the Rhine, that the State of which you are the youngest children, has not forgotten to seize the first opportunity to make you participate in the fruits of its victories.   Your cities will celebrate with grateful joy, the day on which the property plundered from your ancestors, re-taken from a rapacious enemy, by the powerful hand of your King and his warriors, shall re-enter your walls, &c.   (Signed)   SACK,
            President of the Prussian Provinces of the Rhine.

* Vide Duke of Wellington's letter to Lord Castlereagh, and Prince Blucher's to General Mufflin.

"BRUSSELS, July 26.—The French cannon brought from La
Belle Alliance are placed here upon the Esplanade, without the gate
Du Rivage, till they shall be embarked for England. They are
87 in number, as well cannon as howitzers. Some have the cypher
"Louis XIV." others have the words "liberty, equality," and the greater
number the cypher of Napoléon; fifty others are expected in a short
time. We have received from the head-quarters of Prince Augustus
of Prussia, an account of the surrender of Landrecies, to the arms of his
august Sovereign. The capitulation in 9 articles was annexed to the
dispatch. The place is given up to the Prussian troops; the garrison to
march out with the honours of war, and repair either to the French army, or disperse and go home. They kept two cannon, drawn by four
horses. The French troops lay down their arms on the glacis, except
fifty men per battalion, and the company of Veterans, whom his Royal
Highness permits to retain their arms, on account of the honourable,
brave, and distinguished conduct of the garrison. The officers keep
their swords; the subalterns and members of the Legion of Honour,
their side arms, and all their private property. The property of the
inhabitants to be respected, and no one to be molested for his political opinions, or for his conduct previous to the capitulation."

A letter from a Life Guardsman, speaking of the havoc made
among the Cuirassiers of the Imperial Guards at the battle of Waterloo, contains the following homely, but emphatical description :—
" Until we came up with our heavy horses, and our superior weight
of metal, nothing was done with the Cuirassiers, unless one got
now and then a cut at their faces, not one of them gave way; we
therefore galloped at them, and fairly rode them down; when they
were unhorsed, *we cracked them like lobsters in their shells*, and by
the coming up of the cannon afterwards, thousands of them were
squeezed as flat as *pancakes*.

One man of the Scots Greys, from Ayrshire, has eighteen sword
and sabre wounds, the greater number of which were inflicted by
those savages after he was on the ground, dismounted. His name is
Laurie, and a few days previous to the battle, he had accounts of
his father's death, by which this gallant private soldier became possessed of £12,000. He says, that he saved his life in the end only by
calling out in French, as the Enemy were charging over him—" *Oh!
mon Dieu! mon Dieu! mes amis! mes amis!*" by which contrivance
he was taken for one of their own men.

A Prussian hussar made a capture at the battle of Waterloo of five
thousand Napoleons, which he has sent to his family, by the Intendant-General and Counsellor of State, Ribbentrop: a soldier of
the landwehr also obtained possession of five hundred Napoleons.

RELATION

FIDÈLE ET DÉTAILLÉ

DE LA DERNIÈRE CAMPAGNE
DE BUONAPARTE,

TERMINE PAR LA BATAILLE

DE MONT SAINT-JEAN,

DITE DE WATERLOO,

OU DE LA BELLE-ALLIANCE.

Par un Témoin oculaire.

TROISIÈME EDITION,

REVUE ET CORRIGEE.

PARIS, J. G. DENTU, IMPRIMEUR-LIBRAIRE,
RUE DU PONT DE LODI, No. 5, PRES LE PONT-NEUF, 1815.

A faithful and detailed Relation of the final Campaign of Buonaparté, *terminated by the Battle of* Mont St. John, *otherwise called of* Waterloo, *or of* La Belle Alliance, *by an Eye-Witness.*

Fas mihi quod vidi referre.

The landing of Buonaparté at Cannes, operated as a thunder-bolt upon every honest and truly patriotic Frenchman; upon all, in a word, who sincerely wished the repose and welfare of their country. In fact, they could expect from this event nothing but disastrous results, already announced by a civil war which appeared inevitable.

Nevertheless, by a concurrence of circumstances as extraordinary as unforeseen, the imminent danger towards which we were precipitated, was for a while lulled. Who could credit it!—this man, pursued by the general hatred of a nation, on which he had drawn every scourge, found in its bosom a mass of people disposed to assist his most culpable projects.

The whole Army scandalously broke their oaths of allegiance to the best of Kings, even turned their arms against him, and forced him ere long to abandon his Capital. The well-disposed part of the king-

g

dom had the mortification of seeing Buonaparté arrive
even at Paris, and arrive too in some degree trium-
phantly.

No sooner did he re-appear, than he employed
every means to deceive those people whom he had
already pressed under his iron yoke, for the purpose
of extorting from them yet greater sacrifices, and
plunging them into an abyss of misery from which
they could only rise with himself.

Meanwhile, through his myrmidons, he caused the
most injurious and absurd reports to be circulated
against the King, while he kept in alarm the holders
of national lands; and, to attach to his cause a
numerous class of citizens he had so long oppressed,
affected to follow their principles. He proclaimed
with loud effrontery, that he was in perfect understanding with Austria, of which the speedy arrival of
Maria Louisa would furnish the happiest proof.

Shaken by such positive assurances, France resigned herself, for some time, to the flattering hope of
avoiding that war she had herself declared against all
Europe, by once more receiving, and in despite of
treaties, the man she had for ever proscribed. Even
those thinking Frenchmen whose ideas had not been
misled either by self-interest or false notions of
independence, still sought to create to themselves
illusion, and wished to believe Buonaparté incapable
of such atrocious deceit. Restrained by an ignorant
and enthusiastic multitude, they could only offer
their silent vows for the salvation of their country.

Thus, by perfidious insinuations, by lies artfully fa-
bricated and more impudently supported, Buonaparté succeeded in restoring to France the confidence
he stood in need of, to engage her in the contest he
was preparing. Thus, to the eternal shame of the
nation, the constant Disturber of its repose, the Devas-
tator of Europe, the monster to whom France owes
all its misfortunes, at the moment when he resigned
the people to a host of new enemies his very name
had roused to vengeance, even at that moment he
was in some measure hailed as their Deliverer.

He declares his wish for peace! He invokes the

treaty of Paris—not to legitimate his rights to supreme power, which were already sufficiently consecrated by his bayonets—but he calls an assembly of the people, of whom he exacts no other services, nor imposes other obligations, than to proclaim the war he brings, a *national* one. Thirsting for vengeance, and a slave to the same ambition by which he had already fallen, he dreams but of victory and conquests; and if he succeeds so far as to persuade the nation he still respects her, he only manœuvres to render her the instrument of his mad projects. Impatient to figure once more on the horrid scene of battle, anticipating the moment when, restored to power, he may command even over death itself, he urges with incredible activity the formation of his armies.

At every quarter troops were embodied, organized, and dispatched to the frontiers. In a few days, France is transformed into a vast camp. While a first and numerous army moves towards Belgium, others are collected in Alsace, in Lorraine, Franche-Comté, at the foot of the Alps, and under the Pyrenean mountains.

The Powers of Europe knew too well the character of this perfidious man, to deliberate one moment on the part they had to take. Declarations issued from the Congress of Vienna, to announce their determination. The intercourse from France was most carefully intercepted, while innumerable armies were approaching its frontiers.

There was nothing to be hoped from the mediation of Austria; and all Europe rose up to hurl from his throne, a second time, the man whom rebellion and perjury had just placed there, and who dared again brave it by threats of fresh aggression to force its acknowledgment of him.

During these movements, the Deputies of the Departments assembled at Paris to assist at the Champ de Mai,* where the vain and absurd formality of examining the votes on his Additional Act of the Constitutions of the Empire, was to be performed. There,

* The Field of May.

among a great number of upright and learned men,
were found many names the Revolution had stamped
with an infamous celebrity; and a crowd of military
men without resources, and incapable of other political views than an exclusive preponderance founded
on their sabres. Into such hands were committed the
destinies of France; and the *Acte Additionel*, that audacious system of despotism, was ratified by men
who, with the words of freedom in their mouths, were
only the interpreters of their Master's will. The undi-
gested opinions of a few thousand individuals from
that class of people the least qualified to be invested
with deliberative power, and the greatest proportion
from an ignorant, undiscerning soldiery, was impudently adopted as the expression of the national will.
France, compressed by terror and treated by its own
army as a conquered country, was compelled to
receive those laws which consecrated its servitude.

Meanwhile the French armies concentrated on the
frontiers; that of the North, the most numerous of
them all, occupied at the beginning of June extensive
contonments *par échelons* in the departments of the
North and the Aisne. Its head-quarters were at
Laon. It occupied Valenciennes and Maubeuge. Its
right communicated with the army of the Moselle,
and its left was covered by Lisle. Chiefly composed
of old soldiers, the enthusiastic spirit of this army
was intense in favour of Buonaparté. This army
lived on the best possible terms with the people about
the Aisne, who, beholding in this war a national one,
sought only to preserve their country from fresh
invasions, and set themselves with avidity to the
construction of such fortifications as were conceived
necessary for their defence.

The National Guards were armed at a moment;
and the whole populace testified their intention of
rising in mass on the approach of the enemy. The
same spirit was manifested in all those departments
of France which had been invaded in 1814, with the
exception of that of the North, who openly avowed
contrary sentiments, and did not dissemble their dis-
like to the presence of these troops. They could

not draw from thence a single military resource, and the National Guards peremptorily refused to march. The Army counted on the effective co-operation, at the moment of hostilities, of all the inhabitants generally; and the latter, persuaded that the Allies had only been able to enter France through a succession of treasons, had an entire confidence in the Army. The latter, therefore, awaited in self-security, the commencement of the campaign, but, impatient for battle, vented their spleen against the tardiness of the Allies.

Such was the state of affairs, when they learned that the Guards, who had quitted Paris after the Champ de Mai, were directed by forced marches on Laon; that Buonaparté followed them some days after, and had suddenly appeared on the frontiers. He arrived, in fact, as soon as they at Vervins, where he put himself at the head of the army, which drew round him from all its quarters.

It is still to be asked by what enchantment Buonaparté succeeded in so fascinating the eyes of an immense population, and of an army, that the one saw without fear all the calamities of war burst on them, and the other audaciously braved all the Powers of Europe leagued against them. Certain it is, however, that he was received every where with loud and unanimous shouts of acclamation.

It did not generally appear he had any idea of attacking; but rather that he had drawn thither his troops to form a line of defence. He however showed in his movements his usual activity, and lost no opportunity of presenting himself before his soldiers.

On arriving at Beaumont, the army of the North joined that of the Ardennes, under command of Vandamme, and established its head-quarters at Fumay. That of the Moselle, under General Gerard, departed by forced marches for Metz. The army of the North thus was composed of five bodies of infantry, commanded by Lieutenant-Generals D'Erlon, Reille, Vandamme, Gerard, and Count de Lobau. The cavalry, under Grouchy, was formed into four divisions under the orders of Generals Pajol, Excelmans, Milhaud, and Kellerman.

The Imperial Guard, of 20,000 men, formed the kernel of this splendid army, which was strengthened by a body of artillery well disciplined, provided with an excellent train, and pontoon corps. Beside the batteries attached to each division, each corps had its park of reserve. The Guard, particularly, had a magnificent train of artillery, almost wholly composed of pieces new cast. The whole might be estimated at 150,000 effective men, of whom 20,000 were cavalry; and 300 pieces of cannon.

Still, in the very bosom of their own country, those troops failed in that discipline which forms the strength of armies. Without feelings for their unfortunate compatriots, who showed every degree of zeal in furnishing them subsistence, the French soldiers treated them with the utmost cruelty; and, conceiving they had an unquestionable right to plunder, abandoned themselves to every species of excess.

In every place they ransacked the houses, broke open coffers, ill-treated the peasants, and took every thing at discretion. "There is war," said they, "it cannot be carried on without us, and therefore we have free play." And, pursuant to this kind of reasoning, they gave entire scope to that thirst for plunder improved by ten years warfare, and outrage only to be paralleled by the exterminating incursions of the barbarians of old. Roving from house to house, from granary to granary, from cellar to cellar, they did not return till loaded with spoil, after destroying every thing they left behind. Too happy that cottager who, accused but of having too well concealed his cash, escaped their vengeance by leaving his all to destruction.

Dreadful to be credited! their officers, for the most part, tolerated these infamous proceedings. "Why," said they with a sort of satisfaction, "is there not a magazine? the soldiery must live." And the soldiers not only *lived;* but the officer, it will be easily believed, lived in abundance, and did not much trouble himself upon whom. Is this the loyal, disinterested, generous, and delicate character that distinguished the French officer? No, surely! But other times, other manners; and it was reserved to the officers of Buonaparté to exhibit to history, a physiognomy novel and strange.

Doubtless there were many men of honour and morality attached to this army, who lamented such disorders, and served with regret amidst these rebellious troops, whose atrocities enhanced their crime; but, hurried on by the force of circumstances, they sought apology for the violation of their oaths, in the need to prevent at all events the invasion of their native frontiers. Moreover, it was impossible to restrain these excesses; the soldiers could no longer be controlled; and the superior officers were aware that such devastations had been constantly practised by the troops under Buonaparté's immediate command; and that it was one of his most powerful engines to conciliate their devotion and stimulate their courage.

The country was covered with rich crops, that promised the most abundant of harvests: but ill betide the lands that lay in their way; still more unhappy the neighbourhood of the camps. It seemed as though, by a determinate motive of studied destruction, they sought out for that purpose the richest fields. In an instant all disappeared under the scythe and sword, to be made forage for the cavalry and thatch for the canteens.

The interior administration of the army was deranged by acts of equal anarchy. An implacable hatred seemed to animate the different corps against each other, and displayed itself in acts of open hostility. No mutual confidence, no fraternity of arms, no interchange of generous feelings; pride, selfishness, and thirst of prey, reigned throughout. Often, when the commandant of a division, or regiment, arrived at the post it was destined to occupy, he seized every thing without consideration for those who were to follow. Guards were placed in every house that presented any resource, and by the mere right of preoccupation opposed all division of the spoil. The sentries were often attacked, and real warfare ensued. Many were thus wounded, and not a few killed on the spot.

The Imperial Guard, as being the immediate Janissaries of the Despot, comported itself with extreme arrogance towards the other troops, and was detested throughout; while repulsive and disdainful towards the other corps within its contact, it was not less tormented by them, whenever its numbers were too few to dictate the law. . The different denominations of cavalry, not only were at open war among themselves, but insulted the foot by every means and on every occasion, and the infantry in turn threatened them with its bayonets.

Actuated by such a spirit, the troops approached the frontiers as the defenders of the State! Their marches were rapid and long, and the weather, though stormy, tolerably fine; nor were the roads so cut up as to retard the artillery, or camp equipages. Their movements, therefore, almost partook of precipitation. It was evidently the intention to surprise the Enemy by a sudden approach; and these forced marches gave rise to the reports of a sudden irruption into Belgium. On the 14th, this whole army had joined and formed in line on the extreme frontiers.

It was then that the uncertainty in which they had remained respecting these manœuvres was done away, by the following proclamation, which was read at the head of every division:

" Soldiers !

"This day is the anniversary of Marengo and of Friedland, which twice decided the fate of Europe. Then, as after the battles of Austerlitz and Wagram, we were too generous. We trusted to the oaths and protestations of Princes, whom we left upon their thrones. Now, however, coalesced among themselves, they conspire against our independence, and the most sacred rights of France. They have begun the most unjust of aggressions; are not they and we the same men still?

"Soldiers! At Jena, against these same Prussians, now so arrogant, you were as one to three, and at Montmirail, one to six!

"Let those among you that have been prisoners in England, describe their *pontoons* (the prison ships), and tell the miseries they there endured.

"The Saxons, the Belgians, Hanoverians, soldiers of the Rhine, all groan at being compelled to lend their arms to Princes, enemies of justice and the rights of nations. They know the Coalation is insatiable. After having devoured twelve millions of Poles, twelve millions of Italians, a million of Saxons, six million of Belgians, it seeks to devour the whole second order of States in Germany.

" A moment of prosperity has blinded these senseless Princes. The oppression and humiliation of France are beyond their power. If they enter France, they will there find a grave.

" Soldiers! We have forced marches to make, battles to offer, perils to encounter; but with constancy, victory will remain ours. The rights, the honour, and the weal of France, shall be reconquered.

" To every Frenchman who has a heart, the hour is come to conquer or die."

It is scarcely necessary to say, that this proclamation was received with transports of joy and loud acclamations by a multitude of ignorant soldiers, to whom a few high-sounding words they do not comprehend, seem the very acme of eloquence.

Nor need we mention that ridiculously pompous proclamation. It wears the same stamp with all his other productions, and only differs from them in greater extravagance and absurdity. Whoever weighed the incoherent declamation of that vain-glorious prophet, looked on it with pity. Meanwhile it augmented the public inquietude by laying open the whole extent of the dangers Buonaparté meant to brave.

The chiefs, however, were enraptured with the precision of their routes, and recognized, they said, the presence of the *great man* in those scientific combinations, by which all the masses of the army, after encumbering each other's march, seemed all at once to rise from the ground, and find themselves ranged in line by the effect of magic. So great is the power of prepossession.

The 15th, at break of day, this army broke up for the Belgic territory. The 2d division attacked the Prussian outposts, and pursued them with vigour as far as Marchienne-au-Pont; the cavalry of this body had to charge several corps of infantry different times, which they drove back, took some hundreds of prisoners, and the Prussians hastened to recross the Sambre.

The light cavalry of the centre followed the 2d division on the road to Charleroi, and, brushing away in different charges such of the Enemy as they met,

drove the whole to the other side. While numerous
sharp-shooters defended the approach to the bridge
the Prussians were employed in rendering it impassable, in order to retard our march and afford them
time to evacuate the city; but being too closely pushed, they were not able to destroy it effectually, and
our men soon removed all difficulties to their passage
over it. About noon their work was finished, and
the light cavalry took possession of Charleroi.

On the other hand, the 2d body, which had effected
its march to Marchienne, advanced on Gosselies, a
large town situated on the road to Brussels, with the
intention of intercepting at that quarter, the troops
driven out of Charleroi. The Prussians, surprised at
so sudden an attack, and pursued by the light troops,
retired in great disorder to Fleurus, where their main
body was concentrated. They were attacked several
times by our advanced guard, who afforded them no
time to take any positions. The presence of Buonaparté so electrified the French troops, there was no
possibility of restraining them. They rushed on the
Enemy without firing a shot; charging them so furiously with the bayonet, that nothing could resist
their shock.

The squadrons doing duty under Buonaparté charged the infantry several times, and it was in one of
those charges that General Letort, colonel of the
Dragoons of the Guard, received a mortal wound.

The French, in a word, after the most obstinate and
sanguinary encounters, carried all the positions opposed by the Enemy to their advance; towards night
they ceased the pursuit; and Buonaparté, leaving the
3d corps on the road to Namur, and the 2d at Gosselies on that to Brussels, returned with his head-
quarters to Charleroi.

The result of these engagements was, a thousand
prisoners, the passage of the Sambre, and the possession of Charleroi; but the principal advantage
derived from it was, to sustain the confidence of the
army by the gaining an early success; and, according to Buonaparté's general method of acting, every
thing was put in effort to make the most of it. The

prisoners were divided into parties, and passed before the troops in the rear. The soldiers cried out—" Long live the Emperor!"—It was what was expected, and the aim was answered.

The whole French army encamped on the Belgic territories, surrounded by the new subjects of the kingdom of the Low Countries, who hailed us as their liberators! Yet some of the villagers, who drew near at the cry of " Long live the Emperor," did not appear very enthusiastic in the cause. They received us rather as conquerors, whose goodwill it was requisite to conciliate, and their acclamations evidently expressed—" We are willing to become Frenchmen, if your bayonets carry law with them; but in mercy do not pillage us, do not lay waste our lands, treat us as your countrymen." These supplications were unheeded; though our soldiers placed unlimited confidence in their amicable demonstrations, they conducted themselves towards them as avowed enemies. Plunder and devastation marked their way; and wherever they pitched at night, that place was a desert in the morning!

No sooner had our troops taken a momentary position near some village, than they spread like a torrent through the unfortunate habitations; liquors, provisions, moveables, linen, clothes, every thing disappeared in an instant. Each village, where we had encamped, was left next day a heap of ruins, or rather of rubbish, scattered with the broken fragments of household furniture. Its environs, generally covered with rich crops, appeared destroyed by some dreadful hail-storm; while the places where our bivouacs had lighted up their watch-fires, black and scattered, seemed to point the spots where the thunderbolts had fallen.

The instant we quitted, the inhabitants, plunged in silent despair, rushed from their hiding-places in half-naked swarms, to search for the dispersed relics of their furniture or utensils, and collected what could be found.*

* Ought we, as many well-intentioned persons pretend, to shun disclosure, under the pretext that it is needful to spare the honour of France, and not jus-

It appeared from information obtained, that the Prussian advanced posts, although on their guard, had been surprized; and, far from expecting so serious and lively an attack, the Allies were preparing to enter in a few days upon the French territory. The inhabitants, too, were astonished at our appearance, when they thought us anxiously employed in securing our own frontiers. They gave a very bad account of the misconduct and exactions of the Prussians.

Each one speculated for himself on the probable result of the campaign, according to his information. The Enemy's army not being collected, was not prepared to concentrate itself. If pursued with vivacity, the different corps would be separately turned on all points, and would make little defence. Wellington was not prepared; disconcerted by so unexpected a movement, his whole plan was frustrated, since he had lost the initiative, and could not resume his ground. In short, their confidence in Buonaparté knew no bounds; his combinations, as sure in their results, as admirable in their conceptions, were either to annihilate the English, or drive them to their ships. A speedy arrival on the Rhine was to take place amidst universal acclamation of the inhabitants of Belgium, risen in mass for their deliverance, and the whole rushing with transport into the ranks of their old companions in arms.

The 16th, at 4 A. M., the columns which remained on the right bank of the Sambre, put themselves in march and passed the river, when the whole army advanced forward.

The command of the left wing, consisting of the

---

tify the future reprisals of hostile armies on its territory? Should we with this intent refuse to trace the picture of excesses committed by our troops, and stifle the reproach due to their misdeeds? Did we even suppress the mention of such deplorable acts of revolting Vandalism, they would not be the less notorious; and our silence might draw down on France, the injurious surmise that she owns and approves them. We ought not then to hesitate in denouncing them before the face of day, as atrocious abuses of force and confidence, which she most formally disavows, and so by holding them up to public indignation, do away the stain that otherwise would fall on herself. Thus will a three-fold duty be performed, to efface national dishonour, to convey shame to the breasts of the culpable, and to testify the horror which all must feel for deeds of violence, that invariably call down on their perpetrators, scorn and hatred implacable, and the whole weight of a terrible, though haply a protracted vengeance.

1st and 2d divisions of infantry, and four corps of cavalry, was given to Ney, who arrived the evening
before at head-quarters, and received orders to march
by Gosselies and Frasnes on the road to Brussels.

The centre, composed of the 3d, 4th, and 6th divisions, the reserve, and a numerous body of cavalry,
forming the mass of the army, directed itself upon
Fleurus. Marshal Grouchy, with the cavalry of
Pajol, and some battalions of foot, manœuvred towards the village of Sombref on the Namur road.

In forming out of Fleurus, they presently descried
the Prussian army; the chief masses of which appeared in close columns, crowning the upland levels
that surround the mill of Bussi, and stretching in amphitheatre through the whole length of a sloping
hill, in front of which was a deep ravine, tufted
with thickets, that extended in front of the entire
line. Its right rested on the village of St. Amand,
its centre at Ligny, and its left stretched beyond the
reach of sight towards Sombref, Gembloux, and the
road to Namur. All these villages, which are large
and built on uneven and broken ground, are in front
of the ravine, and were lined with infantry.

Having reconnoitred them, Buonaparté took his
measures for the attack. The 1st corps, forming part
of the left, was placed with the divisions of heavy
cavalry behind the village of Frasnes on the right,
and near the Brussels road, in order to direct itself
on such points where its presence should be necessary.
The 3d advanced in columns of attack on St. Amand,
the 4th on Ligny, supported by the Guard; the 6th
corps, and a numerous reserve of cavalry, under
Marshal Grouchy, with the right divisions, marched
on Sombref.

The 3d corps began the attack on the village of
St. Amand, and, after meeting a very obstinate resistance, carried it by the bayonet, but was driven out
again after being in possession of a part of it. The
4th corps threw itself, in its turn, upon Ligny; and
the two wings successively became engaged, the left
at Frasnes, and the right at Sombref. In a few moments the affair was general, and a heavy cannonade,

which, perpetually increased, was heard along the whole line.

The combat was maintained on both sides with equal obstinacy ; each soldier seemed to meet his adversary with personal rancour, and each had resolved, it is evident, to give no quarter.　The villages which were the scenes of action, were taken and re-taken over and over, with dreadful carnage ; and a defence made by the Prussians in the church of St. Amand, rendered the result of the day so dubious, that Buonaparté sent, with great haste, the 1st division to save that point.

By this movement, the left, which had obtained considerable advantage over the English line, and driven it from the heights of Frasnes, back to the farm of Quatre-bras, and taken position there, became materially weakened ; and the total loss of the battle was risked through the imprudence of Buonaparté in not advising Marshal Ney, that he had drawn off a part of his forces.

The 1st corps had parted about an hour to make towards St. Amand, when the English army, strengthened with numerous reinforcements under the Prince of Orange, resumed the offensive, and vigorously repulsed our light troops, and the columns they preceded.　Their cavalry were ranged upon the high road to Brussels, while the infantry occupied the entire skirts of an extensive wood, which stretched along the left of that road.　From the whole outline of this forest, ran a hollow way, resembling a ravine.　In front to the road, were fields of rye of considerable extent.　The French line were in possession of the right side of the road to a certain height.

All on a sudden, the fields were covered with numerous battalions in solid columns, supported by a formidable cavalry, which boldly advancing, threatened to break our line.　Our troops appeared intimidated, and fell back in a kind of panic.　The moment was urgent, and it was necessary to bring up at the instant our reserve. Marshal Ney, little alarmed by this circumstance, as he relied on the arrival of the 1st corps, sent orders for them to charge the

Enemy. But what was his surprise and embarrassment, on learning that Buonaparte had disposed of
them elsewhere!

He immediately ordered the 8th and 11th Cuirassiers, who were at hand, to charge the first battalions.
The charge was made with the greatest bravery; but
these battalions, covered by a wood filled with infantry, opened conjointly so terrible a fire, that the Cuirassiers, unable to penetrate further, were compelled
to make a short turn and retreat in disorder. It was
in this charge, which, however unfortunate, was executed with daring valour, that a cuirassier of the 11th
regiment took a standard of the 64th regiment of the
English line.

This repulse, with the crowds of wounded soldiery
and cuirassiers who fell back, or were conveyed to
the rear of the army, spread dismay. Equipages,
hospital-waggons, cantineers, servants, the swarm of
non-combatants that follow an army, and who, according to the orders given, all made a precipitate escape,
hurrying with them every thing that stood in the way
along the road to Charleroi; which was presently
choaked. The rout was complete, and spread with
rapidity. Every one fled in confusion, crying, " The
Enemy, the Enemy!"

The evil, however, was reparable. The Cuirassiers of General Roussel advanced at full trot towards the English, but had not occasion to charge.
Our infantry fell back in good and close order, opposing a vigorous resistance, and checked the Enemy.
Led off at length to the heights of Frasnes, it formed
again, but had little further share in the affair of the
day. In a short time, order was restored in the rear,
and the fugitives halted the moment they were assured of not being pursued.

Meanwhile the 1st corps detached from the left
wing had remained useless; and when it came up, the
3d had taken the village of St. Amand. It was ordered, therefore, to return to its former position; thus
marching and countermarching, it was not brought
into action on any one point.

The fire still continued very briskly along the line,

particularly towards Ligny, the point of the greatest strength, and of course most directed against. The cannonading did not cease an instant; and, by what we could judge, our artillery did considerable mischief among the great body of Prussian troops that were posted in mass on the heights and slopes, which formed an open amphitheatre to us. Our troops, almost hid behind the uneven grounds, were less exposed to the Enemy's artillery; who, however unsuccessful, did not relax their fire.

Towards seven P. M. we were masters of the villages, but the Prussians still kept their positions behind the ravine; at this moment it was that Buonaparté, who from the commencement had manœuvred so as at a proper time to have the power of transporting a great force beyond the ravine, directed his guard and the whole of his reserve on the village of Ligny. This bold movement, the execution of which what had passed on the left wing had retarded, was intended to cut off from the main body the right of the Prussian army behind St. Amand, and intercept their retreat upon Namur. Instantly the Guards, supported by a strong cavalry and powerful artillery, pressed forward to the ravine, which they cleared amidst a shower of balls, and the combat became dreadful. But nothing could withstand the impetuosity of the French Grenadiers, who cut their way with the most horrible carnage, our cavalry charging at the same time on every side. At length, after the most obstinate defence, the Prussians were driven back, and left us masters of the field of battle, covered with dead, the dying, the wounded, some prisoners, and a few field-pieces. The Guards immediately possessed themselves of the slopes and uplands which were evacuated, and our cavalry pursued the fugitives.

During this decisive operation at Ligny, the 3d corps were endeavouring to employ the Prussian right wing, in order to divert their attention from what had passed. But they readily saw through our design, and made good their retreat to Gembloux and Namur.

The French army prepared to push their success;

but the approach of night, and fatigues of the day, prevented it. They contented themselves with taking possession of all the Prussian posts, and at ten o'clock the fire had ceased along the whole line.

Various extravagant reports circulated in our army respecting this battle. Marshal Blücher had, in fact, a horse killed under him; he was stunned by the fall, and surrounded by French Cuirassiers; it was to the darkness of the night alone he owed his safety. But notwithstanding the Prussians must have severely suffered, their loss was never known, nor ever attended to in our Orders.

On the left, where the English were engaged, both parties maintained their ground and their positions.

The death of the Duke of Brunswick was announced, killed from the fire of the division commanded by Jerome Buonaparté; and also the death of General Hill. The first intelligence was confirmed the following day, and urged our French Generals to interweave, for the purpose of currying favour with the Ex-King of Westphalia, some unbecoming pleasantries on the fatality that seemed to pursue the unfortunate Duke, who, placed in constant opposition with the conqueror of his States, was condemned to die by his hand. And the latter, they augured hence, was again called to be his successor. It was added, that Jerome himself had been struck by a spent bullet. We will not stop to examine the truth of a fact of so trivial importance : but it is to be observed this sort of shots never reach any but great personages, whose valour it is interesting to enhance.

But every one agreed that Buonaparté had obtained his end in separating the Prussians and the English, and that, having so much weakened the former, he had now only the latter to encounter.

It was to realize the hope of exterminating the English, that on the 17th, at day-break, Buonaparté leaving behind him the 3d and 4th corps, together with the cavalry of General Pajol, under command of Marshal Grouchy, to watch the Prussians, marched with his reserve, and the 6th corps, towards Quatrebras.

h

The English appeared to occupy the same positions as on the day preceding; and the French army remained till 11 o'clock A. M. observing them, and waiting for the troops from the right, whose arrival was delayed by heavy rains and cross-roads almost impracticable.

Arrangements were made for the attack, and the united corps advanced in front of battle, along the heights of Frasnes, when it was perceived that the English had manœuvred so as to mask their retreat. The troops we saw on the plain, at the entrance of the wood, and on the road, were only a strong rear-guard to cover the same. Buonaparté set out in pursuit of them with his cavalry, and all the army urged its march to Brussels.

The ardour of the soldiers during this rapid pursuit was incredible. In the dexterous and admirably executed retreat of the English, they chose only to see their total defeat, the abandonment of Brussels, and their refuge on board their ships.

We again crossed the plains of Quatre-bras, strewed with dead, among whom were vast numbers of wounded Frenchmen, who had not been removed. We had time to ascertain how murderous the affair had been on both sides; but, from all appearance, the English loss was the greatest. The plains which lay between the road and the wood, where they were in position, but particularly the skirt of the wood, and the hollow way behind it, was buried beneath hills of slain, of whom the greatest portion were Scotchmen. Their costume, composed of a kind of folded jacket, of brown stuff chequered with blue stripes, which not descending so low as the knees leaves the leg nearly bare, singularly attracted the attention of our French soldiery, who gave them the appellation of *Sans-culottes*.

Buonaparté, with his advance, followed the English till night, and only stopped at the entrance of the forest of Soigné, when he met a degree of resistance not to be surmounted on that day. After having cannonaded them as long as the light permitted, he took up his head-quarters at the farm of

Caillon, near Planchenois. The different corps of
the army encamped at Genappe and its neighbourhood.

The night was dreadful, the wind blew a tempest,
and the rain fell in unceasing torrents; the troops
slept on the mud and among the dripping corn, and
so did the inhabitants of the farms and villages
round, driven naked from their burning cottages by
these more than Tartarian Frenchmen, whom pretended deserters, sent purposely by the English Staff,
made to believe the latter were abandoned by the
Belgians, and in full retreat towards their vessels.

However, at break of day, how great was their
astonishment to find the English had not only maintained their evening position, but were prepared to
defend it! Buonaparté, who dreamed they had escaped, exclaimed in a transport of joy: "I have
them then at last, these English!"

With unheard-of impatience, and without ascer-
taining whether Grouchy had, or not, succeeded in
keeping the Prussians in check; without inquiring
either the force or the position of his enemy, he hurried on his rear, and prepared for action.

The French army, presenting an effective force of
120,000 men, was ranged by ten o'clock on the heights
opposite to those the English were seen to occupy, in
front of the Forest of Soigné, which they held.

In the centre were perceived, behind the village of
Mount St. John, strong bodies of infantry that covered a vast plain, in front of which redoubts were
distinctly seen, of dark earth newly thrown up, extending beyond that whole line along the skirts of the
forest, lessening as they extended, and covered with
batteries. Its right rested on the village of Merke-
Braine, having in front the farm of Hougoumont,
surrounded by a wood intersected with different ravines or deep sinuosities; its left stretched far towards Wavres, also covered by a ravine, and the
farm of La Haye Sainte; it was impossible to ascertain its dispositions farther than Smouhen, where
the Brunswick troops were placed, and where it
was presumed the line terminated. In general,

except on the great plain, which was considered to be the centre of the English army, few troops were to be seen; but was it not to be conjectured, as it was afterwards ascertained during the business, that they were concealed in the hollows which separated the plains from the forest, and in the forest itself. Except on the great plain, few troops appeared in view. The head-quarters of Lord Wellington were at Waterloo, in the rear of his lines, which it will be seen crossed the two high roads of Brussels and of Nivelles.

The instant the French troops were come up, Buonaparté, who had placed himself on a mound at a small distance from the farm where he had slept, on the right of the road, ordered the cannonade to begin. He walked to and fro alone, with folded arms, a little in front of his Staff. The weather was stormy; there fell at intervals some short showers.

The 2d corps was on the left, and marched against the farm of Hougoumont. The 1st had its left on the road, and advanced upon the centre of the line. The 6th occupied the right. The Guard was in reserve upon the height. The cavalry was distributed upon different points; but its strongest columns were disposed on the wings, and particularly the right one.

About noon, the first discharge of cannon was heard from the French lines, and numerous light troops in front opened their fires. The left made a lively attack on the farm of Hougoumont, the buildings of which had been crenellated for defence, by the infantry, who maintained themselves with great obstinacy. Horse and foot advanced together against the corps placed in the rear of that farm, and who were throwing into it a continual reinforcement. After an hour's contest, the English appeared to retire a little, and the French army closed its advance. The artillery was in front of the whole line, and the infantry followed up in columns.

Our troops became thus engaged by degrees, not without sustaining great losses under the difficulties of uneven hilly ground, deep ditches, and ravines, where they were checked at every step, by fresh columns concealed till the moment we came up to them.

Every inch of ground was disputed on both sides, and neither gave way till every means of resistance was exhausted. The smallest hillock, the most trivial embankment was frequently taken and retaken several times. Repeated charges of cavalry took place; the field of battle was heaped with dead, and the firing, instead of slackening, became more and more violent. Both sides contended with equal fury, and the defence was as obstinate as the attack was impetuous.

It was speedily reported, that very strong columns were marching, the bayonet in front, upon Mount St. John, at the same time that the cavalry of the wings were to charge the batteries, which appeared to be very little protected. This grand movement, from the result of which so much might be expected, was impatiently waited for; but the obstinate perseverance of the English in maintaining their position in the villages which flanked their wings, retarded it. They successively sent battalions towards the farms of Hougoumont and La Haye Sainte, which our cavalry as frequently drove back; yet, those villages, though pressed with unparalleled vigour, still defended themselves. Eager to drive the Enemy from Hougoumont, who appeared resolved not to retire, we decided to set fire to it, at the same time sending a reinforcement against La Haye Sainte, which we carried after a most sanguinary contest.

The English artillery made dreadful havock in our ranks: we were so completely exposed, that their ricochets passed easily through all the lines, and fell in the midst of our equipage, which was placed behind on the road, and its environs. A number of shells too burst amongst them, and rendered it indispensable for the train to retire to a greater distance. This was not done without considerable disorder, which the English clearly perceived. Our artillery re-opened their fire with equal vivacity; but probably with much less effect, as their masses could only be levelled against by approximation, being almost entirely masked by the inequalities of the ground. The continuous detonation of more than 600 pieces of artillery; the fire of the battalions and light troops; the frequent explosion of caissoons, blown up by shells which reached them; the hissing of balls and grape-shot; the clash of arms; the tumultuous roar of the charges, and shouts of the soldiery—all created an effect of sound, the pen is impotent to describe; and all this within a narrow space, the two armies being close to each other, and their respective lines contracted into the shortest length possible.

However, in spite of obstacles and dangers, the French army was sensibly gaining ground.

The support of the two British wings being carried we passed the ravine, and made our advances amidst a deluge of balls and grape shot. A strong column approached Mount St. John, whence a terrific fire was pouring. The French cavalry at the same time rushed to carry the guns on the plains, but was charged in its turn by the Enemy's horse, who issued in a body from the hollows where they had lain in ambuscade, and the slaughter became horrible. Neither side gave way one step: fresh columns reinforce them; the charge is repeated. Three times the French are on the point of forcing the positions, and three times they are driven back!

These three assaults, made without interruption, and with all the characteristic impetuosity of the French, caused considerable loss to the Enemy, and called for the most vigorous resistance on their part. Lord Wellington exposed himself very much; and, in order to direct in person, the efforts of his troops, several times threw himself into the midst of the medley to animate them by his presence. The Prince of Orange, who was with the right wing, was wounded at the head of his troops.

The English, however, if the reports are to be credited, were very near being broken; it is strongly affirmed, that for a considerable time, great disorder prevailed in their rear, and they caused their equipages to retrograde with precipitancy, and file off towards Brussels, in much confusion.

But, however that may have been, it is not less true, that they repulsed with insurmountable firmness all our efforts, and knew how to frustrate them, by concealing from our observation, whatever trouble or apprehensions might have been produced from such furious attacks, so often repeated, and so obstinately upheld.

A general uneasiness now prevailed through our army. Several dismounted batteries were withdrawing; numbers of the wounded, detached from the columns, by their reports spread an alarm, and universal silence succeeded the shouts of victory with which the day had begun. All the troops (with the single exception of the infantry of the Guard) were engaged, and exposed to the deadliest fire; the action still continuing with the same fury, yet presenting nothing decisive.

It was near 7 o'clock. Buonaparté, still pacing the ground he had from the first placed himself on, contemplated with a ferocious eye this horrid butchery. The more the difficulties multiplied, the more determined was his obstinacy. And, far from fearing to drive to madness, an army who placed their unbounded confidence in him, he pressed on fresh troops without ceasing; ordering them to advance, charge bayonet in front, and carry every thing before them! In vain was he repeatedly told, that the affair was bad on many points, that the troops were shaken—" Forwards!" he cried—" forwards!"

A general officer had informed him how impossible it was to sustain the position he was in, as one of the batteries was annihilating him; and requested to know what he should do to elude its destructive fire. " Carry it!" was the reply—and he turned his back on the Aide-de-Camp.

An English officer, wounded, was brought before him. He made some inquiries of him, and amongst others: " What was the strength of their army?" The officer replied, very considerable, and had just been reinforced by 60,000 men—" So much the better," he answered: " the more there are, the longer we shall fight." He sent off several expresses towards France, and repeatedly exclaimed, in a tone of distraction, to his Secretary, "Above all, fail not to say the victory is mine!"

At this juncture, and at the moment when all his attempts proved abortive, it was announced to him, that powerful bodies of Prussians were opening on our right flank, and threatening our rear; but he treated the news as an idle tale, and then answered, that they had kept a bad look-out, for those pretended Prussians were nothing but Grouchy's corps. Several of the Aides-de-camp who came to report this news he even abused, and dismissed them with ill-humour.—" Be off! said he, you are frightened; ride up to the columns that are deploying, and you will find they are Grouchy's."

After so peremptory an answer, many of them, ashamed to have been mistaken, advanced heedlessly towards the Prussian jagers, and, notwithstanding the lively fire directed against them, got near enough to be either killed or taken. He was, however, obliged to yield to evidence, when these columns commenced a serious attack on our right wing. A part of the 6th division was sent to sustain this new shock, till those of Marshal Grouchy, on whom the greatest dependence was placed, should arrive; and it was even announced through the army that they were absolutely in line.

It appears from the reports, that a part of Marshal Blucher's army, which from the 16th concentrated itself in the environs of Wavres, had eluded the vigilance of Marshal Grouchy, and being joined by the 4th Prussian corps, under General Bulow, had rapidly joined the English line, to co-operate with Lord Wellington.

Marshal Grouchy had, in reality, briskly pursued the Prussians during their retreat to Wavres, and attacked in that place the portion of the Enemy which remained there. He was, therefore, engaged at the same moment we were, against a small division, which he mistook for the whole of the Prussian army, and over which he continued to obtain signal advantages: but, favoured as they were by the difficulties of a hilly country, intersected with woods and ravines, these corps made a sufficiently obstinate resistance, if not to stop his march, at least to impede it very considerably. Thus they succeeded in holding him in play at a distance from the principal seat of action.

He could not, therefore, be of any assistance to us; and hence it was that the English received a considerable reinforcement, whose concerted intervention put them in a situation no longer to fear our most vigorous attacks; but, on the other hand, to resume the the offensive, and presently to overpower us. Confidence was restored amongst them, and, calculating their manœuvres by the favourable circumstances that occurred, they resisted our efforts with all their force, and with an ardor that seemed to redouble itself.

It is evident that this operation had been preconcerted by the two Generals-in-chief, and that the English defended their positions with such invincible tenacity, only to give the Prussians time to effect that combined movement, on which the success of the battle depended, and the signal of which was waited for from one moment to the other.

Buonaparté, whose resolutions nothing could change, thought the moment was arrived to determine the day: he formed a fourth column of attack, almost entirely composed of his Guard, and led on the charge upon Mount St. John, after directing his orders on every point to second this movement, on which fate seemed to hang. Those old warriors entered the plain with their accustomed intrepidity, and courage was restored through the whole line. The Guard made several charges, but was constantly repulsed, crushed by a terrible artillery that each minute seemed to multiply. These invincible grenadiers beheld the grape-shot make day through their ranks; they closed promptly and coolly their shattered files; nothing intimidates them; nothing stops them but death or mortal wound; but the hour of defeat had sounded! Enormous masses of British infantry, supported by an immense cavalry we had nothing to oppose to, (for our own had already met its destruction,) descend in fury, surround, and cry out to them to surrender. " The Guard never surrenders ; if called on, it dies !" was the reply. No more quarter is given, almost the whole fall fighting in desperation.

This tremendous massacre continues as long as their resistance. At length, the fragment that remained, quit their ranks, and rush in utter confusion towards their first positions, doubtless in hopes to rally there.

Meanwhile the Prussians arrived on our right, advance, and charge what troops remain on that point. The cannonade, and a brisk fire of musketry, were heard in the rear of that line, as it approached, louder and louder. Our troops endeavoured to maintain the combat, but gradually lost ground. At last, our right wing evidently fell back, and the Prussians, who out-flanked it, were on the point of opening on the road, when the report ran that the Guard was repulsed, and when its scattered and maimed battalions were seen to rush back in confusion ; an universal panic seized the army, which disbanded itself on every point, and sought safety in instant flight. In vain, Buonaparté, for a last effort, collected some battalions of the old and young Guard, which had been least engaged, and led them on. All in vain ! Intimidated by the scene, and pulverized by the cannon, this feeble reserve was presently overthrown.

The army then spontaneously, and all at the same time, left its posts, and spread like a torrent in all directions. The cannoneers abandon their guns. The waggon-train cut their traces ; infantry, cavalry, all arms mingled in utter confusion, fly along the road and through the fields. Equipages of all sorts that had been arranged in park along the highway, and withdrawn in disorder, choak the road, and render it impassable.

However, the cry of " *Sauve qui peut,*" was no where heard ; and this general rout was the consequence of a spontaneous movement whose causes remain to this moment unknown, or for which it would be very difficult to assign any other than the knowledge the soldiery had acquired of the perils of our situation; for the French soldier is never, like those of almost all other nations, wholly passive. He observes, he reasons, and never under any circumstances places in his chiefs so blind a confidence as may prevent him from submitting their operations to his own judgment.

No order nor route had been given. The Commanders, swept along by the flying torrent, were separated from their corps; not a single file of men to rally to; no arrangements dreamt of, for an orderly retreat. The Guard, heretofore *Invincibles*, fled foremost of the multitude. Night came on, and added to the confusion.

The Enemy detached a numerous cavalry in pursuit of the fugitives. A part of them took possession of the whole hospital-train on the road, while formidable columns advanced on each flank. All the household carriages of Buonaparté fell first to the Prussians, with mountains of other baggage. All the cannons were taken in the batteries where they had served, along with the caissoons and trains. In a word, the whole *matériel* of our army disappeared in less than one half hour!

The English and Prussian Commanders, having completely effected their junction, met at the farm of La Belle Alliance. The British cavalry being greatly fatigued, that of the Prussians was sent forward, and did not give us a moment's repose.

Arrived at Genappe, they barricaded the entrance, and threw up all possible obstacles, in hopes to pass there the night. Presently a few shots fired by the Prussian cavalry, who were by this time close at their heels, spread the alarm; the bivouac is raised, and all in flight again more confused than before.

No one knew what was become of Buonaparté, who had disappeared. According to some he had perished in the strife; and this account being brought to a well-known general officer, he exclaimed, as Megret did after the death of Charles XII., at Frederickstadt, " *Voilà la pièce finie.*" Others reported he had been unhorsed and made prisoner. The same incertitude prevailed respect-

ing the fate of Marshal Ney, of the Major-general,
and of the principal number of the general Staff.

The former, who was Commandant-in-chief of the
1st and 2d corps had directed in person the different
attacks made on the centre, and was constantly seen
in the thickest of the action.   It appears that until
the moment there was a certainty of its not being
Grouchy's division which approached from the right,
but a body of Prussian troops, he had conceived us
to have the best of the affair, and anticipated the
liveliest hopes of a fortunate issue; but when he saw
Buonaparté maintain against demonstration, that
Grouchy was forming into line, and ostentatiously
circulate this falsehood through the ranks, he supposed it was his purpose to deceive the whole army
in order to inspire it with a fatal confidence.

From that time his opinion changed, and he no
longer acted with the same coolness and self-collec-
tion ; but it must be avowed that not one reproach was
made against him by the army on his change of conduct,
and his bravery was never suspected ; he merely partook the general anxiety and discouragement. It was
indeed obvious that from the opening of the campaign
he appeared profoundly dissatisfied, but dissimulated
his feelings in presence of the public.   There subsisted between him and Buonaparté a certain misunderstanding, and a kind of reciprocal distrust very
difficult to fathom, but not the less evident.   There
is every reason to believe too that he entertained a
jealousy of Marshal Grouchy, which Buonaparté
himself seemed manifestly to adopt.   Such dissen-
tions between the principal chiefs, must necessarily
have cramped the course of their operations, and disturbed the unity of their plans.

A great number of persons declared to have seen
Buonaparté in the midst of the crowd, and perfectly
distinguished him by his grey capotte and pye-balled
horse.

This last story was the true one.   When the last
battalions of the Guard were overthrown, Buonaparté was hurried away with them, surrounded on

all sides by the Enemy, into a cyder orchard, near the farm of Caillon. There he was met by two cavaliers of the Guard, who conducted him cautiously through the Prussian parties that were scouring the country, but who, fortunately for him, were all employed in stopping and plundering the equipages. He was known and recognized in many places, and often heard the whisper run: " The Emperor!—the Emperor!"—words of alarm which caused his instant removal from the spot wherever heard.

After a flight harassed by the Enemy through the whole night, the sad relics of our army reached at the point of day, part of them Charleroi, and the rest to Marchienne, where they hastened to repass the Sambre. The remaining equipages meanwhile, impeded by their gradual accumulation on the two roads which lead to the bridges of Charleroi and Marchienne, were overtaken by the Prussians, abandoned by their train and drivers, and thus the last cannon and military carriage fell into the power of the Enemy, who made at the same time a great number of prisoners.

The Sambre once crossed by the fraction of our army, we hoped to be able to halt, and bivouacs were established in the orchards and meadows on its right bank; but an alarm was given, that the Prussians were nigh. Without waiting orders; without attempting to destroy, or even turn adrift the bridges, without making a single reconnoissance, the flight recommenced with all its disorder: the whole started at once, and each for his own account directs his steps he knows not where.

At a little distance from Charleroi are two roads, one leading to Avesnes, the other to Philippeville. Having no direction, and seeing none of the superior officers, they divided into two parties; the most numerous one taking that of Avesnes, by which they had marched before, and the other that to Philippeville. A great number of scattered men threw themselves into the surrounding woods to avoid the Enemy's cavalry, and thus this brilliant army gradually dispersed and disappeared. It was the latter

road that Buonaparté chose for his retreat. Once
more a fugitive from his own army, he abandons it
without further effort, in the midst of dangers he seems
to take pleasure in aggravating, by delivering it up to
anarchy and dissolution.

Wandering and deserted, thousands of insulated
soldiers run about the country, spreading alarm as
they pass. The wretched inhabitants hear almost
at the same moment the success of the French army,
and its annihilation, and find themselves the prey of
an Enemy whom victory, won with its blood, must
render more ferocious. Every town shuts its gates
against the fugitives, and repelling by force those who
flee thither for safety, oblige them to seek shelter in
the neighbouring hamlets, where they practise every
sort of excess.

It was in quality of a runaway that Buonaparté,
in the moment of general dismay, sought safety, and
presented himself at the gates of Philippeville. He
wanted their protection from the hot pursuit of the
Prussians, who traced him in all directions. He had
the humiliation to be refused admittance, till the
Governor came out and recognized him, when forthwith the gates were closed.

Numbers of soldiers dispersing that way, to whom it
was soon known their illustrious Emperor was in this
place, conceived it their duty to encamp around him.
Buonaparté, however, prudently judged that such an
assemblage might make his asylum known to the
Enemy; he therefore sent orders for them to continue their route: but having, like a wise general,
analized the means of acting on the sentiments of an
army after such a defeat, he insured the prompt execution of his orders, by sending emissaries from the
town, who called out: " The Cossacks—save yourselves—the Cossacks—haste!"

It was these unfortunates who, in accents of despair and grief, spread along their journey the dreadful news, that the Emperor was blockaded at Philippeville. This was looked on as a certainty, but
conceived to be only a measure forming one part of
his grand preconceptions. However, after passing a

few hours at Philippeville, his Majesty withdrew from thence, and departed for Mezieres. Night came on as he passed under the walls of Rocroi, where they supposed he would have slept: a number of people appeared on the ramparts crying—" Long live the Emperor!"—while he remained in sight; but he probably found the night more convenient for continuing his route. There entered the town a few officers and attendants, with some horses only. All his carriages and equipage had been seized by the Enemy.

The great portion of the shattered army, which had withdrawn to Avesnes and Laon, experienced the deepest anxiety as to the fate of Buonaparté. They were ignorant of what had befallen him, but, persuaded that not being amongst them, he had found a grave in the same field of honour with the brave fellows he had led to death, lamented the fate reserved for a chief so dear. When they learn he is arrived at Paris, full of life and good health!—oh! shame eternal!—how paint the indignation they must have felt!

Since the affair of Ligny, there had been no communication from the right of the army, under Marshal Grouchy. The people, therefore, remained in ignorance of what they were become; and reports were circulated, that, for want of knowing the issue of the battle of Mount St. John, they had been surrounded by the allies at Wavre, and, unable to effect a retreat, had laid down their arms; Vandamme being in the number of the killed.

This fine French army then, sacrificed with its predecessors, had ceased to exist!—It seemed as though Buonaparté become furious at having seen some thousands of brave men escape his rage, the monster had stalked from his den in Elba, solely to devour the remainder. And if in fact he might have the credit of such intention, his every action during this short and unhappy campaign, would be in consonance therewith. But let us rather ascribe these enormous errors to his unskilful and presumptuous rashness, and to his well-known and incorrigible mania of advancing always in blind confidence, without plan or

any calculation of the chances of war. It is evident
that system, so uniformly adopted and persevered in
by Buonaparté, being become known to the Allied
Generals, had opened the pit-fall, in which his own
pitiable self-security precipitated him; for, whatever
their foreign bulletins may advance, with the intention, no doubt, of enhancing the glory of their generals, and the bravery of the men, it is clear that the
position of Mount St. John had been reconnoitred,
designed and marked out with the full purpose to
draw him thither with his army, and there give him
battle; for only a Buonaparté, infallible in his own
opinion, could have failed to see through it. The calculated retreat of the English on so strong a position, the obstinacy with which they maintained it, the
facility they had for masking their troops and artillery
in an immense forest, and beyond all that, the redoubts and open batteries they had raised, would
have awakened mistrust in almost any other general.
What further strengthens the supposition is, the erec-
tion of a wooden observatory, which had been raised
on a knoll in front of the forest, where with a good
telescope every movement as far as the Sambre might
be distinguished. It was certainly erected to watch
us, and could not have been the work of twenty-four
hours.

In every hypothesis, prudence called on him to reconnoitre the ground, and ascertain the dispositions
of the Enemy; and could the most unexperienced
general commit the error of making an attack without first placing himself in communication with his
right wing, or at least being fully aware of its operations? Besides, supposing that we had forced the
English line, which could not have been done without very considerable loss, what had been our advantage?—Behind them was a forest of 15 leagues long
by 5 broad; the road through it was but a narrow
defile, where 10,000 men and a few pieces of artillery
would have stopped the progress of the greatest
army.

Great fault was found with the charge of our officers, to whose ill success they ascribed all the mis-

chief that ensued.   They were accused of not having
met boldly the Enemy's battalions, though they had
brought away one standard ; and some went so far
as to surmise treason.   Rumours like these spread
presently through the whole army; and, to counteract
the bad impression, it was studiously propagated that
several generals who had become traitors, among the
rest, General Bourmont, had been delivered to a military commission, and shot.

Every thing, however, was lost; and the destruction of the French army was the more inevitable from
its right being turned, and no provision made for a
retreat.   Yet, (who will credit it?) Buonaparté alone
appeared to make light of the dangers which threatened
him.   Yet will he advance again, and flatters himself still with a few battalions to overturn a force that
had resisted his whole army!

And this is the man who passes " for the first Captain
of the age!"—Yet, it will not be doubted, that at
Mount St. John, Buonaparté displayed the whole
measure of his faculties ; he had too much need of
victory, not to put forth all his energies to obtain it.
Either then, it must be admitted, all his former victories were due to chance, or that his intellects were
deranged on the 18th of June; for his combinations
of that day could not otherwise be termed judicious,
than in so much as we pre-suppose his formal determination to cause the assassination of his whole
army.   Such at least was the opinion of his most
consummate Generals on this day, who exclaimed in
the violence of despair—" The man is not himself!
What would he have?   He loses his understanding!"

It is, however, pretended by some, that setting
aside all disadvantages of ground, the manner in
which he directed the attacks, and the evolutions he
commanded, bore strong resemblance to those of
Marengo, in so much that if on a sudden, at the
moment when the victorious English army broke
from their positions to rush upon us, a formidable column had issued from the ground, commanded by a
Desaix, it is more than probable the chances had
turned to our advantage.

i

If then Marshal Grouchy had appeared at the instant, he would have played most truly the part of Desaix, and it is beyond a doubt the victory had been ours. But he was too distant from the theatre of action to figure there so effectually. That consideration aggravates the inconceivable errors committed at Mount St. John by Buonaparté, whom nothing compelled to hazard so abruptly a decisive battle, and who, instead of reducing his right wing to an absolute nullity by neglecting to secure his communications with it, might without inconvenience have waited till it had rejoined. One day—a few hours even—would have sufficed to accomplish this most essential point, which would have placed every probability of a successful termination on our side: nor can the disasters that ensued from that circumstance be ascribed to unforeseen misfortune; for it is clear, that no measures had been taken to acquire any certain knowledge of the march of Grouchy's corps, or of the difficulties it might have encountered. And arrangements were made, which implied a full certainty, that that body having perfectly repulsed the Prussians, its prompt co-operation might be implicitly relied on.

It is generally believed, that when Buonaparté saw the affair turning so badly, he charged with the greatest bravery at the head of his Guard; that he had two horses killed under him, and courted death in the midst of the English several times. This desperation was proof of a disturbed mind. We must, therefore, deeply deplore the fate of an army committed to the hands of a man marked by such invincible obstinacy—with whom there can be no alternative, but to conquer or die!

The battle of Mount St. John was, assuredly, one of the most murderous that ever has been recorded. The French army, consisting of 120,000 men, after certainly displaying prodigious valour, was almost totally destroyed; 300 pieces of cannon, all the caissoons and equipages, fell into the power of the Enemy, as well as an innumerable mass of prisoners; and the bodies of more than 20,000 Frenchmen, mangled

with grape-shot, strewed the field. The English,
likewise, suffered great losses; but not comparable
to those of the French, from the superior advantage
afforded by their position. Nevertheless, it is presumed the Allied Armies had at least as many as
20,000 killed. There is reason to believe, that at the
commencement of the action, their forces were nearly equal; but the English army was, in fact, much
stronger through its entrenchments, and became considerably augmented by the effective co-operation of
the Prussians.

It was easy to predict the consequences of this
fight. The scattered fragments of the French army
rallied in the environs of Laon and of Rheims, but,
weak and discouraged, were incapable of opposing
the immediate entrance of the Allies into the capital.
They presently made their appearance before the barriers of Paris, when some resistance was first presented, on the arrival of those corps which had composed the right wing of the army.

This right wing, which was supposed to have been
destroyed, had with singular good fortune retreated
by Namur, and, after marching eight days in the
midst of the Allies, and parallel with them, joined at
length the remainder of our army, without having
met any considerable loss.

Thus, seventy thousand men were concentrated
before Paris, and threatened to defend that capital.
But what could so small a force effect against the
united arms of all Europe, which were approaching
with rapid strides towards their central point?—
After some days spent in a resistance extremely alarming to the inhabitants, whose safety was thereby
endangered to an indefinite extent, they succeeded in
overcoming the obstinacy of the troops, who had determined to hold out to the last extremity, and were
resolved to exact for that purpose the greatest sacrifices. In thus gradually disposing them to accept a
capitulation, and extorting, it may be said, in this
manner their consent to evacuate Paris, France in
reality gained a signal victory; the results of which

are incalculable, and perhaps saved the capital from
entire destruction.

The battle of Mount St. John, therefore, by the
occupation of Paris, and re-establishment of the legitimate Government, terminated the frightful strife
in which Buonaparté had engaged us. No doubt,
the momentary destruction of so many thousands of
men was a dreadful catastrophe; but it was the
prompt and unexpected issue of a frightful war,
which might probably have ravaged France for an indefinite period. Even had their efforts been unanimous, yet must she have yielded finally to all the
united energies of Europe put forth against her; and
meanwhile, a prey to wild devastation, trampled under foot by numerous enemies, her soil would only
have been ceded, when covered with dead, and encumbered with the sad ruins of burning villages, her
inhabitants had abandoned them in despair to the discretion of soldiers, whose need is destruction.

History has shown by frequent and terrible exam-
ples, that men whom the power of arms has raised
above all law, no longer recognize the ties of patriotism. They form a corps apart, and treat with un-
distinguishing fury their own or foreign lands. And
what protection could be sought from an army, whose
whole allegiance and devotion were centered in the
individual Buonaparté, and who avowed themselves,
in face of the world, to be the blind instruments of
his will?—Accustomed to a wandering life of plunder, and imbued with the sole genius of destruction,
they exhibited a system of military cosmopolitism. It
breathed only war, for war and unchecked rapine
were the object of its vows. After having ravaged
the rest of Europe, France was still a virgin land,
that presented to them a wide and fertile field of de-
predation. The spirit of disorder and indiscipline
this army carried along with it every where, victorious
or fugitive, had become contagious, and spread not
only among the foreign troops who served in its ranks,
but among those they opposed. France could not,
therefore, have expected a better lot than those unhappy lands their presence had desolated.

Though unfortunately it is too notorious, that the French in their incursions into the neighbouring states, set an example of rapine and exaction, it is no less certain they have been well imitated, if not excelled by those of the foreign troops, who seem to have made it a point of honour to resemble them in this particular. And there is one nation, to whom perhaps it belongs of right to exercise the most cruel reprisals, that may well serve as a model thereof. But whatever be the inducements to such a scandalous abuse of military power, its perpetrators blindly light up a volcano, that assuredly will one day explode under their own feet; for, it cannot be denied, it is the afflicting excesses with which the French armies are reproached, that have drawn down on their native land the resentment of all Europe, and provoked that terrible re-active visitation, under which we now groan. In every point of view, therefore, they have been the heralds of greater evil to France, than to the countries that have had to undergo them. May then this tremendous lesson not pass unheeded by the nations, but enlighten their views of policy and public interest, for the common good of them all!

Necessarily subversive of every principle and of all morality; the destroyer of law and justice; the sworn enemy to civilization—there can exist neither government nor society where Military Despotism reigns. Peace without is impossible, because man is governed by his interest, and the thirst of power is interwoven in his nature. Soldiers, therefore, called at first to the honourable task of maintaining the rights of their fellow-citizens, soon forget their mandatory characters, and, aspiring to engross the wealth, honours, and offices of state, do not hesitate in the choice of means. War, above all, is the element they breathe, and hence a Military Government finds occasion to be for ever at war.

An exclusive preponderance, therefore, of the military profession is the greatest evil which can befall a state. Crushed beneath the weight of their own power, all conquering nations have been conquered

in their turn.   And what country has had to feel
more than France, the weight of this austere truth?
That Military Government, for which she has made
such great sacrifices; these splendid conquests, this
glory of arms, have led her from victory to victory,
to the verge of destruction.

The same deplorable system has made us retrograde with rapid strides towards the ages of barba-
rism.   Factious legions, as in the periods of anarchy
of the Roman Republic, acknowledging no other law
than their own will, called to reign over the nations
they oppressed, the General who had captivated their
choice; or, like the Janissaries of the East, raised and
deposed their own Despot at their pleasure.

It is highly essential, therefore, that all efforts
be combined against this Vandalism, which threatens
to replunge us in the gulph of barbarian darkness.
It is now time that order should succeed to anarchy,
and the authority of laws to the sway of violence.

Buonaparté's Conduct during and after the Battle, with Opinion,
Conversation, &c. collected from various sources.

The following details will give a correct idea of the dangers
which Buonaparté personally underwent on the memorable day of
Waterloo.   These details were furnished by an eye-witness of the
whole, and may be relied on:

" From two o'clock until a quarter before seven, Buonaparté commanded all the operations and movements from a position where he
remained without any danger whatever to his own person: he was
at least a cannon-shot and a half off: nothing in short could reach
him.

" When he was at length convinced, that the corps d'armée
which he had so long and so obstinately taken for that of Marshal
Grouchy, was in reality a Prussian corps, he seemed to think that
the affair was desperate, and that he had no other resource than to
make a great effort with the reserve of his Guard, composed of
15,000 men.   This part he accordingly took.

" At this moment he assumed an appearance of resolution, which
re-animated a little those who surrounded him.

" He advanced, saying—" Let every one follow me," (*Tout le
monde en arrière!*) which evidently signified that he wished to be
in front.   In fact, he made this movement at first, and headed, for
about ten minutes, the formidable column which remained to him
as his forlon hope; but when he arrived within 200 toises (1200 feet)
from three solid squares of Allied troops which occupied a ridge, with
a formidable artillery, (and which ridge it was necessary to carry),

he suddenly stopped under the broken ground of a sand-pit, or ravine, and a little on one side, out of the direction of the cannon balls.

" This fine and terrible column, which he had some time headed, found him here, as it passed and defiled before him in order to advance, taking a demi-tour to the bottom of the hillock, and directly in front of the Enemy's squares, which Buonaparté himself could not see from the lateral point which he occupied, although it is very true that he was close enough to the Enemy's batteries. As the corps passed him, he smiled, and addressed to them expressions of confidence and encouragement. The march of these old warriors was very firm, and there was something solemn in it.—Their appearance was very fierce. A kind of savage silence reigned among them. There was in their looks a mixture of surprise and discontent, occasioned by their unexpected meeting with Buonaparté, who, as they thought, was at their head.

" In proportion as they ranged up the eminence, and darted forward on the squares which occupied its summit, the artillery vomited death upon them, and killed them in masses. This part of the scene came directly under Buonaparté's eyes, without his being able to see what passsed on the height itself, as he still kept himself, as it were, enveloped in the corner of the ravine. It was then precisely a quarter of an hour from seven o'clock, and it was at this very moment that the decisive crisis of the battle commenced.

" Buonaparté had then six persons close to him—these were, his brother Jerome, and Generals Bertrand, Drouet, Bernard, Douhers, and Labedoyere. At every step which he took, or seemed to take, to put his own person in front, Generals Bertrand and Drouet threw themselves before his horse's head, and exclaimed in a pathetic accent—' Ah ! Sire, what are you going to do ! Consider that the safety of France and the army depends entirely upon you. All is lost, if any accident should happen to you.'

" Buonaparté yielded to their entreaties with a zeal or apparent effort, which he seemed to gain over himself. But one thing appeared very singular, namely, that the two men who knew so well how to moderate his ardour, and to retain him, were the only persons whom he never sent to reconnoitre the state of the battle, while he sent the rest twenty times into the midst of the fire to carry orders, or bring him information. One of them having told him, that the Duke of Wellington had been for a long time in front, and at the head of one of his squares, he exhibited a sort of grin, which showed evidently, that this part of the narrative vexed him much.

" Jerome having thought proper to take aside, and whisper with one of his brother's Aides-de-Camp, to whom he spoke his mind very freely, Buonaparté sent him (Jerome) several times into the middle of the fire, as if to get rid of such an importunate critic. Jerome, in fact, took it greatly to heart, that his brother did not profit of this occasion, to die in a glorious manner; and I distinctly heard him say to General Bertrand—' Can it be possible that he will not seek death here ? Never will he find a more glorious grave !'

" At nightfall, Buonaparté disappeared from us, under pretext of going himself to ascertain the state of things, and put himself at the

head of the Guards, to animate them. Before I conclude, there is
a peculiarity which deserves to be noticed, namely, that before
effecting his personal retreat, in order to get rid of impertinent
witnesses, he directed all those around him to carry different orders
at once, the result of which could not concern him in the least."

" Capt. Erskine, who was made prisoner in the battle of the 16th,
was brought before Buonaparté for examination. Being asked by
Buonaparté " Who commands the cavalry?" he was answered,
" Lord Uxbridge." " No, Paget," replied Buonaparté. The officer
then explained that they meant the same person, and Buonaparté
nodded assent. He was then asked, " Who commanded in chief?"
and was answered, " the Duke of Wellington;" upon which he observed, " No, that cannot be, for he is sick." It seems that his
Grace had received a fall from his horse, on the 14th, and was
reported to be indisposed in consequence, and Buonaparté had received intelligence to that effect. The conversation continued in this
line for a considerable time, during which Buonaparté showed himself perfectly acquainted with the strength and position of the
several divisions of the Allied Armies, and the names of their several Commanders. As they were successively mentioned, Buonaparté
occasionally remarked, " Oh! yes, this division cannot be up in
time.—This division cannot be up in a day," and so on. Upon
some difficulty in the conversation, one of his Aides-de-Camp, who
spoke English well, interpreted after, and he, it appeared, had been
in London about ten days before. On the conversation being ended,
a surgeon was ordered to give his attention, and was placed, with
another officer, under three guards—on retiring, they were put to
quarters, which happened to be the cock-loft of a house ; from
hence, on the following morning, they looked secretly, and saw the
whole of the French army march to their positions : knowing the
disparity of force, he trembled to think of the result ; and noticing
particularly the enthusiasm and devotion of the troops—in this state
of anxiety, they silently waited some hours, fearing every moment
to hear the crisis ; at length they heard a great bustle of men and
horses ; upon coming nearer, they discovered them to be French :—all
is now lost, victory is gained, and these are the messengers. On
coming to the town, they however found them flying French ; then
was their joy superior to their former dejection: but in their helpless
situation, they dare not show themselves, as they certainly would
have been shot—but after an hour, the black Brunswickers came
riding through, then they came out of their lurking-places, and
joined their comrades ; it is to be observed, that their guards had
long left them."

LA COSTE'S NARRATIVE.*

" Three officers, early in the morning of the Sunday 18th June,
inquired for him, and asked him how long he had lived in the country,
and upon hearing his reply, wrote three lines upon a piece of paper,
and sent an officer with him to Buonaparté at six. B. asked him if
he knew the different roads. C. answered, yes, and explained them
upon a chart which was lying before B. Coste said that from eight to
one B. was forming his troops for the *general* engagement, which

* Vide Waterloo Letter following, in which a slight variation may be noticed.

began at one. From one to four, B. was dismounted, and remained in the same position, (viz. a little above Hougoumont, towards the left). From four to seven, he was upon the roof of Coste's house, one-eighth of a mile beyond Belle Alliance. At seven he moved in the high road between Belle Alliance and Mount St. Jean, three quarters of a mile from Coste's house. That B. remained there till half-past eight, when finding that the Prussians were coming upon his flank, and that the English by their desperate attack, had thrown his troops into utter confusion, said to Bertrand, " *Sauvons-nous;*" he then immediately galloped off; and that he never spoke for four hours. B. was not seen either to eat or drink during the day, and in Coste's opinion, he considered victory as certain till seven in the evening, when he was cheered with victory by his troops."

Waterloo, August 15.

" Opposite the Inn, at a cottage where the Earl of Uxbridge was carried, you are shown a neat garden ; in the centre of four paths, a little hillock, with a weeping willow and shrubs planted near the spot, shows the sepulchre of his Lordship's leg :* in an inclosure, further behind this cottage, are interred several English Officers; one only, Colonel Fitzgerald, of the Life Guards, has a stone, with an inscription over him ; many have been taken up and transmitted to England : you then proceed to Waterloo, the house of Jean Baptiste La Coste, called Belle Alliance, from whom I obtained the following particulars :—

" About five in the morning, he was taken prisoner to serve as guide, and conducted with his hands tied behind him (that he might not escape as a former man had done) to another house belonging to him, opposite to which Buonaparté had slept. Observing the French soldiers plundering and destroying this house, he cried. Buonaparté asked what he cried for ? " Because your soldiers are destroying all my property, and my family have no where to put their heads." Buonaparté said, " Do you not know that I am Emperor, and can recompense you an hundred times as much ?" He was placed on a horse immediately between Buonaparté and his first Aide-de-Camp, his saddle being tied to the saddle of a trooper behind him, that he might not escape. They proceeded a little beyond Belle Alliance, and Buonaparté took the ground on a small eminence on the opposite side ; a sort of body guard of twelve pieces of artillery, very light, surrounding them. From this spot, he could command both lines. He first observed : " How steadily those troops take the ground ! how beautifully those cavalry form ! *regardez ces chevaux gris!* † Qui

---

* You are also shown the chair on which his Lordship sat during the operation, exactly as it remained ; and they still remember the gallant Earl's heroic sentiments at the moment of this severe trial : but he was not seen to wince in the least, not even by contortion of features, consoling those about him in saying : " Who would not lose a leg for such a victory ? It is true, I have a limb less ; but I have a higher name in the eyes of my country." The interview between the Noble Duke and his Lordship, upon his visit to Brussels, after the battle, on the Sunday, is described as the most feeling that can be imagined. The Duke in displaying the purest sympathetic affection had a fine contrast in the heroic firmness of the Noble Earl.   Editor.

† Meaning the Scots Greys. N. B. Col. Cheney of the Greys, on whom the command of that regiment devolved on the 18th June, in consequence of the death of Col. Hamilton and the wounds of other officers, had six horses killed under him, yet almost by miracle, himself escaped without a wound.

sont ces beaux cavaliers? Ce sont de braves troupes, mais dans une demi-heure je les couperai en pièces." Observing how the chasms in the British squadrons were filled up the instant they were made by his artillery, he exclaimed *" Quelles braves troupes! comme ils se travaillent, ils travaillent très-bien, très-bien!"* He asked La Coste the particulars of every house, tree, wood, rising ground, &c., with which he seemed well informed, holding a map in his left hand, and intent upon the action all the day, incessantly taking snuff from his waistcoat pocket, in large pinches, of which he violently snuffed up about half, throwing the other from him, with a violent exertion of the arm, and thumb and finger, as if from vexation ; this was all the refreshment he took for fourteen hours : he frequently placed his left hand upon the back of La Coste's horse, to speak to the Aide-de-Camp on the other side of him. Seeing La Coste flinch at the shower of shot, he replied; " Do not stir, my friend, a shot will kill you equally in the back as the front, or wound you more disgracefully." About eight, hearing the fire of the Prussians on the right of his rear flank, leaning his hand on the neck of La Coste's horse, and seeing the British cavalry, from their right and left flanks, making a tremendous charge that would have encircled his personal position, he exclaimed, addressing himself to Bertrand, " *Il faut que nous nous sauvons,*" retreating, with all his staff, about forty yards along the road ; and within about twenty yards of the house Belle Alliance, he halted, and putting the glass to his eye, saw the British cavalry, intermingled *pele-mele,* and furiously cutting the French troops to pieces. He exclaimed, " *Qu'ils sont terribles ses Chevaux Gris!*" (meaning the Scots Greys, which had particularly during the day, and at that moment, attracted his attention), " *Il faut nous dépêcher, nous dépêcher.*" They, and all the cavalry, commenced a gallop, till they got about three leagues beyond Charleroi, where they halted, and pitched a tent upon a grass-plat, about nine at night. A fire was kindled, and refreshments placed upon a chair, which Buonaparté took the first for fourteen hours, standing with his back to the fire, with his hands generally behind him, conversing with a circle of nine, whose horses La Coste had been ordered to hold, till the party, about two in the morning, broke up, when each taking his horse, Bertrand gave La Coste a Napoleon d'or, which he exchanged, after a twenty-four hours fast, to refresh himself and family.

" This statement of La Coste contradicts the account of the new guard, crying to the old, " *Se sauve qui peut ;*" that expression might easily have changed, in running through the army, from the first text, " *Il faut que nous nous sauvons.*" About an hour before the rout, Buonaparté exclaimed : " I shall cut them to pieces, yet it is a pity to destroy such brave troops."

" The latter part corresponds much with an account I had by an officer, that accompanied me in this inspection. About an hour before the finish, he said an Aide-de-Camp came to the Duke of Wellington, telling him that the 5th division was reduced from 4000 to 400, and that their keeping their post was wholly ineffectual; " I cannot help it," said the Chief, " they must keep the ground with myself to the last man. Would to God the night or Blucher would come !" Near an hour after the fire was heard by the British in the

rear of Buonaparté's right flank—" We will beat them yet," cried he.
The charge was sounded, the most dreadful havock commenced, and a
victory closed the 18th day of June, which established a British generalship and the British army as the first in Europe.

" On the left of all, the Brunswickers, in a firm square, made a
breastwork of carnage; the Scots brigade next.   A brigade of Hanoverian Landwehr on their right, forming their square aukwardly,
Colonel Cameron of the 92nd, who was killed afterwards, called to
them to form as *they* did, which they obeyed, and stood; the next, a
Dutch Brigade, by not forming alertly, were cut to pieces.   This
battle proved the fact, of what we vulgarly call *bottom.*"

Premature Proclamation, dated Lacken, June 17, 1815.

So confident was Buonaparte of getting to Brussels, that several
bales of Proclamations were found among his baggage, dated from
" Our Palace of Lacken," a royal residence near that city.

" Proclamation to the Belgians and Inhabitants of the left Bank of the Rhine.

" The ephemeral success of my Enemies detached you for a
moment from my Empire; in my exile, upon a rock in the sea, I
heard your complaint, the God of Battles has decided the fate of
your beautiful provinces; Napoleon is among you; you are worthy
to be Frenchmen; rise in mass, join my invincible phalanxes to ex-
terminate the remainder of these barbarians, who are your enemies
and mine: they fly with rage and despair in their hearts.

At the Imperial Palace of Lacken, June 17, 1815.
(Signed)   NAPOLEON.
By the Emperor,
The Major-General of the Army,
    COUNT BERTRAND.

BUONAPARTE AFTER THE BATTLE OF WATERLOO.

It was on the 20th of June, at nine at night, that the fugitive from
Waterloo arrived at Paris.   He first saw Madame de St. Leu (Louis
Buonaparté's wife), then Maret and Regnault de St. Jean d'Angely.
The following are the details of this interview.   M. St. Didier was
present.

The night was far advanced,   Maret sat in a corner of the room,
with an alarmed countenance—Regnault stood before a table,
making pencil-marks on a piece of paper before him—Buonaparté
walked up and down, biting his nails and taking snuff.   He stopped
all at once.   " Where is the Bulletin?"

Regnault.—There it is, corrected.

Buonaparté.—Let us see.   (Regnault began reading it.)

Buonaparté.—(During two-thirds of it,) It was gained. When Regnault had finished, he said with a sigh—It is lost!

Buonaparté.—It is lost, and—my glory with it.

Regnault.—You have fifty victories to oppose to one defeat.

Maret.—The defeat is decisive; the Emperor is in the right.

Buonaparté.—They are not accustomed to conquer. They will abuse the victory.

Maret.—Those whose cowardice Wellington's bravery has made triumphant, are more dangerous, and more your enemies, than the English and Prussians.

Regnault.—The republicans will grieve; but they will try to profit by the circumstance.

Buonaparté.—They will do well; at least the glory and liberty of the country will remain untouched. If the Royalists succeed, it will be by the support of foreigners.

Maret.—The courage of the Royalists is in the head of Wellington, and the arm of Blucher.

Regnault.—What most presses is, to stop Blucher and Wellington.

Maret.—How? The army exists no more, and the frontier is uncovered.

Regnault.—The frontier is uncovered, but the army exists; it requires only being rallied.

Buonaparté.—It will rally itself; we must reorganize and repair its losses.

Maret.—Are you sure of Soult and Grouchy?

Buonaparté.—Grouchy is an honest man, but feeble. Soult has given pledges.

Regnault.—The army will re-organize itself, but the corps are incomplete.

Buonaparté.—Assemble the ministers.—I will have the Chambers know all to-night.

Maret.—Parties will be agitating.

Regnault.—The parties, agitated for a long time, will know each other, measure their strength, and make efforts.

Buonaparté.—So much the better. The masks will fall off. For the public I mean. As for me, a long time has ——— Summon the Ministers. We will make a report—tell the truth. If all patriotism and honour are not dead, the Chambers will not refuse men and money.

Maret.—They will speak of sparing water and engines, when the house is on fire.

Regnault.—They have stupidly reproached Dictatorship. It is now that it will save all!

Buonaparté.—I have recommended a constitutional monarchy—convoke the Ministers.

Maret.—No Dictatorship. But also no indignities. If we are attacked, we will defend ourselves.

Buonaparté.—Ah! my Old Guard! will they defend themselves like thee?

They separated!—Maret remained with the Emperor, who, in spite of his fatigue, received several visits, at which I was not present. From my window, I saw among the carriages those of Cambaceres, Decres, Caulaincourt, and the two Carnots.

For two days and nights meetings and committees succeed each other in the Elysée Palace, without producing any result. The Emperor's anxiety seemed to increase. Much business seemed to be doing, and yet nothing was determined. The time, was, however, pressing. The Chambers had assembled, and from the violence of the discussions it was plain that the parties stood opposed to each other; the necessity of an abdication was already spoken of with much freedom.

I heard the noise of a carriage which suddenly stopped at the Palace; it was Prince Lucien's. Napoleon turned pale on seeing him; he went down, however, and met his brother in the garden. The Prince drew the Emperor aside into the closest walk in the garden. I followed at a distance by turnings which I knew, and I arrived behind a thicket of verdure which concealed me from them. It is probable I heard only the last part of their conversation.

Prince Lucien.—Where is your firmness now? Abandon this irresolution. You know the consequence of not having the courage to dare.

The Emperor.—I have dared too much.

The Prince.—Yes, too much, and too little. Dare once again. You deliberate when it is proper you should act. Others are acting and not deliberating; they will pronounce your forfeiture.

The Emperor.—Forfeiture! Let us see Davoust.

They returned into the Palace, and the Prince of Eckmuhl was sent for. I am not certain what was proposed to him, nor what he replied; but it appeared that he would attempt nothing against the independence of the national representation.

Prince Lucien, much agitated, soon drove off in his carriage. I heard him say to his Secretary, " What can I say to you? The smoke of Mont St. Jean, has turned his head."

The Emperor shut himself hermetically in a retired cabinet, and did not come out for an hour. He had asked for a jelly and coffee, and a valet-de-chambre sent it into him by a boy, who, during his service in the Palace, had been particularly noticed by Napoleon, and of whom he seemed very fond. The boy looked seriously at the Emperor, who was sitting motionless, with his hands over his eyes.— " Eat some," said the boy, " it will do you good." The Emperor asked—" Are you not from Gonesse?"—" No, Sire, I come from Pierre Fite."—" And your parents have a cottage and some acres there?"—" Yes, Sire."—" That is a happy life!" His head, which he had for a moment raised, he then sunk again upon his hands.

Napoleon soon after returned to his great Cabinet, where he found me opening a dispatch. " Is there any thing new there?" said the Emperor. " It contains a letter addressed to his Majesty himself." Buonaparté read what follows:—

" The chastisement of a hero consists in his fall. Your's is resolved on, and in order that history may consider it as legal as your contemporaries will believe it just, the public authority is about to pronounce it. Your accomplices will not then have it in their power to describe it as the work of the bayonets of Kalmucks. You may, however, prevent this. Take to yourself the honour of descending from a throne from which you may be dragged. This is the advice of a candid Enemy who has often admired you, who never feared you; and who, at the price of his blood, would have wished to have had to revere in you, the saviour of that world, of which you had been the scourge. That enemy cannot leave him whom his genius and the national will have raised to sovereignty, without saying to him what his friends, if any yet remain to him, ought to say—*Abdicate*."

That I should abdicate? biting his lips and crushing the letter in his hand. What think you of it? said he, to two of the Ministers, the Duke of Bassano and Regnault St. Jean d'Angley, who had just entered—the former was silent.—" I understand you," said Napoleon, affecting gaiety, " you agree with the anonymous writer. Well, Count Regnault, what is your opinion?"—" With men and money you might still repel the attacks of your assailants; but without them, what can you do but yield?"—" I am able to resist."—" Public opinion is with the Chambers, and it is the opinion of the Chambers, that a sacrifice is required."

Here General Solignac, Member of the Chamber of Deputies, was announced. Solignac! exclaimed the Emperor—he has not spoke to me these five years, what can he want?—The Ministers withdrew, and Solignac was immediately admitted.

I was not present at the conversation, I shall therefore quote the words in which the General has stated it himself:—

" It was settled; the Chamber had determined to exclude Napoleon from the throne; but it was wished to show regard for the army in proceedings concerning the person of its Chief, whose power and glory the troops had so long been accustomed to respect. There was also reason to fear, that the Decree of its forfeiture might be made the pretext of an insurrection. The capital might become the scene of serious troubles, and the country be involved in a civil war. It appeared necessary, therefore, in order to avoid these evils, that the abdication of Napoleon should proceed from himself, and be considered as a voluntary act of devotedness for the country.

" To obtain this object, I employed the means of persuasion which appeared to me best calculated for success. After an hour and a half's conversation, Napoleon at last yielded to my urgent recommendations. He appeared touched with the frankness and energy with which I spoke, while at the same time I preserved the respect which was due to his rank, and still more to his misfortunes. In a word, I left the Emperor with the assurance that he would transmit his act of abdication, and I arrived at the Chamber of Representatives before the forfeiture, which was then under consideration, became the subject of positive Decree."

Respecting a Protection for Buonaparté.

Head-Quarters, *June* 28.

" Monsieur le Comte.—I have had the honour to receive your Excellency's letter of the 25th. I have already written to the Commissioners named to treat with the Allied Powers for Peace, upon the proposition for a suspension of hostilities ; a reply which your Excellency has seen, and to which I have nothing to add. As to what regards a passport and protection for Napoleon Buonaparté to go to the United States of America, I must inform your Excellency, that I have no authority from my Government to give any sort of answer whatever to that demand. I have the honour to be, Mons. le Comte, with the highest consideration, your obedient servant,

(Signed)   " WELLINGTON."

To Count Bignon.

Napoleon arrived at Rochfort, July 3, and resided at the Prefect's house until the 8th, when he embarked in a boat ; on the 9th he landed on the Isle of Aix ; 10th, he was fearful, from the English cruizers, to put to sea ; on the following day he sent a flag of truce to the Bellerophon ; 11th, he heard of the dissolution of the Chambers at Paris, and entrance of the King ; 12th, landed his suite and baggage at the Isle of Aix ; 13th and 14th, went on board the Epervier, thinking an escape hazardous, and on the other hand fearing arrest. On July 15th, at day-break, Buonaparté came on board the Bellerophon at Rochefort ; Captain Maitland dispatched a frigate to England, with the intelligence of his surrender ; and the officer, who brought this news, was also the bearer of the following letter, written by Napoleon to the Prince Regent :

Copy of Buonaparté's Letter to his Royal Highness the Prince Regent : forwarded to England by General Gourgaud, in the Slaney, on the 14th *of July.*

Rochefort, 13 *Juillet*, 1815.

" Altesse Royale,
" En butte aux factions qui divisent mon pays, et a l'inimitie des plus grandes puissances de l'Europe, j'ai terminé ma carriere politique ; et je viens, comme Themistocle, m'asseoir sur les foyers du peuple Britannique. Je me mets sous la protection de ses lois ; que je reclame de V. A. R. comme le plus puissant, le plus constant, et le plus genereux de mes enemies.   " NAPOLEON."

" Your Royal Highness,
" Exposed to the factions which divide my country, and to the enmity of the greatest Powers of Europe, I have terminated my political career, and I come, like Themistocles, to throw myself upon the hospitality *(m'asseoir sur le foyer)* of the British nation. I place myself under the protection of its laws, which (protection) I claim from your Royal Highness, as the most powerful, the most constant, and the most generous of my enemies.

" *Rochefort,* 13th *July,* 1815."   " NAPOLEON."

" When Napoleon first boarded the Bellerophon, he said to Captain Maitland: " I am come to claim the protection of your Prince and Country," and shortly after said with his usual quickness: " Come, Captain Maitland, suppose we walk over your ship." To this the Captain replied, by saying, that the decks were then washing, and that the ship was consequently not in a state to be inspected; that he had better wait an hour or so, &c. To this Buonaparté rejoined, " No, no, Captain Maitland, let us go now; I have been accustomed to wet and dry, and confusion, &c. for upwards of 20 years, and I must see her in her present state." He did so, and inspected her with all the alacrity, minuteness, and curiosity, so characteristic of him, walking several times over the ship; after this, he expressed himself highly delighted with the admirable economy of a British man-of-war. One day, addressing an old marine, he asked him " how long he had served?" The reply was, " sixteen years," —" Where are your marks of distinction then?" —" I have none," answered the marine. Buonaparté shrugged up his soldiers, and retired.

The Bellerophon arrived in Torbay, on the 24th of July, with Buonaparté, and his suite, consisting of 50 persons, on board. On the 26th, she arrived in Plymouth Sound, and cast anchor.

On the voyage from Rochefort, the officers and crew of the Bellerophon seem to have treated Buonaparté, who was at times unwell, and in bad spirits, with all the respect they would have shown to a reigning Sovereign; and although, on his arrival at Plymouth, orders were issued by the British Government to consider and treat him merely as a General. " By your King, I have been acknowledged first Consul of France, and by all others as Emperor." It appears these orders were but indifferently attended to, so much had he ingratiated himself with all on board during his short voyage. The following letters will give an idea of the curiosity and bustle excited at Plymouth, by the presence of this man:—

Plymouth, July 29th, 1815.

" Yesterday the curiosity of thousands was gratified by the most ample view of the Ex-Emperor. There were at 4. P. M. upwards of 1000 boats in the Sound. The scene at this time beggared all description. The guard-boats, strongly manned, dashed through the water, running against every boat that happened to be too near. The centinels of the Bellerophon, and of the guard frigates, the Eurotas and Liffey, were every moment presenting their pieces to intimidate the curious multitude. At last a movement was observed on board the Bellerophon—the seaman were seen pressing to the forecastle, the booms became covered, and, with unsatiated curiosity, they pressed so closely on the centinels, that they were obliged to clear the gangways. The marines were now also noticed on the poop, and the officers and seamen, by a simultaneous movement uncovered, without orders. A moment after, to gratify the people in the boats, as well as to view the sublime spectacle before him, the object of boundless curiosity advanced to the starboard gangway: the mass of boats endeavoured to precipitate themselves on the ship —the guard-boats dashed furiously through the water—some boats were struck—persons overturned into the sea—the centinels presented their pieces:—all in vain; the force was overwhelming—screams and curses were alternately heard—the next moment all was calm—the Emperor was bowing to the multitude—he stood before them six or seven minutes, and retired for a short time. In this manner was the time spent during the whole of Friday, till eight in the evening. Buonaparté certainly is endeavouring to gratify the spectators as much as possible. Hitherto none have boarded the ship but Lord Keith, and Mr. Penn, the pilot, of Cawsand. The time when Buonaparté is most seen, is from 3 o'clock until eight P. M. The boats get near enough to view his features distinctly, and even to hear him speak. On Friday, Gen. Brown was along-side, and was pointed out to him by an Officer. Buonaparté instantly addressed him in a complimentary manner, in French, which was answered by the General. On Thursday, Sir R. Strachan was also pointed out to him, and he bowed to Sir Richard most courteously, which was returned.

" Plymouth, July 31.

" The boats get within thirty yards of the Bellerophon, and Buonaparté is seen at the gangway for twenty minutes at a time. He always leaves the cabin, and walks to the quarter-deck and gangway, while the cloth is laying for dinner.

" I observed his person particularly, and can describe him thus: He is about five feet seven inches in height, very strongly made and well proportioned; very broad and deep chest; legs and thighs proportioned with great symmetry and strength; a small, round, and handsome foot. His countenance is sallow, and, as it were, deeply tinged by hot climates; but the most commanding air I ever saw. His eyes grey, and the most piercing that you can imagine. His glance, you fancy, searches into your inmost thoughts. His hair dark brown, and no appearance of grey. His features are handsome now; and when younger, he must have been a very handsome man. He is rather fat, and his belly protuberant; but he appears active notwithstanding. His step and demeanour altogether commanding. He looks about forty-five or forty-six years of age. In fact, he is very like the picture exhibited of him. He is extremely curious, and never passes any thing remarkable in the ship, inquiring minutely about it. He also stops and asks the officers divers questions relative to the time they have been in the service, what actions, &c.; and he caused all of us to be introduced to him the first day he came on board. He has also asked several questions about the marines, particularly those who appeared to have been some time in the service, and about the warrant-officers, midshipmen, seamen, &c. He was but a very short time on board, when he asked that the boatswain might be sent for, in order that he might look at him, and was very inquisitive as to the nature of his duty. He dresses in green uniform, with red facings, and edged with red, two plain gold epaulets, the lappels of the coat cut round and turned back, white waistcoat and breeches, and military boots and spurs, the Grand Cross of the Legion of Honour on his left breast. He professes his intention (if he is allowed to reside in England) to adopt the English customs and

manners, and declares that he will never meddle with politics any more.
The army which left Paris, and united with others on the Loire,
wanted him to join them and resume his title, which he refused to
do.   He declares that not another ' *goutte de sang*' shall be shed
on his account.   Fortunate indeed, it would have been, if he really
had been of this opinion some years back ! "

Buonaparté continued in the Bellerophon, till Monday the 7th
instant, when he was transferred to the Northumberland man-of-war,
which, under the command of Admiral Sir George Cockburn, who
was appointed to convey him to St. Helena.

Sir Henry Bunbury, accompanied by the Hon. Mr. Bathurst,
charged with the communication of the determination of Government
to Buonaparté, were conveyed on board the Bellerophon, by Lord
Keith's yacht.   Sir Henry was introduced to the Ex-Emperor ; and,
after mutual salutations, he read to him the resolution of the Cabinet,
by which he was informed of his intended transportation to the Island
of St. Helena, with four of his friends, to be chosen by himself, and
twelve domestics.   He received this intimation without any mark of
surprise, as he said he had been apprised of the determinations: but
he protested against it in the most emphatic manner ; and, in a speech
of three quarters of an hour, delivered with great coolness, self-possession, and ability, reasoned against the outrageous proceeding.   He
recapitulated the circumstances under which he had been forced, he
said, by the breach of the treaty made with him by the Sovereigns
of Europe, to quit the Island of Elba---that he had exerted himself
to prevent the renewal of hostilities---but that when they became
unavoidable, and that the fortune of war had decided against him,
he yielded to the voice of his enemies; and as they had declared in the
face of the world that it was against him only that they had taken
up arms, he abdicated the Imperial Crown of France, in the full
confidence that the Allies would be faithful to their solemn declaration, and leave his country to the settlement of their own affairs ;
then, unarmed, and with the view of seeking an asylum as a private
individual in England, he had first sought to be received under the
King's allegiance, and under the protection of our laws, and had,
finally, voluntarily put himself into the British power.   In this predi-
cament, he felt himself entitled to protest against the measure now
announced to him, and in a long argument, in which he shewed himself to be well versed in our laws, he reasoned against the act.

Sir H. Bunbury and Mr. Bathurst say, that his manner was tem-
perate, his language eloquent, and that he conducted himself
throughout in the most prepossessing way.   The account they give of
his persuasive manner, is, we understand, highly interesting.   Sir
Henry answered to his discourse, that he had no commission, but to
make known to him the resolution of his Majesty's Ministers—but
said, that he should faithfully report the reasons that he had stated
against the proceeding.

Before the Northumberland sailed, a yacht or large boat, with several gentlemen of the Pay-Office, had arrived to pay the ship, who,
availing themselves of the opportunity presented by the folding
doors of the cabin being open, beheld, to their surprise, Buonaparté

playing at *vingt-un* with his companions as cheerfully as if nothing had happened to him. When Sir G. Cockburn saw Buonaparté for the first time, he simply pulled off his hat, in the same manner as he would have done to another General, and said : " How do you do, *General* Buonaparté?" which was returned by him in a manner equally laconic, but with his head uncovered. Every thing was so well conducted in this removal, that the greatest order prevailed, and so little was it known at Torbay, off which place it occurred, that very few boats were present to witness it. The Northumberland has part of the military on board, and is full of stores and baggage. The cabin is neatly fitted up, and the after-part divided in the centre, for sleeping, one side of which is occupied by Buonaparté, and the other by Sir George Cockburn.

Liberty having been afforded to Buonaparté and his companions to procure from England, any articles of luxury or accommodation they may desire, they have sent frequently ashore, and having purchased a billiard-table, wines of the most costly description, an immense quantity of playing-cards, chessmen, &c. and the best books procurable in the English language, (the Ex-Emperor having suddenly grown exceeding fond of that language !) Buonaparté solicited Mr. O'Meara, Surgeon of the Bellerophon, to attend him in the same capacity, which Lord Keith has consented to do, and an exchange between the Bellerophon and the Northumberland was in consequence speedily effected. Buonaparté endeavoured to make him forget his duty, even at the commencement, by offering a salary of 500*l.* per annum; but this gentleman rejected the overture, and said, that the pay of his King was enough to satisfy him !

The Northumberland sailed from Portsmouth on Friday last, and on nearing Torbay on Sunday, perceived two line-of-battle ships approaching her, which proved to be the Bellerophon, with Buonaparté on board, and the Tonnant with Lord Keith. In a few hours the Northumberland hailed them, and asked after Buonaparté, who, she was informed, had not come out of his cabin for some days. The ships came to anchor off Torbay.

General Bertrand went first on board the Tonnant, where he dined with Lord Keith and Sir G. Cockburn. He is a man of about fifty years of age, and extremely well behaved. At dinner, Sir George gave him a general explanation of his instructions with respect to Buonaparté; one of which was, that his baggage must be inspected before it was received on board the Northumberland. Bertrand expressed his opinion strongly against the measure of sending the Emperor (as he and all the suite constantly styled him) to St. Helena, when his wish and expectation was to live quietly in England, under the protection of the English laws. Lord Keith and Sir George Cockburn did not enter into any discussion on the subject. After dinner Lord Keith and Sir G. Cockburn, accompanied by Bertrand, went in the Admiral's yacht towards the Bellerophon. Previously to their arrival, Buonaparté's arms and pistols were taken from him—not without considerable altercation and objections on the part of the French officers.

Those who were not to acccompany him were sent on board the Eurotas frigate. They expressed great reluctance at the separation,

k

particularly the Polish officers.   Buonaparté took leave of them in-
dividually.   A Colonel Pistowki, a Pole, was peculiarly desirous of
accompanying him.   He had received 17 wounds in the service of
Buonaparté, and said he would serve in any capacity, however
menial, if he could be allowed to go with him to St. Helena.   The
orders for sending off the Polish Lancers were peremptory, and he
was removed to the Eurotas.   Savary and Lallemand, however, were
not among those sent on board the frigate—they were left in the Bellerophon.

When Lord Keith and Sir George Cockburn went on board the
Bellerophon, on Sunday afternoon, Buonaparté was upon deck
to receive them, dressed in a green coat with red facings, two epaulets, white waistcoat and breeches, silk stockings, the star of the
Legion of Honour, and *chapeau bras*, with the three-coloured
cockade.   His face is remarkably plump, and his head rather bald
on the top.   After the usual salutations, Lord Keith, addressing
himself to Buonaparté, acquainted him with his intended transfer
from the Bellerophon to the Northumberland.   Buonaparté immediately protested with great vehemence against this act of the British
Government—he did not expect it—he did not conceive that any
objection could be made to his residing in England quietly, for the
remainder of his life.   No answer was returned by either Lord Keith,
or Sir G. Cockburn.   A British officer, who stood near, observed
to him, that if he had not been sent to St. Helena, he would have
been delivered up to the Emperor of Russia.

Buonaparté—" *Dieu me garde des Russes!*" (God keep me from
the Russians.)   In making this reply, he looked at General Bertrand,
and shrugged up his shoulders.

Sir G. Cockburn—" At what hour to-morrow morning shall I
come, General, and receive you on board the Northumberland?"

Buonaparté, with some surprise at being styled merely General—
" At ten o'clock."

Bertrand, Madame Bertrand, Savary, Lallemand, Count and
Countess Montholon, were standing near Buonaparté.   Sir G. Cockburn asked him if he wanted any thing before they put to sea?   Bertrand replied, fifty packs of cards, a backgammon and domino table,
and Madame Bertrand desired to have some articles of furniture,
which, it was said, should be furnished forthwith.

An officer who stood near him, said—" You would have been
taken, if you had remained at Rochefort another hour, and sent off
to Paris."   Buonaparté turned his eye upon the speaker—but did not
speak a word.   He next addressed Sir G. Cockburn, and asked several questions about St. Helena.   " Is there any hunting or shooting
there?—where am I to reside?"   He then abruptly changed the
subject, and burst into more invectives against the Government, to
which no answer was returned.   He then expressed some indignation
at being styled General—saying, " You have sent ambassadors to me
as a Sovereign Potentate—you have acknowledged me as First
Consul."—He took a great deal of snuff whilst speaking.   After reminding him, that the Northumberland's barge would come for
him at ten on Monday morning, Lord Keith and Sir G. Cockburn
retired.

Early on Monday morning, Sir George Cockburn went on board the Bellerophon, to superintend the inspection of Buonaparté's baggage; it consisted of two services of plate, several articles in gold, a superb toilet of plate, books, beds, &c. They found but 4000 gold Napoleons, and these were sealed up and detained. They were all sent on board the Northumberland about eleven o'clock. At half-past eleven o'clock, Lord Keith, in the barge of the Tonnant, went on board the Bellerophon, to receive Buonaparté, and those who were to accompany him. Buonaparté, before their arrival and afterwards, addressed himself to Captain Maitland and the officers of the Bellerophon. After descending the ladder into the barge, he pulled off his hat to them again. Lord Keith received in the barge the following personages:—Buonaparté, General Bertrand and Madame Bertrand, with their children; Count and Countess Montholon. and child; Count Las Cassas,* General Gorgaud; nine men and three women servants. Buonaparté's surgeon refused to accompany him, upon which the surgeon of the Bellerophon offered to supply his place. Buonaparté was this day dressed in a cocked hat much worn, with a tri-coloured cockade; his coat was buttoned close round him—a plain green one with a red collar; he had three orders—two crosses, and a large silver star, with the inscription *Honneur et Patrie;* white breeches, silk stockings, and gold buckles.

About twelve o'clock the Tonnant's barge reached the Northumberland. Bertrand stepped first upon deck, Buonaparté next, mounting the side of the ship with the activity of a seaman. The marines were drawn out and received him, but merely as a General, presenting arms to him. He pulled off his hat. As soon as he was upon deck, he said to Sir George Cockburn—"*Je suis à vos ordres.*" He bowed to Lord Lowther and Mr. Lyttleton, who were near the Admiral, and spoke to them a few words, to which they replied. To an officer he said, "*Dans quel corps servez-vous?*" (In what corps do you serve?)—The officer replied, "In the artillery." Buonaparté immediately rejoined, "*Je sors de ce service moi-même.*" (I was originally in that service myself.) After taking leave of the officers who had accompanied him from the Bellerophon, and embracing the nephew of Josephine, who was not going to St. Helena, he went into the after-cabin, where, besides his principal companions, were assembled Lord Keith, Sir G. Cockburn, Lord Lowther, the Honourable Mr. Lyttleton, &c.

Bertrand asked what we should have done had we taken Buonaparté at sea?—As we were doing now, was the reply.

Lord Lowther and the Hon. Mr. Lyttleton now entered into very earnest conversation with him, which continued for two hours. As he was very communicative, and seemed desirous of a very free conversation with these two young gentlemen, they availed themselves of the opportunity, and entered into a review of much of his conduct. We understand that they asked him how he came to commit the impolicy of attacking Spain—the motives for the Berlin and Milan decrees—the war against Russia—the refusal of the terms of

---

* This person has long been resident in England, and published a work, entitled Le Sage's Historical Atlas.

peace offered him before the first capture of Paris, &c.   To all these questions, we hear, he gave full answers, not avoiding, but rather encouraging the discussion.

His cabin in the Northumberland is fitted up with great elegance. His bed is peculiarly handsome, and the linen upon it very fine.   His toilet is of silver.   Among other articles upon it is a magnificent snuff-box, upon which is embossed, in gold, an eagle with a crown flying from Elba to the coast of France—the Eagle just seeing the coast of France, and the respective distances, are admirably executed.

The following are a few passages of the conversation which Lord Lowther and Mr. Lyttleton had with Buonaparté, when he was transhipped from the Bellerophon to the Northumberland.

Buonaparté, whilst remonstrating against his detention, said, " You do not know my character.   You ought to have placed confidence in my word of honour."

One of the Gentlemen said—" Shall I speak the plain truth to you ?"

Buonaparté.—" Speak it."

—— " I must then tell you, that since your invasion of Spain, no Englishman could put trust even in your most solemn engagements."

B.—" I was called to Spain by Charles IV. to assist him against his son."

—— " No—according to my opinion, to place King Joseph on the throne."

B.—" I had a grand political system.   It was necessary to establish a counterpoise to your enormous power on the sea ; and, besides, that was only what had been done by the Bourbons," or words to that effect.

—— " It must be confessed, however, General, that France under your sceptre was much more to be feared than during the latter years of Louis XIV.'s reign.   She was also aggrandized," &c.

B.—" England on her part had become more powerful."   Here he referred to our colonies, and particularly to our acquisitions in India.

—— " Many well-informed men are of opinion that England loses more than she gains by the possession of that overgrown and remote Empire."

B.—" I wished to revive Spain ; to do much of that which the Cortes afterwards attempted to do."

He was then recalled to the main point, and reminded of the character of the transaction by which he obtained possession of the Spanish Crown, to which he made no answer, but took a new line of argument on the subject of his detention, and after much discussion, concluded by saying—" Well, I have been deceived in relying upon your generosity.   Replace me in the position from which you took me," (or words to that effect.)

Speaking of his invasion of France, he said with great vehemence —" I was then a Sovereign.   I had a right to make war.   The King of France had not kept his promises."

He afterwards said exultingly, and laughing and shaking his head —" I made war on the King of France with 600 men."

He said, that, in confining him as we did, we were " acting like a little aristocratic power, and not like a great free people,"

Of Mr. Fox he said, he knew him, and had seen him at the Thuilleries—" He had not your prejudices."

—— " Mr. Fox, General, was a zealous patriot with regard to his own country, and besides a citizen of the world."

B.— " He sincerely wished for peace, and I wished for it also. His death prevented the conclusion of peace.   The others were not sincere."

At one time he observed—" I do not say that I have not for twenty years endeavoured to ruin England ; and then, as if correcting himself for having inadvertently said more than was prudent— " that is to say, to lower you—I wished to force you to be just—at least less unjust."

He was asked his opinion of the British infantry?

B.—" Long wars make good soldiers—the cavalry of both nations," he said, " was excellent—our artillery had derived much improvement from the French."

Of the Duke of Wellington he seemed at this time to avoid giving any opinion.

To a question about Louis XVIII.

B.—" He is a good sort of man, too fond of the table and pretty sayings. He is not calculated for the French.   The Duchess of Angouleme is the only man in the family. The French must have such a man as myself."

He broke out into some invectives against the conduct of the Allies ; called it perfidious, treacherous.

Touching upon St. Helena, he seemed not only indignant, but surprised at being sent there.

B.—" I would have given my word of honour to have remained quiet, and to have held no political correspondence in England. I would have pledged myself not to quit the place assigned me, but to live as a simple individual."

—— " That seems to be next to impossible ; for though you have had great reverses, you could never so far forget what you had been as to conceive yourself to be, or conduct yourself as a simple individual."

B.—" But why not let me remain in England upon my parole of honour ?"

—— " You forget that some hundreds of French officers violated their parole of honour, and that not only you did not express any indignation against them, but received them with particular distinction—Lefebvre Desnouettes for instance !"

Buonaparté made no remark upon this.

Of the Prince Regent he spoke in the highest terms, adding, that he was the only Sovereign in Europe that had been consistent, constant, and vigorous ; that it was he who had been the real cause of defeating all his designs, and destroying his power.

Letter from Capt. Paget.

" I have been some hours in Buonaparté's company, and have had conversation with him. He says, never was a battle so se-

verely contested as that of Waterloo. His troops knew and felt, that
they never had more to gain, or more to lose, than at that time; and
never had they fought harder, and they were only overcome by the
superiority of British intrepidity. He was astonished at the firmness with which his charges were received and repulsed by our
troops: he spoke highly of our cavalry, and acknwledged that if the
Earl of Uxbridge had not been wounded, he would have been the
Earl's prisoner in two minutes; and he feels no hesitation in saying,
that the Duke of Wellington was a better General than himself. I
mention this circumstance, because in his voyage to Elba, when it
was remarked that the Duke was the best General of the age, he
answered: " We have never met yet."

*Translation of the Protest presented by Buonaparté to Lord Keith,
against his transportation to St. Helena:—*

" I protest solemnly, in the face of Heaven and of men, against
the violation of my most sacred rights, by the forcible disposal of
my person, and of my liberty. I came freely on board the Bellerophon; I am not the prisioner, I am the guest of England.

" Once seated on board the Bellerophon, I was immediately entitled to the hospitality *(je fus sur le foyer)* of the British people.
If the Government, by giving orders to the Captain of the Bellerophon to receive me and my suite, intended merely to lay a snare for
me, it has forfeited its honour and sullied its flag.

" If this act be consummated, it will be in vain that the English
will talk to Europe of their integrity, of their laws, of their liberty.
The British faith will be lost, in the hospitality of the Bellerophon.

" I appeal therefore to history; it will say, that an Enemy who
made war for twenty years on the people of England, came freely,
in his misfortune, to seek an asylum under its laws. What more
striking proof could he give of his esteem and of his confidence?
But how did they answer it in England? They pretended to hold
out an hospitable hand to this Enemy, and when he surrendered
himself to them in good faith, they sacrificed him.

On board the Bellerophon, at Sea.   " NAPOLEON."

His Majesty's ship Northumberland, lat. 34, 53, *long.* 13, 45.
August the 22d, 1815.

" Conversing one day about the siege of St. Jean d'Acre, Buonaparté observed, " that when Sir Sidney Smith was there, he distributed several proclamations among the French troops, which made
them *waver a little.*" In order to obviate this, he published an
Order, in which he " asserted that the English Commodore was
mad," and it concluded with prohibiting all communication with
him. This, he added, " had the desired effect, and so enraged Sir
Sidney, that he sent him a challenge to single combat, which was
declined," and Napoleon returning at the same time for answer, that
" when he brought the Duke of Marlborough to meet him, he would
accept it." He stated most positively, " that he *would then have*

taken Acre, if the English had not taken his battering train," and added, in English and French: "Had it not been for you English, I would have been Emperor of the East; but wherever a ship could get, I was always sure to find some of the English to oppose me."

" He spoke of the invasion of England as his first determination, and said that he intended to have landed as near Chatham as possible, and to have dashed at once for London. He admitted the great probability of his not succeeding, and that he might have been killed in the attempt. That this scheme was not put into effect, he says, was owing to Admiral Villeneuve not obeying the orders he received. He was particularly inquisitive as to the climate of England, and said that the cause of so many suicides was the humidness of the atmosphere.

" The anxiety of the English to see him when on board the Bellerophon, flattered his vanity in the extreme, and he would frequently stand at the gangway purposely to afford the gaping and wondering multitude an opportunity of beholding his person. At this time he had invariably a spy-glass in his hand, which he frequently used in observing the spectators.

" He appeared greatly pleased with the beauty of our fair countrywomen, and was always wishing to know their names, families, and any circumstance that could be communicated to him concerning them.

" Buonaparté gives great credit to our infantry and our artillery. He said, " the British infantry is now what the French was ten years back, and that the cavalry is greatly inferior to the infantry in every thing but appearance." He found great fault with the construction of the bits, which he says " are so bad that the men cannot manage their horses." Bertrand and the others assented to the truth of this observation.

" One day Buonaparté was speaking of the Duke of Wellington, and observed, " he did not expect he would have given him battle, but that he would have retreated, and waited for the Russians and other reinforcements, in which case, he says, he must have been finally beaten; but that he was extremely happy to find Lord Wellington did not decline the combat," adding, that " he made qnite *certain* of obtaining the *victory*." He also said, " that he knew of the advance of the Prussians, but that he did not regard it of much consequence; and that he was betrayed by some of his Generals." He further said, " that the universal consternation among his troops taking place at a time of *darkness*, he was not able to rally the fugitives *by showing his person to them, which he is convinced would have effectually restored order had it been day-light; but that, in consequence of its being dark, he was borne away by the crowd, and obliged to* fly himself."

" On being asked why he had not given himself up to Austria? He replied, " What, give myself up to a nation without laws, honour, or faith! No: the moment I had got there, I should have been put into a dungeon, and never heard of more. In giving myself up to the English, I have given myself up to a nation with honourable and just laws, which afford protection to every person."

" One day he observed, he " ought to have *died* the day he entered Moscow, as ever since he had experienced a continual series of disasters." He further observed, he " would have made peace at Dresden, and also afterwards, if it had not been for the advice of the Duke of Bassano, who persuaded him against it."*

" The invasion of Spain, Buonaparté says, he undertook at the special desire of Talleyrand, who was continually urging him to that measure, invariably pointing out the absolute necessity of its being undertaken, and, if possible accomplished at all hazards.

" It is astonishing the detestation in which Fouché is held by Buonaparté and all his followers, who never mention his name but with the greatest contempt; and they say, " it was entirely owing to this Creature that Buonaparté abdicated in favour of his Son; and that he was continually carrying on a clandestine correspondence with the Allies."

" The respect that is still paid to Buonaparté by his suite is very great; as an instance, I shall mention that he was one day playing at chess with Montholon, who is by far the best player of the two. Buonaparté had evidently the worst of the game, when Montholon made purposely an improper movement, which was speedily observed by the former, and he ultimately was the victor. Montholon praised the superior skill of his Master (as he termed him), and declared himself " not competent to encounter such an excellent player again;" at which Buonaparté was highly pleased. At this game, or Vingt-un, Buonaparté generally passes his time; but was much hurt when the Admiral insisted that neither of these games, nor any other, should be played on Sundays.

" He has been very inquisitive as to the climate, &c. of St. Helena, and declares that he shall be more comfortable there than in Austria. Temperance, he says, is the only means of preserving health, and adds, that he never was ill but twice in his life, and on one of those occasions only applied a blister. Montholon's wife has been unwell, and he inquired of the surgeon how she was. He said, rather better, but that he thought the fear of the tropical climates preyed on her mind. Buonaparté replied, nearly in the words of Shakespeare, " Doctor, thou cannot administer to a mind diseased." The force with which this remark was made, was observed by every one near, and apparently related to his own feelings.

" Bertrand and his wife are continually with Buonaparté, and the whole are more reconciled to their future destiny.

" Sir George Cockburn and Buonaparté are on excellent terms, as he is, indeed, with all the officers of the ship; they frequently play at cards, &c. in which, occasionally they have the advantage of each other.

" Hitherto our passage has been very favourable, and no particular occurrence has taken place since we sailed from Torbay."

* This strongly confirms the statement in the recent publication of M. Pradt, Archbishop of Malines, and Ambassador at Warsaw.

PRINCE BLUCHER'S LETTERS.

To his Excellency the General Count Kalkreuth, Governor of Berlin.

Head Quarters at Genappe, June 19, 1815, ¼ *past* 5, A. M.

" I hereby acquaint your Excellency, that in conjunction with the English army, under the Duke of Wellington, I obtained the completest victory that it is possible to gain, over Napoleon Buonaparté. The battle was fought in the neighbourhood of a few insulated houses, lying on the road from this place to Brussels, and called La Belle Alliance; and I think there cannot be a better name for this important day. The French army is in a state of entire disorganization, and a prodigious quantity of artillery is taken. Time does not allow me to give your Excellency any further particulars at this moment. I reserve to myself the communication of the details, and beg your Excellency to publish this joyful news to the good people of Berlin. " BLÜCHER."

To the Princess Blucher, written immediately after the Battle.

" My dear Wife,

" You well remember what I promised you, and I have kept my word. The Enemy's superiority of numbers obliged me to give way on the 17th; but on the 18th, in conjunction with my friend Wellington, I put an end at once to Buonaparté's dancing. His army is completely routed, and the whole of his artillery, baggage, caissons, and equipages, are in my hands; the insignia of all the various orders he had worn, are just brought me, having been found in his carriage, in a casket. I had two horses killed under me yesterday. It will soon be all over with Buonaparté. " BLÜCHER."

" P. S. (Written by the Prince's son, on the road to Genappe.) Father Blucher embraced Wellington in such a hearty manner, that every body who were present, said it was the most affecting scene that could be imagined."

To Major-General Von Dobschutz, Military Governor of the Prussian Provinces on the Rhine.

Head Quarters at Merbes-le-Chateau, June 21.

" Sir,

" It is with great pleasure I inform you, that the consequences of the victory of the 18th continue to prove more and more brilliant. The Enemy's Army is entirely broken up, and has lost, as near as we can calculate, 300 cannon; not a regiment of the Enemy's is together, and subordination has ceased among them. During the battle of the 18th, a French corps had penetrated to Wavre, to operate on our line of communication, and hinder us from supporting the Duke of Wellington; this corps of the Enemy, was yesterday forced back, by Lieutenant-General Von Thielmann, who was opposed to it at Wavre, as far as Namur, and Lieutenant-General Thielmann probably occupied that place yesterday evening. Maubeuge was surrounded yesterday, and Landrecies and Avesnes will be so to-morrow, " BLÜCHER."

From another official Letter.—Gosselies, June 20.

" I have recovered from my fall, but I have had again a horse wounded. I believe now that we shall not so soon have any considerable battles, perhaps not at all. The victory is the most complete that ever was gained. Napoleon escaped in the night, without either hat or sword. I send both sword and hat to-day to the King. His most magnificently embroidered state mantle and his carriage are in my hands, as his perspective glass with which he observed us during the battle. His jewels and all his valuables are the booty of our troops. Of his equipage he has nothing left.

" Many a private soldier has got 5 or 600 dollars in booty. Napoleon was in the carriage to retreat, when he was surprised by our troops: he leaped out, jumped upon his horse without his sword, losing his hat, which fell off, and so he probably escaped under favour of the night. The consequences of this victory are incalculable, and Napoleon's ruin will be the result of it.

" BLUCHER."

Paris, Oct. 19, 1815.

" Sir,

" As my conduct has been publickly animadverted upon, for not having allowed the property plundered from Prussia by a banditti to remain in the Museum of the Louvre; I have only to remark, that ably supported by the Illustrious Wellington, I pursued the thieves, who had despoiled many of the Nations of Europe of their inestimable Monuments of the Fine Arts; I attacked and dispersed them, and restored to my country the plunder they had unjustly taken, spurning the idea of negotiating with the French Commissioners on this subject: they may now thank Providence, for our not following their base example. " BLUCHER."

To General Count Mufflin, Governor of Paris, &c.

Letter from an Officer of high Rank in the Prussian Army.
Genappe sur Oise, near Guise, June 24, 1815

" The army has behaved gloriously. The 3d corps had to cover our rear, while we were engaged: it had some severe attacks to support, and fought without interruption on the 18th, 19th, and 20th; it was at first in a critical situation, but extricated itself very well; if we had lost the battle this was our only dependence.

" Never was any battle so fine as ours at La Belle Alliance, never battle so decisive, and never was an enemy so completely destroyed. With some corps of the army we had got unperceived into the rear of the Enemy, who with great superiority of numbers, and still greater impetuosity, had attacked the Duke of Wellington, and kept ourselves concealed in a wood.

" Just as the fate of t he day was dubious, the British Army had lost considerable ground, and the Enemy was ready to strike another blow against it, we resolved, though our columns were for the most part not come up, to make the attack with two brigades only: we therefore burst out of the wood, exactly in the rear of the Enemy, and opened our fire. The Enemy was now in a desperate situation; but fought, however, with a desperation suitable to it, and turned all his reserve against us. We maintained our position. The Enemy brought up fresh troops against us; but we also became stronger every quarter of an hour: the firing became so violent, that the Enemy's cannon-balls flew by us without ceasing, not to mention our own fire; I could scarcely hear the notices that were brought, and give the necessary orders; and, though my voice is very powerful, I was obliged to exert it to the utmost, in order to be heard. As our troops continued to be reinforced, we advanced cautiously, but incessantly: it was a grand sight to see our battalions formed into square masses, descend from the heights, which rise like terraces, preceded by their batteries and sharp-shooters. After an obstinate resistance the Enemy's army was broken, and fled in the utmost disorder. General Gneisenau, resolved to leave him not a moment's repose, put himself at the head of the troops, encouraged the tired men to follow him, and so with only a few cannon, which we fired from time to time, we drove him from all his bivouacs, and continually firing and cutting him down, we pursued till we at last reached the Guards. Buonaparté had intended to stop at Genappe; but when he heard our cannon, and our cavalry and infantry, though few in number, come up, he escaped from his carriage, defending himself with his pistols. Besides his hat and sword, his seal-ring was also taken, and now blazes on the hand of the hero, Gneisenau. We have got all his baggage, even his diamonds. The fusileers sold four or five diamonds as large as a pea, or even larger, for a few francs. We have a large quantity of diamonds of a middle size, and one of the size of a pigeon's egg: the fusileers have chosen out the finest as a present to the King. The subaltern officers of this battalion dine now upon silver. We did not halt till day-break. It was the finest night of my life; the moon beautifully illuminated the scene, and the weather was mild. General Gneisenau had again a horse killed by a cannon-ball in the last battle, another twice wounded by musket-balls, his sabre once beat out of the scabbard, and once shot to pieces."

Letter from Duffeldorf.—June 26.

"Buonaparté's costly travelling carriage, which is provided with every convenience, and which was taken by the 15th Prussian regiment of infantry of the line, arrived here yesterday afternoon. What various thoughts and feelings must the sight of this carriage inspire! It was naturally an object of general curiosity. Upon being examined, it was found to contain several private drawers, filled with various articles of value; among other things, some articles belonging to Buonaparté's toilet; various articles for the table, mostly massy gold: besides this carriage, it seems that seven other state carriages were taken, among which is the magnificent state coach, in which he intended to make his entry into Brussels, drawn by eight cream-coloured stallions; there were taken, besides, eighty Arabian horses, all his baggage, diamonds, treasures, &c. &c.

"The travelling library taken, consisted of near 800 volumes."

Head-quarters of the Allied Sovereigns.*---Saarbruck, July 3d, 1815.

"It is seldom that a grand political plan has been executed with such an active and successful co-operation of all the parties as the present. No greater importance was for a moment attached to Buonaparté's enterprize, than it deserved. The declarations of the

* This Letter is attributed to Gentz.

13th of March and the 12th of May, equally show the immutable
sentiments of the High Allies, and the just appreciation of what the
Disturber of the peace of the world, returned from Elba, could effect.
It occurred to nobody to believe any lasting effects of his appearance. The peace of Europe was established; the invasion of Buonaparté was rather a breaking of the peace in the light of an offence
against the police, than a political breach of the repose of Europe:
the first great occasion, on which all the European States had to
show that they formed one and the same re-united whole. Too
weak to destroy a work which rested on such firm foundations; the
Enemy was powerful enough to cause to the world incalculable,
though transitory evils. It was, therefore, to be proved by the
energy of the great penal measures against the last attempt to involve
Europe in flames by unworthy means, whether the union of its
Princes would be durable, whether amidst the difficult negociations
concerning the *meum* and *tuum*, and the particular pretensions of
each individual, the great public spirit of the years 1813 and 1814
had really maintained itself unimpaired.

" Every possible doubt of this nature is for ever and irrevocably
silenced by the events themselves.

" The political and military tactics of Napoleon were well known
to divide in order to command, *politically* by separate negociations,
militarily by partial attacks on his adversaries, executed with an
immense display of force: to divide and cut them off from each
other, was more especially the line he had to follow in this new
enterprize; as he could depend on finding in his own party the unity
of guilt and desperation, and as the union of the Princes opposed
to him, seemed, from the diversity of the several interests, to become more intricate and artificial with the accession of every new
member.

" His political attacks were directed, as had been foreseen, first
against Austria; in such a critical situation as his was, nothing short
of the defection of so great a power as Austria could throw a weight
into his scale. He has brought into play the most sacred private
feelings, which, in the great mind of him who was to be gained by
them, had been long since repressed within their due limits; he gave
clearly to understand the immense present advantages which a
union with him would have placed in the hands of the House
of Austria. All was in vain: posterity will judge whether
Austria has worthily terminated a twenty-years struggle, whether
the ancient pillars of her throne, justice and an innate conscien-
tiousness in her policy, have been forgotten by her, at a moment
when an indubitable preponderance (the highest aim of short-
sighted cabinets) was offered to her; posterity will only doubt whether Austria has shown more magnanimity in prosperity or adversity.

" In a military point of view, it was with certainty to be foreseen that he would make a concentrated attack upon one of the
wings of the great theatre of war, which extended from the Apen-
nines and the Alps along the Rhine; Italy and the Netherlands
were the first and most natural objects of his operations. Now by
a rare union of political and military activity, the first of these objects, Italy, was wrenched from his hands; so that the Alps, whose
summits, supported by his only Ally, he fancied he could threaten,

became his most vulnerable frontier, is evident to the whole world.

" The more difficult it was for him to separate himself from Paris, as it was decided that he must renounce Italy for ever, and that he could find only in France a place for his usurped throne, the more unalterably was the plan of operations prescribed to him, which he had to adopt, and by which he was to meet his ruin. It was necessary that the Power which the most nearly threatened Paris, should be first, if not annihilated, at least shaken.

" According to the first plan of the Allies, three armies were to penetrate into France at once, independent of each other, but tending to a common centre. That of the Upper Rhine under Field-Marshal Prince Schwartzenberg, that of the Lower Rhine under Field-Marshal Prince Blucher, and that of the Netherlands under Field-Marshal the Duke of Wellington. The Russian armies, which according to the usual calculations could not come up till a later period, were to form the Reserve, as the Austrian army in Italy, was to come to support the South of France immediately after the completion of the conquest of Italy.

" The turn that affairs took in Italy, induced the great British Commander, strenuously to urge the union of the two armies of the Lower Rhine and the Netherlands. With what reciprocal regard, this union, this *belle alliance* was accomplished, neither of the two Commanders becoming subordinate to the other, and how just was the military conception in which this union originated, has been proved by the most brilliant result : the heroism and the energy of the execution were no more than Europe justly expected from the two Generals and their armies.

" But that the Lower Rhine could be uncovered, without causing a break in the whole undertaking, and that the urgent representations of the Duke of Wellington could be attended to, for this, Europe is indebted to the unparalleled exertions of the Prussian Government, which had assembled upon the Rhine, before the end of June, a force that, according to the most favourable calculations, would have achieved the utmost that could be expected, had it arrived by the same time upon the Elbe; so that it was able immediately to enter into the great line, and to fill up the interval between the army of the Upper Rhine and that of the Netherlands.

" Thus, by a perfectly united exertion of all the great Powers of Europe, was Buonaparté defeated, both in the cabinet and the field. The remembrance of this great moment, so truly glorious for all the leading Sovereigns, will never be extinguished. Posterity, in complete possession of all the details of these events, will acknowledge how much it owes, in particular, to his Majesty the Emperor of Austria."　　　　　　　　　　*From the Austrian Observer.*

Letter from the Duke of Wellington to Sir Charles Flint.

" Would you credit it, Napoleon overthrown by the gallantry of a British army !—But I am quite heart-broken by the loss I have sustained; my friends, my poor soldiers—how many of them have I to regret !—I shall follow up this tide of success, and I shall not be satisfied even with this victory, if it be not followed by the total overthrow of Buonaparté."

Duke of Wellington to Lord Castlereagh.---Paris, Sept. 23d, 1815.

" There has been a good deal of discussion lately, respecting the the measures which I have been under the necessity of adopting, in order to get for the King of the Netherlands, his pictures, &c. from the Museums ; and lest these reports should reach the Prince Regent, I wish to trouble your Lordship with the following statement of what has passed, for his Royal Highness's information.

" Shortly after the arrival of the Sovereigns at Paris, the Minister of the King of the Netherlands claimed the pictures, &c. belonging to his Sovereign, equally with those of other Powers ; for, as I learn, he never could get any satisfactory reply from the French Government. After several conversations with me, he addressed to your Lordship an official note, which was laid before the Ministers of the Allied Sovereigns assembled in conference ; and the subject was taken into consideration, repeatedly, with a view to discover a mode of doing justice to the claimants of the specimens of the arts in the Museum, without injuring the feelings of the King of France

" In the mean time the Prussians had obtained from his Majesty, not only all the pictures really Prussian, but those belonging to the Prussian Territories on the left of the Rhine, and the pictures, &c. belonging to all the Allies of his Prussian Majesty ; and the subject pressed for an early decision, when your Lordship wrote your note of the ————, on which it was fully discussed.

" The Ministers of the King of the Netherlands, still having no satisfactory answer from the French Government, applied to me as the Commander-in-Chief of the army of the King of the Netherlands, to know whether I had any objection to employ his Majesty's troops to obtain possession of what was his undoubted property ? I referred this application again to the Ministers of the Allied Courts, and no objection having been stated, I considered it my duty to take the necessary measures to obtain what was his right.

" I accordingly spoke to the Prince de Talleyrand upon the subject, explained to him what had passed in conference, and the grounds I had for thinking that the King of the Netherlands had a right to the pictures, and begged him to state the case to the King, and to ask his Majesty to do me the favour to point out the mode of effecting the object of the King of the Netherlands, which should be the least offensive to his Majesty. The Prince de Talleyrand promised me an answer the following evening, which not having received, I called upon him at night, and had another discussion with him on the subject ; in which he informed me, that the King could give no orders upon it, that I might act as I thought proper, and that I might communicate with M. Denon. I sent my Aide-de-Camp, Col. Freemantle to M. Denon in the morning, who informed him that he had no orders to give any pictures out of the gallery, and that he could give none without the use of force.

" I then sent Colonel Freemantle, to the Prince de Talleyrand to inform him of this answer, and to acquaint him that the troops would go the next morning, at 12 o'clock, to take possession of the King of Netherlands pictures, and to point out, if any disturbance resulted from this measure, the King's Ministers, and not I, were responsible. Colonel Freemantle also informed M. Denon, that the same measure would be adopted.

"'It was not necessary, however, to send the troops, as a Prussian guard had always remained in possession of the gallery, and the pictures were taken without the necessity of calling for those of the army under my command, excepting as a working party to assist in taking them down and packing them.

"It has been stated, that in being the instrument in removing the pictures belonging to the King of the Netherlands from the gallery of the Thuilleries, I had been guilty of a breach of a treaty, which I had myself made; and as there is no mention of the Museum in the Treaty of the 25th of March, and it now appears, that the Treaty meant, is the Military Convention of Paris, it is necessary I should show how that Convention affects the Museum.

"It is not now necessary to discuss the question, whether the Allies were or not at war with France: there is no doubt whatever, that their armies entered Paris under a Military Convention, concluded with an officer of the Government; the Prefect of the Department, as an army officer, being the representative of each of the authorities existing at Paris at the moment, and authorized by those authorities to treat and conclude for them.

The article of the Convention which it is supposed has been broken, is the 11th, which relates to public property. I positively deny that this article refers at all to the Museum, or Gallery of Pictures.

"The French Commissioners, in the original *projet*, proposed an article to provide for the security of this description of property: Prince Blucher would not consent; as he said there were pictures in the gallery, which had been taken from Prussia, which his Majesty Louis the 18th had promised to restore, but which had never been restored. I stated this circumstance to the French Commissioners; and they then offered to adopt the article, with an exception of the Prussian pictures. To this offer I answered, that I stood there as the Ally of all the nations in Europe; and any thing that was granted to Prussia, I must claim for other nations. I added, that I had no instructions regarding the Museum, or any grounds on which to form a judgment how the Sovereigns would act; that they certainly would insist upon the King's performing his engagement, and that I recommended that the article should be omitted altogether, and the question should be reserved for the decision of the Sovereigns, when they should arrive.

"Thus, the question regarding the Museum stands, and the Treaty or Convention of Paris is silent upon it: but there was a communication upon the subject, which reserved it for the decision of the Sovereigns.

"Supposing the silence of the treaty of Paris of May 1814, regarding the Museum, gave the French Government an undisputed claim to its contents upon all future occasions; it will not be found that this claim was broken by this transaction. Thus I acted for the French Government at the time I considered that the successful army had a right, and would touch the contents of the Museum; and they made an attempt to save them by an article in the Military Convention. This article was rejected, and the claim of the Allies to their pictures was broadly advanced by the negociators on their part, and this was stated as the ground for rejecting the article. Not only then the Military Convention did not itself guarantee the possession ; but the transaction above recited, tended to weaken the claim of possession by the French Government, which is founded upon the silence of the Treaty of Paris of May 1814.

" The Allies, having the contents of the Museum justly in their power, cannot do otherwise than restore them to the countries from which, contrary to the practice of civilized warfare, they had been torn during the disastrous periods of the French Revolution, and the tyranny of Buonaparté.

" The conduct of the Allies regarding the Museum, at the period of the treaty of Paris, might be fairly attributed to their desire to conciliate the French army, and to consolidate the reconciliation with Europe, which the army at that period manifested a disposition to effect.

" But the circumstances are now entirely different : the army disappointed the reasonable expectations of the world, and seized the earliest opportunity of rebelling against their Sovereign ; and of giving their services to the common Enemy of mankind, with a view to the revival of the disastrous period which had passed, and of the scenes of plunder which the world had made such gigantic efforts to get rid of.

The army having been defeated by the armies of Europe, they have been disbanded by the united Councils of the Sovereigns, and no reasons can exist why the Powers of Europe should not do justice to their own subjects, from any view to conciliate that army again ; neither has it once appeared to me to be necessary that the Allied Sovereigns should omit this opportunity to do justice, and to gratify their own subjects, in order to gratify the people of France.

" The feeling of the people of France upon this subject, must be founded on national vanity only. It must be a desire to retain these specimens of the arts, not because Paris is the fittest depository for them, (as on that subject, artists, connoisseurs, and all who have written upon it, admit that the whole ought to be removed to their ancient seats,) and because they were obtained by military success, of which they are the trophies.

" The same feeling which induces the people of France to wish to retain the pictures and statues of other nations, would naturally induce other nations to wish, now that success is on their side, that the property should be returned to its rightful owners, and the Allied Sovereigns must feel a desire to gratify them.

" It is besides on many accounts desirable, as well for their own happiness as that of the world, that the people of France, if they do not already see that Europe is too strong for them, should be made sensible of it ; and that, whatever may be the extent at any time, of their momentary and partial success against any one, or any number of the individual Powers in Europe, that the day of retribution must come. Not only then would it, in my opinion, be unjust in the Sovereigns to gratify the people of France on the subject, at the expense of their own people ; but the sacrifice they would make, would be impolitic, as it would deprive them of the opportunity of giving the people of France a great moral lesson.

" I am, &c.

Paris, Sep. **23,** 1815.   " WELLINGTON."

EXPLANATION

of the movements, and of the battles fought during the 15th, 16th, 17th and 18th of June, 1815, by the French Army under the command of Buonaparté, and the Anglo-Prussian Army commanded by the Duke of Wellington and Prince Blucher.

The 15th of June, the French attacked the Prussians upon the Sambre, towards Thuin, A. They repulsed them, and passed the Sambre to Charleroi, B, and to Marchienne-au-Pont, C; they took Charleroi, B, the Prussians, commanded by General Ziethen retreated with precipitation through Gosselies, D, upon Fleurus, E; they concentrated at Sombref, F; they occupied the villages, viz. of Ligny, 1, Saint Amand, 2, and Bry, 3, situated in front of their position. The English Army united again at Nivelles, G. The French attacked a brigade of the Belgic Army at Frasnes, H, and obliged them to retreat upon Quartre Bras, I.

On the 16th, the Belgians recovered their lost ground; but Lord Wellington caused his army to retrograde in the morning to take their position at Quartre Bras, I. Battle of Ligny. The left of the French is in advance to Frasnes, H, and towards Quartre Bras, I; the centre at Ligny, 1, and the right towards Sombref, F. The English and the Prussians were attacked at the same time. Marshal Blucher being overcome, retreats upon Tilly, J, and marches all night to arrive at Wavre, K, where they concentrated.

On the 17th, General Thielmann retreated to Sombref, F, upon Gembloux, L, where he joined the fourth Prussian corps, of which a part marched towards Mont Saint Guibert, M. The French following up their success; one part of the army pursue the Prussians, the other marched against Lord Wellington, who retreated to Quartre Bras, I, upon Genappe, N, and from thence to Waterloo, O, where he took his position, supported by the forest of Soigne, and the cavalry on the roads to Brussels and Nivelles, G; his right extended to Merke-Braine, P, and his left towards Ter-la-haye, Q, communicating with Wavre, K, by Ohain, R. The ravines, and the farms of Hougoumont, S, and of La Haye Sainte, T, covered the wings of the English army, whose centre rested on the plains of Mont St. Jean, U. The bivouacks were established near the observatory, V.

On the 18th, the French attacked the English position, and commenced the fire at Hougoumont, S, by which they got possession also of La Haye Sainte, T. The centre of the English army, occupying in force the heights of Mont Saint Jean, U, is vigorously attacked. Planchenoit, W, and the farm of La Belle Alliance, X, is occupied by the French; it was towards this point, that Bulow directed himself, at the same time that Marshal Blucher bore down upon Ohain, R, for to act in junction. Æ is the place where the Prince of Orange was wounded. The Prussians marched through Saint Lambert, Y, and Frischemont, Z, from whence they debouched towards Smouhen,* on the right of the French, to decide the affair.

PART II.

A

COMPLETE SERIES

OF

OFFICIAL ACCOUNTS,

Published by Authority,

VIZ.

FIELD MARSHAL DUKE OF WELLINGTON's — FIELD
MARSHAL PRINCE BLUCHER's—THE HANOVERIAN
— DUTCH — RUSSIAN — AUSTRIAN —
SPANISH AND FRENCH.

Communicating the Details to their respective Governments

OF THE

CAMPAIGN IN THE NETHERLANDS,

AND

RELATIVE OPERATIONS;

WITH OTHER DOCUMENTS

" THE very important results from the Battle of Waterloo
so teem with suggestions, that infinitely more must be
trusted to the reader's reflection and sensibility than can be
offered on paper to his eye. The effect of these events is
so grand, their succession to each other is so rapid, and, at
the same time, so towering in the scale of importance,—their
variety is so precipitate and wild, that one feels, in relation
to this political crisis, much in the same way as when
surrounded by the most sublime and abrupt scenes of nature
—as if it would be impertinent to throw in the petty voice
of remark amongst so much that outstrips the power and
speculation of individuals. There is a pitch of activity of
mind, excited by the vastness of surrounding objects, which
silences language by a conviction of its inability; and there
is a rush in the tide of success which produces a vague but

A

serious impression, akin to alarm, occasioned by the faculties finding themselves at a loss. The break-up of what appeared so strong, the instantaneous discomfiture and dispersion of what appeared so formidable, the unbounded triumph of what appeared so beset with doubts and difficulties, which we have witnessed, cause the result to assume altogether the air of a stupendous phenomenon. Amidst this union of violence and rapidity, we feel ourselves rather carried than carrying, we seem the object of some over-ruling influence, rather than the fulfillers of our own designs. The interval has been so small since Bonaparte declared himself impregnable in French feeling and strength, —since we heard of armies on armies collected to resent as well as resist invasion,—since we were dazzled and astounded with oath-taking ceremonials, with the imposing display of a throne, the steps of which were crowded with devoted children, —that, now, when we find this man absolutely stripped, and rendered destitute by one blow,—his unrestrainable and all-confident soldiery scattered and dissipated by one encounter, —and France, " the beautiful and invincible," laid open to her heart, defenceless and bare, by one defeat,—we startle in that feeling of scepticism which is sometimes produced by the overpowering nature of the conviction of a reality. It may be said, we believe,—and under all the circumstances, without any violation of generosity,—that the two extremes of previous boasting and subsequent depression and disgrace, could have happened in no country of Europe, within the same space of time, but *France;* and we apprehend it may be said, consistently, under all the circumstances, both with truth and decency, that the succession of the latter to the former could not have been so rapidly forced on such an enemy, by any other country than *England.* Neither the taunt nor the self-congratulation would be worth writing, unless connected with the vindication of true principles. Every triumph of policy, with such a bias, is a benefit gained for mankind generally.

" It is the proud distinction of the British troops, that they are alike to be depended upon in " doing or in suffering,"

while the French are nothing unless they are *doing :* the
latter must be carried out of themselves to reach to any
thing that is great, and when the artificial stimulus fails,
or is checked, they drop back into their natures, which do
not well sustain them. Their British adversaries, on the
other hand, have no occasion to go beyond the essential
qualities of their character, and their efforts being thus
sounder in motive, are more substantial in effect. The
difference may be represented by calling one the rock, and
the other the foaming spray which it beats back. During
the whole course of the war in Spain, this difference was
very perceptible,—but never has it been exhibited on so
grand a scale as in the late battles in the Netherlands.
The French were impetuous and desperate in their charges,
—the British were immoveable and calm in receiving them :
wherever any number, no matter how small, of British
troops could be thrown forward to meet the enemy, there
was the enemy, no matter how strong, or how triumphant
over others, abruptly stopped. Moral superiority took the
aspect of a physical obstacle, which must be annihilated to
be removed. In the grand result the French have felt, the
world has seen, and posterity will know, that England's
sons are the best in the fight, and that they are capable of
the mightiest exertions of every kind. Their country alone
has held out without interval or faltering : their country
alone has entirely escaped degradation in these times of
misfortune : she alone has assisted all, and held her own
head high without assistance. Our enemy has now experienced the superiority of England in every way ; all his
publications, for many years, have avowed that his great
design was to ruin England ; his measures have all been
directed to this end. He has tried to effect it at sea, on
shore, singly, and by alliances,—he has tried to effect it by
commercial, financial, and *sentimental* means. We have
destroyed him at sea, we have beaten him on shore ; we
have repelled him singly, we have conquered him with our
Allies : we tired him out of his anti-commercial system, and
our finances have also triumphed, without the commis-

sion of any breach of faith to our creditors. We have, exposed the meanness and falsehood of his sentiments. Lastly, in one great battle,—England, away from her own shores, has, in the teeth of superior numbers, beaten the collected might of France on her own frontier, headed by an Imperial General whose superiority over all Captains, ancient or modern, the public voice of France has asserted, and sworn, in prose and poetry, in harangues and writings, —in insolence, in perfidy, and falsehood. In one battle, England has dealt to France a blow that has gone to her heart, and sent her reeling and tumbling backward on a throne, which, in theatrical show at least, she had sworn to defend to the last drop of her blood, in behalf of which, she, but the other day, held forth the boldest language of defiance;—a throne which was said to present a superb spectacle, a sublime spectacle, an imposing spectacle, and heaven knows how many spectacles besides. This throne has tumbled down like rotten wood under her stagger and fall: her soldiers have disappeared, like the smoke of her cannon, after the prodigious noise they made;—and, between her frontier and the neighbourhood of her capital, scarcely an arm has been raised to preserve the " fine country,"—to vindicate the honour of the " great nation,"— to fulfil the " destiny" which had " decreed France to be the Queen of the West."

" If it be true, which has been taken for granted by some, that it was the will of the people of France that Bonaparte should reign over them,—the ruin of that person at one blow, the instantaneous desertion of him in the teeth of engagements to support him to the last, and the breaking up of a national army by one defeat, form a more severe humiliation of the French than any which they have inflicted on other countries. Nothing that has been done by them to Prussia or to Austria was so severely disgraceful to the vanquished as this which has fallen on themselves, supposing that they were enlisted in Bonaparte's cause. Assuming, on the other hand, that Bonaparte's return was a measure of violence, that it was offensive to the public

sentiment of France,—what is to be said of a people that
are thus to be wrested to and fro,—knocked like a shuttle-
cock from one government to another,—and all the while
debating about their " destinies, and their deliberations,
and their high attitude,"—deriving that self-satisfaction
from words which they ought to seek in things.—Some, we
know, feel a distrust and disheartenedness from the utter
overthrow of Bonaparte, in consequence of regarding it as
the overthrow of intellect; but, if the matter be properly
considered, it will appear that a grand vindication has been
effected of those principles which combine intellect, morality, and freedom together. It has been proved, that it
is only from this union that the invincibility of character
can spring, into whose contemplation the idea of yielding
is never admitted, which acquires strong feeling from serious
reflection, and its keenest enthusiasm from a sober sense of
self-respect. This is a description of character which at
least applies better to England than to France; the triumph
of the latter over the former, therefore, would have been a
most melancholy event as a proof of the little practical
worth of those domestic virtues, social comforts, and public
rights which England possesses in a superior degree to
France. But the victory of England is an assurance that
they are of sterling worth; that, although they may demand
some self-denials, yet that they well repay them; that
Providence has a sacred store, from which it bestows its
most splendid and imperishable gifts on those, who wil-
lingly forfeit, for their sake, the easy pleasures that are within
the reach of indolence and sensuality. It would, indeed,
have been a miserable thing for the hopes of the world, if a
perjured and unprincipled soldiery, a careless and fickle
people, a perfidious and declamatory government, had, in
the terrible and decisive struggle of faculty and heart,
gained the day: but the great fight of Waterloo has, with
the instrumentality of English heroism, connected the political and moral qualities which philanthropists enforce, with
that public strength which is the common ambition of the
gross as well as of the enlightened.

" We rejoice in the victory which England has gained ; and we have no doubt, that the cause of political freedom, in France, will be benefited by what has happened. . Bonaparte's fall has proved, we think, that he was not supported by the opinion of the French, and, if not so supported, his return was a piece of ruffian-violence, and his pretensions, since his return, sheer knavish imposition."

We now proceed to give the words of the original documents, as issued by the respective governments, as the best elucidation of the glorious events, which cannot fail to fix an emulative record of English valour to the latest posterity.

OFFICIAL BULLETIN.

Downing Street, June, 22, 1815.*

" The Duke of Wellington's dispatch, dated Waterloo, the 19th of June, states, that on the preceding day Bonaparte attacked, with his whole force, the British line, supported by a corps of Prussians; which attack, after a long and sanguinary conflict, terminated in the complete Overthrow of the Enemy's Army, with the loss of ONE HUNDRED AND FIFTY PIECES OF CANNON, AND TWO EAGLES. During the night, the Prussians, under Marshal Blucher, who joined in the pursuit of the enemy, captured SIXTY GUNS, and a large part of Bonaparte's BAGGAGE. The Allied Armies continued to pursue the enemy. Two French Generals were taken."

* The first news of the commencement of hostilities was known in London at four o'clock on Tuesday, June 20, 1815, by the following means :—The Hon. Mr: Butler, and the knight of Kerry, were travelling on pleasure, in the Netherlands, on Thursday the 15th, intending to sleep that night at Charleroi ; but hearing the firing of the Prussians and French, they proceeded back to Brussels, at about o'clock, where they communicated what they had heard. They remained at Brussels until half past one on the Sunday, having, in the interim, witnessed the effect of the variety of reports, and consequent confusion, which is accurately detailed in the first part of this work ; and having given their endeavours to help the wounded to quarters, &c. on Monday, three o'clock, they reached Ostend, and sailed in the Leveret frigate on Tuesday morning ; at five o'clock they were at Deal, and arrived in London at four o'clock in the afternoon, where they delivered to Lord Melville the dispatches they had been entrusted with by Admiral Markham, who sent home word all he knew, had seen, or believed, which contained, in substance, communicated verbally by the Duke's aid de camp, the Duke of Wellington's entire confidence in his dispositions, and ultimate success of the battle he then had to fight.

It is but due to observe, that the great expedition in this communication, is attributed to the particular exertions of Mr. Tournier, the courier who accompanied the above gentlemen, whose experience and foresight led him to avoid the common road, which, as he predicted, had become completely choked in its facilities for travellers.—EDITOR.

London Gazette Extraordinary.

Downing Street, June 22d, 1815.

Major the Honourable H. Percy, arrived late last night with a dispatch from Field Marshal the Duke of Wellington, K.G. to Earl Bathurst, his Majesty's Principal Secretary of State for the War Department, of which the following is a copy:

My Lord,   *Waterloo, June* 19th, 1815.

Bonaparte having collected the 1st, 2d, 3d, 4th, and 6th, corps of the French army and the Imperial Guards, and nearly all the cavalry, on the Sambre, and between that river and the Meuse, between the 10th and the 14th of the month, advanced on the 15th and attacked the Prussian posts at Thuin and Lobez, on the Sambre, at day-light in the morning.

I did not hear of these events till the evening of the 15th, and I immediately ordered the troops to prepare to march; and afterwards to march to their left, as soon as I had intelligence from other quarters to prove that the enemy's move ment upon Charleroi was the real attack.

The enemy drove the Prussian posts from the Sambre on that day; and General Ziethen, who commanded the corps which had been at Charleroi, retired upon Fleurus; and Marshal Prince Blucher concentrated the Prussian army upon Sombref, holding the villages in front of his position of St. Amand and Ligny.

The enemy continued his march along the road from Charleroi towards Brussels, and on the same evening, the 15th, attacked a brigade of the army of the Netherlands, under Prince de Weimar, posted at Frasne, and forced it back to the farm house on the same road, called Les Quatre Bras.

The Prince of Orange immediately reinforced this brigade with another of the same division, under General Perponcher, and, in the morning early, regained part of the ground which had been lost, so as to have the command of the communication leading from Nivelles and Brussels, with Marshal Blucher's position.

In the meantime, I had directed the whole army to march upon Les Quatre Bras, and the 5th division, under Lieutenant General Sir Thomas Picton, arrived at about half-past two in the day, followed by the corps of troops under the Duke of Brunswick, and afterwards by the contingent of Nassau.

At this time the enemy commenced an attack upon Prince Blucher with his whole force, excepting the 1st and 2d corps; and a corps of cavalry under General Kellerman, with which he attacked our post at Les Quatre Bras.

The Prussian army maintained their position with their usual gallantry and perseverance, against a great disparity of numbers, as the 4th corps of their army, under General Bulow, had not joined, and I was not able to assist them as I wished, as I was attacked myself, and the troops, the cavalry in particular, which had a long distance to march, had not arrived.

We maintained our position also, and completely defeated and repulsed all the enemy's attempts to get possession of it. The enemy repeatedly attacked us with a large body of infantry and cavalry, supported by a numerous and powerful artillery; he made several charges with the cavalry upon our infantry, but all were repulsed in the steadiest manner. In this affair, his Royal Highness the Prince of Orange, the Duke of Brunswick, and Lieutenant-General Sir Thomas Picton, and Major-General Sir James Kempt, and Sir Denis Pack, who were engaged from the commencement of the enemy's attack, highly distinguished themselves, as well as Lieutenant-General Charles Baron Alten, Major General Sir C. Halket, Lieutenant-General Cooke, and Major-Generals Maitland and Byng, as they successively arrived. The troops of the 5th division, and those of the Brunswick corps, were long and severely engaged, and conducted themselves with the utmost gallantry. I must particularly mention the 28th, 42d, 79th, 92d regiments, and the battalion of Hanoverians.

Our loss was great, as your Lordship will perceive by the

inclosed return; and I have particularly to regret His Serene
Highness the Duke of Brunswick, who fell, fighting gallantly, at the head of his troops.

Although Marshal Blucher had maintained his position at
Sombref, he still found himself much weakened by the
severity of the contest in which he had been engaged, and,
as the fourth corps had not arrived, he determined to fall
back, and concentrated his army upon Wavre; and he
marched in the night after the action was over.

This movement of the Marshal's rendered necessary a
corresponding one on my part; and I retired from the farm
of Quatre Bras upon Genappe, and thence upon Waterloo
the next morning, the 17th, at ten o'clock.

The enemy made no effort to pursue Marshal Blucher.
On the contrary, a patrole which I sent to Sambref, in the
morning, found all quiet, and the enemy's videttes fell back
as the patrol advanced. Neither did he attempt to molest
our march to the rear, although made in the middle of the day,
excepting by following with a large body of cavalry, brought
(from his right) the cavalry under the Earl of Uxbridge.

This gave Lord Uxbridge an opportunity of charging
them with the 1st Life Guards, upon their debouché from
the village of Genappe, upon which occasion his Lordship
has declared himself to be well satisfied with that regiment.

The position which I took up, in front of Waterloo,
crossed the high roads from Charleroi and Nivelles, and had
its right thrown back to a ravine near Merke Braine, which
was occupied, and its left extended to a height above the
hamlet Ter-la-Haye, which was likewise occupied. In front
of the right centre, and near the Nivelles road, we occupied
the house and garden of Hougoumont, which covered the
return of that flank; and, in front of the left centre, we occupied the farm of La Haye Sainte. By our left we communicated with Marshal Prince Blucher, at Wavre, through
Ohain; and the Marshal had promised me, that in case we
should be attacked, he would support me with one or more
corps, as might be necessary.

The enemy collected his army, with the exception of the

third corps, which had been sent to observe Marshal Blucher, on a range of heights in our front, in the course of the night of the 17th and yesterday morning; and at about ten o'clock he commenced a furious attack upon our post at Hougoumont. I had occupied that post with a detachment from General Byng's brigade of Guards, which was in position in its rear; and it was for some time under the command of Lieutenant-Colonel Macdonald, and afterwards of Colonel Home; and I am happy to add, that it was maintained, throughout the day, with the utmost gallantry by these brave troops, notwithstanding the repeated efforts of large bodies of the enemy to obtain possession of it.

This attack upon the right of our centre was accompained by a very heavy cannonade upon our whole line, which was destined to support the repeated attacks of cavalry and infantry occasionally mixed, but sometimes separate, which were made upon it. In one of these, the enemy carried the farm house of La Haye Sainte, as the detachment of the light battalion of the legion which occupied it had expended all its ammunition, and the enemy occupied the only communication there was with them.

The enemy repeatedly charged our infantry with his cavalry; but these attacks were uniformly unsuccessful, and they afforded opportunities to our cavalry to charge, in one of which, Lord E. Somerset's brigade, Life Guards, Royal Horse Guards, and 1st Dragoon Guards, highly distinguished themselves; as did that of Major General Sir W. Ponsonby, having taken many prisoners and an eagle.

These attacks were repeated till about seven in the evening, when the enemy made a desperate effort with the cavalry and infantry, supported by the fire of artillery, to force our left centre, near the farm of La Haye Sainte, which, after a severe contest, was defeated; and having observed that the troops retired from this attack in great confusion, and that the march of General Bulow's corps by Frichermont upon Planchenoit and La Belle Alliance, had begun to take effect; and as I could perceive the fire of his cannon, and as Marshal Prince Blucher had joined in person, with a corps of his army to the left of our line by Ohain, I determined to attack the enemy, and immediately advanced the whole line of infantry, supported by the cavalry and artillery. The attack succeeded in every point; the enemy was forced from his position on the heights, and fled in the utmost confusion, leaving behind him, as far as I could judge, ONE HUNDRED AND FIFTY PIECES OF CANNON, with their ammunition, which fell into our hands.

I continued the pursuit till long after dark, and then discontinued it, only on account of the fatigue of our troops, who had been engaged during twelve hours, and because I found myself on the same road with Marshal Blucher, who assured me of his intention to follow the enemy throughout the night; he has sent me word this morning, that he had taken 60 pieces of cannon belonging to the Imperial Guard, and several carriages, baggage, &c. belonging to Bonaparte, in Genappe.

I propose to move, this morning, upon Nivelles, and not to discontinue my operations.

Your Lordship will observe, that such a desperate action could not be fought, and such advantages could not be gained, without great loss; and, I am sorry to add, that our's has been immense. In Lieutenant-General Sir Thomas Picton, his Majesty has sustained the loss of an Officer who has frequently distinguished himself in his service; and he fell, gloriously leading his division to a charge with bayonets, by which one of the most serious attacks made by the enemy on our position, was defeated.

The Earl of Uxbridge, after having successfully got through this arduous day, received a wound, by almost the last shot fired, which will, I am afraid, deprive his Majesty for sometime of his services.

His Royal Highness the Prince of Orange distinguished himself by his gallantry and conduct till he received a wound from a musket ball, through the shoulder, which obliged him to quit the field.

It gives me the greatest satisfaction to assure your Lordship, that the army never, upon any occasion, conducted itself better. The division of Guards, under Lieutenant-General Cooke, who is severely wounded, Major-General Maitland and Major General Byng, set an example which was followed by all; and there is no Officer, nor description of troops, that did not behave well.

I must, however, particularly mention, for His Royal Highness's approbation, Lieutenant-General Sir H. Clinton, Major-General Adam, Lieutenant-General Charles Baron Alten, severely wounded; Major-General Sir Colin Halket, severely wounded; Colonel Ompteda, Colonel Mitchele, commanding a brigade of the 4th division; Major-Generals Sir James Kempt and Sir Denis Pack, Major-General Lambert, Major-General Lord E. Somerset, Major-General Sir W. Ponsonby, Major-General Sir C. Grant, and Major-General Sir H. Vivian; Major-General Sir O. Vandeleur; Major-General Count Dornberg. I am also particularly indebted to General Lord Hill for his assistance and conduct upon this, as upon all former occasions.

The Artillery and Engineer departments were conducted much to my satisfaction by Colonel Sir G. Wood, and Colonel Smyth; and I had every reason to be satisfied with the conduct of the Adjutant-General Major-General Barnes, who was wounded, and of the Quarter-Master-General, Colonel Delancy, who was killed by a cannon shot in the middle of the action. This officer is a serious loss to his Majesty's service, and to me at this moment. I was likewise much indebted to the assistance of Lieutenant-Colonel Lord Fitzroy Somerset, who was severely wounded, and of the Officers composing my personal staff, who have suffered severely in this action. Lieutenant-Colonel the Honourable Sir Alexander Gordon, who has died of his wounds, was a most promising officer, and is a serious loss to his Majesty's service.

General Kruse, of the Nassau service, likewise conducted himself much to my satisfaction, as did General Trip, commanding the heavy brigade of cavalry, and General Vanhope, commanding a brigade of infantry of the King of the Netherlands.

General Pozzo di Borgo, General Baron Vincent, General Muffling, and General Alava, were in the field during the action, and rendered me every assistance in their power Baron Vincent is wounded, but I hope not severely; and General Pozzo di Borgo received a contusion.

I should not do justice to my feelings, or to Marshal Blucher and the Prussian army, if I did not attribute the successful result of this arduous day to the cordial and timely assistance received from them.

The operation of General Bulow upon the enemy's flank, was a most decisive one; and, even if I had not found myself in a situation to make the attack, which produced the final result, it would have forced the enemy to retire, if his attacks should have failed, and would have prevented him from taking advantage of them, if they should unfortunately have succeeded.

I send, with this dispatch, two eagles, taken by the troops in this action, which Major Percy will have the honour of laying at the feet of his Royal Highness—I beg leave to recommend him to your Lordship's protection.

I have the honour, &c.

(Signed)   WELLINGTON.

P. S. Since writing the above, I have received a report, that Major-General Sir W. Ponsonby is killed; and, in announcing this intelligence to your Lordship, I have to add the expression of my grief for the fate of an Officer, who had already rendered very brilliant and important services, and who was an ornament to his profession.

2d P. S. I have not yet got the returns of killed and wounded, but I inclose a list of Officers killed and wounded on the two days, as far as the same can be made out without the returns; and I am very happy to add, that Colonel Delancy is not dead, and that strong hopes of his recovery are entertained.

HANOVERIAN ACCOUNT.

Extract from a Report of Lieutenant-General Charles Von Alten, to His Royal Highness Field-Marshal and Governor-General the Duke of Cambridge, dated Brussels, June 20th, 1815. (Original in this Work.)

On the evening of the 15th, the troops broke up from their cantonments, which were very widely separated. The Duke of Wellington concentrated the troops in the environs of Brussels, at Genappe. The Hereditary Prince of Orange, under whose command my division was, advanced to Quatre Bras, where the roads from Mons to Namur, and from Brussels to Charleroi, intersect each other. The French had divided their army and attacked the Prussians, the Duke of Wellington, and our corps, at one and the same time. The Hereditary Prince posted us between Quatre Bras and Sart à Maveline in such a manner that the right wing occupied the former, and the left the latter village. The troops marched up, under a most violent cannonade, from the enemy. A wood on the right of Quatre Bras, was alternately taken on our part and by the French. The cannonade on both sides was extremely brisk. The enemy repeatedly attempted to force our left wing; I detached the field battalion of Lüneburg to drive him out of the village of Pierremont in our front. Lieutenant-Colonel Klenke executed this commission with great intrepidity, took the village and maintained it against the reiterated attacks of the enemy. Upon this, the enemy's infantry advanced in several columns, against which I detached the field-battalions of Grubenhagen, Osnabrück, and Bremen. With the assistance of the artillery of the German Legion, under Captain Cleves, the troops repulsed the enemy. On the right wing the enemy's cavalry ventured to make several attacks, but, by the gallantry of the troops, prevented it from breaking through them. On this occasion, the battalion of the Landwehr of Lüneburg, under the command of Lieutenant-Colonel Von Ramdohr, particularly distinguished itself. It suffered the enemy's cavalry to approach to the distance of thirty paces, and then received it with a volley, by which it was repulsed with great loss. We were so fortunate as to maintain our position; but, as the Prussian army, on our left wing, had sustained a considerable check, we were obliged to fall back, on the 17th, upon Genappe, in which movement my division formed the rear-guard. As the enemy appeared, in the afternoon, in very great force, we retreated to Mont St. Jean, on the road to Brussels.

Here the whole army of the Duke of Wellington had assembled; and it took a position on the heights in front of this village, so that the left wing was supported upon the village of Frichermont, and the right on the *chaussée* from Brussels to Nivelles. The *chaussée* from Genappe to Brussels intersected the centre of the army, which was formed by my division. I sent the second light battalion of the King's German Legion, under Major Baring, to occupy the farm-house of La Haye Sainte, situate just before the left wing of my division. A company of Hanoverian Yagers, and two light companies of the English Guards, were thrown into the farm-house of Hougoumont and the small wood before it, in front of the right wing.

The infantry of the corps of His Royal Highness the Prince of Orange, to which my division belonged, was marched up in columns *en echiquier*, the battalions being placed two and two beside one another, in such a manner that they might immediately deploy or form into squares. Between the columns there was a sufficient space for the passage of the cavalry and artillery stationed behind the squares. The corps of General Lord Hill was posted in reserve, at Braine la Leud, and, at the same time, covered the *chaussée* from Nivelles to Brussels. Beyond this *chaussée* there was some cavalry for the purpose of watching the motions of the enemy.

About one o'clock, the enemy sent his *tirailleurs* upon the wood in front of our right wing, where a smart engagement ensued. This post was of great importance to us, as the enemy would have gained, in its possession, a height which would have endangered our right flank. He caused strong columns of infantry, supported by artillery, to advance successively upon this post, the maintenance of which were committed to the British Guards, who defended it with undaunted gallantry.

The battle became general upon the whole line. The enemy brought up against us a numerous artillery, under cover of which a column of several thousand men pushed on upon the *chaussée* of Genappe, but it was repulsed by the two light battalions and the 8th battalion of the line of the King's German Legion, and the field-battalion of Lüneburg. Behind this column the enemy's cavalry advanced with such impetuosity, as to overthrow the infantry acting *en debandage*, and to penetrate to the hill among the squares posted *en echiquier*. The troops remained immoveable till the English cavalry came up and repulsed the enemy; the squares most exposed on this occasion, were commanded by Lieutenant-Colonel Von Wurmb and Major Von Schkopp. Lieutenant-Colonel Von Langrehr had already been brought wounded to the rear. The fire of the

enemy's artillery now became brisker, and it was kept up
on both sides with a vehemence, such as few of the oldest
soldiers had, perhaps, ever witnessed. The attacks of the
enemy's infantry and cavalry were several times repeated,
and in different quarters. Bonaparte was determined to
break through the centre, and thus to open for himself the
way to Brussels. One column was repulsed by Colonel
Von Ompteda, who put himself at the head of his battalion. Meanwhile, the enemy kept advancing nearer, and
continually bringing up fresh troops. His artillery played
upon our squares at the distance of 150 paces. Not one of
them gave way; the dead were pushed aside, and the ranks
filled up again. Several went to meet the enemy's cavalry,
and, by their heavy fire, compelled it to retreat. At
length, some of them, which were almost entirely cut in
pieces, fell back; they retreated, however, in good order,
and immediately advanced again when they were ordered.
The Duke of Wellington was a constant eye-witness of their
conduct. This hero was always at that point where the
danger was the greatest; and the Prince of Orange displayed
a courage worthy of his illustrious ancestors. It was his
corps, against which the main force of the enemy, led on
by Bonaparte in person, was directed. At this critical
moment, the Prussian General, Von Bülow, who had hastened to our assistance with 30,000 men, attacked the
enemy in his flank. The victory was our's; the enemy fled
in all directions, leaving behind the greatest part of his
artillery. About 200 pieces of cannon and several eagles
have been taken. The number of prisoners brought in
cannot be accurately stated, but it amounts to many thousands.

These two days have, indeed, cost us much, and, with
the deepest regret, I have to inform your Royal Highness,
that the greatest part of our most distinguished officers
have fallen. Among these I reckon particularly, Colonels
Von Ompteda and Du Plat, and Lieutenant-Colonels Von
Wurmb and Von Langrehr. We have, to be sure, this
consolation, that these men have covered their graves with
glory, and that the Hanoverians have established their
reputation for valour. As an eye-witness, indeed, I can
only bear testimony concerning the field-battalions of
Bremen, Lüneburg, Verden, Grubenhagen, and the Duke
of York, belonging to my division, and affirm, that they
have rendered themselves worthy of being recorded in the
annals of our army; but a highly favourable report has also
been made to me of some of the brigades of the Landwehr,
which were in the engagement. Colonel Halkett bestows
particular praise on the battalion of Osnabrück. Of our
cavalry, the Duke of Cumberland's regiment only was pre-

sent at the conflict, but was not advanced to the attack. It was for some time much exposed to the fire of the artillery, by which it sustained considerable loss.

Though every officer and soldier, whom I had an opportunity of observing, has done his duty, still I feel it incumbent upon me to make particular mention of some of them who pre-eminently signalized themselves on these arduous days; and, I venture to hope, that your Royal Highness, as you are so disposed to reward merit, will confer on them marks of your satisfaction and approbation, than which, nothing is for them a more powerful stimulus.

Major-General Count Von Kielmansegge gave the most brilliant example of courage and intrepidity to his brigade, and constantly supported me with all his might.

The conduct of Lieutenant-Colonels Von Klencke, Von Wurmb, and Von Langrehr, of Majors Von Schkopp, Von Bülow, and 'Von Stockhausen, deserves the highest praise. According to report received from Colonel Halkett, I think I may, with justice, recommend Major Count Münster also to your Royal Highness. He fought with the battalion of Osnabrück Landwehr against Napoleon's Guards, and overthrew them.

I am not less grateful to the Officers of my staff, and especially to Colonel Von Berger, as chief of the *etat-major*, who never quitted my side on the 16th and 18th, and who, by his counsel and exertions, rendered me the greatest service. The meritorious talents of this officer are known to your Royal Highness; and, severely wounded as I was, I should not have been able to retain the chief command of the Hanoverian troops, had not Colonel Berger's contusion permitted him to perform its principal duties.

On Major Heise, of the King's German Legion, whom your Royal Highness assigned to me as Military Secretary, I must bestow the deserved encomium, that he evinced on these two days, a zeal and activity which reflect upon him the highest honour.

Majors Kunze and Von Schlütter, who had no specific sphere of action, as I had only the command of the division, nevertheless seized every opportunity to afford me assistance, and, therefore, I cannot pass them by unnoticed in this report.

Lieutenant Count Von Kielmansegge was, likewise, very serviceable to me. It is, as yet, impossible for me to name all the officers who have distinguished themselves on these days, as I have not yet received the reports of the brigadiers. I shall collect them, however and send your Royal Highness an extract, that you may be made acquainted with them all, if possible. Thus, too, the Lists of Dead, Wounded, and Missing, had not yet been completed, because the army put itself in motion again immediately. I hope to be able to transmit them in a few days. The names of the killed shall shortly follow.

I have still to remark to your Royal Highness, that the wound which I received at the conclusion of the engagement, will not prevent me from retaining the command of the Hanoverians; if you shall be pleased to continue to entrust me with it under these circumstances. I hope, in a few weeks, to be completely recovered.

The official Lists of Killed, Wounded, and Missing, of the Hanoverian brigades of Count Kielmansegge and Colonel Halkett, and the battery under Captain Braun, only have yet been received, and are subjoined.

OFFICERS KILLED.

Artillery.—Lieut. Von Schulze.

Infantry.— 1st Bremen battalion, Lieut.-Col. Von Langrehr. 1st Lüneburg batt. Capt. Von Bobart; Ensign Von Plato. 1st Grubenhagen batt. Lieut.-Col. Von Wurmb. Bremervörde batt. of Landwehr, Lieut. Löper; Ensign Von Holt. 2d batt. of the Duke of York's, Lieut. Uffel; Ensign Berghoff.

OFFICERS SEVERELY WOUNDED.

General Staff.—Lieut.-Gen. Von Alten.

Artillery.—Capt. Braun.

Infantry.—1st Bremen batt. Lieut.-Col. Von Langrehr, (since dead of his wounds;) Major Müller; Capt. Von Lepel; Capt. Bazoldo; Lieut. Von Quistorp, 1; Lieut. Von Quistorp, 2. 1st Verden batt. Major Von Schkopp; Capt. Jacobi; Adjut. Gerhard; Lieutenants Selig, Suffenplan, Brandis, 1, and Brandis, 2. 1st batt. of the Duke of York's: Capt. Von Pawel; Lieutenants Moll and Marenholz. 1st Lüneburg batt. Lieut. Völger; Capt. Korfes. 1st Grubenhagen batt. Lieut. Westpfahl; Ensigns Ernst and Stiepel. Bremervörde batt. of Landwehr: Lieut. Warnecke; Ensign Wilke. 2d batt. of the Duke of York's: Capt. Gotthardt; Ensigns Niehencke and Meyer. 3d batt. of the Duke of York's: Major Von der Büsche-Hünefeld. Saltzgitter batt. of Landwehr: Lieut. Von Spangenberg.

OFFICERS SLIGHTLY WOUNDED.

General Staff.—Colonel Von Berger.

Infantry.—1st Bremen batt. Lieut. Wehner; Ensigns Bruel and Meyer. 1st Verden batt. Capt. Von Baudomer. 1st batt. of the Duke of York's: Major Von Bülow; Ensigns Müller and Rabius. 1st Lüneburg batt. Lieut. Col. A. Von Klencke; Lieut. Von Plato; Ensigns Von Weihe and Sachse. 1st Grubenhagen batt. Capt. Bauer; Lieut. Marwedel; Ensign Von Bülow. Bremervörde batt. of Landwehr: Lieut. Meyer; Ensign Holthusen. 2d batt. of the Duke of York's: Major Count Von Münster; Capt. Quentin; Lieutenants Winckler and Riechers. Saltzgitter batt. of Landwehr: Capt. Von Hammerstein.

MISSING.

Infantry.—1st Lüneburg batt. Major Von Dachenhausen. 1st Grubenhagen batt. Lieut. Von Lütken. Bremervörde batt. of Landwehr: Lieut. Ehlers; Ensign Ress. Saltzgitter batt. of Landwehr: Assistant Surgeons, Töpken and Homeier.

A. VON BERGER,
Colonel and Chief of the General Staff.

To his Excellency the Hanoverian Lieutenant-General Sir Charles Alten.

GEORGE, Prince Regent, acting for and in the name of His Majesty, our father George III. by the grace of God, King, &c. communicate to you, by these presents, our gracious intentions.

" Noble, beloved, and loyal, if on the one hand we are deeply afflicted at the considerable loss which our Hanoverian corps, confided to your orders, has suffered in the memorable battles of the 16th and 18th of last month, we have had reason, on the other hand, to feel peculiar satisfaction at learning the eulogiums which you bestow in your account, upon the distinguished courage and bravery of our valiant Hanoverians, a testimony upon which we set the higher value, as it comes from you, from a general who has combated in so many battles for his country and the good cause, and has constantly distinguished himself by his talents and his bravery.

" It very sincerely afflicts us to see you among the number of those who are wounded; and it is, however, with pleasure that we perceive you were able to retain the command of your troops, and that you have the hope of being entirely recovered in a few weeks.

" We have been very glad at receiving, with your narration, the copy of the report which you made on the 20th of last month, to our beloved brother the Duke of Cambridge, upon the said battles, by which we have been perfectly informed of the plan of the battle, and of all the circumstances which have accompanied it. It will be the object of our particular solicitude to recompense all those who have gloriously distinguished themselves before the enemy, and we certainly shall not fail also to provide for the widows and orphans of those who have fallen fighting for their country. We wait, for this end, only for the proposals of our beloved brother the Duke of Cambridge, whom your farther reports will soon enable to realize our intentions.

" We charge you to express to the Hanoverian army, under your command, our entire satisfaction with their good conduct in the said battles: assuring you, at the same time, that it is perfectly well known to me how much is to be ascribed to the talents and bravery with which you commanded them.—It is with sentiments of affection and favour, &c. &c.

" GEORGE, Prince Regent.

(Signed)
" Carlton House, July 7, 1815."

After having given the General such a flattering mark of his esteem, His Royal Highness has deigned, by a later resolution, to confer upon him and his descendants the title of Count, as a recompense for his distinguished services in the war in Spain, and in the battle of Waterloo.

B 2

His Royal Highness has been further pleased to testify his high
satisfaction with the Hanoverian troops who were present in this last
battle, and to permit them to bear, like the English troops, on their
colours and on their uniforms, the word " Waterloo."

DUTCH ACCOUNT.

*Reports of William Prince of Orange, to His Majesty the King of the
Netherlands.   (Original in this Work.)*

Head-quarters, Nivelles, 17th June, 1815, two in the morning.

Very early on the morning of the 15th, the Prussian army was
attacked in its position, which it abandoned, and retired from Charleroi, by Gosselies, as far as the environs of Fleurus. As soon as I
was apprised of this attack, I gave the necessary orders to the corps
of troops under my command. The result of what took place in the
Prussian army was, that the battalion of Orange Nassau, which, together with a battery of light artillery, occupied the village of Frasne,
were attacked at five o'clock in the evening of the 15th. These
troops maintained themselves in their position on the height of this
village, and at a short distance from the road, called Quatre-Bras.
The skirmishing ceased, upon this point, at eight o'clock in the
evening.

As soon as I was informed of this attack, I gave orders for the
third division, as well as to two English divisions, to move upon
Nivelles; and to the second to maintain the position of Quatre-Bras.
Only a part of the second division was enabled to move thither immediately, in consequence of the brigade, under the orders of Major-
General Byland, not being able to leave Nivelles prior to the arrival
of other troops at that place.

The firing of the tirailleurs commenced at five o'clock yesterday
morning, on this point, and was kept up on both sides until mid-day,
without any result. About two o'clock the attack became much
more severe, especially on the part of the cavalry and artillery. The
brigade of light cavalry, under the command of General Van Merlen,
was not able to come up before four o'clock; previous to which time
I had no cavalry to oppose to the enemy. Seeing of how great importance it was to preserve the position on the heights of the road,
called Quatre-Bras, I was fortunate in maintaining them against an
enemy who, in every respect, was superior to me in forces.

Having been attacked by the two corps d'armée, commanded by
Generals D'Erlon and Reille, and having succeeded in checking
them, the Duke of Wellington had time enough to assemble a sufficient force to foil the projects of the enemy. The result of this
attack has been, that, after a very obstinate contest, which lasted till
nine o'clock in the evening, we not only checked the enemy, but
even repulsed him.

The Prussian army, which was also attacked yesterday, maintained its principal position; and there is no doubt, but that Napoleon, with very considerable forces, directed an attack upon the
whole line.

Our troops bivouacked upon the field of battle, whither I shall
immediately proceed, in expectation of the probability that Napoleon

will endeavour, this day, to execute the project of yesterday. The Duke of Wellington has concentrated, upon this point, as many troops as he was able to collect.

I experience a lively pleasure in being able to announce to your Majesty, that your troops, and the infantry and artillery in particular, fought with great courage.

Circumstances having prevented my receiving the reports from the different corps concerning their loss, I am unable to acquaint you with it: but I shall have the honour of doing so as soon as possible.

(Signed)   WILLIAM Prince of Orange.

Brussels, June 22, 1815.

After the battle of the 16th, of which I had the honour of giving an account of to your Majesty, on the 17th, at two in the morning, from the head-quarters at Nivelles, the Duke of Wellington keeping his line with the Prussian army, in the morning, made a movement, the result of which was, that the army found itself in position upon the heights in front of Waterloo, where it bivouacked; the enemy's cavalry, which followed the movements of the army, was, in different attacks, repulsed with loss by the British cavalry.

On the 18th, at day break, we discovered the enemy in our front: at ten o'clock he showed a disposition to attack. The army of Bonaparte was composed of the first, second, third, fourth, and sixth corps, the Imperial Guards, and nearly the whole of his cavalry, and a train of artillery, consisting of many hundred pieces of cannon. About eleven o'clock the enemy unmasked a small battery, under the cover of the fire of which, his tirailleurs advanced against our right wing, and, immediately after, his attack was directed against a farm surrounded with copse wood, which was situate a short way in front of this wing, and on the left of the road leading to Nivelles. The enemy made the most furious, but fruitless, attacks to possess himself of this farm. At noon, the cannonade became violent; and before half past twelve, the battle was extended along the whole line. The French repeatedly attacked our two wings; but, as their principal object was to pierce the right of our centre, they employed all their means to accomplish it. Some columns of the enemy's cavalry advanced boldly against us: but, notwithstanding the inconceivable violence with which they renewed their attacks, from three o'clock in the afternoon until the end of the battle, they never succeeded in making our line waver. The enemy was constantly repulsed, as well from the fire of the squares as by the charges of our cavalry: it is impossible to depict to your Majesty the fury with which they fought, especially during the last six hours.

I was unfortunate in not being able to see the end of this glorious and important battle, having received, half an hour before the defeat of the enemy, a ball through my left shoulder, which compelled me to quit the field of battle.

It is with the most lively satisfaction that I am able to inform your Majesty, that your troops, of all arms, have fought with the greatest courage. In the charges of cavalry, the brigade of carabineers attracted particular notice. The division of Lieutenant-General Chassé was not engaged until late; and, as I was not personally able to quit the centre, I had placed it, for the day, under the orders of General

Lord Hill, commanding the second corps of the army. I have
heard that this division, likewise, conducted itself with much bravery,
and that Lieutenant-General Chassé, as also the two commanders of
brigades, very satisfactorily acquitted themselves of their duty.

I cannot, at this moment, make any detail to your Majesty, of
the loss we have sustained, not having received the returns. I am
obliged, nevertheless, with the most profound regret, to state, that it
is considerable.

The Generals of Division have requested me to speak of those who
have particularly distinguished themselves; and I feel it a duty to
name those to your Majesty of whose conduct I was myself an eye-
witness, viz.—

The Lieutenant-Generals Collaert and De Perponcher; the first is
wounded. The brave and experienced officer, Major-General Van
Merlen, died of his wounds upon the field of battle. I take this
opportunity of recommending his widow and children to your Majesty's kind consideration.—— Major-General Trip distinguished
himself as much by his intelligence as his gallantry.——Major-
General Ghigny.——The Commanders of the three regiments of
carabineers, Lieutenant-Colonel Coenegracht, dead of his wounds,
Colonel De Bruyn, and Lieutenant-Colonel Lechleitner.——Lieut.-
Colonel Weslenberg, commanding the battalion of militia, No. 5,
who is a very excellent officer, conducted his battalion very ably, and
behaved extremely well in the battle of the 16th.——Major Hegman,
of the third battalion of Nassau, wounded. Majors Merex and De
Bryas, of the carabineers, No. 2, the last wounded. Major de la
Sarraz, of the artillery. Major-General De Constant Rebecque,
Quarter-Master-General, performed his duty with the greatest credit,
and rendered great services.——I yet have to bear testimony to your
Majesty, of my satisfaction of the conduct of my Adjutants-Major,
Van Limburg Stirum, wounded on the 16th, and on the 18th, Col.
de Caylar, and Major Ampt, had each a horse shot under them; and
Lieutenant-Colonel Cruquenbourg had two.

I have charged my Adjutant, Van Hooft, to transmit this report to
your Majesty. I take the liberty of recommending him to your
favourable consideration.

(Signed)   WILLIAM Prince of Orange.

LOSS OF THE DUTCH.

Officers killed or missing - - - - -	27
Wounded - - - - - - -	115
Rank and file killed or missing - - - -	2058
Wounded - - - - - - -	1936
Total - - - - - - -	4136
Horses killed - - - - - -	1630

MARSHAL BLUCHER'S OFFICIAL REPORT OF THE OPERATIONS OF THE PRUSSIAN ARMY OF THE LOWER RHINE.

It was on the 15th of this month, that Napoleon, after having collected, on the 14th, five corps of his army, and the several corps of the guard, between Maubeuge and Beaumont, commenced hostilities. The points of concentration of the four Prussian corps, were Fleurus, Namur, Ciney, and Hannut; the situation of which made it possible to unite the army, in one of these points, in 24 hours.

On the 15th, Napoleon advanced by Thuin, upon the two banks of the Sambre, against Charleroi. General Ziethen had collected the first corps near Fleurus, and had, on that day, a very warm action with the enemy, who, after having taken Charleroi, directed his march upon Fleurus. General Ziethen maintained himself in his position near that place.

Field Marshal Blucher intending to fight a great battle with the enemy as soon as possible, the three other corps of the Prussian army were consequently directed upon Sombref, a league and a half from Fleurus, where the 2d and 3d corps were to arrive on the 15th, and the 4th corps on the 16th.

Lord Wellington had united his army between Ath and Nivelles, which enabled him to assist Field Marshal Blucher, in case the battle should be fought on the 15th.

JUNE 16.—BATTLE OF LIGNY.

The Prussian army was posted on the heights between Brie and Sombref, and beyond the last place, and occupied with a large force the villages of St. Amand and Ligny, situate in its front. Mean time, only three corps of the army had joined; the fourth, which was stationed between Liege and Hannut, had been delayed in its march by several circumstances, and was not yet come up. Nevertheless, Field Marshal Blucher resolved to give battle; Lord Wellington having already put in motion, to support him, a strong division of his army, as well as his whole reserve, stationed in the environs of Brussels, and the fourth corps of the Prussian army being also on the point of arriving.

The battle began at three o'clock in the afternoon. The enemy brought up above 130,000 men. The Prussian army was 80,000 strong. The village of St. Amand was the first point attacked by the enemy, who carried it, after a vigorous resistance.

He then directed his efforts against Ligny. It is a large village, solidly built, situate on a rivulet of the same name. It was there that a contest began which may be considered as one of the most obstinate recorded in history. Villages have often been taken, and retaken: but here the combat continued for five hours in the villages themselves, and the movements, forwards or backwards, were confined to a very narrow space. On both sides fresh troops continually came up. Each army had, behind the part of the village which it occupied, great masses of infantry, which maintained the combat, and were continually renewed by the reinforcements which they received from their rear, as well as from the heights on the right and left. About two hundred cannon were directed from both sides against the village, which was on fire in several places at once. From time to time the combat extended through the whole line, the enemy having also directed numerous troops against the third corps; however, the main contest was near Ligny. Things seemed to take a favourable turn for the Prussian troops, a part of the village of St. Amand having been retaken by a battalion commanded by the Field Marshal in person; in consequence of which advantage we had regained a height, which had been abandoned after the loss of St. Amand. Nevertheless, the battle continued about Ligny with the same fury. The issue seemed to depend on the arrival of the English troops, or on that of the fourth corps of the Prussian army; in fact, the arrival of this last division would have afforded the Field Marshal the means of making, immediately, with the right wing, an attack, from which great success might be expected: but news arrived that the English division, destined to support us, was violently attacked by a corps of the French army, and that it was with great difficulty it had maintained itself in its position at Quatre Bras. The fourth corps of the army did not appear, so that we were forced to maintain, alone, the contest with an army greatly superior in numbers. The evening was already much advanced, and the combat about Ligny continued with the same fury, and the same equality of success; we invoked, but in vain, the arrival of those succours which were so necessary; the danger became every hour more and more urgent; all the divisions were engaged, or had already been so, and there was not any corps at hand able to support them. Suddenly, a division of the enemy's infantry, which, by favour of the night, had made a circuit round the village without being observed, at the same time that some regiments of cuirassiers had forced the passage on the other side, took, in the rear, the main body of our army, which was posted behind the houses. This surprise, on the part of the enemy, was decisive, especially at the moment when our cavalry, also posted on a height behind the village, was repulsed by the enemy's cavalry in repeated attacks.

Our infantry, posted behind Ligny, though forced to retreat, did not suffer itself to be discouraged, either by being surprised by the enemy in the darkness, a circumstance which exaggerates in the mind of man the dangers to which he finds himself exposed, or, by the idea of seeing itself surrounded on all sides. Formed in masses, it coolly repulsed all the attacks of the cavalry, and retreated in good order upon the heights, whence it continued its retrograde movement upon Tilly. In consequence of the sudden irruption of the enemy's cavalry, several of our cannons, in their precipitate retreat, had taken directions which led them to defiles, in which they necessarily fell into disorder; in this manner, 15 pieces fell into the hands of the enemy. At the distance of a quarter of a league from the field of battle, the army formed again. The enemy did not venture to pursue it. The village of Brie remained in our possession during the night, as well as Sombref, where General Thielman had fought with the third corps, and whence he, at daybreak, slowly began to retreat towards Gembloux, where the fourth corps, under General Bulow, had at length arrived during the night. The first and second corps proceeded in the morning behind the defile of Mount St. Guibert. Our loss in killed and wounded was great; the enemy, however, took from us no prisoners, except a part of our wounded. The battle was lost, but not our honour. Our soldiers had fought with a bravery which equalled every expectation; their fortitude remained unshaken, because every one retained his confidence in his own strength. On this day, Field Marshal Blucher had encountered the greatest dangers. A charge of cavalry, led on by himself, had failed. While that of the enemy was vigorously pursuing, a musket shot struck the Field Marshal's horse: the animal, far from being stopped in his career by this wound, began to gallop more furiously till it dropped down dead. The Field Marshal, stunned by the violent fall, lay entangled under the horse. The enemy's cuirassiers, following up their advantage, advanced: our last horseman had already passed by the Field Marshal, an Adjutant alone remained with him, and had just alighted, resolved to share his fate. The danger was great, but Heaven watched over us. The enemy, pursuing their charge, passed rapidly by the Field Marshal without seeing him: the next moment, a second charge of our cavalry having repulsed them, they again passed by him with the same precipitation, not perceiving him, any more than they had done the first time. Then, but not without difficulty, the Field Marshal was disengaged from under the dead horse, and he immediately mounted a dragoon horse.

On the 17th, in the evening, the Prussian army concentrated itself in the environs of Wavre. Napoleon put himself in motion against Lord Wellington upon the great road leading from Charleroi to Brussels. An English division maintained, on the same day, near Quatre Bras, a very severe contest with the enemy. Lord Wellington had taken a position on the road to Brussels, having his right wing leaning upon Braine-la-Leud, the centre near Mont St. Jean, and the left wing against La Haye Sainte. Lord Wellington wrote to the Field Marshal, that he was resolved to accept the battle in this position, if the Field Marshal would support him with two corps of his army. The Field Marshal promised to come with his whole army; he even proposed, in case Napoleon should not attack, that the Allies themselves, with their whole united force, should attack him the next day. This may serve to show how little the battle of the 16th had disorganized the Prussian army, or weakened its moral strength. Thus ended the day of the 17th.

BATTLE OF THE 18th.

At break of day the Prussian army again began to move. The 4th and 2d corps marched by St. Lambert, where they were to take a position, covered by the forest, near Frichemont, to take the enemy in the rear, when the moment should appear favourable. The first corps was to operate by Ohain, on the right flank of the enemy. The third corps was to follow slowly, in order to afford succour in case of need. The battle began about 10 o'clock in the morning. The English army occupied the heights of Mont St. Jean; that of the French was on the heights before Planchenoit: the former was about 80,000 strong; the enemy had above 130,000. In a short time, the battle became general along the whole line. It seems that Napoleon had the design to throw the left wing upon the centre, and thus to effect the separation of the English army from the Prussian, which he believed to be retreating upon Maestricht. For this purpose, he had placed the greatest part of his reserve in the centre, against his right wing, and upon this point he attacked with fury. The English army fought with a valour which it is impossible to surpass. The repeated charges of the Old Guard were baffled by the intrepidity of the Scottish regiments; and at every charge the French cavalry was overthrown by the English cavalry. But the superiority of the enemy in numbers was too great; Napoleon continually brought for-

ward considerable masses, and, with whatever firmness the
English troops maintained themselves in their position, it
was not possible but that such heroic exertions must have a
limit.

It was half-past four o'clock. The excessive difficulties
of the passage by the defile of St. Lambert, had considerably retarded the march of the Prussian columns, so that
only two brigades of the fourth corps had arrived at the
covered position which was assigned to them. The decisive
moment was come; there was not an instant to be lost.
The Generals did not suffer it to escape. They resolved
immediately to begin the attack with the troops which they
had at hand. General Bulow, therefore, with two brigades
and a corps of cavalry, advanced rapidly upon the rear of
the enemy's right wing The enemy did not lose his presence of mind; he instantly turned his reserve against us,
and a murderous conflict began on that side. The combat
remained long uncertain, while the battle with the English
army still continued with the same violence.

Towards six o'clock in the evening, we received the news
that General Thielman, with the third corps, was attacked
near Wavre by a very considerable corps of the enemy, and
that they were already disputing the possession of the town.
The Field Marshal, however, did not suffer himself to be
disturbed by this news; it was on the spot where he was,
and no where else, that the affair was to be decided. A
conflict continually supported by the same obstinacy, and
kept up by fresh troops, could alone insure the victory, and
if it were obtained here, any reverse sustained near Wavre
was of little consequence. The columns, therefore, continued their movements. It was half an hour past seven,
and the issue of the battle was still uncertain. The whole
of the 4th corps, and a part of the 2d, under General Pirch,
had successively come up. The French troops fought with
desperate fury: however, some uncertainty was perceived
in their movements, and it was observed that some pieces
of cannon were retreating. At this moment, the first columns of the corps of General Ziethen arrived on the points
of attack, near the village of Smonhen, on the enemy's
right flank, and instantly charged. This moment decided
the defeat of the enemy. His right wing was broken in
three places; he abandoned his positions. Our troops
rushed forward at the *pas de charge*, and attacked him on
all sides, while, at the same time, the whole English line
advanced.

Circumstances were extremely favourable to the attack
formed by the Prussian army; the ground rose in an amphitheatre, so that our artillery could freely open its fire
from the summit of a great many heights which rose gra-

dually above each other, and in the intervals of which the troops descended into the plain, formed into brigades, and in the greatest order; while fresh corps continually unfolded themselves, issuing from the forest on the height behind us. The enemy, however, still preserved means to retreat, till the village of Planchenoit, which he had on his rear, and which was defended by the guard, was, after several bloody attacks, carried by storm. From that time the retreat became a rout, which soon spread through the whole French army, and, in its dreadful confusion, hurrying away every thing that attempted to stop it, soon assumed the appearance of the flight of an army of barbarians. It was half-past nine. The Field Marshal assembled all the superior officers, and gave orders to send the last horse and the last man in pursuit of the enemy. The van of the army accelerated its march. The French being pursued without intermission, was absolutely disorganized. The causeway presented the appearance of an immense shipwreck; it was covered with an innumerable quantity of cannon, caissons, carriages, baggage, arms, and wrecks of every kind. Those of the enemy who had attempted to repose for a time, and had not expected to be so quickly pursued, were driven from more than nine bivouacs. In some villages they attempted to maintain themselves; but as soon as they heard the beating of our drums, or the sound of the trumpet, they either fled or threw themselves into the houses, where they were cut down or made prisoners. It was moonlight, which greatly favoured the pursuit, for the whole march was but a continued chace, either in the corn fields or the houses.

At Genappe, the enemy had entrenched himself with cannon, and overturned carriages : at our approach, we suddenly heard in the town a great noise and a motion of carriages; at the entrance we were exposed to a brisk fire of musketry; we replied by some cannon shot, followed by a *hurrah*, and, an instant after, the town was ours. It was here that, among many other equipages, the carriage of Napoleon was taken; he had just left it to mount on horseback, and, in his hurry, had forgotten in it his sword and hat. Thus the affairs continued till break of day. About 40,000 men, in the most complete disorder, the remains of the whole army, have saved themselves, retreating through Charleroi, partly without arms, and carrying with them only 27 pieces of their numerous artillery.

The enemy, in his flight, had passed all his fortresses, the only defence of his frontiers, which are now passed by our armies.

At three o'clock, Napoleon had dispatched, from the field of battle, a courier to Paris, with the news that victory was no longer doubtful: a few hours after, he had no longer any army left. We have not yet any exact account of the enemy's loss; it is enough to know, that two-thirds of the whole were killed, wounded, or prisoners: among the latter are Generals Monton, Duhesme, and Compans. Up to this time about 300 cannon, and above 500 caissons, are in our hands.

Few victories have been so complete; and there is certainly no example that an army, two days after losing a battle, engaged in such an action, and so gloriously maintained it. Honour be to troops capable of so much firmness and valour! In the middle of the position occupied by the French army, and exactly upon the height, is a farm, called *La Belle Alliance.* The march of all the Prussian columns was directed towards this farm, which was visible from every side. It was there that Napoleon was during the battle; it was thence that he gave his orders, that he flattered himself with the hopes of victory; and it was there that his ruin was decided. There, too, it was, that, by a happy chance, Field Marshal Blucher and Lord Wellington met in the dark, and mutually saluted each other as victors.

In commemoration of the alliance which now subsists between the English and Prussian nations, of the union of the two armies, and their reciprocal confidence, the Field Marshal desired, that this battle should bear the name of *La Belle Alliance.*

By the order of Field Marshal Blucher,

General GNEISENAU.

N.B. The Prussians lost 33,120. Editor.

PROCLAMATION,

ADDRESSED BY FIELD MARSHAL PRINCE BLUCHER TO THE ARMY OF THE LOWER RHINE, TO BE READ AT THE HEAD OF EVERY BATTALION.

Brave Officers and Soldiers of the Army of the Lower Rhine—

You have done great things, brave companions in arms. You have fought two battles in three days. The first was unfortunate, and yet your courage was not broken.

You have had to struggle with privations, but you have borne them with fortitude. Immoveable in adverse fortune, after the loss of a bloody battle, you marched with firmness to fight another, relying on the God of battles, and full of confidence in your Commanders, as well as of perseverance in your efforts against presumptuous and perjured enemies, intoxicated with their victory.

It was with these sentiments you marched to support the brave English, who were maintaining the most arduous contest with unparalleled firmness. But the hour which was to decide this great struggle has struck, and has shewn who was to give the law, whether an adventurer, or Governments who are the friends of order. Destiny was still undecided, when you appeared issuing from the forest which concealed you from the enemy, to attack his rear with that coolness, that firmness, that confidence, which characterizes experienced soldiers, resolved to avenge the reverses they had experienced two days before. There, rapid as lightning, you penetrated his already shaken columns. Nothing could stop you in the career of victory. The enemy in his despair turned his artillery upon you; but you poured death into his ranks, and your progress caused in them disorder, dispersion, and, at last, a complete rout. He found himself obliged to abandon to you several hundreds of cannon; and his army is dissolved.

A few days will suffice to annihilate these perjured legions, who were coming to consummate the slavery and the spoliation of the universe.

All great Commanders have regarded it as impossible immediately to renew the combat with a beaten army: you have proved that this opinion is ill founded; you have proved, that resolute warriors may be vanquished, but that their valour is not shaken.

Receive, then, my thanks, incomparable soldiers—objects of all my esteem. You have acquired a great reputation. The annals of Europe will eternize your triumphs. It is on you, immoveable columns of the Prussian monarchy, that the destinies of the King, and his august house, will for ever repose.

Never will Prussia cease to exist, while your sons and your grandsons resemble you.

(Signed)   BLUCHER.

RUSSIAN ACCOUNT.

Copy of a Letter from General Count Pozzo di Borgo to his Excellency Prince Wolkonsky. (Original in this Work.)

I have had the honour of giving your Excellency an account of the advantageous action which the Duke of Wellington had fought on the 4-16 of June, at the place called Les Quatre Bras.* The movement of Prince Blucher having induced his Grace to remove his head-quarters to Waterloo, on the 5-17, he took a position in advance of that place, at the point where the great causeway from Brussels to Namur crosses that which leads to Braine-la-Leud.

Though the ground is open, and without any remarkable feature, it rises almost insensibly upon this point, to the distance of half a league. At the right extremity of the

---

* At present, the Editor has not been able to obtain this Document.

front of this elevation, there is a farm, consisting of a stone house, of a surrounding wall, and of a wood intersected by natural hedges and ditches. It was upon this ground that the Duke resolved to expect the enemy; he placed his batteries, occupied the farm and the garden, and drew up his army along the eminence, protected by its height from the enemy's fire.

The army being composed of different troops, he took the precaution to support each of them by English infantry, all disposed in such a manner as to be able to succour the point threatened.

On the 6 18, towards noon, the French army, commanded by Bonaparte, began the attack; his first efforts were directed against the farm, of which I have made mention; after several attempts, he succeeded, at about half-past one o'clock, in dislodging a part of the troops from it. The Duke hastened to the spot, and ordered two battalions to retake it, and to defend themselves there to the last extremity. His orders were punctually executed.

The enemy then directed two strong columns against our centre. The Duke of Wellington in person, led some battalions of infantry against these columns, and Lord Uxbridge conducted the cavalry. They attacked at the point of the bayonet; the French were overthrown, and their cavalry broken (culbutée). In this charge, one eagle, a standard, and about 1200 prisoners were taken. The victorious troops instantly returned to their positions, and reformed their line.

The attack on the farm did not cease; the enemy penetrated to it, but was never able to establish a footing there.

Bonaparte seeing that he could not obtain any advantage, manœuvred with all his cavalry, and a part of his infantry, against our right, tried to out-flank it with 17,000 cavalry, and began by a most vigorous attack. The Duke made his dispositions in consequence; the cavalry of both armies charged; the squares of infantry remained immoveable, and repulsed every attack: this attempt of the enemy was baffled. At last, about six o'clock, he repeated another attack upon our centre, and succeeded in getting as far as the eminence. The Duke caused him to be attacked, overthrew him, pursued him, and the rout became general.

Prince Blucher had announced, that he would march against the right of the French. On the advance, the two Field Marshals met each other, about half-past eight in the evening.

The army of Lord Wellington did not exceed 50,000 actually engaged. The enemy was far superior, especially in cavalry. The Prince Royal of Orange is wounded in the shoulder; it is hoped that he will recover. Lord Uxbridge has had a thigh fractured. Sir Thomas Picton is killed. The Duke's head-quarters will be at Nivelles this evening. He is gone to Brussels to make up his dispatches *(pour faire son expedition)*.

P.S. Just as I am going to seal my letter, news is brought that 300 cannon are already taken, and also the equipages of Bonaparte, and prisoners innumerable.

AUSTRIAN ACCOUNT.

(Original in this Work.)

Head-quarters of the Allied Sovereigns, Heidelberg, June 21, 1815.

General Baron Vincent having been disabled from writing, in consequence of the Wound he received in the Battle of Waterloo, the Austrian Government gave Publicity to the following Account of the Military Events on the 15th, 16th, 17th, and 18th of June, in the Netherlands, and of the great Victory obtained over Bonaparte and the French Army, by the Duke of Wellington and Prince Blucher.

" On the 12th of June, in the morning, at three o'clock, Napoleon Bonaparte left Paris, and, taking the road by Soissons, Laon, and Avesnes, arrived at Maubeuge on the 13th, in the evening. Soult, as Major, went before him on the 9th, by the way of Lille; as also Jerome Bonaparte, Marshal Mortier, and the guards. All the disposable troops, between the North Sea and the Maese, were collected in five corps d'armée, between the Sambre and the Meuse; 150,000 men, of whom 25,000 were cavalry, with 60 batteries of cannon,* were destined to a grand attack, which was to force Marshal Blucher over the Meuse, and the Duke of Wellington towards Flanders. Even the corps of General Girard, which was stationed about Metz, was made to approach by way of Sedan, in order, in case of need, to serve as a reserve.

" It was, evidently, the internal situation of France that induced Bonaparte to the hazardous step of staking the very flower of his strength against two generals who were fully equal to him. In the first place, it was only on the field of battle that he could become again perfect master of the army, whose creature he was become, and which combined in itself many discordant elements; in the second place, the first, as unimportant, as tumultuous sittings of the new representatives of France, which are before the

---

* Carnot's report to the chamber of representatives, on the 14th of June, officially states, that the French artillery consisted in all of 100 batteries, completely organized, and in the line with the different armies.

public in the journals, showed the internal contradiction and the danger of his position so very clearly, that he could no, longer hesitate to remove his throne from the capital to the camp.

" Thus, it happened, that he opened the campaign just at the moment when the Russian troops had entered into the line of the great force collected upon the Rhine, and when, therefore, no connected system of resistance was possible, except from the centre of France, and when the most fortunate result of his attacks could have no other effect than that of removing him still further from the solution of the problem which was, in fact, before him.

" According to accounts just received from the Netherlands, hostilities began there on the 15th instant. The enemy who had, in the last few days, collected all his forces between the Sambre and the Meuse, and had assembled five corps d'armée, put his columns in motion on the 15th, upon both banks of the Sambre, hoping to surprise the Prussian army in its cantonments, and, by a rapid advance, perhaps, to hinder the different corps from concentrating themselves, and also to prevent the union of the Prussian army under Prince Blucher, with that under the Duke of Wellington. As the two armies were cantoned, with all their troops, at the extreme frontiers of the enemy, their union was not practicable in any point except in the neighbourhood of Brussels. To keep in view this main object, namely, mutual union, and to direct their operations accordingly, was the determination of the two illustrious commanders ; and it was happily attained on the 17th, amidst continual and very bloody battles, by the valour of their troops, and by fresh proofs of their talents. The following, according to the statements of the couriers, who have just arrived, is a summary of these events.

"On the 15th, at half-past five in the morning, the posts of the Prussian first corps, under General Von Ziethen upon both sides of the Sambre, were attacked, and the points of Thuin and Charleroi were taken, after an obstinate resistance from the troops which were stationed there. This General, according to his instructions, retreated fighting, and took a position at Fleurus. Field Marshal Prince Blucher, who had his head-quarters at Namur, assembled at Sombref the second corps, which was lying in the neighbourhood. The Duke of Wellington assembled his troops about Soignies and Braine le Comté. The enemy pushed his posts, this day, to Genappe, in order to interrupt the communication between the two armies. This induced the Duke of Wellington to place his reserve, on the morning of the 16th, at Quatre Bras, in order to approach on his side the Prussian army, and, by thus forcing

c

the enemy to employ a part of his force against the English army, to afford all the aid he could to Prince Blucher. The three corps of the Prussian army collected, on the forenoon of the 16th, had the following position. On the right wing, the village of Brie; before the front, St. Amand; on the left wing, the village of Ligny; the third corps, at Point du Jour.

" On the 16th, in the forenoon, he advanced his columns beyond Charleroi, and soon commenced an attack upon Prince Blucher—against whom he directed his chief force. His strength was estimated at 120,000 foot, and 22,000 cavalry. It consisted of the first, second, third, and fourth corps of the French army, the guards, and the reserves.

" The fourth Prussian corps, which was cantoned in the neighbourhood of Liege, had found it impossible to join the others. The Prussian army was, therefore, far inferior in strength to the enemy. However, it was a considerable mass, and all depended on maintaining the ground with this, in order to give the more remote corps, as well of the Duke of Wellington as of the Prussian army, time to come up. Prince Blucher, intimately persuaded how important this was, resolved to accept the battle, notwithstanding the superiority of the enemy. About three o'clock in the afternoon, large masses of the enemy attacked the village of St. Amand. After a resistance, which cost the enemy very dear, it was taken; recovered again by the Prussian troops, again taken by the enemy; stormed, for the third time, by the Prussians, and, at last, each party remained in possession of one half of it, so that the part called Little St. Amand, and La Haye, remained in the occupation of the Prussian army. It was now five o'clock. The enemy directed his attacks against the village of Ligny, when a combat began that was still more murderous than the former. The village lies on the rivulet Ligny; the enemy had his artillery upon the heights on the further bank; that of the Prussians was planted on the heights upon the hither bank. Amidst alternate attempts to take it from each other, one of the most bloody conflicts, recorded in history, continued here for four hours. Prince Blucher, in person, sword in hand, continually led his troops again to the combat. The battle was, at last, undecided; the village remained here also, half in the possession of each party. Thus the day declined; it was between eight and nine in the evening, when the enemy brought forward his masses of cavalry to attain his object, namely, to cut off the communication of the Prussians with the English army. This induced Field Marshal Blucher to withdraw his army by way of Tilly to Wavre, in order to join the fourth corps of the Prussian army, and to form an immediate junction with the Duke of Wellington.

"The English army had been engaged, on this day, with Marshal Ney and the French cavalry, under General Kellermann; and on that side also the battle had been extremely bloody. The Duke of Wellington had been able to bring up only a part of his troops. However, the enemy had gained no ground, and, at nine o'clock in the morning of the 17th, the Duke was still on the field of battle, and regulated his movement to join with the Prussian army in such a manner, that his army was, on the 18th, at Waterloo.

"The momentary interruption of the communication between the two allied armies, was the cause that the movement of the Prussian army upon Wavre was not known to the Duke till the 17th, in the morning. By this battle of Blucher's, the Duke of Wellington had gained time to collect his army; and, on the 17th, in the forenoon, it stood at Les Quatre Bras. At ten o'clock he put it in motion, and made it take up a position with the right wing, upon Braine la Leud, and the left upon La Haye. The enemy, on his side, followed, the same evening, with large masses, to within a cannon shot of the camp.

"In this position, the Duke was induced not to decline the battle, if Prince Blucher would approach nearer to him. Prince Blucher accepted the proposal, in case the enemy, as it was to be expected, should fall with all his forces on the Duke of Wellington. He resolved, in this case, to march his army, by the way of St. Lambert, into the enemy's flank and rear. Early in the morning of the 18th, the fourth corps marched for this purpose through Wavre. It arrived at half-past eleven, at St. Lambert, and was followed by the second, and then by the first corps.

"As the third corps was on the point of following, it was attacked close to Wavre, by a corps of the enemy, which Bonaparte had detached thither to observe the Prussian army. Prince Blucher left General Thielman with the third corps, to oppose it, and keeping his mind constantly fixed on the grand object, turned all the rest against the mass of the enemy.

"Towards eleven o'clock, the enemy developed from La Belle Alliance, his attacks upon Mont St. Jean,* which was the most important point of Wellington's position, and was occupied by 1000 infantry. A massy wall was raised there as a defence, and two successive violent attacks of the enemy, each with six battalions of infantry, were repulsed. Now Bonaparte advanced his cavalry, and undertook a general attack on the Duke's whole line. This also was repulsed. But the smoke of the cannon and musketry was,

* This is surely a mistake for Hougoumont.

c 2

for a long time, prevented from rising by a heavy tempes-
tuous air, and concealed the approach of the columns of
infantry, which were all directed against the centre.   Fresh
attacks of cavalry were designed to employ the English
infantry, till the French came up, and no infantry less practised, and less cool than the English, could have resisted
such attacks.

" The first French attack, of this description, was repulsed
about two o'clock ; but Bonaparte renewed it five or six
times, till about seven o'clock, with equal courage.   The
English cavalry, of the King's household troops, led on by
Lord Uxbridge, made, about six o'clock, some very brilliant attacks, and cut to pieces two battalions of the old
guard, into whose masses they penetrated.

" About this time, the extraordinary loss of men, and the
necessity of bringing the reserves into the line, made the
situation of the Duke of Wellington critical.   Prince Blucher,
however, had advanced with the fourth corps, over Lasne
and Aguiers, and, about five o'clock, his first cannon-shot
were fired from the heights of Aguiers.   He extended his
left wing towards the Chassée of Genappe, in order to make
his movement quite decisive.   Bonaparte, upon this, threw
some masses of his infantry upon La Haye, Papelotte, and
Frichemont, of which he made himself master ; by which
the armies of Blucher and Wellington were separated.

" Prince Blucher had, however, at an earlier period, directed the first corps from St. Lambert, over Ohain, to
strengthen the Duke's left wing ; and the head of this corps
reached La Haye about seven o'clock, took this village
without much resistance, advanced in masses, and restored
the communication with the fourth corps ; upon which it
advanced, along with it, against La Belle Alliance, in order
to disengage the Duke of Wellington, who was still occupied by a heavy fire of musketry along his whole line, and
had been obliged to withdraw his artillery into the second
position.   When the enemy saw himself taken in the rear,
a flight commenced, which soon became a total rout, when
the two allied armies charged the enemy on all sides.   Field
Marshal Blucher, who was the nearest to Genappe, undertook the pursuit of the enemy, as the two commanders met
at La Belle Alliance about nine in the evening.

" About 11 at night Prince Blucher reached Genappe : the
enemy made a fruitless attempt to maintain himself there ;
he was instantly overthrown. Prince Blucher made his army
march the whole night, in order incessantly to break all the
enemy's masses that were still together : when the courier
came away on the 19th 300 cannon and powder waggons
were already taken, as well as Bonaparte's Field equipage.

" Thus, by the aid of Providence, by the unanimity and

bravery of the two allied armies, and by the talents of their Generals, was obtained one of the greatest and most decisive victories recorded in history.

" The loss of the Allies on these bloody days of the 15th, 16th, 17th, and 18th of June may amount to 30,000 men killed and wounded. Among the superior officers of the English Army killed, were the Duke of Brunswick Oels, Generals Picton, Ponsonby, and Fuller, the Dukes Aids de Camps, the Colonels Gordon and Canning; wounded, the Quarter-Master General of the Army De Lancey, General Sir ——— Barnes, the Prince Royal of the Netherlands, Lord Fitzroy Somerset, the Hereditary Prince of Nassau Weilburg (slightly) and of the Duke of Wellington's Suite, the Austrian General, Baron Vincent, the Russian General, Count Pozzo di Borgo, and almost all the Duke's Aids de Camps.

" The loss of the Prussian Army on the 18th is not mentioned, no reports having been made. On the 15th and 16th there were among the killed, Colonel Von Thieman ; wounded, Generals, Von Holzendorf and Juergass, and of the Suite of Prince Blucher, the English Colonel Harding, and several Aids de Camps. On the 16th the Princes horse fell under him pierced with balls, at the moment of an attack of Cavalry, a part of which rode over him. The contusions thereby occasioned, in the thigh and shoulders, did not however hinder him from leading on his troops in person, in the battle of the 18th.

" On the 19th, the Field Marshal had his head quarters already at Charleroi, and was pursuing the enemy with his accustomed ardour.

" Several French generals and officers came over after the battle, and their number was encreasing every moment.

SPANISH ACCOUNT.

General Miguel Alava, in quality of Minister Plenipotentiary to the King of the Netherlands, from the King of Spain, having shared the dangers of the battle, by the side of the Duke of Wellington, has addressed his court, under the date of the 20th of June, from Brussels, giving an account of the battles of Quatre Bras, and Waterloo.

The following is a Copy of his Dispatch to Don Pedro Cevallos, principal Secretary of State to Ferdinand VII.

(Original in this Work, as a Translation of the whole Gazette.)

Supplement to the Madrid Gazette of Thursday, 13th July, 1815.

Lieutenant-General of the Royal Armies, Don Miguel de Alava, Minister Plenipotentiary of His Majesty in Holland, has addressed to His Excellency Don Pedro Cevallos, First Secretary of State, the following letter:

Most Excellent Sir,

    The short space of time that has intervened between the departure of the last post and the victory of the 18th, has not allowed me to write to your Excellency so diffusely as I could have wished; and although the army is, at this moment, on the point of marching, and I also am going to set out for the Hague to deliver my credentials, which I did not receive till this morning; nevertheless, I will give your Excellency some details respecting this important event, which, possibly, may bring us to the end of the war much sooner than we had any reason to expect.

    I informed your Excellency, under date of the 16th inst. that Bonaparte, marching from Maubeuge and Philippeville, had attacked the Prussian posts on the Sambre, and that, after driving them from Charleroi, he had entered that city on the 15th.

    On the 16th, the Duke of Wellington ordered his army to assemble on the point of Quatre Bras, where the roads cross from Namur to Nivelles, and from Brussels to Charleroi; and he himself proceeded to the same point, at seven in the morning.

    On his arrival, he found the Hereditary Prince of Orange, with a division of his own army, holding the enemy in check, till the other divisions of the army were collected.

    By this time, the British division, under General Picton, had arrived, with which the Duke kept up an unequal contest with more than 30,000 of the enemy, without losing an inch of ground. The British Guards, several regiments of infantry, and the Scottish Brigade, covered themselves with glory on this day; and Lord Wellington told me, on the following day, that he never saw his troops behave better, during the number of years he had commanded them.

    The French Cuirassiers likewise suffered much on their part; for, confiding in their breast-plates, they approached the British squares so near, that they killed officers of the 42d regiment with their swords; but those valiant men, without flinching, kept up so strong a fire, that the whole ground was covered with the Cuirassiers and their horses.

    In the meantime, the troops kept coming up; and the night put an end to the contest in this quarter.

    During this time, Bonaparte was fighting, with the remainder of his forces, against Marshal Blucher, with whom he had commenced a bloody action at five in the afternoon; from which time, till nine in the evening, he was constantly repulsed by the Prussians, with great loss on both sides. But, at that moment, he made his cavalry charge with so much vigour, that they broke the Prussian line of infantry, and introduced disorder and confusion throughout.

    Whether it was that Bonaparte did not perceive this incident, or that he had experienced a great loss; or, what is more probable, that Marshal Blucher had re-established the battle, the fact is, that he derived no advantage whatever from this accident, and that he left him quiet during the whole of the night of the 16th.

    Lord Wellington, who, by the morning of the 17th, had collected the whole of his army in the position of Quatre Bras, was combining his measures to attack the enemy, when he received a dispatch from Marshal Blucher, participating to him the events of the preceding day, together with the incident that had snatched the victory out of his hands; adding, that the loss he had experienced was of such a nature, that he was forced to retreat to Wavre, on our left, where the corps of Bulow would unite with him, and that on the 19th he would be ready for any thing he might wish to undertake.

In consequence of this, Lord Wellington was obliged immediately to retreat, and this he effected in such a manner, that the enemy did not dare to interrupt him in it. He took up a position on Braine le Leud, in front of the great wood of Soignés, as he had previously determined, and placed his head quarters in Waterloo.

I joined the army on that morning, though I had received no orders to that effect, because I believed that I should thus best serve his Majesty, and at the same time fulfil your Excellency's directions; and this determination has afforded me the satisfaction of having been present at the most important battle that has been fought for many centuries, in its consequences, its duration, and the talents of the chiefs who commanded on both sides, and because the peace of the world, and the future security of all Europe, may be said to have depended on its result.

The position occupied by his lordship was very good; but, towards the centre, it had various weak points, which required good troops to guard them, and much science and skill on the part of the general in chief. These qualifications were, however, to be found in abundance in the British troops and their illustrious commander; and, it may be asserted, without offence to any one, that to them both belongs the chief part, or all the glory of this memorable day.

On the right of the position, and a little in advance, was a country-house, the importance of which Lord Wellington quickly perceived, because, without it, the position could not be attacked on that side, and it might therefore be considered as its key.

The Duke confided this important point to three companies of the English Guards, under the command of Lord Saltoun, and laboured, during the night of the 17th, in fortifying it as well as possible, covering its garden, and a wood which served as its park, with Nassau troops, as sharp-shooters.

At half past ten, a movement was observed in the enemy's line, and many officers were seen coming from and going to a particular point, where there was a very considerable corps of infantry, which we afterwards understood to be the Imperial Guard; here was Bonaparte in person, and from this point issued all the orders. In the mean time, the enemy's masses were forming, and every thing announced the approaching combat, which began at half past eleven, the enemy attacking desperately with one of his corps, and, with his usual shouts, the country-house on the right.

The Nassau troops found it necessary to abandon their post; but the enemy met such resistance in the house, that, though they surrounded it on three sides, and attacked it most desperately, they were compelled to desist from their enterprise, leaving a great number of killed and wounded on the spot. Lord Wellington sent fresh English troops, who recovered the wood and garden, and the combat ceased, for the present, on this side.

The enemy then opened a horrible fire of artillery from more than 200 pieces, under cover of which Bonaparte made a general attack, from the centre to the right, with infantry and cavalry, in such numbers, that it required all the skill of his Lordship to post his troops, and all the good qualities of the latter, to resist the attack.

General Picton, who was with his division on the road from Brussels to Charleroi, advanced with the bayonet to receive them; but was unfortunately killed at the moment when the enemy, appalled by the attitude of this division, fired, and then fled.

The English Life Guards then charged with the greatest vigour, and the 49th and 105th French regiments lost their respective eagles in this charge, together with from 2 to 3,000 prisoners. A column of cavalry, at whose head were the Cuirassiers, advanced to charge the Life Guards, and thus save their infantry, but the Guards received them with the greatest valour, and the most sanguinary cavalry fight, perhaps, ever witnessed, was the consequence.

The French Cuirassiers were completely beaten, in spite of their cuirasses, by troops who had nothing of the sort, and lost one of their eagles in this conflict, which was taken by the heavy English cavalry, called the *Royals*.

About this time, accounts came that the Prussian corps of Bulow had arrived at St. Lambert, and that Prince Blucher, with the other, under the command of General Thielman (Ziethen) was advancing, with all haste, to take part in the combat, leaving the other two in Wavre, which had suffered so much in the battle of the 16th, in Fleurus. The arrival of these troops was so much the more necessary, in consequence of the forces of the enemy being more than triple, and our loss having been horrid during an unequal combat, from half past eleven in the morning, till five in the afternoon.

Bonaparte, who did not believe them to be so near, and who reckoned upon destroying Lord Wellington before their arrival, perceived that he had fruitlessly lost more than five hours, and that in the critical position in which he would soon be placed, there remained no other resource but that of desperately attacking the weak part of the English position, and thus, if possible, beat the Duke before his right was turned and attacked by the Prussians.

Henceforward, therefore, the whole was a repetition of attacks by cavalry and infantry, supported by more than 300 pieces of artillery, which unfortunately made horrible ravages in our line, and killed and wounded officers, artillerists, and horses, in the weakest part of the position.

The enemy, aware of this destruction, made a charge with the whole cavalry of his guard, which took some pieces of cannon that could not be withdrawn; but the Duke, who was at this point, charged them with three battalions of English and three of Brunswickers, and compelled them in a moment to abandon the artillery, though we were unable to withdraw them for want of horses; nor did they dare to advance to recover them.

At last, about seven in the evening, Bonaparte made a last effort, and putting himself at the head of his guards, attacked the above point of the English position with such vigour, that he drove back the Brunswickers who occupied part of it; and, for a moment, the victory was undecided, and even more than doubtful.

The Duke, who felt that the moment was most critical, spoke to the Brunswick troops with that ascendancy which every great man possesses, made them return to the charge, and, putting himself at their head, again restored the combat, exposing himself to every kind of personal danger.

Fortunately, at this moment, he perceived the fire of Marshal Blucher, who was attacking the enemy's right with his usual impetuosity; and the moment of decisive attack being come, the Duke put himself at the head of the English Foot-Guards, spoke a few words to them, which were replied to by a general *hurrah*, and his Grace himself leading them on with his hat, they marched at the point of the bayonet, to come to close action with the Imperial Guard. But the latter began a retreat, which was soon converted into flight, and the most complete rout ever witnessed by military men. Entire columns, throwing down their arms and cartouch-boxes, in order to escape the better, abandoned the spot on which they had been formed, where we took possession of 150 pieces of cannon. The rout at Vittoria was not comparable to this, and it only resembles it, inasmuch as on both occasions, they lost all the train of artillery and stores of the army, as well as all the baggage.

The Duke followed the enemy as far as Genappe, where he found the respectable Blucher, and both embraced in the most cordial manner, on the royal road of Charleroi; but finding himself in the same point as the Prussians, and that his army stood in need of rest after so dreadful a struggle, he left to Blucher the charge of following up the enemy, who swore, that he would not leave them a moment of rest. This he is now doing, and yesterday, at noon, he had reached Charleroi, from whence, at night, he intended to proceed on after them.

This is, in substance, what has happened on this memorable day; but the consequences of this event are too visible for me to detain myself in stating them.

Bonaparte, now tottering on his usurped throne, without money and without troops to recruit his armies, has received so mortal a blow, that, according to the report of the prisoners, no other resource is left him, ' than to cut his own throat.'

For this reason, they say, they never saw him expose his person so much, and that he seemed to seek death, in order not to survive a defeat fraught with such fatal consequences to him.

I told your Excellency, under date of the 16th, that his manœuvre appeared to me extremely daring before such generals as Blucher and the Duke: the event has fully justified my prediction. For this reason, I conceive, that his executing it has arisen from nothing else than desperation, at the appearance of the enormous troops about to attack him on all quarters of France, and in order to give one of his customary blows before the Russians and Austrians came up.

His military reputation is lost for ever, and, on this occasion, there is no treason on the part of the Allies, nor bridges blown up before their time, on which to throw the blame: all the shame will fall upon himself.

Numerical superiority, superiority of artillery, all was in his favour; and his having commenced the attack, proves that he had sufficient means to execute it.

In short, this talisman, which, like a charm, had enchanted French military men, has been dashed to pieces on this occasion. Bonaparte has for ever lost his reputation of being invincible; and, henceforward, this reputation will be preserved by an honourable man, who, far from employing this glorious title in disturbing and enslaving Europe, will convert it into an instrument of her felicity, and in procuring for her that peace she so much requires.

The loss of the British is horrid, and of those who were by the side of the Duke, he and myself alone, remained untouched in our persons and horses.

The Duke of Brunswick was killed on the 16th, and the Prince of Orange and his cousin, the Prince of Nassau, aid-de-camp to the Duke of Wellington, received two balls. The Prince of Orange distinguished himself extremely; but, unfortunately, although his wound is not dangerous, it will deprive the army of his important services for some time, and possibly he may lose the use of his left arm.

Lord Uxbridge, general of cavalry, received a wound at the close of the action, which made the amputation of his right leg necessary; an irreparable loss, for it would be difficult to find another chief to lead on the cavalry, with the same courage and skill.

The Duke was unable to refrain from shedding tears, on witnessing the death of so many brave and honourable men, and the loss of so many friends and faithful companions, and nothing but the importance of the triumph can compensate so considerable a loss.

This morning he has proceeded on to Nivelles, and to-morrow he will advance to Mons, from whence he will immediately enter France. The opportunity cannot be better.

I cannot close this dispatch without stating to your Excellency, for the information of his Majesty, that Capt. Don Nicholas de Minuissir, of Doyle's regiment, and of whom I before spoke to your Excellency, as well as of his destination in the army, conducted himself yesterday with the greatest valour and steadiness, having been wounded when the Nassau troops were driven from the garden, he rallied them and made them return to their post. During the action, he had a horse wounded under him, and by his former conduct, as well as by that of this day, he is worthy of receiving from his Majesty a proof of his satisfaction.

This officer is well known in the war-office, as well as to Gen. Don Josef de Zayas, who has duly appreciated his merits.

God preserve your Excellency many years, &c. &c.

(Signed)   MIGUEL de ALAVA.

Brussels, 20th of June, 1815.

To his Excellency, Don Pedro Cevallos, &c. &c.

P. S. The number of prisoners cannot be stated, for they are bringing in great numbers every moment. There are many generals among the prisoners; among whom are the Count de Lobau, aid-de-camp to Bonaparte, and Cambrone, who accompanied him to Elba.

MY LORD,   *Brussels, June* 19th, 1815.

I have to inform your Lordship, in addition to my dispatch of this morning, that we have already got here five thousand prisoners taken in the action of yesterday, and that there are above two thousand more coming in to-morrow: there will probably be many more. Among the prisoners are the Count Lobau, who commanded the 6th corps, and General Cambrone, who commanded a division of the guards. I propose to send the whole to England by Ostend.

I have the honour to be, &c.

Earl Bathurst, &c. WELLINGTON.

ORDER OF THE DAY, June 20, 1815.

" As the army is about to enter the French territory, the troops of the nations which are at present under the command of Field Marshal the Duke of Wellington are desired to recollect that their respective Sovereigns are the Allies of his Majesty the King of France, and that France therefore ought to be treated as a friendly country. It is then required that nothing should be taken either by the Officers or Soldiers, for which payment be not made. The Commissaries of the Army will provide for the wants of the troops in the usual manner, and it is not permitted, either to Officers or Soldiers, to extort contributions. The Commissaries will be authorized, either by the Marshal, or by the Generals who command the troops of the respective nations, in cases where their provisions are not supplied by an English Commissary to make the proper requisitions, for which regular receipts will be given ; and it must be strictly understood, that they will themselves be held responsible for whatever they obtain in the way of requisition, from the inhabitants of France, in the same manner in which they would be esteemed accountable for purchases made for their own Government in the several dominions to which they belong.

(Signed) " J. WATERS, A. A. G."

" I acquaint all Frenchmen, that I enter their country at the head of a victorious army, not as an enemy, the Usurper excepted, who, is the enemy of human nature, and with whom no peace and no truce can be maintained. I pass your boundaries to relieve you from the iron yoke, by which you are oppressed. In consequence of this determination I have given the following orders to my army, and I demand to be informed of any one who shall presume to disobey them. Frenchmen know, that I have a right to require that they should conduct themselves in a manner that will enable me to protect them against those by whom they would be injured. It is therefore necessary, that they should comply with the requisitions that will be made by persons properly authorized, for which a receipt will be given, which they will quietly retain, and avoid all communication or correspondence with the Usurper and his adherents. All those persons who shall absent themselves from their dwellings, after the entrance of this army into France, and all those who shall be found attached to the service of the Usurper, and so absent, shall be considered to be his partizans and public enemies, and their property shall be devoted to the subsistence of the forces.

" Issued at Head-quarters, from Malplaquet,

June 21st, 1815. (Signed) " WELLINGTON."

Extracts of Dispatches received by Earl Bathurst from the Duke of Wellington, 22d and 25th June.

Le Cateau, June 22, 1815.

We have continued in march on the left of the Sambre since I wrote to you. Marshal Blucher crossed that river on the 19th, in pursuit of the enemy, and both armies entered the French territory yesterday; the Prussians by Beaumont,* and the allied army, under my command, by Bavay.—The remains of the French army have retired upon Laon. All accounts agree in stating, that it is in a very wretched state; and that, in addition to its losses in battle, and in prisoners, it is losing vast numbers of men by desertion.—The soldiers quit their regiments in parties, and return to their homes; those of the cavalry and artillery selling their horses to the people of the country.—The third corps, which in my dispatch of the 19th, I informed your Lordship had been detached to observe the Prussian army, remained in the neighbourhood of Wavre till the 20th; it then made good its retreat by Namur and Dinant. This corps is the only one remaining entire.—I am not yet able to transmit your Lordship returns of the killed and wounded in the army in the late actions. It gives me the greatest satisfaction to inform you, that Colonel Delancy is not dead; he is badly wounded, but his recovery is not doubted, and I hope will be early.

Joncourt, June 25, 1815.

Finding that the garrison of Cambray was not very strong, and that the place was not very well supplied with what was wanting for its defence, I sent Lieut.-General Sir Charles Colville there, the day before yesterday, with one brigade of the 4th division, and Sir C. Grant's brigade of cavalry; and, upon his report of the strength of the place, I sent the whole division yesterday morning. I have now the satisfaction of reporting, that Sir Charles Colville took the town by escalade yesterday evening, with trifling loss, and, from the communications which he has since had with the Governor of the citadel, I have every reason to hope that that post will have been surrendered to a Governor sent there by the King of France, to take possession of it, in the course of this day. St. Quentin has been abandoned by the enemy, and is in possession of Marshal Prince Blucher; and the castle of Guise surrendered last night. All accounts concur in stating, that it is impossible for the enemy to collect an army to make head against us. It appears that the French corps which was opposed to the Prussians, on the 13th instant, and had been at Wavre, suffered considerably in its retreat, and lost some of its cannon.

* The fortress of Avesnes, after having been attacked for several hours by the Prussians, surrendered, by capitulation, in the night. It was accelerated by an accident in the explosion of a magazine of 150,000 pounds of powder, destroying nearly the whole town, and 400 persons. EDITOR.

[Transmitted by the Duke of Wellington.]

Gory, June 26, 1815.

My Lord.—Lieut. Colonel Sir N. Campbell (Major of the 54th regiment) having asked my leave to go to head-quarters to request your Grace's permission to return to England, I beg leave to take the opportunity of mentioning, that I feel much obliged to him for his conduct in closing, in the town of Cambray, with the light companies of Major General Johnston's brigade, and in leading one of the columns of attack.

The one which he commanded, escaladed, at the angle formed on our right side, by the Valenciennes gateway, and the curtine of the body of the place.

A second, commanded by Colonel William Douglas, of the 91st regiment, and directed by Lieut. Gilbert, Royal Engineers, took advantage of the reduced height in that part of the escarpe (which, on an average, is, on that side, about fifty-five feet) by placing their ladders on a covered communication from this place, to a large ravelin near the Amiens road *.

The Valenciennes gate was broken open by Sir N. Campbell, and draw-bridges let down in about half an hour, when, on entering the town, I found that the attack made by Col. Mitchell's brigade, on the side of the Paris gate, had also succeeded; the one directed by Captain Sharpe, Royal Engineers, forced the outer gates of the Corre Port in the horn-work, and passed both ditches, by means of the rails of the draw-bridges, which they scrambled over by the side; not being able to force the main gate, they escaladed by the breach (the state of which your Grace had observed) in the morning, and before which, although the ditch was said to have twelve feet water, a footing on dry ground was found, by wading through a narrow part in the angle of the gate, within the rampart. I have every reason to be satisfied with the light infantry of the division, who, by their fire, covered the attacks of the parties, of sixty men each, which preceded the column.

The three brigades of artillery of Lieutenant-Colonel Webber Smith, and Majors Knott and Browne, under the direction of Lieutenant-Colonel Hawker, made particularly good practice, and immediately silenced the fire of the enemy's artillery, except from two guns on each flank of the citadel, which could not be got at, and two field pieces on the ramparts of the town, above the Valenciennes gate, and which played upon the troops as they debouched from the cover they had been posted in. Twenty prisoners

* A third column had been formed, but not found necessary.

were made at the horn work of the Paris gate, and about
one hundred and thirty altogether in the town. Their fire
was very slack, and even that, I foresaw, they were forced
to, by the garrison of the citadel. I left the 23d and 91st
regiments in town, with two guns and a troop of Ensdorff
hussars, and I am much indebted to Sir William Douglas
and Colonel Dalmer, for their assistance in preserving
order. Some depredations were committed, but of no
consequence, when the circumstances we entered by are
considered.

From the division, as well as my personal staff, I received every assistance, in the course of the three days
operations.

I am, &c.

(Signed)   CHARLES COLVILLE.

*An Extract received by Earl Bathurst, addressed to his
Lordship by the Duke of Wellington, dated Orvillé,
June 28, 1815.*

My Lord,

The citadel of Cambray surrendered on the evening
of the 25th instant, and the King of France proceeded
there with his Court and his troops on the 26th. I have
given that fort over entirely to his Majesty.

I attacked Péronne, with the 1st brigade of guards,
under Major-General Maitland, on the 26th, in the afternoon. The troops took the hornwork, which covers the
suburb on the left of the Somme, by storm, with but
small loss; and the town immediately afterwards surrendered, on condition that the garrison should lay down their
arms and be allowed to return to their homes.

The troops upon this occasion behaved remarkably well;
and I have great pleasure in reporting the good conduct of
a battery of artillery of the troops of the Netherlands.

I have placed in garrison there two battalions of the
troops of the King of the Netherlands.

The armies under Marshal Blucher and myself have
continued their operations since I last wrote to your Lordship. The necessity which I was under of halting at Cateau,
to allow the pontoons and certain stores to reach me, and
to take Cambray and Peronne, had placed the Marshal
one march before me; but I conceive there is no danger
in this separation between the two armies.

He has one corps this day at Crespy, with detachments
at Villars Coterets and La Ferté Milon; another at Senlis;
and the fourth corps, under General Bulow, towards Paris;
he will have his advanced guard to-morrow at St. Denis
and Gonasse. The army under my command has this day

its right behind St. Just, and its left behind Taub, where the high road from Compeigne joins the high road from Roye to Paris. The reserve is at Roye.

We shall be upon the Oise to-morrow.

It appears, by all accounts, that the enemy's corps collected at Soissons, and under Marshal Grouchy, have not yet retired upon Paris; and Marshal Blucher's troops are already between them and that city.

Dispatch, addressed to Earl Bathurst, by his Grace the Duke of Wellington, dated Orvillé, June 29, 1815.

MY LORD,

Being aware of the anxiety existing in England to receive the returns of killed and wounded in the late actions, I now send Lists of the Officers, (the whole of the killed and wounded will be found at the end in an alphabetical form) and expect to be able to send, this evening, returns of the non-commissioned officers and soldiers. The account of non-commissioned officers and soldiers, British and Hanoverian, killed, wounded, and missing, is between 12 and 13,000.

Your Lordship will see in the inclosed lists the names of some most valuable officers lost to his Majesty's service. Among them I cannot avoid to mention Colonel Cameron of the 92d, and Colonel Sir H. Ellis of the 23d regiments, to whose conduct I have frequently drawn your Lordship's attention, and who at last fell distinguishing themselves at the head of the brave troops which they commanded.

Notwithstanding the glory of the occasion, it is impossible not to lament such men, both on account of the public, and as friends.

I have the honour to be, &c.

WELLINGTON.

Beaumont, June 20.

All the details which we have hitherto collected concerning the flight of the French are confirmed here. Bonaparte passed through this place yesterday, at one o'clock: he had on a grey surtout and a round hat. He took the road to Avesnes. Disorder increases every moment in the French army, and the want of discipline is at the highest pitch. The soldiers think themselves betrayed, and every one manifests his wish to return to his home.

At Beaumont, all fled at the first alarm. Almost at the gate of the town we found a piece of cannon abandoned, and two more on the road to Solre-le-Chateau. They say that the enemy has set on fire a train of pontoons near the village of Clermont. I hope I shall be able to save some of them.

At, Charleroi, our troops found nine cannon and 100 caissons abandoned. The crowd upon the bridge was so great, that Bonaparte was obliged to place there a company with fixed bayonets, to stop the fugitives. This company was overpowered, and then it was impossible to stop the torrent. An inhabitant of that town counted twenty-nine pieces which passed the bridge, and six were left between Charleroi and Sobre-le-Chateau.

(Signed)   ZIETHEN.

My Lord,   *Louvres, June* 30th.
I have the honour of inclosing to your Lordship the returns of the killed and wounded of the army, on the 16th, 17th, and 18th; lists of Officers, &c.

Brigadier General Hardinge, who was employed by me with the Prussian army, is not included in these returns; but he received a severe wound in the battle of the 16th, and has lost his left hand. He had conducted himself, during the time he was so employed, in such a manner as to obtain the approbation of Marshal Prince Blucher and the officers at the Prussian head quarters, as well as mine, and I greatly regret his misfortune.

I have the honour to be, &c. &c.

Earl Bathurst.   (Signed)   WELLINGTON.

The following is a Copy of the Form of Prayer and Thanksgiving for the late Victory; ordered to be read in all Churches.

" O God, the disposer of all human events, without whose aid the strength of man is weakness, and the counsels of the wisest are as nothing, accept our praise and thanksgiving for the signal victory which thou hast recently vouchsafed to the Allied Armies in Flanders.—Grant, O merciful God, that the result of this mighty battle, terrible in conflict, but glorious beyond example in success, may put an end to the miseries of Europe, and staunch the blood of Nations. Bless, we beseech Thee, the Allied Armies with thy continued favour. Stretch forth thy right hand to help and direct them. Let not the glory of their progress be stained by ambition, nor sullied by revenge; but let Thy Holy Spirit support them in danger, control them in victory, and raise them above all temptation to evil, through Jesus Christ our Lord.; to whom with Thee and the Holy Ghost, be all honour and glory now and for ever. *Amen.*"

PROPOSALS FOR COMMISSIONERS.

Laon, June 25, 1815.

The changes which have taken place in the Government of France, by the abdication of the Emperor Napoleon,

accepted in the name of the French people by their representatives, having removed the obstacles which had hindered, till this day, the opening of a negociation, calculated
to prevent the evils of war, between France and the high
Allied Powers, the undersigned Plenipotentiaries have
received full powers for negociating the conclusion and
signature of all acts which may conduce to stop the effusion
of blood, and re-establish, upon a stable foundation, the
general peace of Europe. They have, therefore, the honour
to give this information to His Highness the General in
Chief, Prince Blucher, and to beg him to enable them
immediately to repair to the head-quarters of the Allied
Sovereigns, and to confer previously with him on the
subject of a general suspension of arms between the French
and the Allied Armies, a suspension which has been already
demanded by the French General commanding the van-
guard of the Army of the North, and virtually agreed upon
between our respective out-posts.

The Plenipotentiaries request His Highness the General
in Chief, Prince Blucher, to accept the assurance of their
high consideration.

> Count HORACE SEBASTIANI.
> Count DE LA FORET.
> LA FAYETTE.
> B. CONSTANT, Councillor of State.
> D'ARGENSON.

ABDICATION OF BONAPARTE.

Head-quarters, at La Villette, June 30, 1815.

MY LORD,—Your hostile movements continue, although,
according to their declarations, the motives of the war
which the Allied Sovereigns make upon us no longer exist,
since the Emperor Napoleon has abdicated.

At the moment when blood is again on the point of
flowing, I receive, from Marshal the Duke of Albufera, a
telegraphic despatch, of which I transmit you a copy.
My Lord, I guarantee this armistice on my honour. All
the reasons you might have had to continue hostilities
are destroyed, because you can have no other instruction
from your government than that which the Austrian Generals had from theirs.

I make the formal demand to your Excellency of ceasing
all hostilities, and that we proceed to form an armistice,
awaiting the decision of Congress. I cannot believe, my
Lord, that my request will remain ineffectual; you will
take upon yourself a great responsibility in the eyes of your
noble fellow-countrymen.

D

No other motive but that of putting an end to the effusion of blood, and the interests of my country, have dictated this letter.

If I present myself on the field of battle, with the idea of your talents, I shall carry the conviction of there combating for the most sacred of causes, that of the defence and independence of my country; and, whatever may be the result, I shall merit your esteem.

Accept, I beg you, my Lord, the assurance of my highest consideration.

The Marshal Prince of ECKMUHL, Minister at War.

The same letter was written by His Excellency to Marshal Blucher.

PROCLAMATION OF THE DUTCHESS D'ANGOULEME.

London, June 26, 1815.

" If the voice of your legitimate King has not yet reached you, I now make you hear it. It is in his name, in virtue of the powers he has confided to me, that I address you.

" Faithful Frenchmen! join the daughter of your Kings; she does not bring you war; she speaks to you only of peace and union. She laments the frightful calamities brought upon you by treason and perjury: she cannot look without terror to those of which war may still render you the victims.

" Frenchmen! in the name of the country, of your families, of all that you hold most dear and sacred upon earth, rise all, join yourselves to me, to secure the triumph of the paternal views of the best of Kings.

" Frenchmen! time is precious, victorious armies advance: let a truly national movement, and the expression of our fidelity to our King, at once put an end to a war, not undertaken from ambition and the love of conquest, but from the necessity of saving France and Europe.

" Frenchmen! raise the standard of fidelity, and you shall see me in the midst of you.

(Signed)   " MARIA THERESA."

ADVANCE OF THE ALLIED ARMIES TO PARIS.

Dispatches of the Duke of Wellington, transmitted to Earl Bathurst by Captain Lord Arthur Hill, dated Gonasse, 2d and 4th inst.

" *Gonasse, July 2d,* 1815.

" The enemy attacked the advanced guard of Marshal Prince Blucher's corps at Villars Coterets, on the 28th, but the main body coming up, they were driven off, with the loss of six pieces of cannon, and about 1000 prisoners. It appears that these troops were on the march from Soissons to Paris, and having been driven off that road by the Prussian troops at Villars Corterets, they got upon that of Meaux. They were attacked again upon this road by General Bulow who took from them five hundred prisoners, and drove them across the Marne. They have, however, got into Paris. The advanced guard of the allied army, under my command, crossed the Oise on the 29th, and the whole on the 30th, and we yesterday took up a position with the right on the height of Rochebourg, and the left upon the Bois de Bondy. Field Marshal Prince Blucher having taken the village of Aubervilliers, or Vertus, on the morning of the 30th of June, moved to his right, and crossed the Seine at St. Germain as I advanced, and he will this day have his right at Plessis Pique, his left at St. Cloud, and the reserve at Versailles. The enemy have fortified the heights of Montmartre and the town of St. Denis strongly, and by means of the little rivers Rouillon and La Vielle Mar, they have inundated the ground on the north side of that town, and water having been introduced into the canal de l'Ourcq, and the bank formed into a parapet and batteries, they have a strong position on the side of Paris. The heights of Belleville are likewise strongly fortified, but I am not aware that any defensive works have been thrown up on the left of the Seine. Having collected in Paris all the troops remaining after the battle of the 18th, and all the depots of the whole army, it is supposed the enemy had there about 40 or 50,000 troops of the line and guards, besides the National Guards, a new levy, called Les Tirailleurs de la Garde, and the Federés. I have great pleasure in informing your Lordship that Quesnoy surrendered to his Royal Highness Prince Frederick of the Netherlands, on the 29th of June. I inclose the copy of his Royal Highness's report on this subject, in which your Lordship will observe with satisfaction the intelligence and spirit with which this young Prince conducted this affair. I likewise understand that Bassaume has surrendered to the officer sent there by the king of France to take possession of that town."

(TRANSLATION.)

Petit Wargnies, June 28th, 1815.

" On the day before yesterday I had the honour of receiving your Grace's letter, dated Joncourt, 26th inst. sent by your aid-de-camp, Captain Cathcart, whom I have requested to inform your Excellency, that Marshal Count Rothallier had arrived this morning to summon the place in the name of Louis XVIII. He entered into a negociation with Lieutenant-General Despreaux, Governor of Quesnoy. The only result, however, produced by this, was a very singular reply from the Governor, from which it appeared to me, that he might

possibly be induced to capitulate, and I determined at once on firing
some shells and shot into the town, and of advancing our Tirailleurs
to the very glacis, to annoy them in every quarter, with a view of
making some impression on the Commandant, and of endeavouring
by that means to excite to revolt the National Guards and inhabitants,
who are said to be well disposed towards us. From the information
collected as to the fortifications, there appeared to me no reasonable
chance of taking it by escalade, the ditches being filled with water,
in addition to the inundation which had been made. At eleven
o'clock at night I ordered five howitzers and six six-pounders to open
on the town, and I continued the fire until three o'clock at day break.
The town was at one time on fire in three places, but the fire was
shortly extinguished. Some men were killed in the town, and several
wounded, which appears to have produced exactly the effects which
I wished. Last night, General Anthing, who commands the Indian
brigade, sent an officer with the proposals to the Commandant, according to the authority which I had given to him, and coupled with
a threat of bombardment and assault.

" Upon this, a negociation was entered into, which ended in the
signing of the following capitulation this night; that is to say, that he
would send an officer, with an aid-de-camp of General Anthing, to
Cambray, to ascertain the fact of the residence of the King of France
in that town, and the abdication of Bonaparte in favour of his son, and
that, thereupon, he would give us this night, at six o'clock, possession
of the Porte des Forets, to be occupied by a company of artillery, and
that, the next morning, the garrison should march out of the town;
the National Guards to lay down their arms and return to their
homes; the Commander, and that part of the garrison who were not
National Guards, were to go and receive the orders of Louis XVIII.
in whose name we shall take possession of the town."

CAPTURE OF PARIS.

My Lord,   *Gonasse, July* 4th, 1815.
Field Marshal Prince Blucher was strongly opposed by
the enemy in taking the position on the left of the Seine,
which I reported in my dispatch of the 2d instant, that he
intended to take up on that day, particularly on the heights
of St. Cloud and Meudon; but the gallantry of the Prussian troops, under General Ziethen, surmounted every obstacle, and they succeeded finally in establishing themselves
on the heights of Meudon, and in the village of Issy. The
French attacked them again in Issy, at three o'clock in the
morning of the 3d, but were repulsed with considerable loss;
and finding that Paris was then open on its vulnerable side,
that a communication was opened between the two Allied
Armies by a bridge which I had established at Argenteuil,
and that a British corps was likewise moving upon the left
of the Seine, towards the Pont de Neuilly, the enemy sent
to desire that the firing might cease on both sides of the
Seine, with a view to the negociation, at the Palace of St.

Cloud, of a Military Convention between the armies, under which the French army should evacuate Paris.

Officers accordingly met on both sides at St. Cloud, and I inclose the copy of the Military Convention which was agreed to last night and which had been ratified by Marshal Prince Blucher and me, and by the Prince d'Echmuhl on the part of the French army. This Convention decides all the military questions at this moment existing here, and touches nothing political. General Lord Hill has marched to take possession of the posts evacuated by agreement this day, and I propose to-morrow to take possession of Montmartre. I send this dispatch by my aid-de-camp, Captain Lord Arthur Hill, by way of Calais. He will be able to inform your Lordship of any further particulars, and I beg leave to recommend him to your favour and protection.

I have, &c.

To Earl Bathurst.   (Signed)   WELLINGTON.

The 3d of July, 1815, the Commissioners named by the Commanders in Chief of the respective armies, that is to say, the Baron Bignon, holding the Portefeuille of Foreign Affairs; the Count Guillemont, Chief of the General Staff of the French army; the Count de Bondy, Prefect of the Department of the Seine, being furnished with the full powers of his Excellency, the Marshal Prince of Echmuhl, Commander in Chief of the French army on one side; and Major-General Baron Muffling, furnished with the full powers of his Highness the Field Marshal-Prince Blucher, Commander in Chief of the Prussian army; and Colonel Hervey, furnished with the full powers of his Excellency the Duke of Wellington, Commander in Chief of the English army on the other side, have agreed to the following Articles:—

Art. I. There shall be a suspension of arms between the Allied armies commanded by his Highness the Prince Blucher, and his Excellency the Duke of Wellington, and the French army under the walls of Paris.

Art. II. The French army shall put itself in march to-morrow, to take up its position behind the Loire. Paris shall be completely evacuated in three days; and the movement behind the Loire shall be effected within eight days.

Art. III. The French army shall take with it all its materiel, field artillery, military chest, horses, and property of regiments, without exception. All persons belonging to the depôts shall be removed, as well as those belonging to the different branches of administration, which belong to the army.

Art. IV. The sick and wounded, and the medical officers whom it may be necessary to leave with them, are placed under the special protection of the Commanders in Chief of the English and Prussian armies.

Art. V. The military and those holding employments, to whom the foregoing article relates, shall be at liberty, immediately after their recovery, to rejoin the corps to which they belong.

Art. VI. The wives and children of all individuals belonging to the

French army, shall be at liberty to remain in Paris. The wives shall be allowed to quit Paris for the purpose of rejoining the army, and to carry with them their property, and that of their husbands.

Art. VII. The officers of the line employed with the Federés, or with the Tirailleurs of the National Guard, may either join the army or return to their homes, or the places of their birth.

Art. VIII. To-morrow, the 4th of July, at mid-day, St. Denis, St. Ouen Clichy, and Neuilly, shall be given up. The day after to-morrow, the 5th, at the same hour, Montmartre shall be given up. The third day, the 6th, all the barriers shall be given up.

Art. IX. The duty of the city of Paris shall continue to be done by the National Guard, and by the corps of the municipal gendarmerie.

Art. X. The Commanders in Chief of the English and Prussian armies engage to respect, and to make those under their command respect, the actual authorities, so long as they shall exist.

Art. XI. Public property, with the exception of that which relates to war, whether it belongs to the Government, or depends upon the Municipal Authority, shall be respected, and the Allied Powers will not interfere in any manner with its administration and management.

Art. XII. Private persons and property shall be equally respected. The inhabitants, and, in general, all individuals who shall be in the capital shall continue to enjoy their rights and liberties without being disturbed or called to account, either as to the situations which they hold, or may have held, or as to their conduct or political opinions.

Art. XIII. The foreign troops shall not interpose any obstacles to the provisioning of the capital, and will protect, on the contrary, the arrival and the free circulation of the articles which are destined for it.

Art. XIV. The present Convention shall be observed, and shall serve to regulate the mutual relations until the conclusion of peace. In case of rupture, it must be denounced in the usual forms, at least ten days before-hand.

Art. XV. If difficulties arise in the execution of any one of the articles of the present Convention, the interpretation of it shall be made in favour of the French army, and of the city of Paris.

Art. XVI. The present Convention is declared common to all the Allied armies, provided it be ratified by the Powers on which these armies are dependent.

Art. XVII. The ratifications shall be exchanged to-morrow, the 4th of July, at six o'clock in the morning, at the bridge of Neuilly.

Art. XVIII. Commissioners shall be named by the respective parties, in order to watch over the execution of the present Convention.

Done and signed at St. Cloud, in triplicate, by the Commissioners above named, the day and year before mentioned.

(Signed)   The Baron BIGNON.
        Count GUILLEMONT.
        Count De BONDY.
        The Baron De MUFFLING.
        F. B. HERVEY, Colonel.

Approved and ratified, the present Suspension of Arms, at Paris, the 3d of July, 1815.

Approved (Signed) Marshal the Prince D'ECHMUHL.

My Lord,   *Paris, July* 8th, 1815.

In consequence of the Convention with the enemy, of which I transmitted your Lordship the copy in my dispatch of the 4th, the troops under my command, and that of Field-Marshal Prince Blucher, occupied the barriers of Paris on the 6th, and entered the city yesterday; which has ever since been perfectly quiet.

The King of France entered Paris this day.

I have the honour to be, &c.

Earl Bathurst, &c.   WELLINGTON.

Immediately after the Arrangement, under which Paris was surrendered, the following was issued:

GENERAL ORDER.

" 1. The Field-Marshal has great satisfaction in announcing to the troops under his command, that he has, in concert with Field-Marshal Prince Blucher, concluded a Military Convention with the Commander in Chief of the French Army, near Paris, by which the enemy is to evacuate St. Denis, St. Ouen, Clichy, and Neuilly, this day at noon; the heights of Montmartre to-morrow at noon; and Paris next day.

" 2. The Field-Marshal congratulates the Army upon this result of their glorious victory. He desires that the troops may employ the leisure of this day and to-morrow, to clean their arms, clothes, and appointments, as it is his intention that they should pass him in review.

" 3. Major-General Sir Manley Power, K. C. B. is appointed to the Staff of this Army.

" (Signed)   J. WATERS, Lt. Col. A. A. G."

Paris, July 9th.

Yesterday the King made his public entry into his capital at three in the afternoon. His Majesty left St. Denis at two o'clock. Numerous detachments from the National Guard of Paris went to meet the King, and to range themselves among the faithful adherents who served to form his Majesty's retinue. No ceremonial had, however, been ordered. The public enthusiasm and brilliant testimonies of general joy alone embellished this family festival. The King's carriage was preceded and followed by his military household. Around it we observed several Marshals, followed by a great number of General Officers, who had always accompanied the King. The inhabitants of Paris and the neighbouring towns covered the road. All, as well as the National Guard, had assumed the white cockade, making the air resound with cries of *Vive le Roi!*

Count Chabrol, Prefect of the Seine, accompanied by the Municipal Body, waited the arrival of the King at the barrier of St. Denis. At four o'clock, the acclamations of an immense multitude announced the approach of a procession, which defiled amidst a thousand times repeated cries of *Vive le Roi!*

AUSTRIAN PROCLAMATION.

" Frenchmen!—Twenty years of trouble and misfortunes had oppressed Europe. One man's insatiable thirst of dominion and conquest, while depopulating and ruining France, had desolated the remotest countries; and the world saw, with astonishment, the disasters of the middle ages, reproduced in an enlightened age.

" All Europe rose. One cry of indignation served to rally all nations.

" It depended on the Allied Powers, in 1814, to exercise upon France a just vengeance, which she had but too much provoked ; but great monarchs united for an only and sacred cause—the re-establishment of peace in Europe—knew how to distinguish between the promoter of so many evils and the people, whom he had made use of to oppress the world.

" The Allied Sovereigns declared, under the walls of Paris, that they could never make either peace or truce with Napoleon Bonaparte. The capital rose against the oppressor of Europe. France, by a spontaneous movement, rallied itself to the principles which were to restore and to guarantee her liberty and peace.

" The Allied Armies entered Paris as friends. So many years of misfortunes, the spoliation of so many countries, the death of millions of brave men, who fell on the field of battle, or victims of the scourges inseparable from war, all was buried in oblivion.

" Bonaparte solemnly abdicated a power which he had exercised but for the misfortunes of the world. Europe had from that time no enemy more to combat.

" Napoleon Bonaparte has re-appeared in France; he has found all Europe in arms against him.

" Frenchmen!—It is for you to decide on peace or war. Europe desires peace with France—it makes war only upon the Usurper of the French Throne. France, by admitting Napoleon Bonaparte, has overthrown the first basis on which its relations with other Powers were built.

" Europe does not wish to encroach on the rights of any nation, but she will never allow France, under a Chief but lately proscribed by herself, again to threaten the repose of her neighbours.

" Europe desires to enjoy the first benefit of peace; it desires to disarm, and it cannot do this as long as Napoleon Bonaparte is on the Throne of France. Europe, in short, desires peace, and because it desires it, will never negociate with him whom it regards as a perpetual obstacle to peace.

" Already, in the plains of Brabant, Heaven has confounded this criminal enterprise. The Allied Armies are going to pass the frontiers of France; they will protect the peaceable citizens—they will combat the soldiers of Bonaparte—they will treat as friends the provinces which shall declare against him—and they will know no other enemies than those who shall support his cause.

" Field Marshal Prince SCHWARTZENBERG.
" *Head-quarters at Heidelberg, June 23, 1815.*"

AUSTRIAN ORDER OF THE DAY.

Carlsrhue, Head-quarters, June 24.

" Soldiers of the Austrian Army of the Rhine!

" Napoleon, whose ambitious plans, and lust of conquest, armed all Europe against him, was conquered by you and your Allies. Returning from the exile into which the generosity of the victors had sent him, he again attacks the repose, the welfare, the peace, the security of all States ; provokes, by his guilty arrogance, the armies of United Europe to combat for the inviolability of their frontiers, the honour of their country, the happiness of their fellow-citizens— these most sacred of all possessions, which this man, to whom nothing is sacred, and who has become the scourge of humanity, has been attacking and endeavouring to destroy for so many years. Thus, brave soldiers of the Austrian army, a new and vast career of glory is opened to you. I know that you will distinguish it by new victories, and that your new deeds in arms will render still more dear to me the proud satisfaction of calling myself your General. It is as honourable to you as agreeable to me, that I have only to recal the remembrance of your ancient exploits to animate you to new ones. The victories of Culm, Leipsic, Brienne, and Paris, are so many illustrious garlands that crown your standards ; continue worthy of your glory by combating, as you did formerly, and by adding fresh laurels to those you have already gained.

" Great things have been already performed ; your brethren in Italy have, with their arms, opened themselves a way into the heart of the enemy's country, and their victorious banners wave in the capital of the kingdom of Naples. Those in Flanders, gained, on the 18th inst. one of the most memorable victories recorded in history. Those victorious armies have their eyes fixed upon you, and summon you to similar exploits. Let the recollection of what you have been on so many a hard-fought day—let the feeling of what you owe to yourselves animate you to become constantly more worthy of your ancient glory, by combatting for your Emperor, your honour, and your country.

" SCHWARTZENBERG, Field Marshal."

BAVARIAN ORDER OF THE DAY.

Soldiers! in three days you have marched from the Rhine, in hopes of contributing to the operations of the allied armies in the Netherlands. These victorious armies have anticipated you. A great and decisive victory crowned their efforts in the battle of the 18th. It is now for us and the allied armies on the Upper Rhine, to annihilate the enemy's corps which oppose us. Soldiers! to-morrow we attack the enemy ; march against him with courage and perseverance. His Royal Highness our Crown Prince is among us ; his Royal Highness his younger brother is with the van-guard. The Crown Prince will be witness to your actions. Honour and protect the property of the peaceable French inhabitants ; it is not upon them that we make war: it is against Napoleon and his adherents that our swords are drawn.

Come on, then, against him and them? Come on, then, for King and Country, for our Allies, and for Germany !

Given at our head-quarters, at Hoinburg, June 22, 1815.
(Signed)   PRINCE WREDE, Field Marshal.

BAVARIAN PROCLAMATION.

Frenchmen! the manner in which we, yesterday, entered your country, may prove to you that we are not the enemies of the peaceable inhabitants I have pardoned even such of your fellow-countrymen as have been taken with arms in their hands, and also might have been deservedly shot as banditti. But, considering that these armed ruffians, who scour the country under the name of free corps, to plunder their fellow-citizens, are a scourge which Bonaparte has brought upon France, which has been already made sufficiently unhappy by the unbounded ambition of this enemy of the repose and happiness of the world. I command,——

I. That every one who belongs to these free corps, or is taken with arms in his hands, without belonging to the troops of the line, and wearing their uniform, shall be brought before a court martial, and shot in twenty-four hours.

II. That every town or commune, in which any of the allies shall be murdered, shall be punished; for the first offence, the town with a contribution of 200.000 francs, and the village one of 50,000. On a repetition of the offence, the town, or village, shall be plundered and burnt.

III. Within twenty-four hours after the entrance of the allied armies, every town, or commune, shall deliver up its arms and military effects at the chief place of the prefecture or subprefecture.

IV. Every town, or commune, in which, twenty-four hours after the entrance of the allied troops, arms or military effects shall be found, shall pay a contribution, the town of 200,000, the village of 50,000 francs. The house of the owner of these arms, shall be plundered and pulled down, and the owner brought before a court-martial, and shot in twenty-four hours. If the owner of the arms should have absconded, his family, or the mayor, or the principal inhabitants, shall be punished in a military manner, as protectors of highwaymen.

Frenchmen! make yourselves easy. Our victorious armies will not disturb the repose of the peaceable citizen. Europe has taken up arms again only to conquer, for itself and for you, the peace and the happiness of which a single usurper threatens to rob it for the second time.

Given at my head-quarters, at Sargemines, 24th June, 1815.

Field Marshal Prince WREDE.

RUSSIAN PROCLAMATION.

" Frenchmen!—Europe, united at the Congress of Vienna, has informed you of your true interests, by the acts of the 13th of March and the 12th of May. It comes in arms to prove to you that it has not spoken in vain. It desires peace ; it has need of it ; it must be confirmed by its amicable relations with you : it can have none, it never can have any, with the man who pretends to govern you. A fatal infatuation may have made the French soldier forget for a moment the laws of honour, and have extorted a perjury from him. An ephemeral power, supported by all kinds of illusion, may have misled some Magistrates into the paths of error. But this power totters, soon it will wholly disappear. The combined army of the North convinced you of it on the day of the 18th of June ; our armies are marching to convince you of it in their turn.

" Frenchmen, it is still time!—Reject the man who, again chaining all your liberties to his car, threatens social order, and brings into your native country all nations in arms. Be restored to yourselves, and all Europe salutes you as friends, and offers you peace. It does more:—From this moment, it considers all Frenchmen, who are not ranged under the standards of Bonaparte, and who do not adhere to his cause, as friends. We have consequently the order to protect them, to leave them the peaceable enjoyment of what they possess, and to support the laudable efforts which they shall make to replace France in the relative situation which the Treaty of Paris had re-established between her and all the European Nations.

" God, justice, the wishes of all nations second us. Frenchmen, come to meet us; our cause is yours; your happiness, your glory, your power, are still necessary to the happiness, the glory, and the power of the nations who are going to combat for you.

(Signed)   " Marshal Count BARCLAY DE TOLLY.
" *Head-quarters, Oppenheim, June 23.*"

THE DUTCH ORDER OF THE DAY.

Brussels, June 27.

" His Majesty, informed by my reports of the glorious victories to which you have contributed, with so much bravery and fidelity, has charged me with the commission equally agreeable and flattering to my heart, to testify to you, my Fellow-citizens, his entire satisfaction with your conduct in the several actions that have taken place. I cannot give you, brave warriors of the Netherlands, a stronger proof of the approbation of our beloved and august Sovereign, than by making you acquainted with the tenor of the letter which his Majesty has addressed to me, and which is conceived in these terms:—"

" *The Hague, June 24.*

" Your reports of the 17th and 22d inst. have given me inexpressible satisfaction.

" As a sovereign and a father I doubly feel the joy which the happy result of so many obstinate combats has generally excited, for I have the certainty, that my troops have had a glorious share in them, and have seen, in the Son of their Prince, a brave example of the most dangerous duties they have to perform.

" I desire that you will acquaint, with my complete satisfaction, all the brave warriors of the Netherlands, who fought under your command at Quatre Bras, and at La Belle Alliance. Tell them, that all their fellow countrymen have their eyes fixed on them with admiration and gratitude, and are proud of the firmness and courage which they have displayed. Let them know, that the blood they have shed has irrevocably effaced the last doubt that might have subsisted on the solidity of this new kingdom, and the union of its inhabitants. Assure them, that they shall always have in me a true friend of their noble profession, and a protector of valour and of all military merit.

" Do you yourself find the reward of your devotion, and an alleviation of your wounds in the honour of being to the brave warriors of the Netherlands, the organ of the sentiments consecrated to them by their King and country.   (Signed)   " WILLIAM."

" Continue then, my countrymen, to walk in the path of honour, your King acknowledges your services, and the country honours you. As for me, I feel my wounds only because they keep me for a time at a distance from you. My most ardent desire is to join you, again to combat the common enemy, and bravely to lavish our blood and our lives for the King and country.

(Signed) " WILLIAM Prince of Orange."

THE SWISS PROCLAMATION.

GENERAL ORDER ADDRESSED TO COL. D'AFFRY, COMMANDANT
OF DIVISION, AT BASLE.

" Switzerland, faithful to its old principles, had declared itself for the defence of its frontiers. A Convention with the Powers armed for the restoration of the repose of Europe consecrated this declaration. On the part of Switzerland no hostile step was taken against multiplied offences. The communications with Switzerland were intercepted without previous notice, and dispositions made for attack. In the mean time, the flower of the French, commanded by Napoleon Bonaparte, was completely routed, on the plains of Flanders, by Wellington and Blucher.

" When Bonaparte had brought to Paris the news of his own defeat, and it was seen that they could no longer shake the torches of war over all Europe, but that the avengers of perjury, and of the rupture of peace, would advance without halting, the authors of those calamities endeavoured to avert their consequences by a stroke of the pen. Bonaparte again renounced that throne, after having, fifteen months before, formally abandoned, for himself and his posterity, that bloody sceptre of iron with which he had so long oppressed Europe. At that moment, his Generals sent heralds to the right bank, and to the centre of our army, to ask a suspension of arms, though no hostilities had yet taken place. While this request, accompanied by a promise that nothing hostile should be undertaken against us, was transmitted to the authorities of the confederation, on the same day, the 28th, in the evening, all at once, against the law of nations, without any reason, the fortress of Huningen bombarded the town of Basle, thus breaking their word of honour, always held sacred by brave soldiers, and attacking the Swiss territory by the mischief they have inflicted on our confederates of Basle.

" Soldiers, arm to punish the authors of injustice. We must watch that no part of our frontiers be violated by an enemy without faith. Call to mind the invasion of 1798; the atrocity of bombarding a town without its being besieged, without notification, and without cause, is a repetition of the same perfidy. We must put it out of the power of such an enemy to injure us; therefore, comrades' prepare to combat for justice and honour, for liberty and country. May God bless the powerful confederation, of which we form a part, and to which the most sacred duty attaches us.

" BACHMANN,
" General in Chief of the Confederation.

" Head-quarters, at Berne, June 29, 1815."

BLUCHER'S FAREWELL TO THE BRAVE BELGIANS.

" Marshal Prince Blucher to the brave Belgians.

" My army being on the point of entering the French territory, we cannot leave you, brave Belgians! without bidding you farewell; and without expressing our lively gratitude for the hospitality which you have shown to our soldiers. We have had an opportunity of appreciating your virtues. You are a brave, a loyal, and a noble people. At the moment when danger seemed to threaten you, we were called to give you aid: we hastened to obey the call, and it was much against our will that we found ourselves compelled, by circumstances, to wait so long for the commencement of the contest, which we should have been glad to see begin sooner. The presence of our troops have been burdensome to your country; but we have paid, with our blood, the debt of gratitude which we owed you, and a paternal government will find means to indemnify such among you as have suffered the most by the quartering of our troops.

" Adieu, brave Belgians! The remembrance of the hospitable reception you have afforded us, as well as the recollection of your virtues, will be eternally engraven on our hearts. May the God of peace protect your fine country! May he remove from it, for a long period, the troubles of war! May you be as happy as you deserve to be! Farewell!

" BLUCHER."

" *Head-quarters, Marbes le Chateau, June 21st, 1815.*"

From the Duke of Wellington, to the Mayor of Brussels.

Paris, August 13th, 1815.

MR. MAYOR,

I take this opportunity to write to you, in order to thank you to request you to make known my gratitude to the inhabitants of Brussels and the environs, for the care and kindness they have shown to the wounded officers and soldiers of the army under my command.* The services which we have had in our power to render the city of Brussels, in saving it from the hands of a cruel enemy, by the efforts

---

* The acts of humanity of the inhabitants of Brussels, if particularized, would occupy many pages. But it ought not to be left unknown, the signal service of the Mayor on this occasion;— he literally and figuratively gave wine and beer when water was required. An inhabitant, of the name of Troyaux, made his whole establishment a complete hospital, finding, without any previous consideration for remuneration, every possible comfort and subsistence for the unfortunate needing his kindnesses. A female, who had realized a little independence by selling lace, lodged and relieved the distresses of a great many. The fair sex, indiscriminately, in high or low circumstances, were animated with the most solicitous attention. The regard of these brave people towards the English, was brotherly and affectionate; and many of the inhabitants went to find our countrymen in the field, and brought them to their homes; and crowds met them on the road with refreshments of every kind. E.

that have been made, and by the bravery of the troops. almost under its very walls, give us reason to hope that the
inhabitants would relieve, as far as lay in their power, those
who had been the victims.   But, I did not expect the tender
care, the kindness, which the inhabitants have displayed
towards us, and I beg you to believe, and to let them know,
that their conduct has made upon us all an impression which
will never be effaced from our memory.

I well know of what value, on such occasions, is the example of the magistrates, and I beg you, Mr. Mayor, to believe, that I duly appreciate that which you have given.

I have the honour to be, Mr. Mayor,
            Your most obedient, and humble Servant,
    (Signed)   WELLINGTON, *Prince of Waterloo.*

TO THE PREFECT OF THE DEPARTMENT OF THE SEINE.

Paris, July 10, 1815.

" Sir,—Your agreeable letter of the 9th, which I have had the honour to receive this morning, has been in the original, as you desired,
to His Highness Prince Blucher, of Wahstadt.

" After the reiterated orders which I have received, for the raising
of the contributions, imposed by this Prince, on the city of Paris, it
is not long in my power to avoid those coercive measures which are
rendered necessary, by the tergiversations employed, to elude my
propositions.   At the receipt of this letter, you and several of the
inhabitants of Paris are placed as hostages under a military guard,
and if we do not receive, this very day, a part of the contribution in
question, you, as well as the other hostages, will be conveyed to the
fortress of Graudenz, in West Prussia.—This measure has been dictated to me by the Commander-in-Chief.   You and your fellow-
citizens cannot tax it with injustice, when I remind you of the over-
tures which I have, several times, made you respecting the demands
of Prince Blucher.—You know that, in 1806, 1807, and 1808,
Prussia, under the administration of M. Daru, not only lost its
prosperity, but was ruined by the enormous mass of requisitions and
exactions to which it was subjected : you know what was done in
1809, 1810, and 1811, to exhaust the kingdom; nor can I dissemble, that in 1812, though then in alliance with France, several
of our Provinces suffered treatment, of which the most cruel enemy
would hardly have been guilty.   It was in 1813, that we shook off
the yoke of tyranny : the victorious arms of the allies delivered France
from a dynasty under which that fine country had groaned for so
many years.

" The inconceivable efforts which Prussia made to support the
great contest, after six years of oppression, signalized by all kinds of
extortion and arbitrary treatment, put it out of our power to make a
suitable provision for the equipment, the pay, and other wants of the
armies again called forth to combat Bonaparte and his adherents.
France, now delivered, cannot refuse its gratitude to the conquerors
of the common enemy, when one reflects on the persevering courage

and patience, in the midst of numberless privations, which they have shown during the most extraordinary efforts; but this gratitude must not consist, as in 1814, in empty words, but in deeds. You pretend that the contribution of 100 millions of francs exceeds the ability of your city.—Ask Count Daru, what Berlin (a city of one quarter of the size of yours) was obliged to furnish? and you will be convinced it greatly exceeds the demands of Prince Blucher from the capital of France.—If we treated your provinces as you did ours, from 1806 to 1812, the contribution to be imposed, according to that standard, might exceed your ability. But far from using reprisals, we have hitherto demanded only the reimbursement of the expenses of the war; for the budgets of our finances have no head for the exorbitant impositions levied in foreign countries, such as were found in the budgets of France, previous to the year 1814. Last year the conquest of Paris ended the war. In this campaign, the same conquest has been the object of our labours; to attain it we have been forced to make promises to the troops—not such promises as the French leader made to his army before the defeats on the Katzbach, near Calne and Dennewitz, which hindered him from performing them, but such as generous conquerors make to modest soldiers, whose welfare they value, and whose courage they know how to appreciate.*

" It is by the contribution that these promises must be fulfilled ; and I cannot conceive, Sir, how it happened, that in these three days that we have been negociating on this subject, you have not got together a sum on account sufficient to show your good will to the Prince, who must not be deceived in his hope of fulfilling his promise to his soldiers, who are used to depend on his word. You, and those who have neglected, or rather prevented, the payment of a sum in part, are the persons to whom Paris must impute the disagreeable consequences of this neglect. I am sorry, Sir, that having a particular esteem for you, l am obliged to make this declaration. I must add, that the measures taken on this occasion are no violation of the Convention of Paris, since they fall only on those who show disobedience or coolness in the execution of our orders. Accept the assurance, &c. (Signed) " RIBBENTHROP."

---

* The Editor begs to add the reported account of the several exactions made by the French during the last twenty years ; viz. In Flanders, Brabant, and Holland, in 1794 and 1795, 14 millions sterling: in Italy, at different times, 17 millions; in Brabant, Flanders, and Holland, since taking possession of them, 48 millions; in the Austrian states, 13 millions; in Prussia, 25 millions (150 millions of dollars); in Hamburgh, Saxony, Westphalia, and Hanover, 23 millions; in Spain and Portugal, before and after the war, 35 millions, together 175 millions sterling, the seventh part of what is now demanded from France. Besides this are to be reckoned the expenses caused by the presence and support of the French troops, the English subsidies, taxes, and loans on account of the war (700 millions) the whole will amount to 958 millions; add to this the above 175 millions, and the whole makes the enormous sum of 1,133, millions sterling, the 45th part of what France has now to pay.

This letter was written in German, which the Prefect not understanding, begged the bearer to translate it for him, which he readily did. The Prefect suffered himself to be arrested, but stopped his journey to Graudenz by making a payment.

June 23.

Thanks of both houses of Parliament were given to the Duke of Wellington, officers, and men; and also to His Royal Highness the Duke of York, Captain General, and Commander-in-Chief of His Majesty's forces, for his effective and unremitted exertions in the discharge of the duties of his high and important situation, during the period of upwards of Twenty years, in the course of which time, the British army has attained a state of discipline and skill before unknown to it, and which exertions, under Providence, have been in a great degree the means of acquiring for this country the high military glory which it enjoys among the nations of Europe.

EXTRACT FROM THE SPEECH OF THE PRINCE REGENT TO PARLIAMENT UPON CLOSING THE SESSIONS.   *July 12th,* 1815.

" Under such circumstances you will have seen with just pride and satisfaction, the splendid success with which it has pleased Divine Providence to bless his Majesty's arms, and those of his Allies.

" Whilst the glorious and ever-memorable victory obtained at Waterloo, by Field Marshals the Duke of Wellington and Prince Blucher, has added fresh lustre to the characters of those great commanders, and has exalted the military reputation of this country beyond all former example, it has, at the same time, produced the most decisive effects on the operations of the war, by delivering from invasion the dominions of the King of the Netherlands, and by placing, in the short space of fifteen days, the city of Paris, and a large part of the kingdom of France, in the military occupation of the Allied Armies."

THE ADDRESS OF THE CITY OF LONDON.

July 5th.   " To his Royal Highness the Prince of Wales, Regent of the United Kingdom of Great Britain and Ireland ;
" The Dutiful and Loyal Address of the Lord Mayor, Aldermen, and Commons of the City of London, in Common Council assembled.
" May it please your Royal Highness,
" We, his Majesty's most dutiful and loyal subjects, the Lord Mayor, Aldermen, and Commons of the City of London, in Common Council assembled, beg leave to approach your Royal Highness with the sincerest affection to your Royal Person, and with the warmest congratulations upon the glorious victory obtained, by the Allied **Army,**

on the eighteenth of June, under the command of Field-Marshal the Duke of Wellington.

" At a period when the tumults of war had subsided, and Peace had begun to shed invaluable blessings over long-contending and hostile nations, it was with indignation and horror we beheld the return of that Person who had been the dreadful Scourge of Europe, from an obscurity, in which the stipulations of a solemn Treaty had bound him to continue.

" We observed with grief, that on his re-appearance, the lawful Sovereign of France was compelled, by a rebellious and faithless sol-diery, to leave his Capital, and to take refuge in the Netherlands.

" We felt assured that the relations of peace and amity which had been so recently entered into by your Royal Highness, in the name of our beloved Sovereign, could not be maintained with this daring Usurper, who had repeatedly manifested, that no Treaty was held sacred by him, longer than suited the purposes of his ambition or re-venge; who had constantly evinced the deepest hatred of the British name and character; and with whom his Majesty's Allies had unani-mously declared the impossibility of making any engagements in the relations of peace and concord.

" Under these difficult circumstances, we beheld, with the highest satisfaction, the wisdom of your Royal Highness, in appointing to the chief command of his Majesty's armies on the Continent, that Illus-trious Hero who had so often led them to conquest and to glory.

" It is with the most heartfelt joy we contemplate the late Victory, as affording another leaf to the page of history, by recording further magnificent deeds to enhance the honour and grandeur of the British Empire; in which will be seen, that a greatly superior force of the veteran armies of France, commanded by a Napoleon Bonaparte, could not withstand the irresistible bravery of British heroes, when guided by a Wellington aided by a Blucher.

" It is with the deepest sorrow we lament the fall of a large portion of these brave defenders of the liberties of Europe; and particularly of an Illustrious Member of your Royal Highness's Family, who had ever evinced the characteristic gallantry of a Prince of the House of Brunswick : but we trust the issue of this great event affords a well-grounded hope, that the power of the Usurper will be destroyed, and the peace of Europe established upon the most solid foundation.

" We shall continue to place our humble reliance on the Divine Goodness, that these results may speedily take place, and that the glory, the peace, and the prosperity of this United Kingdom, under the Government of your Royal Highness, and a long line of succeeding Princes of your Royal Highness's Illustrious House, may endure until the latest period of time.

" We have only further to entreat your Royal Highness, to be as-sured of the continued zeal, loyalty, and affection, of his Majesty's faithful Citizens of London, to support your Royal Highness in bringing this great contest to a speedy and happy termination.

(Signed, by order of the Court,) " HENRY WOODTHORPE."

To which Address, his Royal Highness was pleased to return the following most gracious Answer:—

E

" I receive, with the greatest satisfaction, this loyal and dutiful address.

" By the favour of Divine Providence the first operations of the Allied Armies on the Continent have been attended with the most signal and decisive success; and we may confidently trust, that the high military reputation which this country has acquired by the undaunted valour and consummate discipline of our Troops, and the transcendant genius and heroic example of the great Commander who has constantly led them to Victory, will afford one of the most important securities for the future tranquillity and independence of Europe.

" I deeply lament, with you, the extent of private calamity, occasioned by the loss of many valuable Officers and Men, in the late unexampled contest; and I feel most sensibly the manner in which you have adverted to an Illustrious Member of the House of Brunswick, who closed, on that memorable occasion, a career of honour with a death of glory.

" To the surviving relatives of those who have fallen, it must be a soothing reflection, that they have perished in a just and noble cause, and that the memory of their splendid and inestimable services will be cherished, with admiration and gratitude, to the latest posterity.

" I have a perfect reliance on the stedfast loyalty and public spirit of the Citizens of London, and on your assurances of support in such exertions as may be necessary to bring this most important contest to a speedy and happy termination."

They were all very graciously received, and had the honour to kiss the hand of the Prince Regent.

ABDICATION OF BONAPARTE.

This is one of the consequences that resulted from the brilliant victory of the Duke of Wellington. Never, in the history of the world, did one battle produce an event so important. The fate of Bonaparte and of France has been decided at a blow.

" Paris papers of the 22d and 23d have been received. Bonaparte returned to Paris, from the army, on the 21st. On that day there were very tumultuous debates in the two Houses of Representatives, on the necessity of Bonaparte's abdication. On the 22d, he sent in his abdication in favour of his SON, as NAPOLEON THE SECOND. This abdication was accepted simply without any condition in favour of his Son, and a Provisional Government appointed, consisting of Carnot, Fouche, Caulincourt, Grenier, and another, to treat with the Allied Generals for Peace.

" It was attempted in debate by the Ministers of the Interior, to show that Soult had rallied 60,000 men on the northern frontier; but this was denied by Marshal Ney with warmth, who asserted that 20,000 men was the utmost number that could be mustered, and that the Allies could pass the frontier and be at Paris in six or seven days."

DECLARATION OF BONAPARTE TO THE FRENCH.

Paris, June 23.

" Frenchmen! In commencing a war for maintaining the national independence, I relied on the union of all efforts, of all wills, and the concurrence of all the national authorities. I had reason to hope for success, and I braved all the declarations of the Powers against me.

" Circumstances appear to me changed. I offer myself as a sacrifice to the hatred of the enemies of France.—May they prove sincere in their declarations, and really direct them only against my power! My political life is terminated; and I proclaim my Son, under the title of Napoleon II. Emperor of the French.

" The present Ministers will provisionally form the Council of the Government. The interest which I take in my son, induces me to invite the Chambers to form, without delay, the Regency by a law.

" Unite all for the public safety, in order to remain an independent nation.

(Signed) " NAPOLEON."

" *Malmaison, 25th June,* 1815.
" *Napoleon to the brave Soldiers of the Army before Paris.*

" Soldiers!—While obeying the necessity which removes me from the brave French army, I carry with me the happy certainty that it will justify, by the eminent services which the country expects from it, the praises which our enemies themselves have not been able to refuse it. Soldiers! I shall follow your steps, though absent; I know all the corps, and not one of them will obtain a single advantage over the enemy, but I shall give it credit for the courage it shall have displayed. Both you and me have been calumniated: men, very unfit to appreciate our labours, have seen in the marks of attachment which you have given me, a zeal of which I was the sole object.

" Let your future successes tell them that it was the country above all things which you served by obeying me, and that if I have any share in your affection, I owe it to my ardent love for France, our common mother.

" Soldiers! some efforts more and the coalition is dissolved; Napoleon will recognise you by the blows which you are going to strike.

" Save the honour, the independence of the French. Be to the last the same men that I have known in you for these last twenty years, and you will be invincible.

(Signed) " NAPOLEON."

[" Napoleon reigned 100 days, in which he has spent 600 millions, and lost 150,000 men. France is ravaged by civil war, and the capital besieged by two armies."]

Admiralty Office, July 25, 1815.

Captain Maitland, of the Bellerophon, to J. W. Croker, Esq. dated in Basque Roads, the 14th inst.

For the information of my Lords Commissioners of the Admiralty, I have to acquaint you, that the Count Las Casses and General Allemand this morning came on board his Majesty's ship under my command, with a proposal for me to receive on board Napoleon Bonaparte (who had been secreted at Rochefort) for the purpose of throwing himself on the generosity of His Royal Highness the Prince Regent. —Conceiving myself authorized, by their Lordships' secret order, I have acceded to the proposal, and he is to embark on board this ship to-morrow morning. That no misunderstanding might arise, I have explicitly and clearly explained to the Count Las Casses, that I have no authority whatever for granting terms of any sort; but that all I can do is to convey him and his suite to England, to be received in such manner as His Royal Highness may deem expedient.

Foreign Office, July 21.

From Viscount CASTLEREAGH, *dated Paris, July 17, 1815.*

Since closing my dispatches, of this date, I have received the accompanying communication from this Government.

(TRANSLATION.)

" I have the honour to acquaint your Lordship, that NAPOLEON BONAPARTE, not being able to escape from the English cruisers, or from the guards kept upon the coast, has taken the resolution of going on board the English ship *Bellerophon,* Captain MAITLAND.

" I have the honour to be, &c.

(Signed)   " Le Duc D'OTRANTE.

" To his Excellency Lord Viscount Castlereagh."

Paris, July 17.

Measures had been taken to prevent the escape of Bonaparte. It will be seen, by the following extract of a letter from the Maritime Prefect of Rochefort, to the Minister of the Marine, that the result has been such as there was reason to expect.

" *Rochefort, July 15, ten o'clock at night.*

" To execute the orders of your Excellency, I embarked in my boat, accompanied by Baron Richard, Prefect of Charente-Inferieure. The reports from the roads, of the

14th, had not yet reached me: I was informed by Captain Hilibert, commander of the *Amphytrite* frigate, that Bonaparte had embarked on board the brig *Epervier*, armed as a flag of truce, determined to surrender himself to the English cruizers.

" In fact, at break of day we saw him manœuvre to approach the English ship *Bellerophon*, commanded by Captain Maitland, who, seeing that Bonaparte was coming towards him, mounted a white flag at the mizen-mast. Bonaparte was received on board the English vessel, as also the persons in his suite. The Officer whom I left in observation had informed me of this important news, when General Beker, who arrived a few moments afterwards, confirmed it to me.*

(Signed)   " BONNEFOUX.
" Captain of a vessel, Maritime Prefect."

CESSATION OF HOSTILITIES WITH FRANCE BY SEA.

Paris, July 27th, 1815.

Faithful to the principle of the alliance formed between the Powers of Europe, and only directed against the man who, usurping anew the supreme power in France, made all the evils of war re-appear, his Royal Highness the Prince Regent of England, who has shewn himself so constantly animated by the noble desire of terminating these evils, has been informed that Napoleon Bonaparte had given himself up to the naval force of his Britannic Majesty, has hastened to cause all hostility on the coasts of France immediately to cease. His Excellency Lord Castlereagh has made an official communication of these orders to the Minister of the King, and the following note to that effect has been addressed to Prince Talleyrand :—

Note.—The undersigned, his Britannic Majesty's Principal Secretary of State for Foreign Affairs, has received orders from his Royal Highness the Prince Regent, to inform Prince Talleyrand, for the purpose of its being communicated to his Most Christian Majesty, that as soon as the news was received in England that Bonaparte had been given up to the naval forces of Great Britain, his Royal Highness instantly gave orders to cause all acts of hostility on the coasts of France to cease.—The undersigned communicates with the greatest pleasure to his Highness Prince Talleyrand, a copy of the orders issued on this subject, and embraces this opportunity to renew to him the assurance of his distinguished consideration.

CASTLEREAGH.
Paris, July 24, 1815.

---

* Vide Part I. for an account of Bonaparte, while on board the Bellerophon.

Earl Bathurst to the Lords Commissioners of the Admiralty.

MY LORDS,   *War Department, July* 21, 1815.

Having been this day informed that Napoleon Bonaparte has surrendered to the Honourable Captain Maitland, commanding his Majesty's ship the Bellerophon, his Royal Highness the Prince Regent, eager to seize the opportunity of delivering the ports of France from the restraints which resulted from the state of warfare, in as much as may be compatible with the great object of the alliance of the Sovereigns, the stability of the peace and tranquillity of Europe, has ordered me to let you know, that it is his intention that your Lordships should give orders for the immediate cessation of all acts of hostility against the coast of France, and that his Majesty's ships may allow free navigation to those French ships that sail under the white flag.

I have, &c.   (Signed) BATHURST.

THE MANNER IN WHICH BONAPARTE IS TO BE TREATED.

Letter from Earl Bathurst, Secretary of State, to the Lords of the Admiralty.

MY LORD,   *Downing Street. July* 30*th* 1815.

I wish your Lordships to have the goodness to communicate to Rear Admiral Sir George Cockburn, a Copy of the following Memorial, which is to serve him by way of instruction, to direct his conduct while General Bonaparte remains under his care.   The Prince Regent, in confiding to English Officers a mission of such importance, feels that it is unnecessary to express to them his earnest desire that no greater personal restraint may be employed than what shall be found necessary, faithfully to perform the duties of which the Admiral, as well as the Governor of St. Helena, must never lose sight, namely, the perfectly secure detention of the person of General Bonaparte. , Every thing which, without opposing the grand object, can be granted as an indulgence will, his Royal Highness is convinced, be allowed the General.   The Prince Regent depends further on the well known zeal and resolute character of Sir George Cockburn, that he will not suffer himself to be misled imprudently, to deviate from the performance of his duty.

" BATHURST."

MEMORIAL.

When General Bonaparte leaves the 'Bellerophon' to go on board the 'Northumberland,' it will be the properest moment for Admiral Cockburn to have the effects examined which General Bonaparte may have brought with him.

The Admiral will allow all the baggage, wine, and provisions, which the General may have brought with him, to be taken on board the Northumberland.   Among the baggage, his table service is to be understood as included, unless it be so considerable as to seem rather an article to be converted into money than for real use.

His money, his diamonds, and his saleable effects (consequently bills of exchange also), of whatever kind they may be, must be delivered up. The Admiral will declare to the General that the British Government by no means intends to confiscate his property, but merely to take upon itself the administration of his effects, to hinder him from using them as a means to promote his flight.

The examination shall be made in the presence of a person named by Bonaparte; the inventory of the effects to be retained, shall be signed by this person, as well as by the Rear Admiral, or by the person whom he shall appoint to draw up this inventory.

The interest, or the principal (according as his property is more or less considerable) shall be applied to his support, and in this respect the principal arrangements to be left to him.

For this reason, he can, from time to time, signify his wishes to the Admiral, till the arrival of the new Governor of St. Helena, and afterwards to the latter; and, if no objection is to be made to his proposal, the Admiral or the Governor can give the necessary orders, and the disbursement will be paid by bills on his Majesty's Treasury.

In case of death he can dispose of his property by a last will, and be assured that the contents of his testament shall be faithfully executed.

As an attempt might be made to make a part of his property pass for the property of the persons of his suite, it must be signified, that the property of his attendants is subject to the same regulations.

The disposal of the troops left to guard him must be left to the Governor.

The latter, however, has received a notice, in the case which will be hereafter mentioned, to act according to the desire of the Admiral.

The General must constantly be attended by an Officer appointed by the Admiral, or, if the case occurs, by the Governor. If the General is allowed to go out of the bounds where the sentinels are placed, an orderly man at least must accompany the officer.

When ships arrive, and as long as they are in sight, the General remains confined to the limits where the sentinels are placed. During this time, all communication with the inhabitants is forbidden. His companions in St. Helena are subject during this time to the same rules, and must remain with him. At other times it is left to the judgment of the Admiral or Governor to make the necessary regulations concerning them. It must be signified to the General, that if he makes any attempt to fly, he will then be put under close confinement; and it must be notified to his attendants, that if it should be found that they are plotting to prepare the General's flight, they shall be separated from him, and put under close confinement.

All letters addressed to the General, or to persons in his suite, must be delivered to the Admiral or Governor, who will read them before he suffers them to be delivered to those to whom they are addressed. Letters written by the General or his suite, are subject to the same rule.

No letter that does not come to St. Helena, through the Secretary of State, must be communicated to the General or his attendants, if it is written by a person not living in the island. And their letters, addressed to persons not living in the island, must go under the cover of the Secretary of State.

It will be clearly expressed to the General, that the Governor and Admiral have precise orders to inform his Majesty's Government of all the wishes and representations which the General may desire to address to it; in this respect they need not use any precaution. But the paper on which such request or representation is written, must be communicated to them open, that they may both read it, and when they send it, accompany it with such observations as they may judge necessary.

Till the arrival of the new Governor, the Admiral must be considered as entirely responsible for the person of General Bonaparte, and his Majesty has no doubt of the inclination of the present Governor to concur with the Admiral for that purpose. The Admiral has full power to retain the General on board his ship, or to convey him on board again, when, in his opinion, secure detention of his person cannot be otherwise effected. When the Admiral arrives at St. Helena the Governor will, upon his representation, adopt measures for sending immediately to England, the Cape of Good Hope, or the East Indies, such officers or other persons, in the military corps of St. Helena, as the Admiral, either because they are foreigners, or on account of their character or disposition, shall think it advisable to dismiss the military service in St. Helena.

If there are strangers in the island whose residence in the country shall seem to be with a view of becoming instrumental in the flight of General Bonaparte, he must take measures to remove them. The whole coast of the island, and all ships and boats that visit it, are placed under the *surveillance* of the Admiral. He fixes the place which the boats may visit, and the Governor will send a sufficient guard to the points where the Admiral shall consider this precaution as necessary.

The Admiral will adopt the most vigorous measures to watch over the arrival and departure of every ship, and to prevent all communication with the coast, except such as he shall allow.

Orders will be issued to prevent, after a certain necessary interval, any foreign or mercantile vessel going in future to St. Helena.

If the General should be seized with serious illness, the Admiral and the Governor will each name a physician, who enjoys their confidence, in order to attend the General in common with his own physician; they will give them strict orders to give in, every day, a report on the state of his health.* In case of his death, the Admiral will give orders to convey his body to England.

Given at the War Office, July 30*th,* 1815.

Foreign Office, August 26, 1815.

Lord Bathurst, one of His Majesty's Principal Secretaries of State, has this day notified, by command of His Royal Highness the Prince Regent, to the Ministers of Friendly Powers, resident at this Court, that, in consequence of events which have happened in Europe, it has been deemed expedient, and determined, in conjunction with the Allied Sovereigns, that the Island of St. Helena shall be the place allotted for the future residence of General Napoleon Bonaparte, under such regulations as may be necessary for the perfect security of his person; and, for this purpose, it has been resolved, that all foreign ships and vessels whatever, shall be excluded from all communication with, or approach to, this Island, so long as the said Island shall continue to be the place of residence of the said Napoleon Bonaparte.

---

* By dispatches, which arrived in London, December 4, leaving St. Helena October 23, we learn that Bonaparte landed there on the 17th of that month.

French Movements and previous Arrangements to the Battles of the 15th, 16th, 17th, and 18th of June.

Bonaparte's Portfolio.—Extracts, &c. from Letters, &c. mostly in his own hand-writing, previous to the Battles.

June 11.—Monsieur Count Lavellette,—As I said in my speech this day, that I should depart this night, I wish you would look to it, that no post-horses be taken from the road *by which I* travel: that particular attention be paid to the persons to whom horses are given on the neighbouring roads, and that no courier, or *estaffette*, be sent off.

Other letters, written this day, request Marshal Massena to take the command of the third and fourth divisions, and say, " let Ney come if he wishes to be present at the first battle : he must be at Avesnes by the 13th, where my head quarters will be."

" Acquaint Marshal Suchet, that hostilities will commence on the 16th, and on that day to make himself master of Montmeillan."

June 11.—To the Prince of Eckmuhl (Davoust).—"Look to it, that 240 pieces of naval cannon be placed in battery by the 20th, that I may be without anxiety about the city of Paris."

Speaking of muskets,—" they must be sent quickly, that when we are victorious, I may arm with them the peasants in Belgium, Leige, &c. Give me also a list of Belgian Officers who are here. Send also a Belgian Staff Officer for the suite of the General Staff. These people may become necessary."

June 11.—To the Minister of Marine.—I suppose that you have broken off all communication by sea, and that no person or packet boat dare to pass any more, under any pretence.

June 12.—Set off from Paris and slept at Laon.

June 13.—Slept at Avesnes.

Avesnes, June 13*th*.—To the Major-General.—Give orders for the equipages of the pontoons to repair this evening behind Solre, on the road to Beaumont.

June 13*th*.—To the same.—Since General Vandamme is arrived at Beaumont, I do not think it proper to make him return to Phillippeville, which would fatigue his troops; I prefer letting this General encamp in the first line, a league and a half from Beaumont; I shall review his troops to-morrow. The sixth corps will then be placed a quarter of a league behind. In this case, the army of the Moselle will join to-morrow near Phillippeville; the detachment of Cuirassiers, coming from Alsace, will make this change in the general order.

June 13*th*.—To General Drouet.—Give orders for the division composed of the Chasseurs and Red Lancers to repair this evening in advance of the Solre. Let all the divisions of Chasseurs likewise repair to Solre. All the grenadiers at Avesnes, the grenadiers on horseback, and the dragoons in advance of Avesnes; each corps will have its artillery with it; the reserve artillery in advance of Avesnes.

June 14*th*.—Slept at Beaumont.

June 14*th*.—To Prince Joseph.—Brother,—I remove my headquarters this evening to Beaumont; to-morrow, the 15th, I shall advance to Charleroi, where the Prussian army is, which will occasion a battle, or the retreat of the enemy. The army is fine, and the weather pretty fair; the country perfectly well disposed. I shall write this evening, if the communications are to be made on the 16th, mean time we must prepare. Adieu.

To the Minister at War.—I hope to pass the Sambre to-morrow, the 16th. If the Prussians do not evacuate, we shall have a battle. Suchet must take Montmeillan, and fortify himself there. Recommend that there be 10,000 muskets at Lyons to arm the National Guards. The 300 cannon of the marine must be placed in batteries at Paris; let them be there before the 25th; lastly, let the company of cannoneer —— —— march—let them go *en diligence* to Vincennes, on Thursday. Do not be too prodigal of muskets to the fédérés; we are in great want of them every where, I direct —————— from Maubeuge to Paris—[The blanks are for two words that we cannot decypher. The rest of the letter is quite unintelligible, except a few words; we see that mention is made of the Rhone, of the Saone, of Rapp, who is to defend Alsace to the utmost; of Befort, of Marne, &c. His imperial Majesty seems very uneasy about all this: he has much business on his hands at this moment, and never wrote with more precipitation.]

"   GENERAL ORDER.   *Avesnes, June* 14, 1815.

"   Soldiers!—This day is the anniversary of Marengo and of Friedland, which twice decided the destiny of Europe. Then, as after Austerlitz, as after Wagram, we were too generous! We believed in the protestations and in the oaths of Princes whom we left on the throne! Now, however, coalesced among themselves, they would destroy the independence and the most sacred rights of France. They have commenced the most unjust of aggressions. Let us march, then, to meet them. Are they and we no longer the same men?

"   Soldiers, at Jena, against these same Prussians, now so arrogant, you were one against three, and at Montmirail one against six!

"   Let those among you who have been prisoners of the English, detail to you the hulks, and the frightful miseries which they suffered!

"   The Saxons, the Belgians, the Hanoverians, the soldiers of the Confederation of the Rhine, lament that they are compelled to lend their arms to the cause of Princes, the enemies of justice and of the rights of all nations; they know that this coalition is insatiable! After having devoured twelve millions of Poles, twelve millions of Italians, one million of Saxons, six millions of Belgians, it must devour the states of the second rank of Germany.

"   The madmen! a moment of prosperity blinds them. The oppression and humiliation of the French people are beyond their power. If they enter France, they will there find their tomb.

"   Soldiers! we have forced marches to make, battles to fight, dangers to encounter; but, with steadiness, victory will be ours—the rights, the honour, the happiness of the country will be re-conquered!

"   To every Frenchman who has a heart, the moment is arrived to conquer or perish.   (Signed)   NAPOLEON.

(A true copy.) " The Marshal Duke of DALMATIA, Major-gen."

Beaumont, June 15th *three in the morning.* .—To Prince Joseph.— Brother,—The enemy being in motion to attack us, I march to meet him: hostilities will then begin to-day. Thus I desire that the communications which have been prepared may be made.

Your affectionate Brother.

Charleroi, June 16th, 1815.—To the Minister at War.—My
Cousin,—Send me all the Generals I have demanded, and particularly
General Mouton Duvernet; send me also General Lepic of the
guard; he understands the use of the sabre, (*c'est un bon sabreur*) and
will do well in the grenadiers.

June 16th.—To Prince Joseph.—Brother,—The bulletin will inform you what is passed. I advance my head quarters to Sombref;
we are all in motion. I much regret the loss of General Letort. The
loss yesterday was inconsiderable, and fell chiefly on the four
squadrons of the guard on duty. The confiscation of the property of
the traitors, who hold meetings at Ghent, is necessary. Your affectionate Brother.

FRENCH OFFICIAL* DETAIL OF THE BATTLES WITH THE PRUSSIANS AND ENGLISH, WITH NEY'S OBSERVATIONS.

POSITION OF THE FRENCH ARMY.

On the 14th the army was placed in the following order:
The Imperial Head-quarters at Beaumont.

The first corps, commanded by General Count D'Erlon,
was at Solre-sur-Sambre.

The second corps, commanded by General Reille, was
at Ham-sur-Heure.

The third corps, commanded by General Vandamme, was
on the right of Beaumont.

The fourth corps, commanded by General Girard, was
arriving at Philippeville.

On the 15th, at three in the morning, General Reille
attacked the enemy, and advanced upon Marchiennes-au-
Pont. He had several engagements, in which his cavalry
charged a Prussian battalion, and made 300 prisoners.

At one o'clock in the morning, the Emperor was at
Jamignan-sur-Heure.

General D'Aumont's division of light cavalry sabred two
Prussian battalions, and made 400 prisoners.

General Pajol entered Charleroi at noon. The sappers
and the marines of the guard were with the van to repair
the bridges. They penetrated the first into the town as
sharp-shooters.

General Clari, with the first regiment of hussars, advanced
upon Gosselies, on the road to Brussels, and General Pajol
upon Gilly, on the road to Namur.

At three in the afternoon, General Vandamme, with his
corps, debouched upon Gilly.

Marshal Grouchy arrived with the cavalry of General
Excelmans.

The enemy occupied the left of the position of Fleurus,

* Vide further particulars in the French Officers' Account, Part I.

At five o'clock in the afternoon, the Emperor ordered the attack. The position was turned and carried. The four squadrons, on service, of the guard, commanded by General Letort, broke three squares. The 26th, 27th, and 28th Prussian regiments were put to the rout. Our squadrons sabred 4 or 500 men, and made 150 prisoners.

During this time General Reille passed the Sambre, at Marchiennes-au-Pont, to advance upon Gosselies, with the divisions of Prince Jerome and General Bachelu, attacked the enemy, took from him 250 prisoners, and pursued him on the road to Brussels.

Thus we became masters of the whole position of Fleurus.

At eight in the evening, the Emperor returned to his head-quarters at Charleroi. This day cost the enemy five pieces of cannon, and 2000 men, of whom 1000 are prisoners. Our loss is 10 killed and 80 wounded, chiefly of the squadrons of service which made the charges, and of the three squadrons of the 20th regiment of dragoons, who also charged a square with the greatest intrepidity. Our loss, though trifling as to number, is sensibly felt by the Emperor, on account of the severe wound received by General Letort, his Aid-de-Camp, while charging at the head of the squadrons of service. This is an officer of the most distinguished merit; he is wounded by a ball in the stomach, and the surgeon is apprehensive that his wound will prove mortal.

We have found some magazines at Charleroi. The joy of the Belgians is not to be described. There are villages, where, on the sight of their deliverers, they made dances; and every where it is a transport which comes from the heart.

The Emperor has given the command of the left to the Prince of Moskwa, who had his head-quarters, this evening, at Quatre Chemiers (Quatre Bras), on the road to Brussels.

The Duke of Treviso, to whom the Emperor had given the command of the young guard, has remained at Beaumont, being confined to his bed by a sciatica.

The fourth corps, commanded by General Girard, arrived this evening at Châtel.

General Girard reports, that Lieutenant-General Beaumont, Colonel Clouet, and Captain Villontreys, of the cavalry, have gone over to the enemy. A Lieutenant of the 11th Chasseurs, has also gone over to the enemy. The Major-General has ordered the sentence of the law to be pronounced against these deserters.

Nothing can paint the good spirit and the ardour of the army. It considers, as a happy event, the desertion of this small number of traitors who thus throw off the mask.

BATTLE OF LIGNY-UNDER-FLEURUS.

Paris, June 21.

On the morning of the 16th the army occupied the following position :—

The left wing, commanded by the Marshal Duke of Elchingen, and consisting of the 1st and 2d corps of infantry, and the 2d of cavalry, occupied the positions of Frasne.

The right wing, commanded by Marshal Grouchy, and composed of the 3d and 4th corps of infantry, and the 3d corps of cavalry, occupied the heights in rear of Fleurus.

The Emperor's head-quarters were at Charleroi, where were the Imperial Guard and the 6th corps.

The left wing had orders to march upon Quatre Bras, and the right upon Sombref. The Emperor advanced to Fleurus with his reserve.

The columns of Marshal Grouchy being in march, perceived, after having passed Fleurus, the enemy's army, commanded by Field Marshal Blucher, occupying with its left the heights of the mill of Bussy, the village of Sombref, and extending its cavalry a great way forward on the road to Namur; its right was at St. Amand, and occupied that large village in great force, having before it a ravine which formed its position.

The Emperor reconnoitred the strength and the positions of the enemy, and resolved to attack immediately. It became necessary to change front, the right in advance, and pivoting upon Fleurus.

General Vandamme marched upon St. Amand, General Girard upon Ligny, and Marshal Grouchy upon Sombref. The 4th division of the 2d corps, commanded by General Girard, marched in reserve behind the corps of General Vandamme. The guard was drawn up on the heights of Fleurus, as well as the cuirassiers of General Milhaud.

At three in the afternoon, these dispositions were finished. The division of General Lefol, forming part of the corps of General Vandamme, was first engaged, and made itself master of St. Amand, whence it drove out the enemy at the point of the bayonet. It kept its ground during the whole of the engagement, at the burial-ground and steeple of St. Amand; but that village, which is very extensive, was the theatre of various combats during the evening; the whole corps of General Vandamme was there engaged, and the enemy there fought in considerable force.

General Girard placed as a reserve to the corps of General Vandamme, turned the village by its right, and fought there with its accustomed valour. The respective forces were supported on both sides by about 50 pieces of cannon each.

On the right, General Girard came into action with the 4th corps, at the village of Ligny, which was taken and retaken several times.

Marshal Grouchy, on the extreme right, and General Pajol fought at the village of Sombref. The enemy showed from 80 to 90,000 men, and a great number of cannon.

At seven o'clock we were masters of all the villages situate on the bank of the ravine, which covered the enemy's position ; but he still occupied, with all his masses, the heights of the mill of Bussy.

The Emperor returned with his guard to the village of Ligny ; General Girard directed General Pecheux to debouch with what remained of the reserve, almost all the troops having been engaged in that village.

Eight battalions of the guard debouched with fixed bayonets, and behind them, four squadrons of the guards, the Cuirassiers of General Delort, those of General Milhaud, and the grenadiers of the horse guards. The old guard attacked with the bayonet the enemy's columns, which were on the heights of Bussy, and in an instant covered the field of battle with dead. The squadron of the guard attacked and broke a square, and the Cuirassiers repulsed the enemy in all directions. At half past nine o'clock we had forty pieces of cannon, several carriages, colours, and prisoners, and the enemy sought safety in a precipitate retreat. At ten o'clock the battle was finished, and we found ourselves masters of the field of battle.

General Lutzow, a partisan, was taken prisoner. The prisoners assure us, that Field Marshal Blucher was wounded. The flower of the Prussian army was destroyed in this battle. Its loss could not be less than 15,000 men. Our's was 3,000 killed and wounded.

On the left, Marshal Ney had marched on Quatre Bras with a division, which cut in pieces an English division which was stationed there; but being attacked by the Prince of Orange with 25,000 men, partly English, partly Hanoverians in the pay of England, he retired upon his position at Frasne. There a multiplicity of combats took place; the enemy obstinately endeavoured to force it, but in vain. The Duke of Elchingen waited for the 1st corps, which did not arrive till night; he confined himself to maintaining his position. In a square attacked by the 8th regiment of Cuirassiers, the colours of the 69th regiment of English infantry fell into our hands. The Duke of Brunswick was killed.— The Prince of Orange has been wounded. We are assured that the enemy had many personages and Generals of note killed or wounded; we estimate the loss of the English at from 4 to 5,000 men; our's on this side was very considerable, it amounts to 4,200 killed or wounded. The combat ended with the approach of night. Lord Wellington then evacuated Quatre Bras, and proceeded to Genappe.

In the morning of the 17th, the Emperor repaired to Quatre Bras, whence he marched to attack the English army: he drove it to the entrance of the forest of Soignes with the left wing and the reserve. The right wing advanced by Sombref, in pursuit of Field Marshal Blucher, who was going towards Wavre, where he appeared to wish to take a position.

At ten o'clock in the evening, the English army occupied Mount St. Jean with its centre, and was in position before the forest of Soignes: it would have required three hours to attack it; we were therefore obliged to postpone it till the next day.

The head quarters of the Emperor were established at the farm of Oaillon, near Planchenoit. The rain fell in torrents. Thus, on the 16th, the left wing, the right, and the reserve, were equally engaged, at a distance of about two leagues.

BATTLE OF MOUNT ST. JEAN.

At nine in the morning, the rain having somewhat abated, the 1st corps put itself in motion, and placed itself with the left, on the road to Brussels, and opposite the village of Mount St. Jean, which appeared the centre of the enemy's position. The 2d corps leaned its right upon the road to Brussels, and its left upon a small wood, within cannon shot of the English army. The Cuirassiers were in reserve behind, and the guards in reserve upon the heights. The 6th corps, with the cavalry of General D'Aumont, under the order of Count Lobau, was destined to proceed in rear of our right to oppose a Prussian corps, which appeared to have escaped Marshal Grouchy, and to intend to fall upon our right flank, an intention which had been made known to us by our reports, and by the letter of a Prussian general, inclosing an order of battle, and which was taken by our light troops.

The troops were full of ardour. We estimated the force of the English army at 80,000 men. We supposed that the Prussian corps, which might be in line towards the right, might be 15,000 men. The enemy's force, then, was upwards of 90,000 men, our's less numerous.

At noon, all the preparations being terminated, Prince Jerome, commanding a division of the second corps, and destined to form the extreme left of it, advanced upon the wood of which the enemy occupied a part. The cannonade began. The enemy supported, with 30 pieces of cannon, the troops he had sent to keep the wood. We made also on our side dispositions of artillery. At one o'clock, Prince Jerome was master of all the wood, and the whole English army fell back behind a curtain. Count d'Erlon then attacked the village of Mount St. Jean, and supported his attack with 80 pieces of cannon, which must have occasioned great loss to the English army. All the efforts were made towards the ridge. A brigade of the 1st division of Count d'Erlon took the village of Mount St. Jean; a second brigade was charged by a corps of English cavalry, which occasioned it much loss. At the same moment, a division of English cavalry charged the battery of Count d'Erlon by its right, and disorganised several pieces; but the cuirassiers of General Milhaud charged that division, three regiments of which were broken and cut up.

It was three in the afternoon. The Emperor made the guard advance to place it in the plain upon the ground which the first corps had occupied at the outset of the battle; his corps being already in advance. The Prussian division, whose movement had been foreseen, then engaged with the light troops of Count Lobau, spreading its fire upon our whole right flank. It was expedient, before undertaking any thing elsewhere, to wait for the event of this attack. Hence, all the means in reserve were ready to succour Count Lobau, and overwhelm the Prussian corps when it should be advanced.

This done, the Emperor had the design of leading an attack upon the village of Mount St. Jean, from which we expected decisive success; but, by a movement of impatience so frequent in our military annals, and, which has often been so fatal to us, the cavalry of reserve having perceived a retrograde movement made by the English to shelter themselves from our batteries, from which they suffered so much, crowned the heights of Mount St. Jean, and charged the infantry. This movement, which, made in time, and supported by the reserves, must have decided the day, made in an isolated manner, and before affairs on the right were terminated, became fatal.

Having no means of countermanding it, the enemy showing many masses of cavalry and infantry, and our two divisions of Cuirassiers being engaged, all our cavalry ran at the same moment to support their comrades. There, for three hours, numerous charges were made, which enabled us to penetrate several squares, and to take six standards of the light infantry, an advantage out of proportion with the loss which our cavalry experienced by the grape shot and musket-firing. It was impossible to dispose of our reserves of infantry until we had repulsed the flank attack of the Prussian corps. This attack always prolonged itself perpendicularly upon our right flank. The Emperor sent thither General Duhesme with the young guard, and several batteries of reserve. The enemy was kept in check, repulsed, and fell back—he had exhausted his forces, and we had nothing more to fear. It was this moment that was indicated for an attack upon the centre of the enemy. As the Cuirassiers suffered by the grape-shot, we sent four battalions of the middle guard to protect the Cuirassiers, keep the position, and, if possible, disengage and draw back into the plain a part of our cavalry.

Two other battalions were sent to keep themselves *en potence* upon the extreme left of the division, which had manœuvred upon our flanks, in order not to have any uneasiness on that side—the rest was disposed in reserve, part to occupy the *potence* in rear of Mount St. Jean, part upon the ridge in rear of the field of battle, which formed our position of retreat.

In this state of affairs, the battle was gained; we occupied all the positions, which the enemy occupied at the outset of the battle: our cavalry having been too soon and ill employed, we could no longer hope for decisive success; but Marshal Grouchy having learned the movement of the Prussian corps, marched upon the rear of that corps, which insured us a signal success for next day. After eight hours' fire and charges of infantry and cavalry, all the army saw with joy the battle gained, and the field of battle in our power.

At half-after eight o'clock, the four battalions of the middle guard, who had been sent to the ridge on the other side of Mount St. Jean, in order to support the Cuirassiers, being greatly annoyed by the grape shot, endeavoured to carry the batteries with the bayonet. At the end of the day, a charge directed against their flank, by several English squadrons, put them in disorder. The fugitives recrossed the ravine. Several regiments, near at hand, seeing some troops belonging to the guard in confusion, believed it was the old guard, and in consequence were thrown into disorder. Cries of *all is lost, the guard is driven back,* were heard on every side. The soldiers pretend even that on many points illdisposed persons cried out, *sauve qui peut.* However this may be, a complete panic at once spread itself throughout the whole field of battle, and they threw themselves in the greatest disorder on the line of communication; soldiers, cannoneers, caissons, all pressed to this point; the old guard, which was in reserve, was infected, and was itself hurried along.

In an instant, the whole army was nothing but a mass of confusion; all the soldiers, of all arms, were mixed *pêle-mêle,* and it was utterly impossible to rally a single corps. The enemy, who perceived this astonishing confusion, immediately attacked with their cavalry, and increased the disorder, and such was the confusion, owing to night coming on, that it was impossible to rally the troops, and point out to them their error. Thus a battle terminated, a day of false manœuvres rectified, the greatest success insured for the next day,—all was lost by a moment of panic terror. Even the squadrons of *service*, drawn up by the side of the Emperor, were overthrown and disorganized by these tumultuous waves, and there was then nothing else to be done but to follow the torrent. The parks of reserve, the baggage which had not repassed the Sambre, in short every thing that was on the field of battle, remained in the power of the enemy. It was impossible to wait for the troops on our right; every one knows what the bravest army in the world is when thus mixed and thrown into confusion, and when its organization no longer exists.

The Emperor crossed the Sambre at Charleroi, at five o'clock in the morning of the 19th. Phillippeville and Avesnes have been given as the points of re-union. Prince Jerome, General Morand, and other generals have there already rallied a part of the army. Marshal Grouchy, with the corps on the right, is moving on the Lower Sambre.

The loss of the enemy must have been very great, if we may judge from the number of standards we have taken from them, and from the retrograde movements which he made;—our's cannot be calculated till after the troops shall have been collected. Before the disorder broke out, we had already experienced a very considerable loss, particularly in our cavalry, so fatally, though so bravely engaged. Notwithstanding these losses, this brave cavalry constantly kept the position it had taken from the English; and only abandoned it when the tumult and disorder of the field of battle forced it. In the midst of the night, and the obstacles which encumbered their route, it could not preserve its own organization.

The artillery has, as usual, covered itself with glory. The carriages belonging to the head-quarters remained in their ordinary position: no retrograde movement being judged necessary. In the course of the night, they fell into the enemy's hands.

Such has been the issue of the battle of Mount St. Jean, glorious for the French armies, and yet so fatal.

THE PRINCE OF MOSKWA (MARSHAL NEY) TO HIS EXCELLENCY THE DUKE OF OTRANTO.

M. LE DUC,—The most false and defamatory reports have been spreading for some days over the public mind, upon the conduct which I have pursued during this short and unfortunate campaign. The journals have reported those odious calumnies, and appear to lend them credit. After having fought for twenty-five years for my country, after having shed my blood for its glory and independence, an attempt is made to accuse me of treason; an attempt is made to mark me out to the people, and the army itself, as the author of the disaster it has just experienced.

Forced to break silence, while it is always painful to speak of oneself, and above all, to answer calumnies, I address myself to you, Sir, as the President of the Provisional Government, for the purpose of laying before you a faithful statement of the events I have witnessed. On the 11th of June, I received an order from the Minister of War to repair to the Imperial presence. I had no command, and no information upon the composition and strength of the army. Neither the Emperor nor his Minister had given me any previous hint, from which I could anticipate that I should be employed in the present campaign, I was consequently taken by surprise, without horses, without accoutrements, and without money, and I was obliged to borrow the necessary expenses of my journey. Having arrived on the 12th, at Laon, on the 13th at Avesnes, and on the 14th at Beaumont, I purchased, in this last city, two horses from the Duke of Treviso, with which I repaired, on the 15th, to Charleroi, accompanied by my first aide de-camp, the only officer who attended me. I arrived at the moment when the enemy, attacked by our troops, was retreating upon Fleurus and Gosselies.

The Emperor ordered me immediately to put myself at the head of the 1st and 2d corps of infantry, commanded by Lieutenant Generals d'Erlon and Reille, of the divisions of light cavalry of Lieutenant General Pine, of the division of light cavalry of the guard under the command of Lieutenant Generals Lefebvre Desnouettes and Colbert, and of two divisions of cavalry of the Count Valmy, forming, in all, eight divisions of infantry, and four of cavalry. With these troops, a part of which only I had as yet under my immediate command, I pursued the enemy, and forced him to evacuate Gosselies, Frasnes, Millet, Heppegnies. There they took up a position for the night, with the exception of the 1st corps, which was still at Marchiennes, and which did not join me till the following day.

On the 16th, I received orders to attack the English in their position at Quatre Bras. We advanced towards the enemy with an enthusiasm difficult to be described. Nothing resisted our impetuosity. The battle became general, and victory was no longer doubtful, when, at the moment that I intended to order up the first corps of infantry, which had been left by me in reserve at Frasnes, I learned that the

Emperor had disposed of it without adverting me of the circumstance, as well as of the division of Girard of the second corps, on purpose to direct them upon St. Amand, and to strengthen his left wing, which was vigorously engaged with the Prussians. The shock which this intelligence gave me, confounded me. Having no longer under me more than three divisions, instead of the eight upon which I calculated, I was obliged to renounce the hopes of victory ; and, in spite of all my efforts, in spite of the intrepidity and devotion of my troops, my utmost efforts after that could only maintain me in my position till the close of the day. About nine o'clock, the first corps was sent me by the Emperor, to whom it had been of no service. Thus twenty-five or thirty thousand men were, I may say, paralized, and were idly paraded during the whole of the battle from the right to the left, and the left to the right, without firing a shot.

It is impossible for me, Sir, not to arrest your attention for a moment upon these details, in order to bring before your view all the consequences of this false movement, and, in general, of the bad arrangements during the whole of the day. By what fatality, for example, did the Emperor, instead of leading all his forces against Lord Wellington, who would have been attacked unawares, and could not have resisted, consider this attack as secondary? How did the Emperor, after the passage of the Sambre, conceive it possible to fight two battles on the same day ? It was to oppose forces double our's, and to do what military men who were witnesses of it can scarcely yet comprehend. Instead of this, had he left a corps of observation to watch the Prussians, and marched with his most powerful masses to support me, the English army had undoubtedly been destroyed between Quatre Bras, and Genappes ; and, this position, which seperated the two allied armies, being once in our power, would have opened for the Emperor an opportunity of advancing to the right of the Prussians, and of crushing them in their turn. The general opinion in France, and especially in the army, was, that the Emperor would have bent his whole efforts to annihilate first the English army ; and circumstances were favourable for the accomplishment of such a project: but fate ordered otherwise.

On the 17th, the army marched in the direction of Mount St. Jean.

On the 18th, the battle began at one o'clock, and though the bulletin, which details it, makes no mention of me, it is not necessary for me to mention that I was engaged in it. Lieutenant General Count Drouet has already spoken of that battle, in the House of Peers. His narration is accurate, with the exception of some important facts which he has

passed over in silence, or of which he was ignorant, and which
it is now my duty to declare. About seven o'clock in the
evening, after the most frightful carnage which I have ever
witnessed, General Labedoyere came to me with a message
from the Emperor, that Marshal Grouchy had arrived on
our right, and attacked the left of the English and Prussians
united. This General Officer, in riding along the lines,
spread this intelligence among the soldiers, whose courage
and devotion remained unshaken, and who gave new proofs
of them at that moment, in spite of the fatigue which they
experienced. Immediately after, what was my astonishment,
I should rather say indignation, when I learned, that so far
from Marshal Grouchy having arrived to support us, as the
whole army had been assured, between forty and fifty thousand Prussians attacked our extreme right, and forced it to
retire!

Whether the Emperor was deceived with regard to the
time when the Marshal could support him, or whether the
march of the Marshal was retarded by the efforts of the
enemy, longer than was calculated upon, the fact is, that at
the moment when his arrival was announced to us, he
was only at Wavre upon the Dyle, which to us was the
same as if he had been a hundred leagues from the field of
battle.

A short time afterwards, I saw four regiments of the
middle guard, conducted by the Emperor, arriving. With
these troops, he wished to renew the attack, and to penetrate
the centre of the enemy. He ordered me to lead them
on; generals, officers, and soldiers all displayed the greatest
intrepidity; but this body of troops was too weak to resist,
for a long time, the forces opposed to it by the enemy, and
it was soon necessary to renounce the hope which this
attack had, for a few moments, inspired. General Friant
had been struck with a ball by my side, and I myself had
my horse killed, and fell under it. The brave men who
will return from this terrible battle will, I hope, do me the
justice to say, that they saw me on foot with sword in hand
during the whole of the evening, and that I only quitted
the scene of carnage among the last, and at the moment
when retreat could no longer be prevented. At the same
time, the Prussians continued their offensive movements, and
our right sensibly retired, the English advanced in their turn.
There remained to us still four squares of the Old Guard to
protect the retreat. These brave grenadiers, the choice of
the army, forced successively to retire, yielded ground foot
by foot, till, overwhelmed by numbers, they were almost entirely annihilated. From that moment, a retrograde movement was declared, and the army formed nothing but a
confused mass. There was not, however, a total rout, nor

the cry of *sauve qui peut*, as has been calumniously stated in the bulletin. As for myself, constantly in the rear-guard, which I followed on foot, having all my horses killed, worn out with fatigue, covered with contusions, and having no longer strength to march, I owe my life to a corporal who supported me on the road, and did not abandon me during the retreat. At eleven at night I found Lieutenant General Lefebvre Desnouettes, and one of his officers, Major Schmidt, had the generosity to give me the only horse that remained to him. In this manner I arrived at Marchienne-au-pont at four o'clock in the morning, alone, without any officers of my staff, ignorant of what had become of the Emperor, who, before the end of the battle, had entirely disappeared, and who, I was allowed to believe, might be either killed or taken prisoner. General Pamphele Lacroix, chief of the staff of the second corps, whom I found in this city, having told me that the Emperor was at Charleroi, I was led to suppose that his Majesty was going to put himself at the head of Marshal Grouchy's corps, to cover the Sambre, and to facilitate to the troops the means of rallying towards Avesnes, and, with this persuasion, I went to Beaumont; but parties of cavalry following on too near, and having already intercepted the roads of Maubeuge and Philippeville, I became sensible of the total impossibility of arresting a single soldier on that point to oppose the progress of the victorious enemy. I continued my march upon Avesnes, where I could obtain no intelligence of what had become of the Emperor.

In this state of matters, having no knowledge of his Majesty nor of the Major-General, confusion increasing every moment, and, with the exception of some fragments of regiments of the guard and of the line, every one following his own inclination, I determined immediately to go to Paris by St. Quentin, to disclose, as quickly as possible, the true state of affairs to the Minister of War, that he might send to the army some fresh troops, and take the measures which circumstances rendered necessary. At my arrival at Bourget, three leagues from Paris, I learned that the Emperor had passed there at nine o'clock in the morning.

Such, M. le Duc, is a history of this calamitous campaign.

Now, I ask those who have survived this fine and numerous army, how I can be accused of the disasters of which it has been the victim, and of which your military annals furnish no example. I have, it is said, betrayed my country—I who, to serve it, have shown a zeal which I perhaps have carried to an extravagant height; but this calumny is supported by no fact, by no circumstance. But how can these odious reports, which spread with frightful rapidity, be arrested? If, in the researches which I could make on this subject, I did not fear almost as much to discover as to be ignorant of the truth, I would say, that all was a tendency to convince that I have been unworthily deceived, and that it is attempted to cover, with the pretence of treason, the faults and extravagancies of this campaign; faults which have not been avowed in the bulletins that have appeared, and against which I in vain raised that voice of truth which I will yet cause to resound in the House of Peers. I expect, from the candour of your Excellency, and from your indulgence to me, that you will cause this letter to be inserted in the Journal, and give it the greatest possible publicity.

I renew to your Excellency, &c.
Marshal Prince of MOSKWA.

Paris, June 26, 1815.

REPORT ADDRESSED TO THE EMPEROR,
BY MARSHAL DE GROUCHY.

" *Dinant, June* 20th, 1815.

" It was not till after seven in the evening of the 18th of June, that I received the letter of the Duke of Dalmatia, which directed me to march on St. Lambert, and to attack General Bulow. I fell in with the enemy as I was marching on Wavre. He was immediately driven into Wavre, and General Vandamme's corps attacked that town, and was warmly engaged. The portion of Wavre, on the right of the Dyle, was carried, but much difficulty was experienced in debouching on the other side. General Girard was wounded by a ball in the breast, while endeavouring to carry the mill of Bielge, in order to pass the river, but in which he did not succeed, and Lieutenant General Aix had been killed in the attack on the town. In this state of things, being impatient to co-operate with your Majesty's army on that important day, I detached several corps to force the passage of the Dyle and march against Bulow. The corps of Vandamme, in the meantime, maintained the attack on the Wavre, and on the mill, whence the enemy showed an intention to debouch, but which I did not conceive he was capable of effecting. I arrived at Limale, passed the river, and the heights were carried by the division of Vichery and the cavalry. Night did not permit us to advance farther, and I no longer heard the cannon on the side where your Majesty was engaged.

" I halted in this situation until day-light. Wavre and Bielge were occupied by the Prussians, who, at three in the morning of the 18th, attacked in their turn, wishing to take advantage of the difficult position in which I was, and expecting to drive me into the defile, and take the artillery which had debouched, and make me repass the Dyle. Their efforts were fruitless. The Prussians were repulsed, and the village of Bielge taken. The brave General Penny was killed.

General Vandamme then passed one of his divisions by Bielge, and carried with ease the heights of Wavre, and along the whole of my line the success was complete. I was in front of Rozierne, preparing to march on Brussels, when I received the sad intelligence of the loss of the battle of Waterloo. The officer who brought it informed me, that your Majesty was retreating on the Sambre, without being able to indicate any particular point on which I should direct my march. I ceased to pursue, and began my retrograde movement. The retreating enemy did not think of following me. Learning that the enemy had already passed the Sambre, and was on my flank, and not being sufficiently strong to make a diversion in favour of your Majesty, without compromising that which I commanded, I marched on Namur. At this moment, the rear of the columns were attacked. That of the left made a retrograde movement sooner than was expected, which endangered, for a moment, the retreat of the left; but good dispositions soon repaired every thing, and two pieces which had been taken, were recovered by the brave 20th dragoons, who besides took an howitzer from the enemy. We entered Namur without loss. The long defile which extends from this place to Dinant, in which only a single column can march, and the embarrassment arising from the numerous transports of wounded, rendered it necessary to hold for a considerable time the town, in which I had not the means of blowing up the bridge. I entrusted the defence of Namur to General Vandamme, who, with his usual intrepidity maintained himself there till eight in the evening; so that nothing was left behind, and I occupied Dinant.

"The enemy has lost some thousands of men in the attack on Namur, where the contest was very obstinate; the troops have performed their duty in a manner worthy of praise.

　　　(Signed)　　　　　　　" DE GROUCHY."

PART III.

ALPHABETICAL LIST

OF THE

OFFICERS KILLED & WOUNDED

AND

REGIMENTAL LOSS,

FROM THE OFFICIAL RETURNS;

WITH AN ENUMERATION OF THE

WATERLOO HONOURS AND PRIVILEGES,

And of those entitled thereto ;

AS ALSO,

THE NAMES OF THOSE WHO ARE ADMITTED

INTO

The Most Honourable Military Order of the Bath,

AND

ORDERS OF THE ALLIED SOVEREIGNS;

CONCLUDING WITH

BIOGRAPHICAL AND MILITARY NOTICES

OF THE

FALLEN HEROES.

ALPHABETICAL LIST of KILLED and WOUNDED,*

From the Official Returns, June 16 to June 26, 1815.

A.

Col. Hon. A. Abercromby, Ass. Qua. Mast. Gen. Cold. F. G. *w.*
Lieut. Acres, 73 F. *since dead.*
Capt. Adair, 1 F. G. *do.*
Maj. Gen. Adam, *sev. w.*
Lieut. Albert, 1 Lt. Inf. K. G. Leg. *k.*
Ensign Alderson, 35 F. *sev. right arm amp.*
Lieut. Alstone, 1 F. *w.*
Lt. Gen. Sir C. Alten, K. C. B. *sev. w.*
Adj. Lieut. Anderson, 71 F. *w.*
Lieut. Anderson, 52 F. *sev. left leg amp.*
Ensign Anderson, 1 F. *k.*
Ensign Anderson, 69 F. *sev.*
Adj. Lt. Andrews, 30 F. *w.*
Lieut. Anthony, 40 F. *sev.*
Ensign Appuhn, 4 line, Ger. Leg. *sev.*
Lieut. Armstrong, 1 F. *k.*
Lieut. Arnold, 10 Dr. *sev.*
Major Arguimbeau, 1 F. *w.*
Capt. Ashton, 3 F. G. *k.*
Col. Askew, 1 F. G. *sev. w.*

B.

Lieut. Bacon, 10 Dr. *sev.*
Lieut. Col. Bailey, 30 F. *sev.*
Ensign Bain, 33 F. *sev.*
Lieut. Baird, 3 F. G. *sev.*
Lieut. Baring, 1 Huss. K. G. L. *w.*
Col. Sir A. F Barnard, K. C. B. 95 F. *w.*
Captain Barnard, 2 Dr. *k.*
Major Gen. Sir E. Barnes, K. C. B. Adj. Gen. *sev. w.*
Capt. Barnett, 40 F. *sev.*
Lieut. Barr, 32 F. *sev.*
Lieut. Barrallier, 71 F. *w.*
Lieut. Barton, 1 F. G. *sev.*
Lieut. Hon. S. Barrington, 1 F. G. *k.*
Capt. Battersby, 1 Dr. G. *k.*
Lieut. Batty, 1 F. G. *w.*
Capt. Baynes, R. Art. *w.*
Major Beane, R. Art. *k.*
Capt. Beardesley, 51 F. *sev.*
Lieut. Beatty, 7 Dr. *sev.*
Ensign Becher, 92 F. *k.*

---

* It has been the Editor's great care that this list should be accurate. Should there be any error, if the friends of the party will have the goodness to communicate it, it will, with pleasure, be attended to.

Major Beckwith, Ass. Qua. Mast. Gen.
95 F. *sev.*

Lieut. Beere, 30 F. *k.*

Ensign Behne, 1 Lt. Inf. Ger. Leg. *sev.*

Lieut. Sir G. H. Berkeley, K. C. B. 35
F. Ass. Adj. Gen. *sev.*

Ensign Bennett, 32 F. *sev.*

Lieut. Berger, 5 line, K. G. *L. sev.*

Cornet Hon. H. Bernard, 1 Dr. G. *miss.*
supposed dead.

Lieut. Bertie, 12 Dr. *k.*

Lieut. Birtwhistle, 32 F. *sev.*

Ensign Birtwhistle, 32 F. *sev.*

Lieut. Black, 91 F. *w.*

Lieut. Black, 1 F *w.*

Capt. Blackman, Cold. F. G. *k.*

Capt. Blackwood, 69 F. *k.*

Major Blair, Brig. Maj. 91 F. *sev.*

Lieut. Blois, 1 Dr. *w.*

Lieut. Bloomfield, Roy. Art. *w.*

Lieut. Boase, 32 F. *sev.*

Capt. Bobers, K. G. L. Brig. Maj. *miss.*
supposed killed

Major Boden, 3 line, K. G. L. *sev.*

Capt. Bolton, R. Art. *k.*

Major Basewell, 2 Lt. Inf. K. G. L. *k.*

Lieut. Bosse, 1 Lt. Dr. K. G. L. *w.*

Lieut. Baron Both, 4 line, K. G. L. *w.*

Lieut, Bouverie, R. H. G. *w.*

Lt. Col. Bowater, 3 F. G. *w.*

Capt. Bowles, 28 F. *sev.*

Lieut. Bowers, 13 Dr. *w.*

Lt. Col. Boyce, 13 Dr. *w.*

Capt. Boyce, 32 F. *since dead.*

Lieut. Boyce, 33 F. *k.*

Lieut. Boyd, 4 F. *sev.*

Capt. Boyle, 42 F. *sev.*

Capt. Baron Bothmer, 1 Lt. Dr. K. G. L.
sev.

Lt. Col. Sir H. Bradford, K. C. B. 1 F. G.
Ass. Qua. Mast. Gen. *sev.*

Lieut. Brander, 42 F. *w.*

Ensign Branwell, 92 F. *sev. right leg amp.*

Capt. Braun, Art. K. G. L. *sev.*

Lieut. Brereton, R. Art. *sev.*

Ensign Bridge, 73 F. *sev.*

Adj. Lt. Bridgland, 28 F. *sev.*

Capt. Hon. O. Bridgeman, A. de C. to
Lord Hill, 1 F. G. *w.*

Adj. Lt. Brinckmann, 8 line, K. G. L. *sev.*

Major Bringhurst, 1 Dr. G. *k.*

Lieut. Brooke, 1 Dr. G. *sev. miss. supposed*
to have been killed.

Lieut. Brown, 79 F. *sev.*

Lt. Col. Brown, 79 F. *sev.*

Capt. Brown, 1 F. G. *k.*

Lieut. Browne, 73 F. *sev. since dead.*

Lieut. Hon. M. Browne, 40 F. *sev.*

Capt. Browne, 6 Dr. *sev.*

Lieut. Browne, 4 F. *sev.*

Lieut. Brooke, 1 Dr. G. *sev. missing, sup-*
posed to have been killed.

Lieut. Brookes, 32 F. *w.*

2 Lieut. Bruce, 1 Dr. G. *sev.*

Capt. Bruce, 79 F. *sev.*

Adj. Lieut. Bruggemann, 3 Huss. K. G. L.
killed.

Capt. Brugh, 44 F. *sev.*

Lieut. Gen. Duke of Brunswick Oels, *k.*

Capt. Buchanan, 16 Dr. *k.*

Lieut. Buck, 33 F. *k.*

Lieut. H. Buckley, 15 Dr. *since dead.*

Capt. Buckley, 1 F. *k.*

Lt. Col. Baron Bulow, 1 Lt. Dr. K.G.L.
sev.

Capt. Burgess, 1 F. G. *thigh amp.*

Capt. Bulow, 2 Lt. Dr. G. Leg. *k.*

Lieut. Burke, 44 F. *sev.*

Lieut. Burke, 44 F. *w.*

Major Bull, R. Art. *w.*

Ensign Buller, 30 F. *k.*

Capt. Burney, 44 F. *sev.*

Major H. Baron Bussche, 1 Lt. Inf. K.
G. Leg. *left arm amp.*

Lieut. Busteed, 69 F. *sev.*

Lieut. Butterworth, 32 F. *w.*

Lieut. W. Byam, 15 Dr. *sev.*

Lieut. E. Byam, 15 F. *w.*

C.

Major Cairnes, R. Art. *k.*

Col. J. Cameron, 92 F. *since dead.*

Lieut. Col. D. Cameron, 79 F. *sev.*

Lieut. Col. Cameron, 73 F. *sev.*

Lieut. C. Cameron, 79 F. *sev.*

Lieut. A. Cameron, 79 F. *w.*

Adj. Lieut. Cameron, 1 F. *sev.*

Lieut. D. Cameron, 79 F. *sev.*

Lieut. J. Cameron, 33 F. *since dead.*

Lieut. Donald Cameron, 95 F. *w.*

1 Capt. John Cameron, 79 F. *since dead.*

Lt. Col. C. Campbell, 1 F. *sev.*

Lieut. Campbell, 52 F. *sev.*

Lieut. Campbell, 44 F. *w.*

Lieut. Campbell, 40 F. *w.*

Capt. Neil Campbell, 79 F. *sev.*

Capt. Campbell, 92 F. *sev.*

Capt. Campbell, 71 F. *w.*

Capt. James Campbell, 79 F. *sev.*

Lt. Col. Canning, A. de Camp to the
D. of Wellington, 3 F. G. *since dead.*

Lieut. Carey, 2 Lt. Inf. K. G. L. *w.*

Lieut. Carruthers, 28 F. *sev.*

Lieut. Carruthers, 2 Dr. *since dead.*

Capt. Cassan, 32 F. *sev.*

Lieut. Cathcart, 91 F. *do.*

Major Chambers, 30 F. *k.*

Capt. Chambers, 1 F. G. A. de Camp to
Sir T. Picton, *k.*

Capt. C. Chawner, 95 F. *sev.*

Lieut. Chisholm, 92 F. *k.*

Lieut. Chisholm, 42 F. *w.*

Lieut. Chrichton, 16 Dr. *sev.*

Ensign Christie, 44 F. *do.*

Major Chuden, 4 line, K. G. Leg. *since*
dead.

Ensign Church, 95 F. *sev.*

Lieut. Col. Clarke, 2 Dr. *do.*

Lieut. Clarke, 1 F. *do.*

Lieut. Clarke, 28 F. *since dead.*

Capt. Clarke, 1 Dr. *w.*

Ensign Clark, 40 F. *sev.*

Capt. Claud, Brig. Maj. G. Leg. *k.*

Capt. Hon. B. Clements, 1 F. G. *sev.*

Lieut. Clyde, 23 F. *w.*
Capt. Coane, 73 F. *sev.*
Lieut. R. Cochran, 95 F. *w,*
Lieut. Coen, 28 F. *w.*
Lieut. Coles, 11 Dr. *w.*
Lieut. Colthurst, 32 F. *w.*
Major Gen. Cooke, *left arm amp.*
Lieut. Col. R. H. Cooke, 1 F. G. *sev.*
Ensign Cooke, 44 F. *k.*
Ensign Leo Morse Cooper, 1 F. *sev.*
Ensign A. Cooper, 14 F. *w.*
Lieut. Coote, 71 F. *w.*
Lieut. Cottingham, 52 F. *sev.*
Cornet Cox, 1 L. G. *do.*
Lieut. Coxon, 95 F. *do.*
Lieut. Coxon, 23 Dr. *miss. supposed killed.*
Lieut. Craddock, 27 F *sev.*
Lieut. Crawford, R. Art. *w.*
Capt. Crawford, 3 F. G. *k.*
Ensign Crawford, 79 F. *w.*
Lieut. Croft, 1 F. G. *sev.*
Capt. Crofton, Brig. Maj. 54 F. *k.*
Lieut. Cromie, R. Art. *both legs amp. since dead.*
Capt. Crowe, 32 F. *sev.*
1 Lt. Col. Currie, 90 F. Ass. Adj. Gen. *k.*
Major Cutcliffe, 23 Dr. *sev.*
Capt. H. W. Curzon, D. A. Adj. Gen. 69 F. *k.*

D.

Lieut. Dallas, 32 F. *sev.*
Lt. Col. Dalrymple, 15 Dr. *left leg amp.*
Capt. Dance, 23 Dr. *w.*
Lieut. Daniel, 30 F. *w.*
Capt. Dansey, R. Art. *sev.*
Lt. Col. Dashwood, 3 F. G. *do.*
Cornet Dassell, 3 Huss. G. Leg. *do.*
Adj. Lt. Davis, 32 F. *do.*
Major Davison, 42 F. *since dead*
Lieut. Dawkins, 15 Dr. *w.*
Lieut. Dawson, 52 F. *sev.*
Major Hon. G. Dawson, Ass. Qua. Mast. Gen. 1 Dr. G. *w.*
Lieut. Day, R. Art. *w.*
Ensign Deacon, 73 F. *sev.*
Lieut. Deares, 28 F. *w.*
Lieut. Bar. Decken, 2 line, K. G. L. *sev.*
Capt. De Einem, Brig. Maj. K. G. L. *do.*
Ensign De Gentzkow, 1 Lt. Inf. G. L. *do.*
Capt. De Gilsa, 1 Lt. Inf. K. G. L. *w.*
Lt. De Goeben, Art. K. G. L. *since dead*
Adj. Lieut. De Hartwig, 4 line, K. G. L. *sev.*
Capt. De Hattorf, 1 Lt. Dr. K. G. L. *w.*
Lt. Col. De Jouquieres, 2 Lt. Dr. K. G. L. *w.*
Lieut. De la Farque, 4 line, K. G. L. *sev.*
Col. De Lancy, Q. M. Gen. K. C. B. *since d.*
Ensign De Murreau, 8 line, G. L. *do.*
Ensign De Robertson, 2 Lt. Inf. K. G. L. *killed*
Lt. Col. De Schroeder, 2 line K. G. L. *w.*
Lieut. De Schulzen, Art. K. G. L. *k.*
Capt. De Seighard, 1 Lt. Dr. K. G. L. *w.*
Capt. De Voight, 8 line, G. L. *k.*
Capt. De Wurmb, 5 line G. L. *k.*

Lieut. Col. Sir F. D'Oyly, K. C. B. 1 F. G. *k.*
Capt. Dumaresque, A. de Camp to Gen. Byng, 9 F. *sev.*
Lieut. Col. Dick, 42 F. *do.*
Capt. Diedel, 3 line, G. Leg. *k.*
Capt. Diggle, 52 F. *sev.*
Lieut. Disney, 23 Dr. *w.*
Ensign Ditmas, 27 F. *w.*
Lieut. Dobbs, 1 F. *sev.*
Capt. Joseph Doherty, 13 Dr. *w.*
Lieut. G. Doherty, 13 Dr. *w.*
Major Gen. Sir W. Dornberg, K. C. B. K. Ger. Leg. *sev.*
Lieut. Col. Douglas, 79 F. *do.*
Capt. Hon. S. Douglas, 6 Dr. *do.*
Lieut. Douglas, 7 Dr. *do.*
Lieut. Dowbiggen, 12 Dr. *w.*
Lieut. Col. D'Oyly, 1 F. G. *sev.*
Cornet Drankmeister, 2 Lt. Dr. K. G. L. *killed*
Lieut. Drew, 27 F. *sev.*
Ensign Drury, 33 F. *do.*
Cornet Deichmann, 3 Huss. K. G. L. *k.*
Capt. Dudgeon, 1 F. *sev.*
Lieut. Dunbar, 42 F. *do.*
Adj. Lt. Duperler, 18 Dr. *w.*
Col. Duplat, Ger. Leg. *since dead*

E.

Ensign Eastwood, 73 F. *w.*
Capt. Edgill, 4 F. *w.*
Capt. C. Ecles, Brig. Maj 95 F. *k.*
Col. Sir J. Elley, K. C. B. Dep. Adj. Gen. R. H. G. *sev.*
Lieut. Elliott, 30 F. *w.*
Col. Sir H. W. Ellis, K. C. B. 23 F. *since dead*
Capt. Ellis, 1 F. G. *w.*
Capt. Ellis, 40 F. *sev.*
Capt. Elphinstone, 7 Dr. *do.*
Lieut. Elwes, 71 F. *since dead*
Capt. English, 28 F. *sev.*
Lieut. Erithropel, Art. K. G. L. *do.*
Capt. Hon. E. S. Erskine, 60 F. Dep. Ass Adj. Gen. *left arm amp.*
Capt. Evelyn, 3 F. G. *sev.*
Ensign Eyre, 95 F. *do.*

F.

Capt. Fane, 44 F. *sev.*
Capt. Farmer, 23 F. *k.*
Lt. Col. Fead, 1 F. G. *w.*
Capt. Felix, 95 F. *w.*
Lieut. Fensham, 23 F. *k.*
Capt. Fraser, 42 F. *w.*
Capt. Ferrier, 92 F. *w.*
Lieut. Col. Ferrier, 1 L. G. *k.*
Capt. Fisher, 40 F. *k.*
Lieut. Col. Fitzgerald, 2 L. G. *k.*
Lieut. Fitzgerald, 32 F. *sev.*
Capt. Fitzgerald, 25 F. Dep. Ass. Qua. Mast. Gen. *w.*
Capt. Fitzmaurice, 95 F. *sev.*
Capt. Hon. H. Forbes, 3 F. G. *k.*
Lieut. Forbes, 79 F. *w.*
Cornet Floyer, 3 Huss. G. L. *w,*
2 Lieut. Fludyer, 1 F. G. *sev.*

Ensign Ford, 40 F. *do.*
Capt. Forlong, 33 F. *do.*
Lieut. Foster, 1 Dr. *k.*
Capt. Fortescue, 27 F. *sev.*
Lieut. Foster, R. Art. *do.*
Ensign Franck, 2 Lt. Inf. Ger. Leg. *do.*
Capt. I. I. Fraser, A. de Camp to the E. of Uxbridge, 7 Dr.
C̶a̶p̶t̶.̶ ̶F̶r̶a̶s̶e̶r̶,̶ ̶7̶9̶ ̶D̶.̶1̶2̶
Capt. Fraser, 79 F. *do.*
Ensign A. L. Fraser, 42 F. *w.*
Ensign W. Fraser, 42 F. *w.*
Lieut. Fraser, 79 F. *sev.*
Adj. Lieut. Fricke, 1 Lt. Dr. K. G. L. *w*
Lieut. Fry, 95 F. *v.*
Col. Fuller, 1 Dr. G. *sev. missing,* supposed to have been killed
Major Fullerton, 95 F. *sev.*

G.

Lieut. Gardiner, 95 F. *sev.*
Lieut. J. P. Gairdner, 95 F. *do.*
Capt. Garland, 73 F. *do.*
Lieut. J. Geale, 13 Dr. *since dead*
Lieut. Gerard, 4 F. *w.*
Major Gerrard, 23 Dr. *sev.*
Ensign Gerrard, 42 F. *k.*
Lieut. Gerstlacher, 3 Huss. D. A. Adj. Gen. K. G. L. *missing,* supposed dead
Lieut. Gilbert, 28 F. *sev.*
Capt. Baron Goeben, 1 Lt. Brig. G. L. *k.*
Capt. Baron Goeben, 3 Hus. K. G. L. *w.*
Lieut. Goodenough, 1 Dr. *w.*
Lieut. Col. Sir A. Gordon, K. C. B. 3 F. G. A. de Camp to the Duke of Wellington, *since dead*
Lieut. Gordon, 7 Dr. *sev.*
Lieut. Gordon, 42 F. *k.*
Capt. Gore, 30 F. *w.*
Lieut. Gore, 33 F. *k.*
Major Graham, 1 Dr. G. *missing,* supposed to have been killed
Capt. Grant, 71 F. *sev.*
Capt. Grant, 92 F. *do. since dead.*
Capt. Grey, 10 Dr. *w.*
Lieut. Græme, 2 Lt. Inf. K. G. L. *sev.*
Lieut. Grier, 44 F. *do.*
Lieut. Griffiths, 23 F. *do.*
Major Griffith, 15 Dr. *k.*
2 Lieut. Griffiths, 2 F. G. *sev.*
Q. M. Griffiths, 1 F. *w.*
Capt. Grose, 1 Ft. Gds. *k.*
Capt. Gubbins, 13 Dr. *k.*
Lieut. Gunning, 1 Dr. *w.*
Lieut. Gunning, 10 Dr. *k.*
Capt. Gurwood, 10 Dr. *sev.*

H.

Capt. Haigh, 33 F. *k.*
Lieut. Tho. Haigh, 33 F. *w.*
Maj. Gen. Sir C. Halkett, K. C. B. K. G. L. *sev.*
Lieut. Hall, R. Staff Corps, *sev.*
Lieut. Col. Hamerton, 44 F. *w.*
Lt. Col. Hamilton, 30 F. *sev.*
Lieut. Hamilton, Dep. Ass. Adj. Gen. 46 F. *w.*
Lieut. Col. Hamilton, 2 Dr. *k.*
Major Hamilton, A. de C. to Maj. Gen. Sir E. Barnes, 4 W. I. R. *w.*

Lieut. Handcock, 27 F. *sev.*
Ensign Handcock, 27 F. *sev.*
Lieut. Col. Hankin, 2 Dr. *w.*
Lieut. Baron Hannerstein, 1 Lt. Dr. K. G. L. *sev.*
Brig. Gen. Hardinge, *left hand amp.*
Capt. Harling, 2 Lt. Dr. K. G. L. *sev.*
Col. Harris, 73 F. *sev.*
Capt. Harris, (T. N.) h. p. Major of Brig. *right arm amp.*
Capt. Harrison, 32 F. *sev.*
Lieut. Hart, 33 F. *k.*
Lieut. Hartmann, Art. K. G. L. *sev.*
Capt. Harty, 33 F. *w.*
Lieut. Harvey, R. Art. *right arm amp.*
Lieut. Hassard, 6 Dr. *sev.*
Lieut. Havelock, A. de C. to Maj. Gen. Alten, 43 F. *w.*
Major Hawtyn, 23 F. *k.*
Lieut. James, Lord Hay, A. de C. to Maj. Gen. Maitland, 1 F. G. *k.*
Lieut. Col. Hay, 16 Dr. *w. sev.*
Cornet Hay, 16 Dr. *k.*
Adj. Ensign Hay, 73 F. *sev.*
Capt. Heise, 4 Line K. G. L. *since d.*
Lieut. Heise, 1 Lt. Inf. K. G. L. *sev.*
Cornet Heise, 1 Lt. Inf. G. L. *sev.*
Cornet Heise, Art. G. L. *sev.*
Lieut. Helmrick, 7 Line K. G. L. *sev.*
Capt. Henderson, 71 F. *sev.*
Lieut. Henderson, 27 F. *sev.*
Lieut. Hern, 44 F. *sev.*
Ensign Heselrige, 73 F. *w.*
Capt. Hesketh, 3 F. G. *w.*
Lieut. Hesse, 18 Dr. *sev.*
Ensign Hewett, 92 F. *sev.*
Capt. Heyliger, 7 Dr. *sev.*
Maj. Heyland, 40 F. *k.*
Lieut. Col. Clem. Hill, R. H. G. *w. sev.*
Lieut. Col. Hill, 23 F. *sev.*
Lt. Col. Sir R. C. Hill, Knt. R. H. G. *sev.*
Lieut. Hillyard, 28 F. *w. sev.*
Lieut. Hobbs, 92 F. *sev.*
Capt. Hobhouse, 69 F. *k.*
Ensign Hodder, 69 F. *sev.*
Major Hodge, 7 Dr. *sev.* and *miss.*
Cor. Bar Hodenberg, 3 Huss. K. G. L. *sev.*
Capt. C. Baron Holle, 1 Line Ger. Leg. *k.*
Lieut. Hollis, 73 F. *k.*
Capt. Holmes, 27 F. *k.*
Capt. Holmes, 92 F. *sev.*
Capt. Holzermann, 1 Lt. Bat. G. L. *k.*
Capt. Holzermann, 2 Lt. Inf. K. G. L. *missing,* supposed *k.*
Lieut. Hope, 92 F. *sev.*
Capt. Horan, 32 F. *w.*
Lieut. Horan, 32 F. *sev.*
Major Hare, 27 F. *w.*
Major Hon. F. Howard, 10 Dr. *k.*
Ensign Howard, 33 F. *w.*
Lieut. Hughes, 30 F. *w.*
Lieut. Humbley, 95 F. *sev.*

I.

Lieut. Ingram, 1 F. *sev.*
Lieut. Ingram, 28 F. *since d.*
Ensign Ireland, 27 F. *k.*
Lieut. Irvine, 1 Dr. G. *w.*

Major Irving, 28 F. *sev.*
Lieut. Irving, 13 Dr. *w.*
Lieut. Irwin, 28 F. *sev.*

J.

Lieut. Jagoe, 32 F. *sev.*
Ensign James, 30 F. *k.*
Capt. Jansen, 3 Huss. G. *L. k.*
Lieut. Jeinsen, 3 Line, K. G. *L. sev.*
Major Jessop, A. Q. M. G. 44 F. *sev.*
Lieut. Jobin, 2 Lt. Inf. K. G. *L. w.*
Capt. Johnson, 23 F. *w.*
Capt. Johnston, 95 Ft. *sev.*
Lieut. Johnston, 95 F. *k.*
Major Johnstone, 71 F. *w.*
Capt. Jolliffe, 23 F. *k.*
Lieut. Col. Jones, 71 F. *sev.*

K.

Lieut. Keily, 1 Dr. *sev.*
Capt. Kelly, 28 F. *w.*
Capt. Kelly, 1 L. G. *sev.*
Major Gen. Sir J. Kempt, K. C. B. *sev.*
Capt. Kennedy, 73 F. *k.*
Lieut. Kennedy, 79 F. *k.*
Ensign Kennedy, 1 F. *k.*
Capt. Kessenbruck, 3 Huss. G. *L. k.*
Lieut. Kessler, 2 Lt. Inf. K. G. *L. sev.*
Cornet Kinchant, 2 Dr. *k.*
Lieut. Klingsohr, 5 Line, K. G. *L. sev.*
Capt. Knight, 33 F. *w.*
Ensign Kronhelm, 4 Line, K. G. *L. k.*
Lieut. Kuester, 1 Lt. Inf. K. G. *L. w.*
Lieut. Kuckuck, K. G. *L. sev.*
Lieut. H. Kuckuck, K. G. *L. sev.*
Lieut. Kuhlmann, 1 Lt. Dr. K. G. *L. k.*
Adj. Lieut. Kynock, 79 F. *k.*

L.

Lieut. Lake, 3 F. G. *sev.*
Col. Sir W. De Lancey, K. C. B. 23 F. *since dead.*
Lieut. Lane, 1 F. *arm amp.*
Capt. Langton, A. de C. to Sir J. Picton, 61 F. *w.*
Lieut. Bar. Langworthy, 4 Line, K. G. *L. w.*
Lieut. Lascelles, 1 F. G. *w.*
Lieut. Law, 71 F. *sev.*
Lieut. Lawrence, 32 F. *w.*
Major Leake, 4 Line, K. G. *L. since d.*
Lieut. Leaper, 79 F *sev.*
2 Lieut. Leebody, 23 F. *k.*
Lieut. Leivin, 32 F. *w.*
Lieut. Leonhardt, 1 Lt. Inf. K. G. *L. sev.*
Lieut. Leschen, 3 Line, K. G. *L sev.*
Major L'Estrange, A. de C. to Sir D. Pack, 71 F. *since dead.*
Lieut. Lewin, 71 F. *w.*
Capt. Lind, 1 Life Guards, *k.*
Lieut. Lind, 71 F. *sev.*
Lieut. Lindham, 2 Lt. Inf. K. G. *L. sev.*
Major Lindsay, 69 F. *sev.*
Lieut. Lister, 95 F. *k.*
Capt. Little, 92 F. *k.*
Major Llewellyn, 28 F. *sev.*
Lieut. Lloyd, 73 F. *sev.*
Major W. Lloyd, R. A. *sev.*
Cornet Lockhart, 12 Dr. *k.*
Lieut. Lockwood, 30 F. *sev.*

Lieut. Logan, 92 F. *sev.*
Ensign Logan, 92 F. *w.*
Cornet Lorenz, 2 L. D. G. *L. sev.*
Major Love, 52 F. *sev.*
Lieut. Bar. Lovetzow, 4 Lt. Dr. K. G. *L. k.*
2 Lieut. Lowe, 73 F. *k.*
Capt. Luttrell, 1 F. G. *sev.*
Capt. Lynam, 95 F. *sev.*

M.

Lieut. Col. Sir R. Macara, K. C. B. 42 F. *k.*
Major R. Macdonald, W. R. A. *w.*
Lieut. Col. Macdonald, 92 F. *sev.*
Lt. Col. Macdonell, C. F. G. *sev.*
Capt. Mackay, 79 F. *sev. miss. sup. k.*
Lieut. Mackenzie, 1 Lt. Dr. K. G. *L. sev.*
Lieut. Mackie, 92 F. *sev. since dead.*
Major Maclean, 73 F. *sev. since dead.*
Capt. Macleod, Dep. Ass. Q. M. G. 35 F. *w.*
Ensign Macpherson, 92 F. *k.*
Lieut. Maddocks, 79 F. *sev.*
Lieut. Magniac, 1 Dr. *miss. sup. d.*
Lieut. Bar. Mahrenhohls, 8 Line, K. G. *L. k.*
Lieut. Malcolm, 42 F. *sev.*
Lieut. Manley, 27 F. *sev.*
Lieut. Mann, 1 F. *sev.*
Lieut. Manners, Roy. A. *since dead.*
Lieut. Mansfield, A. de C. to Maj. Gen. Grant, 15 Dr. *w.*
Capt. H. Marschalk, 1 Lt. Bat. K. G. *L. k.*
Lieut. Col. Baron Marsdell, 2 Lt. Dr. K. G. *L. w.*
Capt. Marshall, 79 F. *sev.*
Major Massey, 1 F. *sev.*
Ensign Mathews, 4 F. *w.*
Lieut. M'Arthur, 79 F. *w.*
Ensign M'Bean, 73 F. *sev.*
Adj. Ensign M'Cann, 44 F. *sev.*
Adj. Lieut. M'Clusky, 6 Dr. *k.*
Lieut. M'Connell, 73 F. *k.*
Eusign M'Conchy, 32 F. *sev.*
Capt. M'Cullock, 95 F. *left arm amp.*
Capt. M'Donald, 42 F. *sev.*
Lieut. M'Donald, 92 F. *sev.*
Major M'Donald, 1 Ft. *sev.*
Ensign M'Donald, 92 F. *sev.*
Lieut. M'Donell, 27 F. *sev.*
Lieut. M'Innes, 92 F. *w.*
Lieut. M'Intosh, 92 F. *sev.*
Capt. M'Intosh, 42 F. *do.*
Q. M. M'Intosh, 42 F. *w.*
Capt. M'Intyre, 33 F. *w.*
Ensign M'Kay, 1 F *w.*
Lieut. M'Kenzie, 42 F. *w.*
Lieut. M'Kinlay, 92 F. *sev.*
Lieut. Col. M'Kinnon, Ft. G. *w.*
Capt. M'Nabb, 30 F. *k.*
Lieut M'Phee, 79 F. *w.*
Capt. M'Pherson, 42 F. *w.*
Lieut. M'Pherson, 92 F. *sev.*
Lieut. M'Phorson, 79 F. *k.*
Capt. M'Ray, 79 F. *sev. miss. supposed k.*
Major Meacham, 28 F. *k.*
Lieut. Meaghan, 32 F. *w.*

Capt. Menzies, 42 F. *sev.*
Ensign Metcalfe, 32 F. *w.*
Lieut. Col. Meyer, 3 Huss. K. G. L. *sev*
Lieut. Meyer, 2 Lt. Dr. K. G. L. *w.*
Lieut. Mill, 13 Dr. *w.*
Lieut. Mill, 40 F. *sev.*
Lieut. Millar, 27 F. *sev.*
Lieut. Col. Miller, 1 Ft. Gds. *since d.*
Lieut. Col. Miller, 6 Dr. *sev.*
Lieut. Miller, 1 F. *sev.*
Major Miller, 95 F. *sev.*
Lieut. Milligan, 11 Dr. *sev.*
Lieut. Mills, 2 Dr. *w.*
Lieut. Col. Milnes, 1 Ft. Gds. *since d.*
Lieut. Col. Mitchell, 92 F. *sev.*
Lieut. Molloy, 95 F. *sev.*
Lieut. Moneypenny, 30 F. *w.*
2 Lieut. Montague, 2 Ft. Gds. *w.*
Capt. Montgomerie, 3 Ft. Gds. *w.*
Capt. Hon. R. Moore, Coldst. F. G. *sev.*
Lieut. Moore, 40 F. *sev.*
Lieut. Moore, 11 Dr. *sev.*
Capt. Moray, Ex aide-de-camp to M. Gen. Grant, 13 Dr. *sev.*
Colonel Morice, 69 F. *k.*
Lieut. Morrison, 1 F. *sev.*
Ensign Mountsteven, 28 F. *sev.*
Lieut Muller, 1 line K. G. L. *sev.*
Lieut. Munro, 42 F. *sev.*
Lieut. Murkland, 33 F. *sev.*
Col. Muter, 6 Dr. *w.*
Adj. Lieut. Myers, 7 Dr. *sev.*
Capt. Mylne, 79 F. *sev.*

N.

Capt. Nanne, 1 Lt. Dr. Ger. Leg. *sev.*
Capt. Col. Napier, R. Art. *sev.*
Ensign Nash, 79 F. *w.*
Capt. Naylor, 1 Dr. G. *w.*
Ensign Nettles, 52 F. *k.*
Lieut. Col. Norcott, 95 F. *sev.*

O.

Lieut. Oelkers, 3 Huss. K. G. L. *sev.*
Lieut. Ogle, 33 F. *sev.*
Lieut Col. O'Malley, 44 F. *w.*
Lieut. Ommaney, 1 Dr. *sev.*
Bar. Ompteda, 5 line Ger. Leg. *k.*
Lieut. O'Neill, 1 F. *k.*
Gen. H. R. H. the Pr. of Orange, G.C.B. *w. sev.*
Ensign Ormsby, 14 F. *w.*
Lieut. Orr, 42 F. *sev.*
Lieut. Osten, 16 Dr. *w.*

P.

Maj. Gen. Sir Denis Pack, K. C. B. *w.*
Lieut. Pack, 13 Dr. *w.*
Maj. Packe, Roy. H. G. *k.*
Lieut. Pagan, 33 F. *sev.*
Ensign Page, 73 F. *k.*
Lieut. Pardoe, 1 F. G. *k.*
Maj. J. Parker, Roy. Art. *leg amp.*
Maj. Parkinson, 38 F. *sev.*
Lieut. Peters, 7 Dr. *sev.*
Capt. Peters, 1 Lt. Dr. G. L. *k.*
Lieut. Phelips, 11 Dr. *k.*
Lieut. Gen. Sir T. Picton, G.C.B. *k.*
Lieut. Pigott, 69 F. *sev.*

Maj. Gen. Sir W. Ponsonby, K.C.B. *k.*
Hon. Col. F. Ponsonby, 12 Dr. *w. sev.*
Lieut. Poole, Roy. Art. *sev.*
Major Poole, 2 Dr. *sev.*
Capt. Power, 44 F. *sev.*
Lieut. Powling, 79 F. *sev.*
Lieut. Pratt, 30 F. *sev.*
Lieut. Prendergast, 30 F. *k.*
Lieut. Pringle, Roy. Engin. *w.*
Capt. Purgold, 2 line K. G. L. *sev.*
Lieut. Pym, 13 Dr. *since dead.*

Q.

Col. Quentin, 10 Dr. *w. sev.*
Lieut. Quell, 32 F. *sev.*

R.

Maj. Radclyffe, 1 Dr. *sev.*
Maj. Ramsay, Roy. Art. *k.*
Lieut. Rea, 1 F. *sen.*
Lieut. Reid, 33 F. *sev.*
Lieut. Riefkugel, 2 Lt. Inf. G. L. *sev.*
Brig. Maj. Reignolds, 2 Dr. *k.*
Maj. Bar. Reitzenstein, 1 Lt. Dr. Ger. Leg. *w.*
Col. Reynell, 71 F. *w.*
Lieut. Reynolds, 73 F. *sev.*
Lieut. Reach, 79 F. *sev.*
Lieut. Richardson, 4 F. *sev.*
Lieut. Richardson, 1 L. G. *sev.*
Lieut. Ridgeway, 95 F. *sev.*
Lieut Ritter, 2 Lt. Dr. K. G. L. *sev.*
Lieut. Robb, 40 F. *w.*
Lieut. W. Robe, Roy. Art. *since dead*
Lieut. Roberts, 71 F. *w.*
Capt. Robertson, 73 F. *k.*
Ensign Robertson, 1 F. *k.*
Ensign Robertson, 79 F. *sev.*
Maj. Robertson, 1 line Ger. Leg. *sev. w.*
Capt. Robins, 7 Dr. *sev.*
Lieut Robinson, 32 F. *sev.*
Lieut. Roe, 30 F. *w.*
Lieut. Jas. Rooke, Aide-de-camp to the Prince of Orange, half pay, *w.*
Lieut. T. K. Ross, 92 F. *w.*
Lieut. Col. Ross, 95 F. *sev.*
Lieut. E. Ross, 92 F. *sev.*
Lieut. K. Ross, 92 F. *w.*
Capt. Rougemont, 8 line K. G. L. *w.*
Lieut. Col. Rowan, 52 F. *w.*
Lieut. Ruffo, 6 Dr. *miss. supposed dead*
Lieut. Rumby, 30 F. *sev.*
Lieut. Russell, 44 F. *sev.*

S.

Lieut. Sadler, 8 line, K. G. L. *w.*
Capt. Sandys, 12 Dr. *sev.*
Capt. Sander, 5 line K. G. L. *sev.*
Capt. Schaumann, 2 Lt. Br. G. Leg. *k.*
Capt. Schlutter, 1 line, K. G. L. *sev.*
Adjt. Lieut. Schnath, 1 line King's Ger. Leg. *sev.*
Capt. Selnchen, 3 Huss. K. G. L. *w.*
Capt. Schreiber, 11 Dr. *w.*
Adj. Lieut. Schuck, 5 line K. G. L. *k.*
Lieut. Scott, 1 F. *w.*
Capt. Seymour, Aide-de-camp to the E. of Uxbridge, 60 F. *w.*
Lieut. Shaw, Roy. Horse Guards, *w.*

Lieut. Shelton, 28 F. *w.*
Lieut. G. H. Shenley, 95 F. *sev.*
Lieut. Adj. Shelver, 1 Dr. Gds. *k.*
Capt. W. Shenley, 95 F. *sev.*
Lieut. Sherwood, 15 Dr. *k.*
Adj. Cornet Shipley, 1 Dr. *k.*
Cornet Lemmel Shuldham, 2 Dr.
Lieut. Sidley, 23 F. *w.*
Lieut. Simmons, 95 F. *sev.*
Capt. Simpson, 1 F. G. *sev.*
2 Lieut Simpson, 3 F. G. *since dead.*
Capt. Sinclair, 79 F. *since dead.*
Lieut. W. Smith, Roy. Art. *w.*
Ensign Smith, 27 F. *sev.*
Maj. C. Smyth, Brig. Maj. 95 F. *since d.*
Lieut. Lord Fitzroy Somerset, Mil. Sec.
  1 F. G. *right arm amp.*
Lieut. Spearman, Roy. Art. *since dead.*
Lieut. Squire, 4 F. *w.*
Lieut. Col. E. Stables, 1st F. G. *k.*
Lieut. Stephens, 32 F. *sev.*
Ensign Stevens, 1 F. *w.*
Lieut. G. Stewart, 1 F. *w.*
Lieut. Stewart, 42 F. *sev.*
Lieut. Stewart, 69 F. *sev.*
Ensign Stewart, 32 F. *sev.*
Assistant Surgeon Stewart, 92 F. *w.*
Lieut. Stroud, 44 F. *sev.*
Lieut. Stillwell, 95 F. *since dead*
Capt. Stothart, 3 F. G. *since dead.*
Lieut. Strachan, 73 F. *k.*
Lieut. Strangways, Roy. Art. *w.*
Lieut. Stratton, Royal Sappers and
  Miners, *w.*
Capt. Streatfield, 1 F. G. *sev.*
Col. Hon. W. Stuart, 1 F. G. *w. sev.*
Lieut. Stuart, 2 Dr. *sev.*
Capt. Summer, Coldst. F. G. *sev.*
Capt. Sweeny, 1 Dr. G. *sev. w.*
Cornet Sykes, 1 Dr. *k.*
Lieut. Symes, 1 F. *w.*
Maj. Sympher, Art. K. G. *L. w.*
Capt. A. Sympher, Art. K. G. *L. w.*

T.

Capt. Thackwell, 15 Dr. *left arm amp.*
Adj. Ensign Thain, 33 F. *w.*
Lieut. Col. Thomas. 1 F. G. *k.*
Capt. Thomson, Roy. Eng. *w.*
Maj. Thornhill, Aide-de-camp to the E.
  of Uxbridge, 7. Dr. *sev.*
Capt. Tilee, 2 line Ger. Leg. *k.*
Ensign Todd, 71 F. *k.*
Lieut. Tomkins, 44 F. *k.*
Maj. Toole, 32 F. *w.*
Lieut. Col. Hon. H. G. Townsend, 1 F.
  w. sev.
Lieut. Sig. Trafford, 1 Dr. *w.*
Lieut. Trinmann, 2 Lt Inf. K. G. *L. sev.*
Cornet Tritton, 1 E. D. Ger. Leg. *sev.*
Lieut, Trotter, 2 Dr. *k.*
Lieut. True, 3 Huss. K. G. *L. sev.*

Capt. Tucker, 27 F. *sev.*
Capt. Turner, 1 Dr. G. *sev.*
Capt. Tyler, Aide-de-camp to Sir T.
  Picton. 93 F. *w.*
Lieut. Tyndale. 51 F. *w.*

U.

Earl of Uxbridge, G. C. B. *right leg amp.*

V.

Lieut. Vane, 2 F. G. *sev.*
Maj. Vernon, 2 Dr. *sev.*
Capt. Vernor, 7 Dr *sev.*
Lieut. Vigoureux, 30 F. *sev.*
Ensign Von Lucken, 1 line, K.G.L. *k.*

W.

Lieut. Wall, 23 Dr. *sev.*
Capt. Wallet, 32 F. *w.*
Ensign Walsh, 95 F. *sev.*
Lieut. Warren, 30 F. *sev.*
Lieut. Waters, Ass. Adj. Gen. *w.*
Maj. Watson, 69 F. *sev.*
Lieut. Weymouth, 2 L. G. *missing*
Lieut. Webb, 95 F. *sev.*
Capt. Webber, Roy. Art. *sev.*
Ensign Webster, 44 F. *sev.*
Capt. Weigman, 2 L. B. G. Leg. *k.*
Lieut. Col. West, 3 F. G. *w.*
Cornet Westby, 2 Dr. *k.*
Capt. Baron Westernhagen, 8 line, Ger.
  Leg. *k.*
Lieut. Westmore, 33 F. *sev.*
Capt. Weyland, 16 Dr. *w.*
Capt. Whale, 1 Life Gds. *w.*
Capt. Wharton, 73 F. *sev.*
Capt. Whinyates, Roy. Art. *sev.*
Capt. Whiteford, 15 Dr. *sev.*
Ensign Whetney, 44 F. *do.*
Capt. Whitty, 32 F. *w.*
Lieut. Wightwick, 69 F. *k.*
Capt. Wildman, Aide-de-camp to the
  Earl of Uxbridge, 7 Dr. *w.*
Lieut. Wildman, 1 line K. G. L. *sev.*
Capt. Wilkie, 92 F. *sev.*
Col. Wilkins, 95 F. *do.*
Lieut. Wilkinson, 28 F. *do.*
Lieut. Col. Wilson, 4 F. *w.*
Ensign Wilson, 44 F. *sev.*
Lieut. Winchester, 92 F. *do.*
Capt. Windsor, 1 Dr. *k.*
Adj. Lieut. Winterbottom, 52 F. *sev.*
Lieut. Wolrabe, 1 Lt. Inf. K. G. L. *do.*
Capt. Wood, 10 Dr. *do.*
Lieut. Wood, 11 Dr. *do.*
Lieut. Worsley, 95 F. *do.*
Capt. Wright, Roy. Staff Corps, *w.*
Ensign Wright, 95 F. *do.*
Lieut. Wyndowe, 1 Dr. *w.*
Lieut. Weynham, 2 Dr. *sev*
Lieut. Col. Wyndham, Coldst. F. G. *do.*

Y

Lieut. Younge, 1 F. *k.*
Adj. Lieut. Young, 42 F. *w.*

N.B. Should this list be found inaccurate, any authenticated correction will be received and attended to with pleasure.

LIST OF REGIMENTS

UNDER THE COMMAND OF

𝕱𝖎𝖊𝖑𝖉 𝕸𝖆𝖗𝖘𝖍𝖆𝖑 𝕯𝖚𝖐𝖊 𝖔𝖋 𝖂𝖊𝖑𝖑𝖎𝖓𝖌𝖙𝖔𝖓,

ON SUNDAY, JUNE 18, 1815;

AND THE

TOTAL LOSS

OF THE

BRITISH AND HANOVERIANS,

From June 16th, *to* 26th, 1815.

TO WHICH IS ADDED,

The computed Losses of the Dutch and Prussians,

DURING THE CAMPAIGN IN THE NETHERLANDS.

	OFFICERS.			RANK AND FILE.			
	Kill.	Wou.	Miss.	Kill.	Wou.	Miss.	Total.
General Staff	12	46	3				61
1st Life Guards	2	4		24	49	4	83
2d Life Guards	1		1	16	40	97	155
Royal Horse Guards, Blue	1	4	1	19	61	20	106
1st Dragoon Guards	3	4	4	40	100	124	275
2d Dragoon Guards							
1st, or Royal Dragoons	4	9	1	86	88	9	197
2d, or Royal N. B. Dragoons	6	8		96	89		199
6th Dragoons	1	5	1	72	111	27	217
7th Hussars		7	3	62	109	15	196
10th Hussars	2	6		20	40	26	94
11th Light Dragoons	2	5		10	34	25	76
12th Light Dragoons	2	3		45	61		111
13th Light Dragoons	1	9		11	69	19	109
15th Hussars	2	3		21	48	5	79
16th Light Dragoons	2	4		8	18		32
18th Hussars		2		13	72	17	104
23d Light Dragoons		5	1	14	26	33	79
1st Light Dragoons, K. G. L.	3	11		30	99	10	153
2d Ditto	2	4		19	54	3	82

	OFFICERS.			RANK AND FILE.			
	Kill.	Wou.	Miss.	Kill.	Wou.	Miss.	Total.
1st Hussars, ditto		1		1	5	3	10
2d Hussars, K.G.L.							
3d Ditto ditto	4	8		40	78		130
Royal Artillery	5	26		62	228	10	331
Ditto, K.G.L.							
Royal Engineers		2					2
Royal Staff Corps		2					2
Royal Sappers and Miners		1			2		3
1st Foot Guards							
Ditto, 2d Battalion	3	9		73	353		438
Ditto, 3d Battalion	4	12		101	487		604
2d Cold. Regiment	1	7		54	242	4	308
3d Foot Guards, 2d Battalion	3	9		39	195		246
1st Foot, (Royal Scots) 3d Batt.	8	26		33	295		362
4th Foot, 1st Battalion		9		12	113		134
Ditto, 2d Battalion							
7th Foot, 1st Battalion							
14th Foot, 3d Battalion		3		7	26		36
23d Foot	5	6		13	80		104
25th Foot, 2d Battalion							
27th Foot, 1st Battalion	2	13		103	360		478
28th Foot, ditto	1	19		29	203		252
29th Foot, ditto							
30th Foot, ditto	6	14		51	181	27	279
32d Foot	1	30		49	290		370
33d Ditto	5	17		49	162	58	291
35th Ditto				1			1
37th Ditto, 2d Battallion							
40th Ditto, 1st Battalion	2	10		30	159	18	219

G

	OFFICERS.			RANK AND FILE.			
	Kill.	Wou.	Miss.	Kill.	Wou.	Miss.	Total.
42d Foot, 1st Battalion	3	21		47	266		337
44th Ditto, 2d Battalion	2	18		14	151	17	202
51st Ditto		2		11	29		42
52 Ditto, 1st Battalion	1	8		16	174		199
54th Ditto				2	2		4
59th Ditto					2		2
69th Ditto, 2d Battalion	4	7		51	163	15	240
71st Foot, 1st Battalion	1	14		24	160	3	202
73d Ditto, 2d Battalion	6	16		54	219	41	336
78th Ditto, 2d Battalion							
79th Ditto, 1st Battalion	3	27	1	57	390	1	479
81st Foot, 2d Battalion							
91st Foot		2		1	6		9
92d Ditto	4	27		49	322		402
95th, 1st Battalion	2	15		28	175		220
95th, 2d Ditto		14		34	178	20	246
95th, 3d Ditto		4		3	36	7	50
13th Veteran Battalion							
1st Lt. Infantry Batt. K. G. L.	4	9		37	82	13	145
2d Ditto ditto	3	9	1	40	120	29	202
1st Line Battalion, K. G. L.	1	6		22	69	17	115
2d Ditto ditto	1	2		18	79	7	107
3d Ditto ditto	1	5		17	93	31	147
4th Ditto ditto	1	7		13	77	15	113
5th Ditto ditto	2	3		36	47	74	162
8th Ditto ditto	3	4		44	80	16	147
THE DUTCH LOSS..........	27	115	....	2058	1936	....	4136
THE PRUSSIAN DITTO, *viz.*							
1st Corps, June 15 to July 3	38	200	27	2418	5322	6434	14439
2d Corps, June 15 to 23	29	151	7	1280	3915	2234	7616
3d Corps, June 15 to July 3	16	107	2	834	2636	1129	4724
4th Corps, June 15 to 23	23	148	5	1132	3871	1174	6353
Total Prussian Loss....	....	....	....	....	....	....	33132

WATERLOO HONOURS, PRIVILEGES, &c.

<hr>

BREVET.—*June* 22.—Major the Hon. H. Percy, of the 14th Light Dragoons, Lieut. Col. in the Army.

<hr>

Thanks of both Houses of Parliament, given to His Grace the Duke of Wellington, Prince Blucher, and the Allied Armies, Officers and Soldiers.—June 23d.

Resolved, Nemine Contradicente, That the thanks of this House be given to Field-Marshal the Duke of Wellington, Knight of the Most Noble Order of the Garter, for the consummate ability, unexampled exertion, and irresistible ardour, displayed by him on the 18th of June, on which day the decisive victory over the enemy, commanded by Bonaparte in person, was obtained by his Grace, with the Allied Troops under his command, and in conjunction with the Troops under the command of Marshal Prince Blucher, whereby the military glory of the British nation has been exalted, and the territory of his Majesty's Ally, the King of the Netherlands, has been protected from invasion and spoil.

Resolved, Nem. Con. That the thanks of this House be given to General His Royal Highness the Prince of Orange, Knight Grand Cross of the Most Honourable Military Order of the Bath ; Lieut. Generals the Earl of Uxbridge, K. G. C. B. ; Lord Hill, K. G. C. B.; Sir Henry Clinton, K. G. C. B. ; Charles Baron Alten, Knight, Commander of the Most Honourable Order of the Bath : Major Generals Sir Henry Hinuber, K. C. B. ; Sir John Ormsby Vandeleur, K. C. B.; George Cooke, Sir James Kempt, K. C. B. ; Sir William Dornbeg, K. C. B.; Sir Edward Barnes, K. C. B.; Sir John Byng, K. C. B. ; Sir Denis Pack, K. C. B. ; Lord Edward Somerset, K. C. B.; Sir John Lambert, K. C. B. ; Sir Colquhoun Grant, K. C. B. ; Peregrine Maitland, Sir Colin Halkett, K. C. B.; Frederick Adam, Sir R. H. Vivian, K. C. B. ; and to the several Officers under their command, for their indefatigable zeal and exertions upon the 18th of June.

Resolved, Nem. Con. That this House doth acknowledge, and highly approve, the distinguished valour and discipline displayed by the Non-commissioned Officers and Private Soldiers of his Majesty's Forces, serving under the command of Field-Marshal the Duke of

Wellington, in the glorious victory obtained upon the 18th of June: and that the same be signified to them by the commanding Officers of the several corps, who are desired to thank them for their gallant and exemplary behaviour.

Resolved, Nem. Con. That the thanks of this House be given to the General Officers, Officers, and Men, of the Allied Forces, serving under the immediate command of Field-Marshal the Duke of Wellington, for the distinguished valour and intrepidity displayed by them on the 18th of June, and that his Grace the Duke of Wellington be desired to signify the same to them accordingly.

Resolved, Nem. Con. That the thanks of this House be given to Marshal Prince Blucher, and the Prussian Army, for the cordial and timely assistance afforded by them on the 18th of June, to which the successful result of that arduous day is so mainly to be attributed; and that his Grace the Duke of Wellington be desired to convey to them the Resolution.

Whitehall, June 23.—The Prince Regent has been pleased to grant the dignity of a Marquis of the United Kingdom of Great Britain and Ireland, unto Lieutenant General, Henry William, Earl of Uxbridge, Knight Grand Cross of the Most Honourable and Military Order of the Bath, and the heirs male of his body, lawfully begotten, by the name, style, and title of Marquis of Anglesey.

Address for a National Monument and Monuments to Officers, who fell in the Battle of Waterloo.—June 29th, 1815.

Resolved, Nemine Contradicente, That an humble Address be presented to his Royal Highness the Prince Regent, that he will be graciously pleased to give directions, that a national monument be erected in honour of the splendid victory of Waterloo, and to commemorate the fame of the Officers and Men of the British Army, who fell gloriously upon the 16th and 18th of the present month; and more particularly of Lieut. General Sir Thomas Picton, and Major General the Honourable Sir William Ponsonby; and that Funeral Monuments be also erected in memory of each of those two Officers in the Cathedral Church of Saint Paul, London; and to assure his Royal Highness, that this House will make good the expense attending the same.

The Prince Regent has been pleased, in the name and on the behalf of His Majesty, to grant promotion to the following Majors and Captains, recommended for Brevet Rank, for their conduct in the Battle of Waterloo:

Commissions to be dated 18th of June, 1815.

To be LIEUTENANT COLONELS in the ARMY, *viz.*

Maj. Frederick Reh, 4 L. K. G. L.
Maj. Edward Parkinson, 33 f.
Maj. Fred. de Lutterman, 3 L. K. G. L.
Maj. Hans Baron Bussche, 1 L. B. ditto.
Maj. Frederick de Robertson, 1 L. ditto.
Maj. Philip Baron Gruben, 1 Hus. ditto.
Maj. George Krauchenberg, 3 Hus. ditto.
Maj. Thomas Hunter Blair, 91 f.
Maj. Dawson Kelly, 73 f.
Maj. Robert Bull, R. A.
Maj. Edward Cheney, 2 D.
Maj. Richard Llewellyn, 28 f.
Maj. Augustus Fredericks, 2 L. D. K.G.L.
Maj. Donald M'Donald, 92 f.
Maj. J. P. Bridger, 12 L. D.
Maj. George Home Murray, 16 L. D.
Maj. William Thornhill, 7 L. D.
Maj. J. Lewis Watson, 69 f.
Maj. Aug. Baron Reitzenstein, 1 L. D. K. G. L.
Maj. John Hare, 27 f.
Maj. George Baring, 2 L. I. K. G. L.
Maj. Jonathan Leach, 95 f.
Maj. Peter Brown, 23 f.
Maj. Thomas F. Wade, 42 f.
Maj. Francis Dalmer, 23 f.
Maj. Richard Egerton, 34 f.

Maj. William Chalmers, 52 f.
Maj. John M'Curliffe, 23 L. D.
Maj. John Parker, R. A.
Maj. C. H. Churchill, 1 G.
Maj. George D. Wilson, 4 f.
Maj. John Keightley, 14 f.
Maj. George Miller, 95 f.
Maj. Charles Beckwith, 95 f.
Maj. John Campbell, 42 f.
Maj. William Campbell, 23 f.
Maj. Charles de Petersdorff, 8 L. B. K. G. L.
Maj. James Bourchier, 11 L. D.
Maj. James Grant, 18 L. D.
Maj. Brook Lawrence, 13 L. D.
Maj. John Thomas Keyts, 51 f.
Maj. Augustus Sympher, Art. K. G. L.
Maj. Charles C. Ratclyffe, 1 D.
Maj. Fielding Brown, 40 f.
Maj. Thomas W. Taylor, 10 L. D.
Maj. L. Arquimbeau 1 f.
Maj. Michael Childers, 11 L. D.
Maj. Henry George Smith, 95 f.
Maj. Felix Calvert, 32 f.
Maj. William Stavely, Roy. Stf. Corps.
Maj. Alexander Campbell Wylly, 7 f.
Brev. Maj. Delacy Evans, 5 W. India R.

Commissions dated June 18, 1815.

To be MAJORS in the ARMY, *viz.*

Capt. Michael Turner, 1 D. G.
Capt. Edward Whinyates, R. A.
Capt. Peter Innes, 79 f.
Capt. Edward Kelly, 1 L. G.
Capt. Henry Madox, 6 D.
Capt. Hon. H. E. Irby, 2 Life G.
Capt. Samuel Reed, 71 f.
Capt. Edward Keane, 7 L. D.
Capt. W. Baron Decken, 2 L. B. K.G.L.
Capt. Adam Brugh, 44 f.
Capt. A. Cleves, Art. K. G. L.
Capt. L. de Dreves, 3 L. Bat. K. G. L.
Capt. Lord John Somerset, 63 f.
Capt. Thomas Dyneley, R. A.
Capt. William Verner, 7 L. D.
Capt. Skinner Hancox, 15 L. D.
Capt. W. F. Halsemann, 1 Lt. In. Bat. K. G. L.
Capt. Conyngham Ellis, 40 f.

Capt. George Bowles, Cold. F. G.
Capt. George L. Rudorff, 1 Lt. In. Bat. K. G. L.
Capt. Hon. E. S. Erskine, 60 f.
Capt. William F. Drake, Roy. H. G.
Capt. William Drummond, 3 G.
Capt. James Gunthorpe, 1 G.
Capt. Aug. de Saffe, 1 L. Bat. K. G. L.
Capt. James Shaw, 43 f.
Capt. Lord Charles Fitzroy, 1 G.
Capt. Charles A, F. Bentinck, C. F. G
Capt. Alexander Macdonald, R. A.
Capt. Robert Ellison, 1 F. G.
Capt. Henry Dumaresque, 9 f.
Capt. James Jackson, 37 f.
Capt. Robert Howard, 30 f.
Capt William Eeles, 95 f.
Capt. John Tyler, 93 f.
Capt. Algernon Langton, 61 f.

Lord Arthur Hill, upon the Staff, (commission dated July 27, 1815.)

July, 1815.

The King of the Netherlands has given the Duke of Wellington the title of PRINCE OF WATERLOO, and the States-General have settled an estate upon his family, annually producing 20,000 Dutch florins (2,000*l.*) consisting of woods, &c. in the neighbourhood of La Belle Alliance, Hougoumont, &c.

The King of Saxony has conferred upon the Duke of Wellington his Family Order of " THE CROWN OF RUE."

The Grand Duke of Baden has also conferred upon this Illustrious Personage, his Order of " FIDELITY," of the First Class, accompanied with a Gold Snuff Box, enriched with diamonds of great value.

Whitehall, June 22, 1815.

His Royal Highness the Prince Regent has been pleased, in the name and on behalf of His Majesty, to nominate and appoint Major General Sir James Kempt, K. C. B. to be KNIGHT GRAND CROSS of the Most Honourable MILITARY ORDER OF THE BATH, vice Lieutenant-General Sir T. Picton, deceased.

His Royal Highness has been also pleased to nominate and appoint the following Officers to be KNIGHTS COMMANDERS of the said Order:

Major General G. Cook, vice Major-General Sir R. R. Gillespie; Major-General Maitland, vice Major General Sir W. Ponsonby, deceased; Major-General F. Adam, vice Major-General Sir J. Kempt.

His Royal Highness the Prince Regent has further been pleased to nominate and appoint the undermentioned Officers to be COMPANIONS of the said Most Honourable MILITARY ORDER OF THE BATH, upon the recommendation of Field Marshal the Duke of Wellington, for their services in the battles fought upon the 16th and 18th of June last.

A.

*Col. Hon. A. Abercromby, Cold. Gds.
Lieut.-Col. Stephen G. Adye, Roy. Art.
Lieut.-Col L. Arquimbeau, 1st Foot.
*Col. Henry Askew, 1st Ft. Gds.

B.

Lieut.-Col. N. W. Bailey, 30 F.
Lieut -Col. G. Baring, 2 Lt. In. K. G. L.
Lieut.-Col. Charles Beckwith, 95 F.
Lieut.-Col. Shapland Boyse, 13 Lt. D.
Major F. Preymann, 8 Line, K. G. L.
Lieut.-Col. James P. Bridger, 12 Lt. Dr.
*Lieut.-Col. F. Brooke, 4 Ft.
Lieut.-Col. Andrew Brown, 79 Ft.
Lieut.-Col. Fielding Browne, 40 F.
Lieut. Col. Robert Bull, Royal Art.
*Lieut.-Col. J. Baron Bulow, 1st Lt. Dr. K. G. L.
Lieut.-Col. De Lancey Barclay, 1 Ft. G.
Lieut.-Col. Hans Baron Bussche, 1 Lt. Inf. K. G. L.

C.

Lieut -Col. Alex. Cameron, 95 F.
Lieut.-Col. Duncan Cameron, 79 F.
*Lieut. Col. Colin Campbell, 1 F.
*Lieut -Col. Sir Guy Campbell, Bt. 6 F.
Lieut -Col. John Campbell, 42 F.
Lieut.-Col. William Campbell 23 F.
Lieut.-Col. Edward Cheney, 2 Dr.
Lieut. Col Isaac B. Clarke, 2 D.
Lieut.-Col. Arthur B Clifton, 1 Dr.
Lieut.-Col. George Colquitt, 1 F.G.

Lieut. Col. Richard H Cooke, 1 F. G.
Lieut.-Col. John M Cutcliffe, 23 Dr.

D.

*Lieut -Col. Thomas Dalmer, 23 F.
Lieut.-Col. L. C. Dalrymple, 15 L. D.
*Lieut.-Col. Robert Henry Dick, 42 F.
Lieut.-Col. Philip Dorville, 1 D.
*Lieut.-Col. Neil Douglas, 79 F.
Major Percy Drummond, R. A.

E.

Lieut.-Col. W. K. Elphinstone, 33 F.

F.

Lieut.-Col. G. Fead, 1 F. G.
Lieut.-Col. J. Fremantle, Cold. G.
Maj. J. Fullarton, 95 F.

G.

Lieut.-Col. C. Gold, Royal Art.
*Lieut.-Col. Lord Greenock, Permanent Assist. Q. M. Gen.

H.

Lieut.-Col. Alexander Hamilton, 30 F.
Lieut. Col. J. M Hammerton, 44 F.
Lieut.-Col. John Hare, 27 F.
Col. Hon. William G. Harris, 73 F.
*Lieut.-Col. Frederick Hartwig, 1 L. I. K. G. L.
*Lieut.-Col. James Hay, 16 L. D.
Major Aug. Heise, 2 Lt. Inf. Bat. K. G. L.
*Col. Francis Hepburne, 3 F. G.
*Col. F. B. Hervey, 14 Lt. D.
*Lieut.-Col. John Hicks, 32 F.

Lieut.-Col. Sir R. C. Hill, Royal H. G.
Major Sir George Hoste, Knt. Royal En.

J.

Major John Jessopp, 44 F.
Lieut.-Col. C. de Jonquieres, 2 Lt. D.
  K. G. L.

K.

Major H. Kuhlmann, Art. K. G. L.
Lieut.-Col. Dawson Kelly, 73 F.
*Col. Sir Edw. Kerrison, Knt. 7 Lt. D.
Lieut.-Col. John T. Keyt, 51 F.

L.

Lieut.-Col. P. A. Latour, 23 Lt D.
Lieut.-Col Jonathan Leach, 95 F.
Lieut.-Col. W. Baron Linsingen, 5 L. B.
  K. G. L.
Lieut.-Col. Richard Llewellyn, 28 F.
Lieut. Col. Frederic de Lutterman, 3 L.
  K. G. L.
Lieut.-Col. Hon. E. P. Lygon, 2 Life G.

M.

Lieut.-Col. James Macdonnell, Cold. G.
Lieut.-Col. Alexander Macdonald, R. A.
Lieut.-Col. Donald Macdonald, 92 F.
Major R. Macdonald, 1 F.
Lieut.-Col. Lord Robert Manners, 10 D.
Lieut.-Col. Douglas Mercer, 3 Ft. G.
Lieut.-Col. F. S. Miller, 6 Dr.
Lieut.-Col. George Miller, 95 F.
*Col. H. H. Mitchell, 51 F.
Lieut.-Col. James Mitchell, 92 F.
Lieut.-Col. Archibald Money, 11 Lt. Dr.
Lieut.-Col. George Muller, 2 L. Batt.
  K. G. L.
Lieut.-Col. Hon. Henry Murray, 18 D.
Lieut.-Col. George H. Murray, 16 Lt. D.
Col. Joseph Muter, 6 D.
Lieut.-Col. George Muttlebury, 69 F.

N.

Col. W. Nicolay, Royal Staff Corps.
Lieut.-Col. Robert Nixon, 28 F.
Lieut.-Col. Amos G. Norcott, 95 F.

O.

Lieut.-Col. George O'Malley, 44 F.

P.

Lieut.-Col. John Parker, R. A.
Lieut.-Col Hon H. Percy, 14 Lt. D.
Lieut.-Col. C. de Petersdorff, 8 L. K.G.L.
Col. Hon F. C. Ponsonby, 12 L. D.

Q.

Col. George Quentin, 10 Lt. D.

R.

Lieut.-Col. Frederick Reh, 4 L. K. G. L.
Lieut.-Col. A. Baron Reitzenstein, 1 L. D.
  K. G. L.
Col. Thomas Reynell, 71 F.
Lieut. Col. Samuel Rice, 51 F.
Lieut.-Col. Frederick De Robertson, 1 L.
  Batt. K. G. L.
Major Thomas Rogers, Royal Art.
Lieut.-Col. Henry W. Rooke, 3 F. G.
*Lieut.-Col. John Ross, 95 F.
*Lieut.-Col. Charles Rowan, 52 F.

S.

Lieut.-Col. Lord Saltoun, 1 F. G.
Lieut.-Col. James W. Sleigh, 11 Lt. Dr.
*Lieut.-Col. J. W. Smith, Royal Art.
Lieut.-Col. Henry G. Smith, 95 F.
Col. James C. Smyth, Royal Eng.
Lieut.-Col. W. Stavely, Royal Staff C.
*Col. Hon. W. Stuart, 1 F. G.
Lieut.-Col. A. Sympher, Art. K. G. L.

T.

Lieut.-Col. F. S. Tidy, 14 F.
Lieut.-Col. R. Torrens, 1 W. India R.

V.

*Lieut.-Col. C. A. Vigoureux, 30 F.

W.

Major L. Walker, 71 F.
*Lieut.-Col. John Waters, Assist. A. G.
Lieut.-Col. J. S Williamson, Royal A.
Lieut.-Col. George D. Wilson, 4 F.
Lieut.-Col. Fred. de Wissell, 5 Line B.
  K. G. L.
Lieut.-Col. Aug. de Wissell, 1 Hussars,
  K. G L
Col. Sir George A. Wood, Knt. R. A.
*Col. A. G. Woodford, Cold. G.
Lieut.-Col. Alex. C. Wylly, 7 F.

War Department, Sept. 23, 1815.

Dispatches, of which the following are copies, have been received at this office, by Earl Bathurst, addressed to his Lordship by Field-Marshal the Duke of Wellington.

Paris, August 2, 1815.

MY LORD,—I have the honour to inclose a list of Officers upon whom the Emperor of Austria has conferred the Cross of a Commander and of a Knight respectively of the Order of MARIA THERESA, in testimony of His Imperial Majesty's approbation of their services and conduct, particularly in the late battles in the Netherlands, which I beg your Lordship to lay before His Royal Highness the Prince Regent, and request His Royal Highness's permission for them respectively to accept the same.

I have, &c.　　WELLINGTON.

To be Commanders of the Order of
MARIA THERESA.

Lieut.-Gen. the Marquis of Anglesey, G. C. B.
Lieut.-Gen. Lord Hill, G. C. B.

To be Knights of the Order of
MARIA THERESA.

Lieut.-Gen Sir Henry Clinton, G. C. B.
Maj.-Gen. Sir James Kempt, K. C. B.
Maj.-Gen Sir Edw. Barnes, K. C. B.
Maj.-Gen. Lord Edw. Somerset, K. C. B.
Col. Sir John Elley, K. C. B. R. H. G.
Col. Thomas Reynell, 71 F.

Col. Sir And. Barnard, K. C. B. 95 F.
Col. the Hon. Alex. Abercromby, C. G.
Col. Sir George Wood, R. A.
Col. Sir Colin Campbell, C. G.
Col. Sir John Colborne, K. C. B. 52 F.
Col. Alex. Woodford, C. G.
Col. the Hon. Fred. Ponsonby, 12 L. D.
Col. Felton B. Hervey, 14 L. D.
Col. Carmichael Smith, Royal Eng.
Lieut.-Col. James M'Donnell, C. G.
Lieut.-Col. Sir Robert Hill, Knt. R. H. G.
Lieut.-Col. Lord FitzroySomerset, K.C.B. 1 G.
Lieut.-Col. Robert Dick, 42 F.
Lieut.-Col. Neil Douglas. 79 F.
Lieut.-Col. Lord Saltoun, 1 G.

War Department, Oct. 28, 1815.

Dispatches, of which the following are copies, have been received by Earl Bathurst, addressed to his Lordship by Field-Marshal his Grace the Duke of Wellington, K. G. G. C. B.

Head-quarters, Paris, Oct. 8, 1815.

MY LORD,—I have the honour to annex a further list of General Officers upon whom His Majesty the Emperor of Austria has conferred the Order of MARIA THERESA, in testimony of His Majesty's approbation of their services and conduct, particularly in the late battles fought in the Netherlands, which I beg your Lordship to lay before His Royal Highness the Prince Regent, and request His Royal Highness's permission for them to wear the same.

              I have, &c.   WELLINGTON.

The Earl Bathurst.

Major-Gen. Sir John Byng.
Major-Gen. Sir Frederick Adam.

Major-Gen. Sir Denis Pack.
Major-Gen. Sir Hussey Vivian.

War Department, Sept. 23, 1815.

Dispatches, of which the following are copies, have been received at this office, by Earl Bathurst, addressed to his Lordship by Field-Marshal the Duke of Wellington.

Paris, Aug. 21, 1815.

MY LORD,—I have the honour to inclose a list of Officers upon whom His Imperial Majesty the Emperor of Russia has conferred decorations of different classes of the orders of ST. GEORGE, ANNE, and WLADIMIR, respectively, in testimony of His Imperial Majesty's approbation of their services and conduct, particularly in the late battles fought in the Netherlands, which I beg your Lordship to lay before His Royal Highness the Prince Regent, and request His Royal Highness's permission for them to accept the same.

              I have, &c.   WELLINGTON.

Second Class.

St. George.

Lieut.-Gen. the Marquis of Anglesey.
Lieut.-Gen. Lord Hill.

Third Class.

St. George.

Lieut.-Gen. Sir H. Clinton.
Maj.-Gen. Cooke.
Maj.-Gen. Kempt.

Second Class.

St. Wladimir.

Major-General Sir O. Vandeleur.
Major-General Sir J. Byng.
Major-General Sir D. Pack.

Third Class.

St. Wladimir.

Major-General Lord E. Somerset.
Major-General Sir J. Lambert.
Major-General Sir C. Grant.
Major-General Maitland.
Major-General Sir H. Vivian.
Colonel Mitchell.

Fourth Class.

St. George.

Col. Sir J. Elley, Assist.-Adj.-Gen.
Col. Reynell, 71 F.
Col. Sir A. Barnard, 95 F.
Col. Hon. A. Abercromby, A. Q. M. G.

Col. Sir C. Campbell, A. Q. M. G.
Col. Sir J. Colborne, 52 F.
Col. Woodford, Cold. G.
Col. Hon. F. Ponsonby, 12 Lt. D.
Col. Hervey, Acting Military Sec.
Lieut.-Col. Sir R. Hill, Royal H. G.
Lieut.-Col. Lord F. Somerset, Mil. Sec.
Lieut.-Col. Lord Saltoun, 1 G.

Fourth Class.

St. Wladimir.

Col. Hepburn, 3 G.
Col. Sir G. Wood, R. A.
Col. Muter, 6 Dr.
Col. Carmichael Smyth, R. E.
Lieut.-Col. Macdonnell, G.
Lieut.-Col. Sir H. Bradford, 1 G.
Lieut.-Col. Lord Greenock, A. Q. M. G.
Lieut.-Col. Cooke, 1 G.
Lieut.-Col. Sir C. Broke, A. Q. M. G.
Lieut.-Col. Sir H. G. Berkeley, A.Q.M.G.
Lieut.-Col. Ross, 95 F.
Lieut.-Col. Sir G. Scovell, A. Q. M. G.
Lieut.-Col. Dick, 42 F.
Lieut.-Col. Douglas, 79 F.
Lieut.-Col. Nixon, 28 F.
Lieut.-Col. Lygon, 2 L. G.
Lieut.-Col. Hare, 27 F.

First Class.

St. Anne.

Lieut.-Gen. Charles Count Alten.
Major-Gen. Sir E. Barnes, Adj.-G.
Major-Gen. Adam.

War Department, Oct. 28, 1815.

Dispatches, of which the following are copies, have been received by Earl Bathurst, addressed to his Lordship by Field-Marshal his Grace the Duke of Wellington, K. G. G. C. B.

Head-quarters, Paris, Oct. 8, 1815.

My Lord,—I have the honour to inclose a list of Officers upon whom His Majesty the Emperor of Russia has conferred decorations of the Order of St. Anne, in testimony of His Majesty's approbation of their services and conduct, particularly in the late battles fought in the Netherlands, which I beg your Lordship to lay before His Royal Highness the Prince Regent, and request His Royal Highness's permission for them to wear the same.
I have, &c.

The Earl Bathurst, &c. WELLINGTON.

Second Class of

St. Anne.

Col. F. Von Arentscheildt, 3Hus. K.G.L
Lieut.-Col. R. Torrens, W. I. Reg.
Lieut.-Col. John Waters, A. A. G.
Lieut.-Col. Charles Beckwith, 95 f.
Lieut.-Col. W. Campbell, A.Q.M.G.
Lieut.-Col. Colin Campbell, Roy.Scots.
Lieut.-Col. Arthur Clifton, 1 Dr.
Lieut.-Col. John Hicks, 32 f.
Lieut.-Col. W. Elphinstone, 33 f.

Lieut.-Col. Henry Mitchell, 51 f.
Lieut.-Col. A. G. Norcott, 95 f.
Lieut.-Col. A. Cameron, 95 f.
Lieut.-Col. J. B. Clarke, 2 Dr.
Lieut.-Col. Sir J. May, K.C.B. R.A.
Lieut.-Col. Sir Hew Ross, K.C.B. R.A.
Lieut.-Col. Sir R. Gardiner, K C.B. R.A.
Lieut.-Col. Sir W. Gomm, K.C.B. R.A.
Lieut.-Col. John Bull, R. A.
Major Edward Kelly, 2 L.G.
Major A. M'Donald, R. A.

Head-quarters, Paris, Oct. 8, 1815.

My Lord,—I have the honour to inclose a list of Officers upon whom His Majesty the King of the Low Countries has conferred decorations of different classes of the WILHELM's Order, in testimony of His Majesty's approbation of their services and conduct, particularly in the late battles fought in the Netherlands, which I beg your Lordship to lay before His Royal Highness the Prince Regent, and request His Royal Highness's permission for them to wear the same.

I have, &c.   WELLINGTON.

The Earl Bathurst.

Third Class.

WILHELM'S ORDER.

Lieut.-Gen. Sir Henry Clinton, G.C.B.
Maj.-Gen. Sir Colq. Grant, K.C.B.
Maj.-Gen. Sir Colin Halkett, K.C.B.
Maj.-Gen. Sir George Cooke, K.C B.
Maj.-Gen. Sir James Kempt, K.C.B.
Maj.-Gen. Sir William Dornberg, K.C.B.
Maj.-Gen. Sir Per. Maitland, K.C.B.
Lieut.-Gen. Charles Count Alten, K.C.B.

Fourth Class.

WILHELM'S ORDER.

Hon. Col. Stewart, 1 G.

Col. Fra. Hepburn, 3 G.
Col. Fred. Arentscheildt, 3 Hus.
Col. A.B. Clifton, 1 Dr.
Hon. Lieut.-Col. W. Elphinstone, 33 f.
Lieut.-Col. E. O. Tripp.
Lieut.-Col. Sir Charles Broke, K.C.B.
Lieut.-Col. Sir Henry Bradford, K.C.B.
Lieut.-Col. Sir George Berkeley, K.C.B.
Lieut.-Col. Lord Greenock
Lieut.-Col. R. Nixon, 1 f.
Lieut.-Col. G. Muttlebury, 69 f.
Lieut. Col. Harris.
Lieut.-Col. J. Ross, 95 f.
Lieut. Col. Busche, 1 L.B. K.G.L.
Lieut.-Col. George Baring, 2 L.B. K.G.L.

Whitehall, Oct. 31, 1815.

His Royal Highness the Prince Regent has been pleased, in the name and on behalf of His Majesty, to grant the dignity of a Baron of the United Kingdom of Great Britain and Ireland, unto the Right Honourable Lieutenant-General Rowland Baron Hill, Knight Grand Cross of the Most Honourable Military Order of the Bath, and the heirs male of his body lawfully begotten, by the name, style, and title of Baron Hill, of Almarez, and of Hawkstone and Hardwicke, in the county of Salop, and in default of such issue, to the heirs male lawfully begotten of his late brother John Hill, of Hawkstone, in the said county of Salop, Esq. deceased.

War Department, Oct. 28, 1815.

Dispatches, of which the following are copies, have been received at this office, by Earl Bathurst, addressed to his Lordship by Field-Marshal the Duke of Wellington.

Paris, September 24th, 1815.

My Lord,—I have the honour to inclose a list of Officers upon whom His Majesty the King of Bavaria has conferred decorations of different classes of the Order of MAXIMILIAN JOSEPH, in testimony of His Majesty's approbation of their services and conduct, particularly in the late battles fought in the Netherlands, which I beg your Lordship to lay before His Royal Highness the Prince Regent, and request His Royal Highness's permission for them to accept the same.

I have the honour to be, &c.

(Signed)   WELLINGTON.

To Earl Bathurst, &c. &c. &c.

Names of Officers upon whom His Majesty the King of Bavaria has conferred the Orders of MAXIMILIAN JOSEPH.

Head-quarters, Paris, September 23d, 1815.

Commanders.—Major General Sir Colin Halkett, K.C.B. Major General Sir John Lambert, K.C.B. Major General Sir James Lyon, K.C.B. Major General Sir John Vandeleur, K.C.B.

Knights.—Colonel Sir Colin Campbell, K.C.B. Colonel F. B. Hervey. Colonel Lord Fitzroy Somerset, K.C.B. Lieutenant Colonel Norcott. Lieutenant Colonel Sir Noel Hill, K.C.B. Lieutenant Colonel Freemantle. Major Honourable G. Dawson.

War Office, July 24th, 1815.

The Prince Regent, as a mark of his high approbation of the distinguished bravery and good conduct of the 1st and 2d Life Guards at the battle of Waterloo, on the 18th ultimo, is pleased to declare himself Colonel in Chief of both the Regiments of Life Guards.

War Office, July 25th, 1815.

His Royal Highness the Prince Regent has been pleased, in the name, and on the behalf of his Majesty, to approve of all the British Regiments of cavalry and infantry which were engaged in the battle of Waterloo, being permitted to bear on their colours and appointments, in addition to any other badges or devices that may have heretofore been granted to those regiments, the word " Waterloo," in commemoration of their distinguished services, on the 18th of June, 1815.

Vide List of Regiments, page 262.

War Office, July 29, 1815.

The Prince Regent, as a mark of his Royal approbation of the distinguished gallantry of the Brigade of Foot Guards in the victory of Waterloo, has been pleased, in the name and on the behalf of his Majesty, to approve of all the Ensigns of the three Regiments of Foot Guards having the rank of Lieutenants, and that such rank shall be attached to all the future appointments to Ensigncies in the Foot Guards, in the same manner as the Lieutenants of those regiments obtain their rank of Captain.

His Royal Highness has been pleased to approve of the 1st Regiment of Foot Guards being made a Regiment of Grenadiers, and styled " The 1st, or Grenadier Regiment of Foot Guards," in commemoration of their having defeated the Grenadiers of the French Imperial Guards upon this memorable occasion.

War Office, July 31, 1815.

Sir,—The Prince Regent having taken into his most gracious consideration, the distinguished gallantry manifested upon all occasions by the Officers of the British army, and having more particularly adverted to the conspicuous valour displayed by them in the late glorious victory, gained near Waterloo, by the army under the command of Field Marshal the Duke of Wellington ; and His Royal Highness being desirous of testifying the strong sense entertained by him of their devotion to His Majesty's service, I have the honour to acquaint you, that His Royal Highness has been pleased to order—

First,—That the regulation under which pensions are granted to wounded Officers, shall be revised, and that the pensions which have been, or may be granted to Officers, for the actual loss of eye or limb, or for wounds certified to be equally injurious with the loss of limb, shall not be confined to the amount attached by the scale to the rank which the Officer held at the time when he was wounded, but shall progressively increase, according to the rank to which such Officer may, from time to time, be promoted; the augmentation with regard to the pensions of such Officers, now upon the list, being to take the date from the 18th of June, 1815, inclusive.

Secondly,—That every Subaltern Officer of infantry of the line, who served in the battle of Waterloo, or in any of the actions which immediately preceded it, shall be allowed to account two years' service, in virtue of that victory, in reckoning his services for increase of pay given to Lieutenants of seven years' standing; and every such Subaltern will therefore be entitled to the additional 1s. a-day, whenever he shall have served five years as a Lieutenant.

And, thirdly,—That this regulation shall be extended to every Subaltern of cavalry, and to every Ensign of the Foot Guards, who served in the above-mentioned actions; and every such Subaltern and Ensign will, therefore, be entitled to an additional shilling a-day, after five years' service as Lieutenant in the cavalry, or as Ensign in the Guards.

His Royal Highness being also desirous of marking his sense of the distinguished bravery displayed by the non-commissioned Officers and Soldiers of the British forces, in the victory of Waterloo, has been most graciously pleased to order, that henceforth every non-commissioned officer, trumpeter, drummer, and private man, who served in the battle of Waterloo, or in any of the actions which immediately preceded it, shall be borne upon the muster rolls and pay lists of their respective corps as " Waterloo Men;" and that every " Waterloo Man" shall be allowed to count two years' service in virtue of that victory, in reckoning his services for increase of pay, or for pension when discharged.

It is, however, to be distinctly understood, that this indulgence is not intended in any other manner to affect the conditions of their original enlistment, or to give them any right to their discharge before the expiration of the period for which they have engaged to serve.

The Duke of Wellington has been requested to transmit returns of the Subaltern Officers to whom these orders may be considered by his Grace to apply; together with accurate muster rolls containing the names of all the " Waterloo Men" in each corps; such muster rolls being to be preserved in this Office as a record honourable to the individuals themselves, and as documents by which they will at any future time be enabled to establish their claims to the benefits of this regulation.

I have great pleasure in communicating these instances of the Prince Regent's gracious consideration for the army; and I request that you will be pleased to take the earliest opportunity of announcing the same to the Officers and Men of the corps under your command.

I have the honour to be, Sir,
your most obedient and humble servant,
(Signed)   PALMERSTON.

Circular.   To Paymasters of Regiments.

War Office, July 31, 1815.

" That the Lieutenants of Cavalry and Infantry, who had served more than five years as such, on the 18th of June, 1815, or who may subsequently have completed that period of service, are to receive one shilling per diem for every day's service as Lieutenant beyond five years, it being fully understood that the retrospect is, in no instance, to exceed two years. In like manner, the corporals and privates, distinguished as ' Waterloo Men,' are to receive the benefit of the two years' service retrospectively, in cases in which, by the addition of the two years, they would have completed their respective terms of service, on or previously to the 18th of June, 1815, and the two years' service will, of course, be reckoned in all claims subsequently accruing.

" Such of the officers and men present with the battalion as are now entitled to receive the same, may be settled with accordingly.

" The charges for the officers are to be included in the ordinary accounts of their pay, and those for the men present in a distinct supplementary pay list to the 24th of September; forms of which are to be transmitted from that office.

" The ordinary quarterly pay list to this period will, therefore, be proceeded upon, and rendered as if the Circular of the 31st of July last had not been issued.

" The non-commissioned officers and privates absent are to receive the amount due to them, under directions from that department, which is to be issued as soon as a certified return, signed by the Commanding Officer, Adjutant, and Paymaster, shall have been received. And that, under the present Mutiny Act, soldiers becoming entitled to additional pay on account of service, are allowed to receive the same from the first day of the military quarter in which they completed their period of service; but that rule, being to take effect from the 25th of June last, does not apply to the men who, with the addition of the two years now granted to them, will have completed their term of service on or before the 24th of June last."

" *Addressed to the Paymaster.*"

Officers commanding —— Regiment of ——

Vide List of Regiments, page 262.

His Royal Highness the Prince Regent has conferred upon Lieut.-General Sir Charles Alten, K. C. B. and to his descendants, the title of Count, as a recompense for his distinguished services in the war in Spain, and in the Battle of Waterloo.

His Royal Highness has been further pleased to testify his high satisfaction with the Hanoverian troops, who were present in this last battle, and to permit them to bear, like the English troops, on their colours, and on their uniform, the word " Waterloo."

P. S. Parish of Saxtead, Suffolk, including 6*l.* by the Rector and his Lady, in addition to a pension of 10*l.* per annum, proposed to be settled by him as Rector of Framlington cum Saxtead, during his own life, on SERJEANT JAMES GRAHAM, of the Coldstream, whom his Grace the Duke of Wellington has been pleased to recommend for that purpose, 12*l.* 2*s.* 6*d.* (*Waterloo Subscription.*)

The combined Forces of the Allied Armies which came into France, are estimated as follows:

AUSTRIANS   250,000
PRUSSIANS   250,000
RUSSIANS   200,000
ENGLISH AND HANOVERIANS   80,000
BAVARIANS AND WIRTEMBERGERS .   110,000
                                _____
                                 890,000

Adding to this the Staff with the Sovereigns,&c. near 1,000,000

The Generals appointed to the command of the 150,000 troops to remain in France, *viz.*

> For AUSTRIA—*General Frimont.*
> RUSSIA—*General Woronzow.*
> ENGLAND—*Duke of Wellington.*
> PRUSSIA—*General Gneizenau.*

The chief command to be with the DUKE OF WELLINGTON. Paris is to be occupied by from 10 to 12,000 English, in barracks.

These forces will have a certain number of fortresses, as *points d'appui,* in case of any revolutionary movement. They will be well supplied with field artillery, besides that of the fortresses; having among them not less than 500 pieces of cannon.

PROTOCOL OF THE CONFERENCE BETWEEN THE PLENIPOTENTIARIES OF AUSTRIA, RUSSIA, GREAT BRITAIN, PRUSSIA, AND FRANCE, ON MONDAY, THE SECOND OF OCTOBER, 1815.

AFTER various declarations and conferences between the Plenipotentiaries of Austria, Great Britain, Prussia, and Russia, on the one side; and the Duke of Richelieu, appointed Plenipotentiary of His Majesty the King of France, on the other, it has been agreed upon to-day, that the relations between France and the Allied Powers, armed for the re-establishment and maintenance of the general peace, shall be definitively regulated upon the following bases :—

1. The boundaries of France as they were in 1790, from the North Sea to the Mediterranean, shall form the fundamental principles of

the territorial arrangements, so that those districts and territories of former Belgium, of Germany, and Savoy, which, by the Treaty of Paris of 1814, were annexed to old France, shall remain separated therefrom.

2. Where this principle is departed from, the boundaries of 1790 shall be modified and better arranged, according to mutual conventions and interests, both in regard to civil jurisdiction, so as to cut off inclosed districts, and assign, on both sides, a more regular territory, and also in regard to military jurisdiction, so as to strengthen certain weak parts of the boundaries of the centerminous countries.

In conformity to this principle France cedes to the Allies—

Landau, Saarlouis, Philippeville, and Marienburg, with those circles of territory which are more fully laid down in the plan of Treaty proposed by the four Allied Cabinets, on the 20th September.

Versoy, with the necessary territory, shall be ceded to the Helvetic Confederation, in order to bring the Canton of Geneva in direct communication with Switzerland, and the French line of customs shall be there established in the manner most convenient for the administrative system of both countries.

The works of Huningen shall be demolished. The French Government binds itself to erect no others within a distance of three leagues from Basle.

France relinquishes her rights to the principality of Monaco.

On the other hand, the possession of Avignon and the Venaissin, as well as of the county of Mompelgard, and the possession of every other territory which is included within the French line, shall be anew secured to France.

3. France pays to the Allied Powers, by way of indemnity for the expenses of their last armaments, the sum of 700 millions of francs. A special Commission shall fix the mode, the periods, and the securities for this payment.

4. A military line of the following seventeen fortresses, viz.— Condé, Valenciennes, Bouchain, Cambray, Le Quesnoy, Maubeuge, Landrecies, Avesnes, Rocroy, Givet, Mezieres, Sedan, Mommedy, Thionville, Longwy, Bitche, and the Bridge-head of Fort Louis, shall be occupied by an army of 150,000 men, which the Allied Powers shall appoint. This army, which shall be placed under the command of a general, chosen by these Powers, shall be wholly maintained at the expense of France.

A special Commission shall fix all that relates to its maintenance, which shall be regulated in the best way for supplying all the wants of the army, and, at the same time, the least burdensome for the country.

The longest duration of this military occupation is fixed at five years. However, on the expiration of three years, after the Allied Sovereigns have weighed the situation of things and of mutual interests, as well as the advances which may have been made in the restoration of order and tranquillity in France, they will come to a common decision with the King of France, whether the above term of years may be shortened.

The Plenipotentiaries having definitively adopted these bases, have concerted upon the course to be adopted, in order to arrive, in the shortest possible time, at a formal arrangement, and have consequently determined,

1. That a general Treaty shall be drawn up, upon the bases above laid down, and adding to them such articles as, by common consent, shall be judged necessary to complete it. The French Government will nominate, on its part, the person who is to unite with those whom the four Powers have charged with the drawing up of the Treaty.

2. That the Commissioners appointed for the military affairs shall proceed, conjointly with the Commissioners whom the French Government shall appoint for this purpose, to draw up a plan of Convention to regulate every thing relative to the military occupation, and to the support of the army employed in this occupation. The same Commissioners shall also determine the manner and the periods of the evacuation of all such parts of the French territory as are not comprehended within the line of the military occupation.

3. That a special Commission appointed for that purpose by the contracting parties, shall draw up, without delay, a plan of Convention to regulate the mode, the periods, and the guarantees of the payment of the 700,000,000 of francs, to be stipulated by the general Treaty.

4. The Commission formed to examine the reclamations of several Powers, relatively to the non-execution of certain articles of the Treaty of Paris, shall continue its labours, with the understanding, that it is to communicate them as soon as possible, to the Plenipotentiaries in the principal negociation.

5. That as soon as these Commissioners shall have terminated their labours, the Plenipotentiaries shall unite to examine the results of them,—to determine on the definitive arrangements,- and to sign the principal Treaty, as well as the different particular Conventions. This process verbal having been read, the Plenipotentiaries have approved it, and

(Signed)

RASUMOWSKY,	WESSENBERG,
CASTLEREAGH,	CAPO D'ISTRIA,
RICHELIEU,	HUMBOLDT,
WELLINGTON,	HARDENBERG.

London, Foreign Office, Nov. 23, 1815.

Mr. PLANTA arrived early this morning, from Paris, with the several Treaties and Conventions, for the restoration and maintenance of Peace, between His Britannic Majesty and his Allies, on one part, and His Most Christian Majesty, on the other; signed, at Paris, on *Monday, the 20th instant,* by LORD VISCOUNT CASTLEREAGH, and the Field Marshal his Grace the DUKE OF WELLINGTON, as Plenipotentiaries of His Majesty, and by the DUC DE RICHELIEU, as Plenipotentiary of His Most Christian Majesty.

Printed by J. Barfield,
91, Wardour-Street, Soho.

MILITARY AND BIOGRAPHICAL

NOTICES

OF THE

FALLEN HEROES.

" To record the virtues of the departed brave," is a pleasing though painful task to survivers; and the pen is never perhaps exercised with more immediate advantage, or future benefit, than when paying a due tribute to the worth and excellence of those, with whom Providence has adorned Society for a time, and then by some sudden event has swept them away, and left their image alone to memory.

At the head of these may be placed His Serene Highness the Duke of BRUNSWICK OELS, who was killed on the spot by a wound in his side, whilst fighting gallantly at the head of his troops. His remains were brought to Brunswick near midnight, on the 22d June, accompanied by the physician and servants of his household. Several thousand persons went to meet them. At a mile distance from the town, the horses were taken from the hearse, and drawn by the people to the Palace. This Prince had put his army, amounting to 14,000 men, in mourning ever since his father's death; and made his soldiers swear never to leave it off till they had avenged the insult offered to his father's tomb by the French.

FREDERICK WILLIAM, DUKE OF BRUNSWICK-WOLFEN-BUTTLE, OELS, and BERNSTADT, was the fourth and youngest son of Charles William Ferdinand, the late reigning Duke of Brunswick-Wolfenbuttle, who died on the 10th of November, 1806, at Ottensen, near Altona, in consequence of the wound which he received at the unfortunate battle of Jena. He was doubly allied to the illustrious House which sways the British sceptre*—his mother being the sister of our beloved Monarch, and

---

* The seven sons of William the younger Duke of Brunswick Lunenbourg, furnished the most striking instance of fraternal affection. The right of primogeniture had not yet been introduced into the Dukedom, and the death of each reigning Prince had till then given occasion to a division of power, which must in the end be the means of considerably weakening the grandeur of this sovereignty. Immediately after the death of their father, which happened in 1611, the seven brothers resolved to make a regular family convention, in virtue of which it should no longer be permitted to dismember in future the Ducal Domains; but on the contrary, to unite them under that part of their posterity to whose rule they might hereafter fall. They agreed at the same time, that one out of the seven should marry, and that they would draw lots to determine who should be the prop of their house. They all agreed to this pro-

his sister the wife of the Heir-apparent to the throne. He was born on the 6th of October, 1771, and received the same education as his second and third brothers, who are not much older than himself, till the military profession, for which he was destined, required a course of instruction particularly adapted to that object.

In 1785, he was nominated successor to his uncle, Frederick Augustus, Duke of Oels and Bernstadt, in case he should die without issue; an arrangement which was confirmed by Frederick the Great, and his nephew, Frederick William II. as sovereigns of Silesia.

The Prince soon afterwards went to Lausanne, accompanied by M. Langer, who still holds the situation of librarian at Wolfenbuttle, and who had, a few years before, attended his brother, the hereditary prince, to the same place. After a residence of about two years in Switzerland, the Prince immediately commenced his military career. He was appointed captain in the regiment of infantry then in garrison at Magdeburgh, commanded by Lieutenant-General Langefeld, governor of that place, who died in 1789; a regiment which previously had for its chief the Prince's great uncle, the hero of Crevelt and Minden.

The Prince, who devoted himself with the greatest assiduity and zeal to the duties of his profession, was rapidly promoted. In 1790, at the early age of 19, he was invested with the grand order of the Black Eagle. In the war with France, which commenced in 1792, the Prince accompanied the Prussian army. He gained experience; and the military talents and intrepidity which he more and more developed, were conspicuously displayed by him on every occasion. This courage, this buoyant sense of youthful energy, which banished every idea of personal danger, impelled him, in several instances, beyond the bounds of prudence. On the 27th of November, in the last-mentioned year, he incurred the most imminent danger of his life, in a skirmish which took place in the village of Etsch, near Wurbel. He there received two wounds, and it was a considerable time before he recovered from their effects. The treaty concluded at Basle on the 5th of April, 1795, again gave repose to the Prussian army. Prince Frederick William, after being for some time commander of the regiment of Thadden, at Halle, and afterwards of Kleist's regiment, at Prenzlau, was, in 1800, promoted to the rank of Major-General. The latter regiment had long distinguished itself in the Prussian army, and, under the conduct of the Prince, who bestowed on it the most assiduous attention and many sacrifices, confirmed the character and reputation which it had acquired.

On the 1st of November, 1802, he received, at Carlsruhe, the hand of the Princess Mary Elizabeth Wilhelmina, grand-daughter

posal, and the lot fell upon Duke George, the youngest but one: his elder brother affectionately embraced him, and strictly observed every article agreed upon. The posterity of this George are now in possession of the Throne of England.

of the Grand Duke of Baden. The Prince and his consort seemed to have been created expressly for each other ; and their mutual felicity was augmented by the birth of two sons, on the 30th of October, 1804, and the 25th of April, 1806, both of whom are still living.

His uncle, Frederick Augustus, dying on the 8th of October, 1805, he succeeded to the Duchies of Oels and Bernstadt. The following year was marked by the breaking out of the war, the issue of which is so well known. The Duke was attached to the corps commanded by General Blucher, which, after the most astonishing exertions and the most obstinate resistance, was obliged to submit to the law of necessity. The capitulation of Lubeck put an end to the Duke's military career, for this war ; and the circumstances of the times, with the peculiar relations resulting from them, induced him to apply for his dismission from the Prussian service.

The unexpected decease of his eldest brother, the hereditary prince, in the month of September of the same year, and the agreement concluded by him, with his two brothers, called him, on the decease of his father, to the government of the patrimonial dominions ; which, however, he held but for a short time, Brunswick being, by the Treaty of Tilsit, incorporated with the kingdom of Westphalia.

After this reverse, the Duke resided chiefly at Bruchsal, in Baden ; and here he was doomed to experience a misfortune that afflicted him still more severely. On the 20th of April, 1808, he lost his amiable consort, and with her fled all his happiness. In the flower of her age, having not yet attained her 26th year, this excellent princess, wife, and mother, after being delivered of a still-born daughter, was removed to a better life.

After her death little or nothing was known respecting him. On the rupture between Austria and France, in April, 1809, the Duke was in Bohemia, where he was endeavouring to raise an independent corps of black hussars. More fortunate than Schill, who had already perished at Stralsund, the Duke began his new military career by making an incursion into the kingdom of Saxony, in conjunction with a corps of Austrian troops. They were, however, obliged to evacuate Leipsic and Dresden, on the approach of a considerable force, composed of Dutch and Westphalians. The Duke of Brunswick Oels and General Am Ende, retired from Dresden in a western direction, towards Franconia, into which the Austrians had penetrated from Bohemia in considerable force, under the command of Lieutenant Field-Marshal Kienmayer. The armistice concluded at Znaym, in consequence of the battle of Deutsch Wagram, terminated the contest in that country also, and deprived the Duke of the co-operation of the Austrian troops. They evacuated Dresden, which they had a second time occupied, and withdrew beyond the Bohemian frontiers.

Meanwhile the Duke of Brunswick had likewise evacuated some of the places of which he had taken possession, but still remained in the Erzgebirge, without being pursued either by the Saxons or Westphalians. For some time he appeared undecided whether he should join the Austrians in Bayreuth, or adopt a different plan. It is not, however, improbable, that he proceeded farther to the west, as his advanced posts are said to have been seen near Fulda, in order to mislead his adversaries in respect to his real intentions. Be this as it may, the unfortunate events in the course of July fixed his resolution. He determined to quit Germany, where fortune did not seem to smile on the cause which he had espoused, and to conduct his corps to the English, of whose great preparations for an expedition to the Continent the foreign papers were at that time so full.

The difficulties which opposed the execution of this undertaking were innumerable. It was not till he had travelled a space of near 300 miles that he could hope to reach the coasts of the German Ocean. His route lay through countries which were not wholly destitute of hostile troops.

The current accounts stated the corps of the Duke of Brunswick to have been completely dispersed and annihilated; the inhabitants of Leipsic were, therefore, not a little surprised, when, at three in the morning of the 26th of July, he entered that city with 1,900 men, 700 of whom were cavalry, after a smart action before the inner gates. It is not unlikely that the Duke had reason to be dissatisfied with something which had occurred during his former occupation of this city; for a contribution, though a very moderate one, amounting to no more than 15,000 dollars, was imposed; and this, we believe, was the only requisition of the kind made by the Duke during his whole march. His men also exercised the right of retaliation on several persons who had given them cause of offence during and after their retreat.

On the 27th of July, the Duke arrived at Halle, and, with unparalleled celerity, pursued his route by way of Eisleben, to Halberstadt, which place Colonel Count Wellingerode, Grand Marshal of the Palace to the King of Westphalia, entered with the 5th regiment of foot, on the afternoon of the 30th of July. The The same evening, the Duke's corps appeared before the gates with six pieces of cannon. The enemy, though destitute of cavalry and artillery, made an obstinate resistance, but was at length overpowered, after a bloody conflict, which was continued for some time, in the streets of Halberstadt. The Duke, who had fought in the ranks of his black Hussars, invited his officers to table, (to which he was often accustomed to sit down in public), where he was surrounded by such a concourse of people, that he was frequently obliged to request them to stand back. He appeared simply dressed in the uniform of his corps, and without any other decoration than the order conferred on him by the Prussian Monarch.

He now directed his course towards his native city. Late in the evening of the 31st of July, he entered Brunswick, on whose ramparts, wrapped in a cloak, he passed the night. What must have been the feelings of the Prince, when he beheld the palace, once the residence of his illustrious ancestors, his own cradle, and the theatre of his juvenile years; when he traversed the streets, in which his parent had so often been seen, attended by crowds of happy mortals, who awaited the father of his people, to pay him the eloquent tribute of grateful tears; when he encountered the anxious and timid looks of those who once hoped to see the prosperity and the glory of their country augmented by him, whom alone, from among his three sons, his aged father had deemed worthy to be his successor! These were, perhaps, the most painful moments experienced by this high-spirited Prince, since the sable genius of Auerstadt eclipsed the splendour of the House of Welfs. Fate seemed to show him once more the happy land to which he was the rightful heir, to make him the more keenly sensible of his loss. The reflection, that he had returned to a country which once was his, and which he once hoped to leave, to his hopeful offspring, as a fugitive, to whom those lips which ought to have sworn fealty scarcely durst address the accents of compassion, must have wrung his heart. He, nevertheless, retained sufficient strength of mind to conduct himself with exemplary moderation; and, amidst the gloom of his feelings, he was not abandoned by the light of wisdom. If he could not confer happiness, neither would he involve others in his own calamity; but, in a proclamation, magnanimously recommended to his beloved countrymen, to be obedient to their present rulers.

The Duke durst not take any long repose at Brunswick, as he was closely pressed on all sides. The Westphalian General, Reubel, concentrated 4,000 men of his division at Ohoff; General Gratien had set out with a Dutch division from Erfurt, and was approaching the coasts of the German Ocean; while Lieut. Gen. Ewald, with a corps of Danish troops, crossed from Gluckstadt over the Elbe, into the Hanoverian territory, to cover the banks of that river. General Reubel was nearest to the Duke, who, in his rapid retreat, had daily actions with the advanced guard of the Westphalian troops. That which was fought in the afternoon of the 1st of August, at Oelper, near Brunswick, and in which the Duke's horse was killed by a cannon-ball, was the *eleventh* since the commencement of his retreat in Saxony.

The next morning he quitted his native city; and the movement which he now made, caused it to be generally supposed, that he was proceeding to Zell. Thither the troops under Reubel, and others, accordingly directed their course. The Duke, however, suddenly made his appearance at Hanover, which he entered on the morning of the 3d of August; and, in the afternoon, pursued his route, by way of Neustadt, to Nieuburgh, where he arrived early the next day. Here he crossed the Weser. He broke down the bridges behind him, and reached Hoya on the 4th. In this manner, he hastened along the left bank of the Weser, while part of his corps, in order to make a false demonstration, turned off to Bremen. On the evening of the 5th, this detachment possessed itself of the gates of the city, and hastily departed the next day, to rejoin the corps.

The Duke, meanwhile, continued his march through the Duchy of Oldenburg, and through Delmenhorst, where he passed the night between the 5th and 6th of August; and it appeared as if he was directing his course towards East Frieseland, with a view to embark on the coast of that province. This opinion, however, proved erroneous; for, crossing the Hunta, a small stream which discharges itself into the Wezer at Huntebruck, he seized the corn-ships, which had been lying inactive for years at Elsfleth. In these vessels, he embarked his men in the night of the 6th, and by force procured a sufficient number of hands to navigate them, the surrounding district being chiefly inhabited by sea-faring people. On the morning of the 7th, the Duke hoisted the English flag, set sail, and the following day reached Heligoland, with part of his corps. That island he quitted on the 11th, and with his faithful followers proceeded to England. On the turn of affairs in Europe early in 1814, his Highness quitted England to take possession of his patrimony, recovered from the repacious fangs of the world's disturber, and was devoting his attention to those places of internal improvement begun by his father, when the perfidious conduct of the French again summoned him to assist in the task of humbling that ambitious ruler.

How heartily he espoused the cause of legitimate right and social order, may be conceived from the fact, that though the contingent required of him was no more than 4,000, he actually joined the Allied forces with 14,000; Providence, however, decreed that he should not enjoy those gratifications, nor live to see the results of a victory, of which he so bravely contributed to accomplish, by his personal exertion and valour, and that of his brave followers.* The Hanoverian Government assumes the administration of the Duchy during the Minority of his eldest boy, now 10 years old.

In the battle of Genappe, the brave Lieut.-Col. MACARA, 42d regiment, K. C. B. whose death was deeply avenged by his comrades. He was wounded about the middle of the engagement, and was in the act of being carried off the field, by four of his men, when a party of French unexpectedly surrounded, and made them all prisoners. Perceiving by the Colonel's numerous decorative distinctions, that he was an officer of rank, and possibly considering the difficulty of retaining him as a prisoner, they immediately cut him down, with his faithful attendants.

* *Aix la Chapelle*, 12th July.---" The Duke of Wellington caused twelve pieces of the brass cannon taken from the enemy to be delivered to Colonel Osterman, of the Brunswick Troops, in order to be employed in the monument which is intended to be erected to his memory.

Colonel CAMERON, who nobly fell at the head of his regiment, we have to produce the following honourable testimony of the high consideration of his country:—

" *Whitehall, June* 6*th.*—The Prince Regent being desirous of conferring upon John Cameron, Esq. Col. in the army, Lieut.-Col. of the 92d (Highland) regiment of Foot, and Knight of the Royal Portuguese Military Order of the Tower and Sword, such a mark of his Majesty's royal favour, as may in a special manner evince the sense he entertains of the highly distinguished services of that officer upon divers important occasions, and more especially during the recent glorious and ever memorable campaigns in Portugal, Spain, and France; and particularly the signal intrepidity displayed by him in the action of Arroya de Moulino; in the defence of the pass of Maya; in the brilliant action near Bayonne; in crossing the river Gave de Mouline, at Arriverete; and in compelling a very superior force of the Enemy to abandon the town of Aire; hath been pleased to grant unto the said Col. Cameron, His Majesty's Royal Licence and Authority, that he and his descendants may bear the following crest of honourable augmentation, viz.:—" On a wreath, a Highlander of the 92d regiment, armed and accoutred, up to the middle in water, grasping in his dexter hand a broad sword, and his sinister a banner, inscribed 92d, within a wreath of laurel," and in escrol above, " Arriverete," in allusion to to the signal bravery displayed by him in forcing a passage through the river Gave de Mouline, in face of a very superior body of the Enemy.

June 17th, whilst charging the French Hussars early in the morning, Major HODGE, 7th Hussars. That regiment formed part of the cavalry under the Earl of Uxbridge, and was actively engaged, together with the Life Guards, in covering the retreat of the British Army from the attacks of the Enemy's Lancers and Cuirassiers, as mentioned in the Gazette.

June 17. Near Brussels, in consequence of a severe wound on the preceding day, in his 24th year, Lieut. E. M. WIGHTWICK, 69th regiment of Foot, fifth son of William Wightwick, Esq. of New Romney, Kent.

Lieut.-Gen. Sir THOMAS PICTON, G. C. B. memorable in the Peninsular campaigns, began his Military career September, 1771, in the 12th regiment of foot, upon the reduction of which regiment, we find him to have attained the rank of Captain, and in the bosom of his family in Pembrokeshire, the birth place, and residence of his ancestors for centuries; upon the commencement of the revolutionary war in 1794, he embarked for the West-Indies, where he soon distinguished himself and obtained his Majority in the 68th regiment, and the appointment of Deputy Quarter Master General. Upon the appointment of a new General Officer, he proposed to return to Europe, but was induced to remain at the request of Sir Ralph Abercrombie, who arrived in 1796; this General Officer was fully sensible of the worth of this Officer, at this moment, and took every occasion he could to make his merit conspicuous, and upon the capture of St. Lucie, became the Lieut.-Col. of the 68th, and with his Commanding Officer and friend returned to England, upon the close of the campaign, by the reduction of St. Vincent.

The ensuing campaigns in 1797, from the kindness and friendship of his Commanding Officer, he was honoured, "in being selected as the best Officer to discharge the duty" of Governor in Trinidad; the difficulties of his new situation, however, in the result, occasioned many days and years of anxiety, which was only to be relieved by the esteem, gratitude, and applause of every man of probity and principle in the island, notwithstanding the unparalleled exertions of individuals to sully his character and ruin his fortune, and to render him an object of public clamour. The law, at length, although tardy in reparation, proclaimed him innocent of the charges attributed to him, and vindicated his honour, which from the first he had boldly defended.

In 1809, we find Major General Picton, commanding a brigade of an army sent to rescue Holland from the French, and was at the Siege of Flushing, of which town, after its surrender, he was appointed Governor: he there rendered himself conspicuous for his humanity to the natives, and to the sick and wounded soldiers—during his stay at Walcheron, he caught the fever, and came home enfeebled and emaciated; fortunately for his Country, his health was restored. Instantly, and even before he could be said to have reassumed his tone of health, his active services were required in Portugal, when he commanded the 3d division of the British army; in which command, his zeal, celerity, and courage, soon distinguished itself, and from the situation in which the fortune of war had placed them, became noticed as the fighting division.

In all the battles in the Peninsular war, the division which he commanded was placed in the post of honour, and never failed to justify the confidence reposed in its gallant commander. The capture of Badajoz was principally owing to his resolution and presence of mind, in converting a feint into a real attack, and thus gaining possession of a castle which over-looked the place. His services were continued during the whole of the Peninsula war, excepting that he was obliged from ill-health to resign for a time previous to the battle of Salamanca, when the command of his division was entrusted to the late gallant Sir Edward Pakenham, who bravely led it to victory. Before the battle of Vittoria, our hero was sufficiently recovered to resume the command, and in this battle his division acted in a manner, which at once excited acclamation and surprize, for nearly four hours, did alone sustain the unequal force opposed to it, of which the whole army, from the peculiar nature of the ground, were acting witnesses. General Picton continued with the army until its entrance into France. In a word he was the very soul of honour. The pupil of Sir Ralph Abercrombie, he never disgraced his general and his friend. In private life Sir Thomas Picton was kind, humane, benevolent, and charitable. He discharged with strictness all the social and relative duties; and, in the midst of the severe persecution, never lost that equanimity of temper which pious integrity alone can impart. The Duke of Wellington, in his dispatch, passes a just eulogium on his worth. (See Gazette.) As soon as our army was sent to Flanders, Government, it is stated, offered him the command of a division; but, apprehending the Duke of Wellington, as Commander-in-Chief, would leave the British force to some officer in whom he could not repose the same confidence, he declined the offer, adding, however, if the Duke should personally require his services, he would instantly repair to the army. This requisition was made—and the General left town on June 11th, and on the 18th terminated his honourable career in the field of glory! He had made his will before his departure—he did not expect to return; but observed to a friend, that when he heard of his death, he would hear of a bloody day. Alas! his prediction was too literally verified!—The following pleasing trait in his character may be relied on: Some time after relinquishing the government of Trinidad, the inhabitants voted him 5000*l.* as a testimony of their esteem. When a dreadful fire laid the capital in ashes some time after this, a subscription was opened for the relief of the sufferers, and the General eagerly seized the opportunity of appropriating the 5000*l.* to that object!* His remains were landed at Deal, June the 25th. Minute guns were fired from all the ships in the Downs, while the body was conveyed to the beach, where all the Naval and Military were drawn up to receive it. The body reached Canterbury the same evening, and was deposited in the custody of a guard of honour, in the same room at the Fountain inn, where, on that same day fortnight, the General had dined, on his way to embark. At six on the 26th, the body proceeded, accompanied to the extremity of the City, by the 52d regiment, with reversed arms, the band playing the Dead March in Saul—On the 3d of July, the remains of this distinguished officer were deposited in the family vault, in the burial-ground of St. George's Hanover Square, on the Uxbridge road, attended by his brother, Rev. Edw. Picton, and many officers and gentlemen of distinction. A great concourse of people assembled, to witness the impressive scene. On the coffin was inscribed: " Lieut. Gen. Sir Thomas Picton, aged 57, G. C. B. who fell at the great and decisive battle of Waterloo, in Flanders, on the 18th of June, 1815, between the French Army, commanded by Napoleon Buonaparte, and the English army, commanded by his Grace the Duke of Wellington."

In the list of those who fell gloriously in the hour of victory, stands conspicuous the name of Major ROBERT CAIRNES, of the Royal Horse Artillery. Nature had marked him as her favourite. Endued with a strength and activity of mind that are rarely surpassed, he carried them into his profession with the happiest result to himself and the service. An undaunted bravery, an exquisite sense of honour, a cool and discriminating, though quick judgment, and a steady perseverance, were his peculiar characteristicks as a soldier; a noble and generous temper, an undeviating sweetness of disposition, a most engaging person, and manners highly polished and universally amiable, were his qualifi-

* The Duke of Queensbury, with a nobleness of spirit, offered 5000*l.* to Sir T. Picton, on the close of his prosecution by Col. F. but he politely refused it, with the highest sense of gratitude to the donor.

cations as a member of society; a heart the most affectionate, and an urbanity the most conciliating, completed his character in the different relations of son, brother, and friend. Adored by his family, beloved by his brother officers, and respected by the world, this gallant man met the death his noble spirit ever panted for, in the 30th year of his age, and left behind him unutterable regrets for his fate—to his friends indeed untimely, but to himself matured. The truth of this sketch will be attested by those who knew and loved its subject, while he who traces it is conscious of his inability to do it justice. By the female line, Major Cairnes was the eldest branch of the family of that name, to whom a Baronetcy was granted by patent in the reign of Queen Anne, but which has been dormant since the death of Sir Alexander Cairnes, who was killed at the battle of Minden.

Colonel FERRIER of the Life Guards, fell on the 18th of June He led his regiment to the charge no less than eleven times; and most of the charges were not made till after his head had been laid open by the cut of a sabre, and his body was pierced with a lance.

Lieut.-Col. Sir FRANCIS D'OYLY, K. C. B. of the 1st. regt. of Foot Guards, in his 39th year. He was the third son of the Rev. Matthias D'Oyly, Rector of Buxted, Sussex, and Archdeacon of Lewes. He entered into his Majesty's service, in the 1st regiment of Guards, in the year 1794; and since that period has been engaged in most of the principal military enterprizes which have taken place in the late wars. In the expedition to the Helder, in 1799, he acted as Aide-de-camp to his late uncle, General D'Oyly. In 1804, he accompanied his regiment to Sicily, and remained there about two years. From the first breaking out of the Peninsular war to the close of it, he was, with very little exception, engaged on various military duties in Spain: he was present in the whole of Sir John Moore's campaign and retreat to Corunna; he afterwards spent a considerable time at Cadiz, while that city was besieged by the French; and, lastly, under the Duke of Wellington, he held the situation of Assistant Adjutant-General to one of the divisions of the army, chiefly to that commanded by the Earl of Dalhousie. Holding this situation, he was engaged in all the great engagements which crowned the Duke of Wellington's campaigns with such distinguished success; in the several battles of Salamanca, Vittoria, the Pyrenees, Orthes, &c.; and accompanied Lord Dalhousie's division of the army to Bourdeaux. Having received several medals for the share he bore in these principal engagements, he was created one of the Knights Commanders of the order of the Bath, on the late extension of the honours of that order. During the whole of the late battles on the 16th and 18th of June, he was closely engaged with the Enemy, and for a long time escaped unhurt. At last, towards the close of the action of the 18th, in the very last charge to which his regiment was led against the broken and yielding enemy, he received a wound from a musket-ball in a vital part of his body, and fell dead from his horse. He was a brave and active officer, ardently and zealously attached to his profession, diligent in the pursuit of the knowledge that belongs to it, anxious to bear a part in its more active services, and to share its dangers and its glories. He has fallen, sincerely and deeply lamented by his relations, and by a large circle of friends, whose esteem and regard he had justly conciliated by many valuable and excellent qualities in private life.

Lieut.-Col. RICHARD FITZGERALD, Captain in the 2d regiment of Life Guards. The distinguished share which the brigade of Life Guards had in contributing by their irresistible charges to the glorious result of that ever-memorable day, is a matter of general notoriety, as it was of admiration, to the armies that witnessed its achievements. Among those whose gallantry was crowned with a death of glory, none was more conspicuous than Col. Fitzgerald: he was the only officer of his regiment who was killed; he did not, however fall, till he had the satisfaction of witnessing the triumph of the British army. Towards the close of the action, being advanced in front of his regiment, leading it in pursuit of the flying Enemy, he was killed by a cannon-shot.*

Major HAWLYN, 23d regt. (Royal Welsh Fusileers), an officer who had greatly distinguished himself with his regiment, at the storming of Badajoz, of Salamanca, and in all the operations of the army in the Peninsula.

CHARLES JOLLIFFE, Captain in the 23d regiment, R. W. P. He was the youngest son of T. S. Jolliffe, Esq. of Ammerdown, co. Somerset, formerly representative in Parliament for the borough of Petersfield Constantly engaged in active duty, the first years of his service, after the siege of Copenhagen, were employed in North America and the West Indies. Upon the reduction of Martinique, he returned with his regiment to Halifax, and from thence to Europe; where he served several campaigns in the Peninsula. Scarcely recovered from a severe wound received in the brilliant action of Orthes, he embarked with his battalion for the Netherlands, and, on the memorable 18th of June, fell with his brave comrades in his country's cause! thus defeating the well-founded hope entertained by all who knew his superior merits, of his attaining the highest honours in his profession.

Lieut. FOSTER of the Royals, killed by a cannon-ball on the 18th of June, in the battle of Waterloo, son of the Rev. Mr. Foster, of Kingston, near Taunton.

Lieut. ELLIOT DUNCAN JOHNSON, 95th regiment, by a can-

---

* A plain monument is erected for this Noble Sacrifice to his Country's Honour, in the Church of Waterloo, with the following Inscription: "Sacred to the Memory of Lieut.-Col. Richard Fitzgerald, of the 2nd Reg. of Life Guards of H. B. Majesty, who died gloriously in the Battle of La Belle Alliance, June 18, 1815; in the 41st year of his age. He carries with him the most profound and sincere regrets of his relations and friends. To the most manly fortitude, he added all the virtues that could do honour to the profession, and make him beloved in private life.'

non-shot, third son of Lieut.-Gen. Johnson, of the East India Company's service; a young man whose amiable disposition and engaging manners had endeared him to the regiment, as well as to his numerous family, who in him will long lament the loss of a most affectionate son and brother.

LIEUTENANT-COLONEL CURRIE.—Amongst the gallant heroes who have fallen in the defence of their country, on the ever-memorable 18th of June, on the plains of Waterloo, few are more lamented than Lieutenant-Colonel Currie, of Dalebank, in Annandale, Assistant Adjutant-General on Lord Hill's Staff. This excellent and valuable officer received his commission at the early age of 13, from the Duke of York, in consequence of the meritorious conduct of his father in the army, and, for a period of above 20 years, had been constantly distinguishing himself in actual service. He fought bravely, and was severely wounded, under Sir Ralph Abercrombie, in Egypt; and served for several years in the West Indies, by which his health was greatly impaired. He was also actively employed as an Aide-de-Camp to Lord Hill, the whole of the war in the Peninsula and in France; where he conducted himself with such ability and bravery, as repeatedly on the field of battle to receive the thanks of the Commander-in-Chief; and particularly at Talavera, at the passage of the Douro, Almarez, and Aroyo de Molinos. It is melancholy, although glorious to record, that Lieutenant-Colonel Currie was the tenth of this gallant and amiable family who have nobly sacrificed their lives in defence of their King and country, six of whom have died on the field of battle.

Lieut.-Col. CHARLES FOX CANNING, who fell in the late tremendous conflict at Waterloo, had served with the Duke of Wellington as his Aide-de-Camp during the whole of the Peninsular war, and was with him in every action and siege from the battle of Talavera to that of Orthes. At the termination of the war he went to Brussels, where his regiment was quartered, and was preparing to go into the field with it, when the Duke accidentally met him in the street, when he was received with the usual cordiality, and the next day he had the inexpressible gratification of finding himself restored, without solicitation, to the honourable situation he had held through so many campaigns. The affecting particulars of his last moments we cannot help repeating, as a proof, that among many other splendid qualities, the Duke of Wellington eminently possesses the power of engaging the affections of his officers, whose most anxious thoughts seem always directed toward the safety of their Commander.—Towards the close of the action of the 18th, Lieutenant-Colonel Canning received orders from the Duke to carry a message of importance to a distant part of the line: he had delivered it and was returning, when a grape-shot struck him in the stomach. He fell, and his friend Lord March immediately rode up to his assistance. As he approached him, the Colonel raised himself up, and with eagerness demanded if the Duke was safe? Being assured that he was, he seemed satisfied, and said—" God bless him!" Then taking the hand of the Nobleman who had so kindly come to his assistance, he had just strength enough to say—" God bless you!" and expired.

Captain the Honourable WILLIAM CURZON, who fell in the battle of Waterloo, was the fourth son of Lord Scarsdale. He was educated at the junior department of the Military College, and entering, 1807, the 9th Foot, at the age of 16—he was with this corps in all the great Peninsular operations, and towards their close was promoted to a company in the 69th Regiment, and he was appointed Aide-de-Camp to Lord Aylmer: his conduct acquired then the regard of all, and was honoured by the friendship of the Duke of Wellington and the Prince of Orange, to whose Staff he was this year appointed. On the great day, when in the execution of his duty, riding with his friend Lord March, he received a ball in his chest, and instantly fell on his face, exclaiming, " Good bye, dear March." His gallant companion rendered him every assistance, but in vain. Lord March then, from a movement of the French Cuirassiers, was calling to the Nassau troops to a form a square, and to resist the threatened attack: Captain Curzon even then, forgetful of himself and his situation, hearing his friend animating the Nassau levies, with a self-devotion worthy of the proudest days of Greece and Rome, faintly joined as he was expiring—" That's right, well done, my dear March."

Major-Gen. Sir W. PONSONBY. The remains of this gallant General were deposited in the family vault at Kensington belonging to his noble ancestors in the female line, on the 10th of July. England has not a more accomplished officer, nor society a more amiable man, than was Sir W. Ponsonby. He was naturally diffident, well-bred, and unassuming, with a singleness of mind and simplicity of character, both of which were so strongly expressed in his countenance, as to induce a prepossession, which his genuine worth secured. He owed his appointment solely to his merit, and was selected for that alone by the illustrious Duke, as both himself and family held opposite politicks to his Grace. His conduct justified the choice, for probably a more timely, a more brilliant, and a more successful charge was never made, than by General Ponsonby, on the morning of the 18th, who with his brigade succeeded in making 2000 prisoners, and in taking two Eagles. He fell, covered with wounds and with glory, in his 43d year. Most of those who thus led to the death of their Commander, shared his fate. (*Particulars of his fall, page 17.*)

Col. Sir Wm. DELANCEY, deputy Quarter-Master-General, K. C. B. This brave officer, when he was raised for medical assistance, conceiving his death equally inevitable and near, entreated to be laid down again to abide his fate, without giving useless trouble. In this situation, he remained till the morning, when he was found, in the course of attention to other sufferers, to be still alive; and hopes were for some time entertained of his recovery.

Col. HAMILTON, of the Greys, fell gloriously at the head of his regiment.

In the moment of victory, pierced with honourable wounds, while bravely charging the Enemy, with his gallant and invincible regiment, Col. Sir H. W. ELLIS, 23d regiment, son of the late Major-Gen. Ellis, of Kempsey, near Worcester, and nephew of William Joyner, Esq. of Berkeley, county of Gloucester. Bred up in the army from his earliest youth, this gallant soldier distinguished himself in almost every quarter, where the exertions of the British were called forth, having received no less than nine wounds in different actions, in Holland, Egypt, and the Peninsula. Upon several occasions, he received tokens of his Sovereign's approbation, and rose to considerable rank, at an early period of life, being not more than 35 at the time of his death.

Fell by the side of the Duke of Wellington, with whom he was respectfully remonstrating on remaining within the range of a destructive fire, Lieut.-Col. the Hon. Sir Alexander Gordon, Aide-de-Camp to the Duke of Wellington.

Lieut. RICHARD MAGNIAC, of the 1st Royal Dragoons. He entered the army from a decided predilection for the profession of arms, and actuated by a high sense of honour, and a desire to distinguish himself, fell in his first campaign on that memorable day, " after behaving most gallantly." Although returned as missing in the official returns of the battle, the length of time that has elapsed without any intelligence, compels his afflicted family, with the deepest sorrow to conclude, that he did not survive; and to seek the only consolation that remains to them in the testimonial of his Commanding Officer, " that he died like a brave and gallant soldier in a glorious cause."

Major ROBERT C. PACKE, Royal Horse Guards, (second son of C. J. Packe, Esq. of Prestwould,) who fell at the head of his squadron, in a brilliant charge on the French Imperial Guards.

In the destructive charge of the 1st Life Guards, Capt. MONTAGU LIND, of that regiment, only son of Edward George Lind, Esq. of Stratford Place, and brother to Lord Agar.

In his 23d year, NEWTON CHAMBERS, son of the Hon. Jane Chambers. He was a captain in the 1st Guards, and Aide-de-Camp to Sir T. Picton, by whose side he fell, at the close of the contest, a few minutes after that lamented General.

Capt. HOBHOUSE, 69th regiment of foot, second son of Sir B. Hobhouse, Bart. M. P. He had volunteered, with his accustomed spirit, to act as Sir Colin Halkett's orderly, in conveying commands to the different regiments of the brigades. Whilst on horseback, and riding about in a very hot fire, he displayed a *sangfroid* and courage, which was remarkable to all. At a most critical period of this sanguinary day, when the regiment was closely engaged with a strong body of the Imperial Guard of infantry, being a very conspicuous mark, he was struck by a ball on the cheek, and spoke no more. Thus fell, in his 25th year, a highly estimable man, and one of his country's most promising soldiers.

Lieut. WILLIAM L. ROBE, of the Royal Artillery, son of Colonel Sir William Robe, K. C. B. was one of the most distinguished members of his corps, and the profession terminated his bright career in the battle of Waterloo, near La Hayé Saint. This gallant officer entered the army, the 3d of October, 1806, as a second Lieutenant in the Royal Artillery, and was promoted to a first Lieutenancy, the 28th of June, 1808. During eight years of service, he was thirty-three times in presence of the Enemy in action, frequently at the side of his father, or in the same field. He had the singular honor, as a subaltern officer, to be distinguished for his conduct by the Duke of Wellington, and in consequence a medal and clasp for the battles of the Nivelle, and the Nivé have been transmitted to his family. With his latest breath, he sent a message to his father, to assure him he died like a soldier. The loss of such a son, Sir William Robe must, as a father, ever regret—as a soldier, however, he cannot fail, with noble pride, to consider his having reared him as a service rendered to his country beyond reward. His brother officers, in testimony of their high esteem and personal attachment, have requested to raise to his memory, a tablet in the Church of Waterloo. P

Lieut.-Col. THOMAS, 3rd Battalion, 1st Guards; the worthy young soldier who obtained his rank by merit, was at an early age placed as Ensign in the East Middlesex Militia, from which he volunteered to accompany the expedition to Holland 1799, and received promotion for his gallant conduct there, from the Duke of Gloucester, who also honoured him with his esteem and friendship. At the battle of Salamanca he was particularly mentioned in the dispatches from Lord Wellington for the gallantry of his conduct, and at the termination of the war was promoted to the rank of Lieutenant-Colonel. He possessed a most excellent natural capacity, leaving nothing unaltered which he had once applied to, without seeming to aspire to gain esteem, he was beloved by old and young, his religion was real and unaffected, and his honour and duty to his country, never on his tongue, but ever dearest to his heart in practice.

Capt. THOMAS CASSAN, of the 32nd regiment. This gallant youth, was wounded in the battle of the 18th, but concealed his situation, and continued in the field with that manly resolution, intrepidity, and disregard for personal danger, which always distinguished him; his fall is deservedly regretted by his brother officers and all who knew him. He was the son of the late John Cassan, Esq. Captain 56th regiment, and had been in the 32d regiment from Ensign to Lieutenant and Captain, and had served in the East Indies.

In his 18th year, the Hon. HENRY BOYLE BERNARD, Cornet in the 1st Dragoon Guards, fifth son of the Earl of Bandon; his Lordship lost another son, Hon. FRANCIS BERNARD, 9th Light Dragoons, in the Peninsular Campaign.

Cornet LEMMEL SHULDHAM of the Scotch Greys; a fine youth, beloved and admired by all who knew him. He fell in that glorious and brilliant charge made (about 2 o'clock) by the Heavy Horse upon the Lancers.

June 19. At Brussels, of wounds received the preceding day, Lieut. Col. MILLER, of the Guards. In his last mortal scene, he displayed the soul and spirit of a hero. On being wounded, he sent for Col. Thomas, and said, " I feel I am mortally wounded ; but I am pleased to think it is my fate rather than yours, whose life is involved in that of your young wife." After a pause, he said faintly : " I should like to see the colours of the regiment, before I quit them for ever." They were brought, and waved round his wounded body. His countenance brightened, he smiled, declared himself well satisfied, and was carried from the field.

June 20. At Brussels, of a wound received at Waterloo, Lieut. Col. STABLES, 1st Foot Guards, of Great Ormead, Herts.

Major the Hon. FREDERICK HOWARD, 10th Hussars, second son of the Earl of Carlisle. His remains have been brought over to England. The whole afflicted family of the Earl of Carlisle were so anxious to recover, if possible, the remains of this their gallant relative, that the Duke of York wrote to the Duke of Wellington, requesting that every endeavour might be made to effect it. On inquiry it was found that two serjeants of the 10th Hussars had interred him on the field. They were in consequence dispatched from Paris for this purpose ; and, on traversing this wide field of slaughter were fortunate enough to discover the place of sepulture, from which they immediately dug up the remains of their beloved officer, enclosed them in a leaden shell, with which they were provided, and took them to Brussels, from whence they were conveyed to England.

In consequence of wounds received in the battle of the 16th, Major C. SMYTH, youngest son of the late Right Hon. John Smyth, of Heath, county of York.

Major GRAHAM, King's Dragoon Guards, who fell in a desperate charge of that distinguished corps.

Capt. WINDSOR, 1st Royal Dragoons, son of the late E. Windsor, Esq. of Shrewsbury.

Captain JAMES GUBBINS, 13th Light Dragoons, eldest son of the late James Gubbins, Esq. at Epsom, Surry ; had been in the campaign under the command of the Duke of Wellington, in Portugal, Spain, and France.

Lieut. JOHN PYM, 13th Light Dragoons, fourth son of F. Pym, Esq. M. P.

At Brussels, of wounds received at Waterloo, aged 26, Lieut. J. RALEIGH ELWES, 71st regiment Highland Light Infantry, youngest son of the late Col. H. Elwes, and brother of Sir Wm. H. Elwes, Bart. of Tynemouth, Northumberland. He had been only ten months married to the daughter of Col. Aird, of the Royal Waggon Train.

July 29.   Maj. W. J. LLOYD, Royal Artillery, died at Brussels, of the wound he received in the battle of Waterloo.

In the Church of Waterloo are the two following inscriptions, on plain mural tablets, opposite to each other :

Sacred to the Memory
of

Lieutenant Colonels	Stables
	Sir Francis D'Oyley, Knt.
	Charles Thomas William Miller,
	William Henry Milne,
Captains	Robert Adair,
	Edward Grose,
	Newton Chambers,
	Thomas Brown,
Ensigns	Edward Pardoe,
	James Lord Hay,
	The Hon. S. T. P. Barrington,

of his Britannic Majesty's 1st Regiment of Foot Guards, who fell gloriously in the battles of Quatre-Bras and Waterloo, on the 16th and 18th of June, 1815.

The Officers of the Regiment have erected this Monument in commemoration of the fall of their gallant companions.

To
the Memory
of
Major Edwin Griffith,
Lieutenant Isaac Sherwood,
Lieutenant Henry Buckley,
Officers in the XV.
King's Reg^t. of
Hussars,
[British]
Who fell in the
Battle of
Waterloo,
June, XVIII, MDCCCXV.

This stone was erected by the Officers of that Regiment, as a testimony of their respect.

Dulce et decorum est propatriâ mori.

FIELD MARSHAL THE DUKE OF WELLINGTON, &c.

1769, May 1, born.

1787, March 7, appointed Ensign in the 73d foot. Dec. 25, appointed Lieutenant in the 76th foot.

1788, January 23, exchanged in the 41st regiment.

1789, June 25, exchanged into the 18th dragoons.

1791, Sept. 20, received a company in the 58th foot.

1792, Oct. 31, again exchanged to the 14th dragoons---appointed Major in the 33d foot.

1793, appointed Lieutenant-Colonel.

1794, commanded a brigade of infantry during Lord Moira's retreat through Flanders. Shortly after was employed in the expedition, under Admiral Christian, for the West Indies; and then accompanied his regiment to India.

1795, May 3, received the rank of Colonel by brevet.

1796, May 4, Colonel Wellesley commanded a division in the attack on Serinpagatam, for which he received thanks in public orders from General Harris.

1800, Sept. 5, he intercepted Dhoudia Waugh's force at Conaghull, when Dhoudia himself and a great number of his followers were killed, and the whole body dispersed---for this Colonel Wellesley received the thanks of General Braithwaite, then in command of the forces at Madras, and also of the Governor General in Council.

1802, April 29, obtained the rank of Major General.

1803, April 21, after a forced march of sixty miles, entered Poonah, possession of which had been taken by Holkar.---Sept. 25, Major General Wellesley, with an army consisting only of 4500 men, of whom about 2000 were Europeans, attacked and defeated at Assaye, Scindeah's army, consisting of 38,500 cavalry, 10,500 regular infantry, 500 match-locks, 500 rocket men, and 90 pieces of ordnance. He next turned his attention to the Rajah of Berar's army, which he defeated on the plains of Agra.---Dec. 14, carried by storm the almost impregnable fortress of Gawilghar.---Dec. 16, signed a Treaty of Peace with the Rajah of Berar.---Dec. 30, ditto with Scindeah.

1804, appointed a Knight of the Military Order of the Bath.

1805.---Early in this year he returned to England, a sword, valued at 1000l. was presented to him by the inhabitants of Calcutta : thanks were voted to him by both Houses of Parliament; and his companions in arms presented him with a gold vase, valued at 2,000 guineas.---In the autumn, Sir A. Wellesley accompanied Lord Cathcart to Hanover, and on the return of the army was appointed to a district.

1806, Jan. 30. received the rank of Colonelcy of the 33d regiment.---April 10, married the Hon. Catharine Pakenham, sister of Thomas, Earl of Longford.

1807, defeated a detached army of Danes near Kioge.

1808, April 25, attained the rank of Lieutenant General.---August 17, fought the battle of Roleia; 21, that of Vimeira, and shortly afterwards returned to England.

1809, March 22, returned to Portugal, and appointed by the Prince Regent of Portugal, Marshal General of the Portuguese troops.---May 12, passed the Douro, defeated Soult, and captured Oporto.---July 23, fought the battle of Talavera. August 26, created Viscount Wellington, Baron of Douro, &c.

1810, Sept, 27, fought the battles of Busaco.

1811, May 8, that of Fuentes de Honore, or Almeida.---This year his Lordship was created, by the Prince Regent of Portugal, Conde de Vimeira, and on the 31st of July, received the local rank of General in Spain and Portugal.

1812, Jan. 19, Cuidad Rodrigo carried by storm.---April 7, Badajoz also carried by storm.---July 22, fought the battle of Salamanca.---This year his Lordship was created Marquis of Wellington.

1813, Jan. 1, appointed Colonel of the Horse Guards, Blue.---June 21, fought the battle of Vittoria, was appointed Field Marshal, and the same year a Knight of the Garter.---August 11, the battle of the Pyrenees.

1814, May 3, he was created Marquis Douro and Duke of Wellington.---April 10, Battle of Thoulouse.

1815, June 18, BATTLE OF WATERLOO.---July 3, the City of Paris capitulated to the Duke and Prince Blucher---the British and Prussian forces took possession on the 7th.---July 18, created Prince of Waterloo by the King of the Netherlands.